Practical Cryptography

Practical Cryptography

Niels Ferguson
Bruce Schneier

WILEY

Wiley Publishing, Inc.

Executive Publisher: Robert Ipsen
Executive Editor: Carol A. Long
Editorial Manager: Kathryn A. Malm
Managing Editor: Fred Bernardi

This book is printed on acid-free paper.

Published by Wiley Publishing, Inc., Indianapolis, Indiana
Published simultaneously in Canada

For general information on our other products and services please contact our Customer Care Department within the United States at (800) 762-2974, outside the United States at (317) 572-3993 or fax (317) 572-4002.

Wiley also publishes its books in a variety of electronic formats. Some content that appears in print may not be available in electronic books.

ISBN: 0-471-22894-X (C)
ISBN: 0-471-22357-3 (P)

Printed in the United States of America

10 9 8 7 6 5 4 3 2 1

Contents

Preface

In the past decade, cryptography has done more to damage the security of digital systems than it has to enhance it. Cryptography burst onto the world stage in the early 1990s as the securer of the Internet. Some saw cryptography as a great technological equalizer, a mathematical tool that would put the lowliest privacy-seeking individual on the same footing as the greatest national intelligence agencies. Some saw it as the weapon that would bring about the downfall of nations when governments lost the ability to police people in cyberspace. Others saw it as the perfect and terrifying tool of drug dealers, terrorists, and child pornographers, who would be able to communicate in perfect secrecy. Even those with more realistic attitudes imagined cryptography as a technology that would enable global commerce in this new online world.

Ten years later, none of this has come to pass. Despite the prevalence of cryptography, the Internet's national borders are more apparent than ever. The ability to detect and eavesdrop on criminal communications has more to do with politics and human resources than mathematics. Individuals still don't stand a chance against powerful and well-funded government agencies. And the rise of global commerce had nothing to do with the prevalence of cryptography.

For the most part, cryptography has done little more than give Internet users a false sense of security by promising security but not delivering it. And that's not good for anyone except the attackers.

The reasons for this have less to do with cryptography as a mathematical science, and much more to do with cryptography as an engineering discipline. We have developed, implemented, and fielded cryptographic systems over the past decade. What we've been less effective at is converting the mathematical promise of cryptographic security into a reality of security. As it turns out, this is the hard part.

Too many engineers consider cryptography to be a sort of magic security dust that they can sprinkle over their hardware or software, and which will imbue those products with the mythical property of "security." Too many consumers read product claims like "encrypted" and believe in that same magic security dust. Reviewers are no better, comparing things like key lengths and on that basis, pronouncing one product to be more secure than another.

Security is only as strong as the weakest link, and the mathematics of cryptography is almost never the weakest link. The fundamentals of cryptography are important, but far more important is how those fundamentals are implemented and used. Arguing about whether a key should be 112 bits or 128 bits long is rather like pounding a huge stake into the ground and hoping the attacker runs right into it. You can argue whether the stake should be a mile or a mile-and-a-half high, but the attacker is simply going to walk around the stake. Security is a broad stockade: it's the things around the cryptography that make the cryptography effective.

The cryptographic books of the last decade have contributed to that aura of magic. Book after book extolled the virtues of, say, 112-bit triple-DES without saying much about how its keys should be generated or used. Book after book presented complicated protocols for this or that without any mention of the business and social constraints within which those protocols would have to work. Book after book explained cryptography as a pure mathematical ideal, unsullied by real-world constraints and realities. But it's exactly those real-world constraints and realities that mean the difference between the promise of cryptographic magic and the reality of digital security.

Practical Cryptography is also a book about cryptography, but it's a book about sullied cryptography. Our goal is to explicitly describe the real-world constraints and realities of cryptography, and to talk about how to engineer secure cryptographic systems. In some ways, this book is a sequel to Bruce Schneier's first book, *Applied Cryptography*, which was first published ten years ago. But while *Applied Cryptography* gives a broad overview of cryptography and the myriad possibilities cryptography can offer, this book is narrow and focused. We don't give you dozens of choices; we give you one option and tell you how to implement it correctly. *Applied Cryptography* displays the wondrous possibilities of cryptography as a mathematical science—what is possible and what is attainable; *Practical Cryptography* gives concrete advice to people who design and implement cryptographic systems.

Practical Cryptography is our attempt to bridge the gap between the promise of cryptography and the reality of cryptography. It's our attempt to teach engineers how to use cryptography to increase security.

We're qualified to write this book because we're both seasoned cryptographers. Bruce is well known from his books *Applied Cryptography* and *Secrets and Lies*, and from his newsletter "Crypto-Gram." Niels Ferguson cut his cryptographic teeth building cryptographic payment systems at the CWI (Dutch National Research Institute for Mathematics and Computer Science) in Amsterdam, and later at a Dutch company called DigiCash. Bruce designed the Blowfish encryption algorithm, and both of us were on the team that designed Twofish. Niels's research led to the first example of the current generation of efficient anonymous payment protocols. Our combined list of academic papers runs into three digits.

More importantly, we both have extensive experience in designing and building cryptographic systems. From 1991 to 1999, Bruce's consulting company Counterpane Systems provided design and analysis services to some of the largest computer and financial companies in the world. More recently, Counterpane Internet Security, Inc., has provided Managed Security Monitoring services to large corporations and government agencies worldwide. Niels also worked at Counterpane before founding his own consulting company, MacFergus. We've seen cryptography as it lives and breathes in the real world, as it flounders against the realities of engineering or even worse, against the realities of business. We're qualified to write this book because we've had to write it again and again for our consulting clients.

How to Read this Book

Practical Cryptography is more a narrative than a reference. It follows the design of a cryptographic system from the specific algorithm choices, out-

wards through concentric rings to the infrastructure required to make it
work. We discuss a single cryptographic problem—one of establishing a
means for two people to communicate securely—that's at the heart of almost every cryptographic application. By focusing on one problem and one
design philosophy for solving that problem, it is our belief that we can teach
more about the realities of cryptographic engineering.

We've both published books before, and we know that publishing is an
imperfect science. Try as we might, this book will not be error-free. We're
sorry, but it's simply the way things are. (Oddly enough, cryptographic
systems have the same problem; we'll talk about that in a few chapters.)
While we've endeavored to make this book as perfect as possible, we have a
procedure for ensuring that the inevitable errors get corrected.

- Before reading this book, go to `http://www.macfergus.com/pc` and
  download the current list of corrections.

- If you find an error in the book, please check to see if it is already on
  the list.

- If it is not on the list, please alert us at `practical-cryptography@`
  `macfergus.com`. We will add the error to the list.

We think cryptography is just about the most fun you can have with mathematics. We've tried to imbue this book with that feeling of fun, and we
hope you enjoy the results. Thanks for coming along on our ride.

January 2003   Niels Ferguson   Bruce Schneier
                  Amsterdam   Minneapolis, Minnesota
                  Netherlands   USA
                  niels@macfergus.com   schneier@counterpane.com

Chapter 1

Our Design Philosophy

This book is about security: about how to build secure cryptographic systems. In this book, we are fanatical about security. There is a good reason for this. In all our years of working in this field, we have yet to see an entire system that is secure. That's right. Every system we have analyzed has been broken in one way or another. There are always a few components that are good, but they invariably get used in insecure ways.

If we as a society want to secure our digital future, we will all need to shape up and do better. It is our hope that this book can contribute to that.

This book gives you a great deal of practical information about cryptographic systems, but none of that matters unless we can convince you that security is important enough to do right. Doing it right means being ruthless in many other areas. This will be hard to adjust to. It took us many years to become ruthless enough. There is no point in having just a bit of security. That is like putting up half a fence around a yard, or locking only your front door and leaving your back door wide open. Security is a system property you cannot compromise on. One hole in the fence is all it takes. So everything else has to give way to create enough room for security. From experience, we know that this is a tough sell in the IT industry. Yet it will have to be done if we want to be safe in our digital world.

1.1   The Evils of Performance

The bridge over the Firth of Forth in Scotland has to be seen to be believed. A 19th-century engineering marvel, it is mind-numbingly large (and therefore expensive) compared to the trains that cross it. It is so incredibly over-engineered it is hard to believe your eyes. Yet the designers did the right thing. They were confronted with a problem they had not solved successfully before: building a large steel bridge. They did an astoundingly good job. They succeeded spectacularly; their bridge is still in use today over a century later. That's what good engineering looks like.

Over the years, bridge designers have learned how to build such bridges much more cheaply and efficiently. But the first priority is always to get a bridge that is safe and that works. Efficiency, in the form of reducing cost, is a secondary issue.

We have reversed these priorities in computer security. The primary design objective all too often includes very strict efficiency demands. The first priority is always speed, even in areas where speed is not important. This leads to security cost-cutting, and security is an area of engineering where we really don't have the skills to build a good system even if we are given an unlimited budget. The result is invariably a system that is somewhat efficient, and inevitably a system that is not secure.

There is another side to the Firth of Forth bridge story. In 1878, Thomas Bouch completed the then-longest bridge in the world across the Firth of Tay at Dundee. Bouch used a new design combining cast iron and wrought iron, and the bridge was considered to be an engineering marvel. On the night of December 28, 1879, less than two years later, the bridge collapsed in a heavy storm as a train with 75 people on board crossed the bridge. All perished. It was the major engineering disaster of the time.[1] So when the Firth of Forth bridge was designed a few years later, the designers put in a lot more steel, not only to make the bridge safe but also to make it *look* safe to the public.

---

[1]William McGonagall wrote a famous poem about it, ending with the lines *For the stronger we our houses do build/The less chance we have of being killed.* Advice that is still highly relevant today.

We all know that engineers will sometimes get a design wrong, especially when they do something new. And when they get it wrong sometimes people are killed. But here is a good lesson from Victorian engineers: if it fails, back off and become more conservative. The computer industry has forgotten this lesson. When we have very serious security failures in our computer systems, and we have them every week or so, we just plod along, accepting it as if it were fate. We don't go back to the drawing board and design something more conservative. We just keep throwing a few patches out and hoping this will solve the problem. That is disgraceful.

By now it will be quite clear to you that we will choose security over efficiency any time. How much CPU time are we willing to spend on security? Almost all of it. We wouldn't care if 90% of our CPU cycles were spent on a reliable security system. The lack of computer security is a real hindrance to us, and to most users. That is why people still have to send pieces of paper around with signatures, and why they have to worry about viruses and other attacks on our computer. Digital crooks of the future will know much more and be much better equipped, and computer security will become a larger and larger problem. We have only seen the very beginning of the digital crime wave. If we want to keep using the Internet for business transactions, we will have to secure our computers much better.

There are of course many ways of achieving security. But as Bruce extensively documented in *Secrets and Lies*, good security is always a mixture of prevention, detection, and response [89]. The role for cryptography is in the prevention part, which has to be very good to ensure that the detection and response parts (which can and should include manual intervention) are not overwhelmed. Anyways, cryptography is what this book is about, so we'll concentrate on that.

Yes, yes, we know, you're still screaming about the 90%. But what else are our computers supposed to do? We can only type around 10 characters per second—on a good day—and even the slow machines of a decade ago had no trouble keeping up with that. Today's machines are over a thousand times faster. If we use 90% of the CPU for security, the computer will appear one-tenth as fast. That is about the speed that computers were five years ago. And those computers were more than fast enough for us to get our work done.

There are only a few situations in which we have to wait on the computer. These include waiting for Web pages, printing data, starting certain programs, booting the machine, etc. A good security system would not slow down any of these activities. Modern computers are so fast that it is hard to figure out how to use the cycles in a useful manner. Sure, we can use alpha-blending on screen images, 3D animations, or even voice recognition. But the number-crunching parts of these applications do not perform any security-related actions, so they would not be slowed down by a security system. It is the rest of the system, which is already as fast as it can possibly get on a human time scale, that will have the overhead. And we don't care if that gets ten times slower. Most of the time you wouldn't even notice the overhead. Even in situations where the overhead would be significant, that is just the cost of doing business.

If you are ever tempted to cut a security corner in the name of efficiency, just repeat to yourself: "We already have enough fast, insecure systems. We don't need another one." We have found that other people accept this explanation much more readily than long-winded arguments about degrees of security.

It will be clear by now that our priorities are security first, second, and third, and performance somewhere way down the list. Of course, we still want the system to be as efficient as possible, but not at the expense of security. We understand that this design philosophy is not always possible in the real world. Often the realities of the marketplace trump the need for security. Systems can rarely be developed from scratch, and often need to be secured incrementally or after deployment. Systems need to be backward-compatible with existing, insecure, systems. Both of us have designed many security systems under these constraints, and we can tell you that it's practically impossible to build a good security system that way. The design philosophy of this book is security first and security foremost. It's one we'd like to see adopted more in commercial systems.

1.2   The Evils of Features

There are no complex systems that are secure. Complexity is the worst enemy of security, and it almost always comes in the form of features or options.

We will discuss why complexity cannot be combined with security in greater detail later, but here is the basic argument. Imagine a computer program with 20 different options, each of which can be either on or off. That is more than a million different configurations. To get the program to work, you only need to test the most common combination of options. To make the program secure, you must evaluate each of the million possible configurations that the program can have, and check that each configuration is secure against every possible form of attack. That is impossible to do. And most programs have considerably more than 20 options. If you want to build something secure you have to keep it simple.

A simple system is not necessarily a small system. You can build large systems that are still fairly simple. Complexity is a measure of how many things interact at any one point. If the effect of an option is limited to a small part of the program, then it cannot interact with an option whose effect is limited to another part of the program. To make a large, simple system you have to provide a very clear and simple interface between different parts of the system. Programmers call this modularization. A good simple interface isolates the rest of the system from the details of a module. And that should include any options or features of the module.

We really should not have to write all of this. It is all basic software engineering. Unfortunately, we see very little of it in real-world systems.

One of the things we have tried to do in this book is to define simple interfaces for cryptographic primitives. No features, no options, no special cases, no extra things to remember, just the simplest definition we could come up with. Some of these definitions are new; we developed them while writing the book. They have helped us shape our thinking about good security systems, and we hope it will help you too.

Chapter 2

The Context of Cryptography

Cryptography is the art and science of encryption. At least, that is how it started out. Nowadays it is much broader, covering authentication, digital signatures, and many more elementary security functions. It is still both an art and a science: to build good cryptographic systems requires a scientific background and a healthy dose of the black magic that we call experience.

Cryptography is an extremely varied field. At a cryptography conference, you can encounter a wide range of topics including computer security, higher algebra, economics, quantum physics, civil and criminal law, statistics, chip designs, extreme software optimization, politics, user interface problems, and everything in between. This book concentrates on a very small part of cryptography: the practical side. We hope to show you how to implement cryptography in real-world systems.

This variety is what makes cryptography such a fascinating field to work in. It is a mixture of widely different fields. There is always something new to learn, and new ideas come from all directions. It is also one of the reasons why cryptography is so difficult. It is impossible to understand it all. There is nobody in the world who knows everything about cryptography. There isn't even anybody who knows most of it. We certainly don't know everything there is to know about the subject of this book. So here is your first lesson in cryptography: keep a critical mind. Don't blindly trust anything, even if it is in print.

2.1   The Role of Cryptography

Cryptography by itself is fairly useless. It has to be part of a much larger system. We like to compare cryptography to locks in the physical world. A lock by itself is a singularly useless thing. It needs to be part of a much larger system. This can be a door on a building, a chain, a safe, or something else. The lock is just a small part of a much larger security system. The same goes for cryptography: it is just a small part of a much larger security system.

Even though cryptography is only a small part of the security system, it is a very critical part. Cryptography is the part that has to provide access to some people but not to others. This is very tricky. Most parts of the security system are like walls and fences in that they are designed to keep everybody out. Cryptography takes on the role of the lock: it has to distinguish between "good" access and "bad" access. This is much more difficult than just keeping everybody out. Therefore, the cryptography and its surrounding elements form a natural point of attack for any security system.

This does not imply that cryptography is always the weak point of a system. It rarely is. In real life, even bad cryptography is invariably much better than the rest of the security system. You have probably seen the door to a bank vault, at least in the movies. You know, 10-inch thick, hardened steel, with huge bolts to lock it in place. It certainly looks impressive. We often find the digital equivalent of such a vault door installed in a tent. The people standing around it are arguing over how thick the door should be, rather than spending their time looking at the tent. People love to argue about the exact key length of cryptographic systems, but fixing buffer overflows in Web servers is much less fun. The result is predictable: the attackers find a buffer overflow and never bother attacking the cryptography. Cryptography is only truly useful if the rest of the system is also secure.

There is, however, one reason why cryptography is important to get right, even in systems that have other weaknesses. An attacker who breaks the cryptography has a low chance of being detected. There will be no traces of the attack, since the attacker's access will look just like a "good" access. This is comparable to a real-life break-in. If the burglar uses a crowbar to break in, you will at least see that a break-in has occurred. If the burglar picks the lock, you might never find out that a burglary occurred. Many modes of attack leave traces, or disturb the system in some way. An attack on the cryptography can be fleeting and invisible, allowing the attacker to come back again and again...

2.2   The Weakest Link Property

Print the following sentence in a very large font and paste it along the top of your monitor.

A security system is only as strong as its weakest link.

Look at it every day, and try to understand the implications. The weakest link property is the main reason why security systems are so fiendishly hard to get right.

Every security system consists of a large number of different parts. We must assume that our opponent is smart and that he is going to attack the system at the weakest spot. It doesn't matter how strong the other parts are. Just like in a chain, the weakest link will break first. It doesn't matter how strong the other links in the chain are.

Niels used to work in an office building where all the office doors were locked every night. Sounds very safe, right? The only problem was that the building had a false ceiling. You could lift up the ceiling panels and climb over any door or wall. If you took out the ceiling panels, the whole floor looked like a set of tall cubicles with doors on them. And these doors had locks. Sure, locking the doors made it slightly harder for the burglar, but it also made it harder for the security guard to check the offices during his nightly rounds. It isn't clear at all whether the overall security was improved by locking the doors or whether it was made worse. In this example, the weakest link property prevented the locking of the doors from being very effective. It might have improved the strength of a particular link (the door), but there

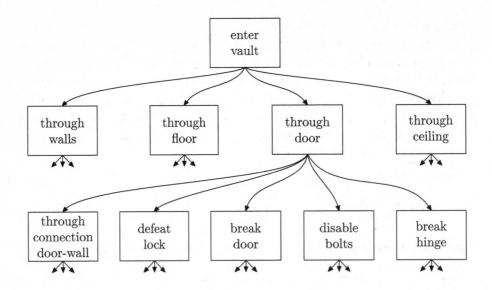

Figure 2.1: Example attack tree for a vault

was another link (the ceiling) that was still weak. The overall effect of locking the doors was at best very small, and its negative side effects could well have exceeded its positive contribution.

To improve the security of a system, we must improve the weakest link. But to do that, we need to know what the links are and which ones are weak. This is best done using a hierarchical tree structure. Each part of a system has multiple links, and each link in turn has sublinks. We can organize the links into what we call an *attack tree*. We give an example in figure 2.1. Let's say that we want to break into a bank vault. The first-level links are the walls, the floor, the door, and the ceiling. Breaking through any one of them gets us into the vault. Let's look at the door in more detail. The door system has its own links: the connection between the door frame and the walls, the lock, the door itself, the bolts that keep the door in the door frame, and the hinges. We could continue by discussing individual lines of attack on the lock, one of which is to acquire a key, which in turn leads to a whole tree about stealing the key in some way.

We can analyze each link and split it up into other links until we are left with single components. Doing this for a real system can be an enormous amount of work, but it provides valuable insight as to possible lines of attack. Trying to secure a system without first doing such an analysis very often leads to useless work. In this book we work only on limited components—the ones that can be solved with cryptography—and the attack tree is so simple that we won't document it explicitly.

The weakest link property affects our work in many ways. For example, it is tempting to assume that users have proper passwords, but in practice they don't. They will choose simple short passwords. Users will go to almost any length not to be bothered by security systems. Writing a password on a sticky note and attaching it to their monitor is just one of many things they might do. You can never ignore issues like this, because they always affect the end result. If you design a system that gives the user a new 12-digit random password every week, then you can be sure he will stick it on his monitor. This weakens an already weak link, and is bad for the overall security.

Strictly speaking, strengthening anything but the weakest link is useless. In practice, things are not so clear-cut. The attacker may not know what the weakest link is and attack a slightly stronger one. The weakest link may be different for different classes of attacker. The strength of any link depends on the attacker's skill and tools. So which link is the weakest depends on the situation. It is therefore worthwhile to strengthen any link that could in a particular situation be the weakest.

2.3   The Adversarial Setting

One of the biggest differences between security systems and almost any other type of engineering is the adversarial setting. Most engineers have to contend with problems like storms, heat, and wear and tear. All of these factors affect designs, but their effect is fairly predictable to an experienced engineer. Not so in security systems. Our opponents are intelligent, clever, malicious, and devious; they'll do things nobody had ever thought of before. They don't play by the rules, and they are completely unpredictable. That is a much harder environment to work in.

Many of us remember the film in which the Tacoma Narrows suspension bridge wobbles and twists in a steady wind until it breaks and falls into the water. It is a famous piece of film, and the collapse taught bridge engineers a valuable lesson. Slender suspension bridges can have a resonance mode in which a steady wind can cause the whole structure to oscillate, and finally break. How do they prevent the same thing from happening with newer bridges? Making the bridge significantly stronger to resist the oscillations would be too expensive. The most common technique used is to change the aerodynamics of the bridge. The deck is made thicker, which makes it much harder for the wind to push up and down on the deck. Sometimes railings are used as spoilers to make the bridge deck behave less like a wing that lifts up in the wind. This works because the wind is fairly predictable, and does not change its behavior in an active attempt to destroy the bridge.

A security engineer has to take a malicious wind into account. What if the wind blows up and down instead of just from the side, and what if it changes directions at the right frequency for the bridge to resonate? Bridge engineers will dismiss this kind of talk out of hand: "Don't be silly, the wind doesn't blow that way." That certainly makes the bridge engineers' jobs much easier. Cryptographers don't have that luxury. Security systems are attacked by clever and malicious attackers. We have to protect against all types of attack.

The adversarial setting is a very harsh environment to work in. There are no rules in this game, and the deck is stacked against us. We talk about an "attacker" in an abstract sense, but we don't know who she is, what she knows, what her goal is, when she attacks, or what her resources are. Since the attack occurs long after we design the system, she has the advantage of five or ten years more research, and can use technology of the future that is not available to us. And with all those advantages, she only has to find a single weak spot in our system, whereas we have to protect all areas. Still, our mission is to build a system that can withstand it all. Welcome to the wonderful world of cryptography.

2.4 Practical Paranoia

To work in this field, you have to become devious yourself. You have to think like a malicious attacker to find weaknesses in your own work. This affects the rest of your life as well. Everybody who works on practical cryptographic systems has experienced this. Once you start thinking about how to attack systems, you apply that to everything around you. You suddenly see how you could cheat the people around you, and how they could cheat you. Cryptographers are professional paranoids. After a while, you learn to separate your professional paranoia from your real-world life, or else you go completely crazy. Most of us manage to preserve some sanity... we think.[1]

Paranoia is very useful in this work. Suppose you work on an electronic payment system. There are several parties involved in this system: the customer, the merchant, the customer's bank, and the merchant's bank. It can be very difficult to figure out what the threats are, so we use the paranoia model. For each participant, we assume that everybody else is part of a big conspiracy to defraud this one participant. If your cryptographic system can survive the paranoia model, it has at least a fighting chance of surviving in the real world.

2.4.1 Attack

Professional paranoia is an essential tool of the trade. With any new system you encounter, the first thing you think of is how you can break it. The sooner you find a weak spot, the sooner you learn more about the new system. Nothing is worse than working on a system for years, only to have somebody come up and say: "But how about if I attack it this way ...?" You really don't want to experience that "Oops" moment.

In this field we make a very strict distinction between attacking somebody's work and attacking somebody personally. Any work is fair game. If somebody proposes something, it is an automatic invitation to attack it. If you break one of our systems, we will applaud the attack and tell everybody about it.[2] We constantly look for weaknesses in any system, because that is the only way to learn how to make more secure systems. This is one thing you will have to learn: an attack on your work is not an attack on you. If you do not learn this you will never survive, so get used to it. Also,

---

[1]But remember: the fact that *you* are not paranoid doesn't mean they are not out to get you.

[2]Depending on the attack, we might kick ourselves for not finding the weakness ourselves, but that is a different issue.

when you attack a system, always be sure to criticize the system, not the designers. Personal attacks in cryptography will get you the same negative response as anywhere else.

This adversarial attitude of cryptographers creates misunderstandings with people not familiar with the field. Outsiders sometimes think we are attacking a person when we attack their work, and then complain about our manners. For example, during one conference in 1999, the AES block cipher proposals were being presented. The proposer of the block cipher Magenta could not attend in person, and had asked a student to represent him. It turned out that Magenta had a serious weakness, and during the five-minute question time after the initial presentation, the proposal was broken by several people in the audience. It was fun. Some of the best cryptographers in the world were being presented with a new block cipher, and they were demolishing it while the rest of the audience watched. That is how we work. Another member of the audience, who had little experience in the field of cryptography, wrote an essay about attending the conference. He thought the student was being attacked personally, and was quite upset at the incredibly rude behavior of the audience. His reaction is understandable. In much of our society an attack on an idea or proposal is automatically taken to be an attack on the author. In cryptography, we simply cannot afford that attitude.

Even worse than this type of incident are the situations which involve people from outside the field who have strayed into cryptography. They take criticism of their work as a personal attack, with all the resulting problems. Sometimes you have to be diplomatic, but that makes it difficult to get the message across. Saying something vague like "There might be some issues with the security aspects" gets a response of "Oh, we'll fix it" even if the basic design is impossible. Experience has shown us that the only way to get the message across is to say be specific and say something like "If you do this and this the security is broken." If it then turns out that the person you are talking to designed the system, you have a problem. There is no neat solution to this.

So the next time someone attacks your work, try not to take it personally. And make sure that when you attack a system, you only criticize the system and not the people behind it.

2.5   Threat Model

Every system can be attacked. The whole point of a security system is to provide access to some people and not to others. In the end, you will always have to trust some people in some way, and these people in turn can attack your system.

It is very important to know what you are trying to protect against. This sounds like a simple question, but it turns out to be a much harder problem than you'd think. What are the threats? Most companies protect their LAN with a firewall, but most of the really harmful attacks are performed by insiders, and a firewall does not protect against insiders at all. It doesn't matter how good your firewall is; it won't protect against a malicious employee. This is a mismatch in the threat model.

Another example is SET. SET is a protocol for online shopping with a credit card. One of its features is that it encrypts the credit card number so that an eavesdropper cannot copy it. That is a good idea. A second feature—that not even the merchant is shown the customer's credit-card number—works less well.

The second property fails because some merchants use the credit card number to look up customer records or to charge surcharges. Entire commerce systems have been based on the assumption that the merchant has access to the customer's credit card number. And then SET tries to take this access away; that is simply not going to happen. When Niels worked with SET several years ago, there was an option for sending the credit card number twice—once encrypted to the bank, and once encrypted to the merchant so that the merchant would get it too. (The SET specifications are so incredibly large and complex that we didn't bother finding out whether this is still the case.)

But even with this option, SET solved the wrong problem. Most credit card numbers that are stolen are not intercepted while in transit between the consumer and the merchant. They are stolen from the merchant's database. SET only protects the information while it is in transit.

SET makes another, more serious, mistake. Recently Niels's bank in the Netherlands offered a SET-enabled credit card. The improved security for online purchases was one of the major selling points. But this turned out to be a bogus argument. It is quite safe to order online with a normal credit card. Your credit card number is not a secret. You give it to every salesperson you buy something from. The real secret is your signature. That is what authorizes the transaction. If a merchant leaks your credit card number, then you might get spurious charges, but as long as there is no handwritten signature (or PIN code) there is no indication of acceptance of the transaction, and therefore no legal basis for the charge. In most jurisdictions you simply complain and get your money back. There might be some inconvenience involved in getting a new credit card with a different number, but that is the extent of the user's exposure. With SET, the situation is different. SET uses a digital signature (explained in chapter 13) by the user to authorize the transaction. That is obviously more secure than using just a credit card number. But think about it. Now the user is liable for any transaction performed by the SET software on his PC. This opens the user up to huge liabilities. What if a virus infects his PC and subverts the SET software? The software might sign the wrong transaction, and cause the user to lose money.

So from the user's point of view, SET offers *worse* security than a plain credit card. Plain credit cards are safe for online shopping because the user can always get his money back from a fraudulent transaction. Using SET increases the user's exposure. So although the overall payment system is better securited, SET transfers the residual risk from the merchant and/or bank to the user. It changes the user's threat model from "It will only cost me money if they forge my signature well enough" to "It will only cost me money if they forge my signature well enough, or if a clever virus infects my PC."

Threat models are important. Whenever you start on a cryptographic security project, sit down and think about what threats you have to protect against. A mistake in your threat analysis can render an entire project meaningless. We won't talk a lot about threat analysis in this book, as we are discussing the limited area of cryptography here, but in any real system you should never forget the threat analysis for each of the participants.

2.6   Cryptography Is Not the Solution

Cryptography is not the solution to your security problems. It might be part of the solution, or it might be part of the problem. In many situations, cryptography starts out by making the problem worse, and it isn't at all clear that using cryptography is an improvement.

How do we protect a car from theft? The easiest way would be to physically protect the car directly. Just don't let anyone near it. This is a bit inconvenient, so instead we install a lock on the car, and carry a car key around. Because the car is locked, we now park it on the street. The thief has two ways of getting the car. He can pick or break the locking system (and we'll include smashing the window in that), or he can steal the car keys, which you still have to protect directly. Note that there are now two lines of attack: the locking system and the key. The introduction of the key has helped the attacker by creating a new line of attack. The major advantage of the car key is that it is much easier to physically protect a key than it is to protect a car. As long as this advantage outweighs the extra risk of the thief attacking the lock, security is improved by having a car key.

In the digital world, things are slightly different. Suppose you have a secret file on your computer that you don't want others to read. You could just protect the file system from unauthorized access. Or you could encrypt the file and protect the key. The encrypted file is no longer a secret, so human nature being what it is, you will probably not protect it very well, just like the car that you park on the street. But where can you store the key? A good key is too long to remember. Some programs store the key on the disk—the very place the secret file was stored in the first place. Now the attacker has two ways of getting the file. Any attack that could recover the secret file in the first situation can now recover the key, which in turn can be used to decrypt the file. Any attack that worked in the first situation also works on the second one, but we have introduced a new point of attack: the attacker could break the encryption system itself. Ultimately, the overall security has been reduced. Therefore, encrypting the file is not the entire solution. It might be part of the solution, but by itself it creates more problems than it solves.

Cryptography has many uses. It is a crucial part of many good security systems. It can also make systems weaker when used in inappropriate ways. In many situations it provides only a feeling of security, but no actual security. This is often all that is required, because that is what most customers want. They want to *feel* secure, but they don't want the hassle that comes with actual security. In situations like this (which are all too common) cryptography is a solution in itself, but any voodoo that the customer believes in would provide the same feeling of security and would work just as well.

2.7   Cryptography Is Very Difficult

Cryptography is fiendishly difficult. Even seasoned experts design systems that are broken a few years later. This is common enough that we are not surprised when it happens. The weakest-link property and the adversarial setting conspire to make life for a cryptographer very hard.

Another significant problem is the lack of testing. There is no known way of testing whether a system is secure. The best we can do is to publish the system and then get other experts to look at it. Note that the second part is not automatic; there are many published systems that nobody has even glanced at since they were published. Even conference and journal papers receive only the most elementary sort of review. These review processes are designed to sift the good papers from the bad ones, not to check the security or correctness of the results. Some checking is done, but a typical reviewer will not have the time to do a thorough analysis of a paper. (After all, reviewers are rarely paid for their work, and when they get 20–30 papers to review in their spare time they are not going to be terribly thorough.)

There are some small areas of cryptography that we understand rather well. This doesn't mean they are simple; it just means that we have been working on them for a few decades now, and we think we know the problems. This book is mostly about those areas. What we have tried to do in this book is to collect the information that we have about designing and building practical cryptographic systems, and bring it all together in one place.

For some reason, people who know very little about cryptography seem to think it is easy. Time and time again we have encountered an electrical engineer or a programmer who has read half a book—more often than not,

Applied Cryptography—and decides to design his own system. So far we have *never* seen this produce a decent result, and we have seen quite a few in the past decade. Suppose a student with two semesters of civil engineering were to design a revolutionary new bridge to span the Bering Strait—would we actually build it and use it without further review? Of course not. But for some reason, when cryptography is involved, people pay for and build systems designed by novices. And because bad cryptography looks just like good cryptography, until it is seriously attacked, some customers are fooled and buy the product.

Do not fall into the trap of thinking that cryptography is easy. It is not.

2.8   Cryptography Is the Easy Part

Even though cryptography itself is difficult, it is still one of the easy parts of a security system. Like a lock, a cryptographic component has fairly well-defined boundaries and requirements. An entire security system is much more difficult to clearly define, since it involves many more aspects. Issues like the organizational procedures used to grant access and the procedures used to check that the other procedures are being followed, are much harder to deal with, as the situation is always changing. Another huge problem in computer security is the atrocious quality of almost all software. Security software cannot be effective if the software on the machine contains thousands of bugs that lead to security holes.

Cryptography is the easy part because there are people who know how to do a reasonably good job. There are experts for hire that will design a cryptographic system for you. They are not cheap, and they are often a pain to work with. They insist on changing other parts of the system to achieve the desired security properties. Still, for all practical purposes, cryptography poses problems that we know how to solve.

The rest of the security system contains problems that we don't know how to solve. Key management and key storage is crucial to any cryptographic system, but most computers have no secure place to store a key. Poor software quality is a problem we don't know how to handle at all. Network security is even harder. And when you add users to the mix, the problem becomes nearly insolvable.

2.9   Background Reading

Anyone interested in cryptography should read David Kahn's *The Code-breakers* [46]. This is a history of cryptography, from ancient times to the 20th century. The stories provide many examples of the problems engineers of cryptographic systems face.

In some ways the book you're holding is a sequel to Bruce's first book *Applied Cryptography* [88]. *Applied Cryptography* covers a much broader range of subjects, and includes the specifications of all the algorithms it discusses. However, it does not go into the engineering details that we talk about in this book.

For facts and precise results, you can't beat the *Handbook of Applied Cryptography*, by Menezes, van Oorschot, and Vanstone [65]. It is an encyclopedia of cryptography; an extremely useful reference book, but just like an encyclopedia, hardly a book to learn the field from.

Bruce's previous book *Secrets and Lies* [89] is a good explanation of computer security in general, and how cryptography fits into that larger picture. And there's no better book on security engineering than Ross Anderson's *Security Engineering* [1]. Both are essential to understand the context of cryptography.

Chapter 3

Introduction to Cryptography

This chapter introduces basic cryptographic concepts and the background information that you will need for the rest of the book.

3.1   Encryption

Encryption is the original goal of cryptography. The generic setting is shown in figure 3.1. Alice and Bob want to communicate with each other. (The use of personal names, particularly Alice, Bob, and Eve, is a tradition in cryptography.) However, in general communication channels are not secure.

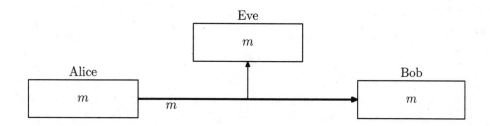

Figure 3.1: How can Alice and Bob communicate securely?

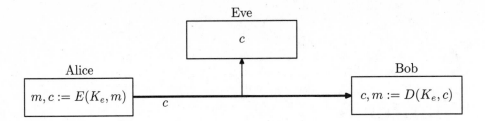

Figure 3.2: Generic setting for encryption

Eve is eavesdropping on the channel. Any message m that Alice sends to Bob is also received by Eve. (The same holds for messages sent by Bob to Alice, but that is the same problem, except with Alice and Bob reversed. As long as we can protect Alice's messages, the same solution will work for Bob's messages, so we concentrate on Alice's messages.) How can Alice and Bob communicate without Eve learning everything?

To prevent Eve from understanding the conversation that Alice and Bob are having, they use encryption as shown in figure 3.2. Alice and Bob first agree on a secret key K_e. They will have to do this via some communication channel that Eve cannot eavesdrop on. Perhaps Alice mails a copy of the key to Bob, or something similar.

When Alice wants to send a message m, she first encrypts it using an encryption function. We write the encryption function as $E(K_e, m)$ and we call the result the *ciphertext* c. (The original message m is called the *plaintext*.) Instead of sending m to Bob, Alice sends the ciphertext $c := E(K_e, m)$. When Bob receives c, he can decrypt it using the decryption function $D(K_e, c)$ to get the original plaintext m that Alice wanted to send to him.

But Eve does not know the key K_e, so when she receives the ciphertext c she cannot decrypt it. A good encryption function makes it impossible to find the plaintext m from the ciphertext c without knowing the key.

This setting has obvious applications for transmitting e-mails, but it also applies to storage. Storing information can be thought of in terms of transmitting a message in time, rather than in space. In that situation Alice and Bob are often the same person, but the same solution applies.

3.1.1   Kerckhoffs' Principle

Bob needs two things to decrypt the ciphertext. He must know the decryption algorithm D, and the key K_e. An important rule is Kerckhoffs' principle: the security of the encryption scheme must depend only on the secrecy of the key K_e, and not on the secrecy of the algorithms.

There are very good reasons for this rule. Algorithms are hard to change. They are built into the software or hardware, which can be difficult to update. In practical situations, the same algorithm is used for a long time. That is just a fact of life. And it is hard enough to keep a simple key secret. Keeping the algorithm secret is far more difficult (and therefore more expensive). Nobody builds a cryptographic system for just two users. Every participant in the system (and there could be millions) uses the same algorithm. Eve would only have to get the algorithm from one of them, and one of them is bound to be easy to subvert. Or she could just steal a laptop with the algorithm on it. And remember our paranoia model? Eve might very well be one of the other users of the system, or even one of its designers.

There are also good reasons why algorithms should be published. From experience, we know that it is very easy to make a small mistake and create a cryptographic algorithm that is weak. If the algorithm isn't public, then nobody will find this fault until the attacker tries to attack it. The attacker can then use the flaw to break the system. As consultants, we have analyzed quite a number of secret encryption algorithms, and *all* of them were weak. This is why there is a healthy distrust of proprietary, confidential, or otherwise secret algorithms. Don't be fooled by the old "Well, if we keep the algorithm secret too, it will only increase security." That is wrong. The potential increase in security is small, and the potential decrease in security is huge. Secret algorithms are often so unbelievably bad that any claim along those lines borders on a demonstration of incompetence.

3.2   Authentication

Alice and Bob have another problem in figure 3.1. Eve can do more than just listen in on the message. Eve could change the message in some way. This requires Eve to have a bit more control over the communication channel,

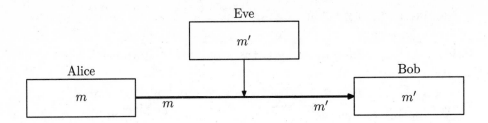

Figure 3.3: How does Bob know who sent the message?

but that is not at all an impossibility. For example, in figure 3.3 Alice tries to send the message m but Eve interferes with the communication channel. Instead of receiving m, Bob receives a different message m'. We assume that Eve also learns the message m that Alice tried to send. Other things that Eve could do are delete a message so that Bob never receives it, insert new messages that she invents, record a message and then send it to Bob later, or change the order of the messages.

Consider the point where Bob has just received a message. Why should Bob believe the message came from Alice? He has no reason to think it did. And if he doesn't know who sent the message, then the message is pretty useless.

To resolve this problem we introduce authentication. Like encryption, authentication uses a secret key that Alice and Bob both know. We'll call the authentication key K_a to distinguish it from the encryption key K_e. Figure 3.4 shows the process of authenticating a message m. When Alice sends the message m she computes a *message authentication code*, or MAC. Alice

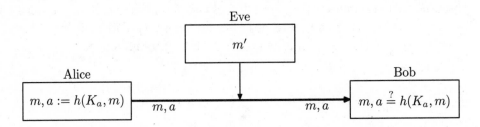

Figure 3.4: Generic setting for authentication

computes the MAC a as $a := h(K_a, m)$ where h is the MAC function and K_a is the authentication key. Alice now sends both m and a to Bob. When Bob receives m and a he recomputes what a should have been, using the key K_a, and checks that the a he receives is correct.

Now Eve wants to modify the message m to a different message m'. If she simply replaces m with m' then Bob will compute $h(K_a, m')$ and compare it to a. But a good MAC function will not give the same result for two different messages, so Bob will recognize that the message is not correct. Given that the message is wrong in one way or another, Bob will just discard the message.

If we assume that Eve does not know the authentication key K_a, then the only way in which Eve can get a message and a valid MAC is to listen to Alice when she sends messages to Bob. This still allows Eve to try some mischief. Eve can record messages and their MACs, and then replay them by sending them to Bob at any later time.

Pure authentication is only a partial solution. Eve can still delete messages that Alice sends. She can also repeat old messages or change the message order. Therefore, authentication is almost always combined with a numbering scheme to number the messages sequentially. If m contains such a message number, then Bob is not fooled by Eve when she replays old messages. Bob will simply see that the message has a correct MAC but the sequence number is that of an old message, so he will discard it.

Authentication in combination with message numbering solves most of the problem. Eve can still stop Alice and Bob from communicating, or delay messages by first deleting them and then sending them to Bob at a later time. But that is about the extent of what she can do.

The best way to look at it is to consider the case where Alice sends a sequence of messages $m_1, m_2, m_3, \ldots$. Bob only accepts messages with a proper MAC and whose message number is strictly greater[1] than the message number of the last message he accepted. So Bob receives a sequence of messages that is a *subsequence* of the sequence that Alice sent. A subsequence is simply the same sequence with zero or more messages deleted.

---

[1] "Strictly greater" means "greater and not equal to."

This is the extent to which cryptography can help in this situation. Bob will receive a subsequence of the messages that Alice sent, but other than deleting certain messages or stopping all communications, Eve cannot manipulate the message traffic. To avoid the loss of information, Alice and Bob will often use a scheme of resending messages that were lost, but that is more application-specific, and not part of the cryptography.

Of course, in many situations Alice and Bob will want to use both encryption and authentication. We will discuss this combination in great detail later. Never confuse the two concepts. Encrypting a message doesn't stop manipulation of its contents, and authenticating a message doesn't keep the message secret. One of the classical mistakes in cryptography is to think that encrypting a message also stops Eve from changing it. It doesn't.

3.3   Public-Key Encryption

To use encryption as we discussed in section 3.1, Alice and Bob must share the key K_e. How did they get far enough along to share a key? Alice couldn't send the key to Bob over the communication channel, as Eve could read the key too. The problem of distributing and managing keys is one of the really difficult parts of cryptography, for which we have only partial solutions.

Alice and Bob could have exchanged the key when they met last month for a drink. But if Alice and Bob are part of a group of 20 friends that like to communicate with each other, then each member of the group would have to exchange a total of 19 keys. All in all the group would have to exchange a total of 190 keys. This is already very complex, and the problem grows with the number of people Alice communicates with.

Establishing cryptographic keys is an age-old problem, and one important contribution to the solution is public-key cryptography. We will first discuss public-key encryption, shown in figure 3.5. We left Eve out of this diagram; from now on, just assume that all communications are always accessible to an enemy like Eve. Apart from Eve's absence, this figure is very similar to figure 3.2. The big difference is that Alice and Bob no longer use the same key, but now use different keys. This is the great idea behind public-key cryptography.

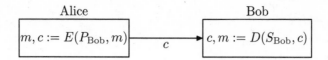

Figure 3.5: Generic setting for public-key encryption

To set things up, Bob first generates a pair of keys $(S_{\text{Bob}}, P_{\text{Bob}})$ using a special algorithm. The two keys are the secret key S_{Bob} and the public key P_{Bob}. Bob then does a surprising thing: he publishes P_{Bob} as his public key. (Why else would it be called a public key?)

When Alice wants to send a message to Bob, she looks up the public key that Bob published. Alice encrypts the message m with the public key P_{Bob} to get the ciphertext c, and sends c to Bob. Bob uses his secret key S_{Bob} and the decryption algorithm to decrypt the message and get the message m.

For this to work, the key-pair generation algorithm, encryption algorithm, and decryption algorithm have to ensure that the decryption actually yields the original message. In other words: $D(S_{\text{Bob}}, E(P_{\text{Bob}}, m)) = m$ must hold for all possible messages m. We'll examine this in more detail later.

Not only are the two keys that Alice and Bob use different, but the encryption and decryption algorithms can also be very different as well. All public-key encryption schemes depend heavily on mathematics. One obvious requirement is that it should not be possible to compute the secret key from the corresponding public key.

This type of encryption is called asymmetric-key encryption, or public-key encryption, as opposed to the symmetric-key encryption or secret-key encryption we discussed earlier.

Public-key cryptography makes the problem of distributing keys a lot simpler. Now Bob only has to distribute a single public key that everybody can use. Alice publishes her public key in the same way, and now Alice and Bob can communicate securely. Even in large groups, each group member only has to publish a single public key, which is quite manageable.

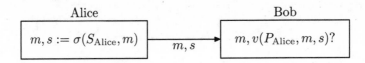

Figure 3.6: Generic setting for digital signature

So why do we bother with secret-key encryption if public-key encryption is so much easier? Because public-key encryption is much less efficient, by several orders of magnitude. Using it for everything is simply too expensive. In practical systems that use public-key cryptography, you almost always see a mixture of public key and secret key algorithms. The public key algorithms are used to establish a secret key, which in turn is used to encrypt the actual data. This combines the flexibility of public-key cryptography with the efficiency of symmetric-key cryptography.

3.4   Digital Signatures

Digital signatures are the public-key equivalent of message authentication codes. The generic setting is shown in figure 3.6. This time it is Alice who uses a key generation algorithm to generate a key pair $(S_{\text{Alice}}, P_{\text{Alice}})$ and publishes her public key P_{Alice}. When she wants to send a signed message m to Bob, she computes a signature $s := \sigma(S_{\text{Alice}}, m)$. She sends m and s to Bob. Bob uses a verification algorithm $v(P_{\text{Alice}}, m, s)$ that uses Alice's public key to verify the signature. The signature works just like a MAC, except that Bob can verify it with the public key, whereas the secret key is required to create a new signature.

Bob only needs to have Alice's public key to verify that the message came from Alice. Interestingly enough, anybody else can get Alice's public key and verify that the message came from Alice. This is why we generally call s a *digital signature*. In a sense, Alice signs the message. If there is ever a dispute, Bob can take m and s to a judge and prove that Alice signed the message.

This is all very nice in theory, and it works too... in theory. In real life, digital signatures aren't nearly as useful as we would like. The main problem is that Alice doesn't compute the signature herself; instead, she has her computer compute the signature. The digital signature is therefore no proof that Alice approved the message, or even saw it on her computer screen. Given the ease with which viruses take over computers, the digital signature actually proves very little. Nonetheless, when used appropriately, digital signatures are extremely useful.

3.5 PKI

Public-key cryptography makes key management simpler, but Alice still has to find Bob's public key. How can she be sure it is Bob's key, and not somebody else's? Maybe Eve created a key pair and published the key while impersonating Bob. The general solution is to use a PKI, or *public key infrastructure*.

The main idea is to have a central authority called the *certificate authority*, or CA. Each user takes his public key to the CA and identifies himself to the CA. The CA then signs the user's public key using a digital signature. The signed message, or *certificate*, states: "I, the CA, have verified that public key P_{Bob} belongs to Bob." The certificate will often include an expiration date and other useful information.

Using certificates, it is much easier for Alice to find Bob's key. We will assume that Alice has the CA's public key, and has verified that this is the correct key. Alice can now retrieve Bob's key from a database, or Bob can e-mail his key to Alice. Alice can verify the certificate on the key using the CA's public key that she already has. This certificate ensures that she has the correct key to communicate with Bob. Similarly, Bob can find Alice's public key and be sure that he is communicating with the right person.

In a PKI, each participant only has to have the CA certify his public key, and know the CA's public key so that he can verify the certificates of other participants. This is far less work than exchanging keys with every party he communicates with. That's the great advantage of a PKI: register once, use everywhere.

For practical reasons, a PKI is often set up with multiple levels of CAs. There is a top-level CA, called the root, which issues certificates on the keys of lower-level CAs, which in turn certify the user keys. The system still behaves in the same way, but now Alice has to check two certificates to verify Bob's key.

A PKI is not the ultimate solution; there are still many problems. First of all, the CA must be trusted by everybody. In some situations, that's easy. The HR department of a company knows all employees, and can take on the role of CA. But there is no entity in the world that is trusted by everybody. The idea that a single PKI can handle the whole world is just plain wrong.

The second problem is one of liability. What if the CA issues a false certificate, or the secret key of the CA is stolen? Alice would be trusting a false certificate, and she might lose a lot of money because of that. Who pays? Obviously Alice can only trust the certificate if the CA is willing to back it up with some kind of insurance. This requires a far more extensive business relationship between Alice and the CA.

There are many companies at the moment that are trying to be the world's CA. VeriSign is probably the best-known one. However, VeriSign explicitly limits its own liability in case it fails to perform its function properly. In most cases the liability is limited to $100. That is far less than what either of us paid for his last order of books: transactions which were secured using certificates signed by VeriSign. That wasn't a problem because payment by credit card is safe for the consumer. However, we won't be buying our next car using a certificate that VeriSign only backs with a $100 guarantee.

For more extensive information on the PKIs and their problems, see chapters 19, 20, and 21.

3.6   Attacks

Having described the most important functions used in cryptography, we will now talk about some attacks. There are many type of attacks, each with its own severity.

3.6.1 Ciphertext-Only

A *ciphertext-only attack* is what most people mean when talking about breaking an encryption system. This is the situation in which Alice and Bob are encrypting their data, and all you as the attacker get to see is the ciphertext. Trying to decrypt a message if you only know the ciphertext is called a ciphertext-only attack. This is the most difficult type of attack, because you have the least amount of information.

3.6.2 Known Plaintext

A *known plaintext attack* is one in which you know both the plaintext and the ciphertext. The object, of course, is to find the encryption key. At first this looks very implausible: how could you know the plaintext? It turns out that there are many situations in which you get to know the plaintext of a communication. Sometimes there are messages that are easy to predict. For example: Alice is away on holiday and has an e-mail autoresponder that sends an "I'm away on holiday" reply to every incoming e-mail. You get an exact copy of this message by sending an e-mail to Alice and reading the reply. When Bob sends an e-mail to Alice, the autoresponder also replies, this time encrypted. Now you have the ciphertext and the plaintext of a message. If you can find the key, you can decrypt all other messages that Alice and Bob exchange.

Another typical situation is where Alice sends the same message to many people, including you. You now have the plaintext and the ciphertexts of the copy she sent to everybody else.

Maybe Alice and Bob are sending drafts of a press release to each other. Once the press release is published, you know the plaintext and the ciphertext.

Even if you don't know the entire plaintext, you often know part of it. E-mails will have a predictable start, or a fixed signature at the end. The header of an IP packet is highly predictable. Such predictable data leads to a partially known plaintext, and we classify this under known plaintext attacks.

A known plaintext attack is more powerful than a ciphertext-only attack. You, as the attacker, get more information than in the ciphertext-only case. Extra information can only help you.

3.6.3   Chosen Plaintext

The next level of control is to let you choose the plaintext. This is a more powerful type of attack than a known plaintext attack. Now you get to select specially prepared plaintexts, chosen to make it easy to attack the system. You can choose any number of plaintexts and get the corresponding ciphertexts. Again, this is not unrealistic in practice. There are quite a large number of situations in which an attacker can choose the data that is being encrypted. Quite often Alice will get information from some outside source (e.g., one that can be influenced by the attacker) and then forward that information to Bob in encrypted form.

Chosen plaintext attacks are not unreasonable in any way. A good encryption algorithm has no trouble withstanding a chosen plaintext attack. If anyone ever tries to convince you that a chosen plaintext attack is not practical, you can bet that his shiny new encryption algorithm is so weak that it cannot even withstand a chosen plaintext attack.

There are two variations on this attack. In the offline attack, you prepare a list of all the plaintexts you want to have encrypted before you get the ciphertexts. In the online attack, you can choose new plaintexts depending on the ciphertexts you've already received. Most of the time this distinction can be ignored. We will normally talk about the online version of the attack which is the more powerful of the two.

3.6.4   Chosen Ciphertext

The term "chosen ciphertext" is a misnomer. It should really be called a "chosen ciphertext and plaintext attack," but that is too long. In a chosen plaintext attack, you get to choose plaintext values. In a chosen ciphertext attack, you get to choose both plaintext values and ciphertext values. For every plaintext that you choose you get the corresponding ciphertext, and for any ciphertext you choose you get the corresponding plaintext.

Obviously the chosen ciphertext attack is more powerful than a chosen plaintext attack as the attacker has more freedom. The goal still is to recover the key. Again, any reasonable encryption scheme has no trouble surviving a chosen ciphertext attack.

3.6.5 Distinguishing Attacks

The attacks described above recover the plaintext or the encryption key. There are attacks that do not recover the encryption key, but let you decrypt a specific other message. There are also attacks that do not recover a message, but reveal some partial information about the message. There are too many forms of attack to list here, and new forms of attack are thought up all the time. So what should we defend against?

The best solution is to define a distinguishing attack. A distinguishing attack is any nontrivial method that detects a difference between the ideal cipher and the actual cipher. This covers all the attacks we have discussed so far, as well as any yet-to-be-discovered attacks. Of course, we will have to define what the ideal cipher is.

Isn't this all rather far-fetched? Well, no. Our experience shows that you really want your building blocks to be perfect. Some encryption functions have imperfections that cause them to fail the distinguishing attack definition, but other than that they are perfectly satisfactory encryption functions. Every time you use them, you have to check that these imperfections do not lead to any problems. In a system with multiple building blocks, you also have to check whether any combination of imperfections leads to problems. This quickly becomes unworkable, and in practice we have found actual systems that exhibit weaknesses due to known imperfections in their building blocks.

3.6.6 Birthday

Birthday attacks are named after the birthday paradox. If you have 23 people in a room, the chance that two of them will have the same birthday exceeds 50%. That is a surprisingly large probability, given that there are 365 possible birthdays.

So what is a birthday attack? It is an attack that depends on the fact that duplicate values, also called *collisions*, appear much faster than you would expect. Suppose a system for secure financial transactions uses a fresh 64-bit authentication key for each transaction. (For simplicity we assume that no encryption is used.) There are 2^{64} ($=18 \cdot 10^{18}$, or eighteen billion billion) possible key values, so this should be quite difficult to break, right? Wrong! After seeing about 2^{32} transactions, the attacker can expect that two transactions use the same key. Suppose the first authenticated message is always the same "Are you ready to receive a transaction?" message. If two transactions use the same authentication key, then the MAC values on their first messages will also be the same, which is easy to detect for the attacker. But knowing that the two keys are the same, the attacker can now insert the messages from the older transaction into the newer transaction while it is going on. As they are authenticated by the correct key, these bogus messages will be accepted, which is a clear break of the financial transaction system.

In general: if an element can take on N different values, then you can expect the first collision after choosing about $\sqrt{N}$ random elements. We're leaving out the exact details here, but $\sqrt{N}$ is fairly close. For the birthday paradox, we have $N = 365$ and $\sqrt{N} \approx 19$. The number of people required before the chance of a duplicate birthday exceeds 50% is in fact 23, but the $\sqrt{N}$ is close enough for our purposes. One way of looking at this is that if you choose k elements, then there are $k(k-1)/2$ pairs of elements, each of which has a $1/N$ chance of being a pair of equal values. So the chance of finding a collision is close to $k(k-1)/2N$. When $k \approx \sqrt{N}$ then this chance is close to 50%.[2]

Most of the time we talk about n-bit values. As there are 2^n possible values, you need $\sqrt{2^n} = 2^{n/2}$ elements in the set before you expect a collision. We will often talk about this as the $2^{n/2}$ bound, or the birthday bound.

3.6.7   Meet in the Middle

Meet-in-the-middle attacks are the cousins of birthday attacks. (Together we call them *collision attacks*.) They are more common and more useful.

---

[2]These are only approximations, but good enough for our purposes.

Instead of waiting for a key to repeat, you can build a table of keys that you have chosen yourself.

Let's go back to our previous example of the financial transaction system that uses a fresh 64-bit key to authenticate each transaction. By using a meet-in-the-middle attack the attacker can break the system even further. Here is how he does it: he chooses 2^{32} different 64-bit keys at random. For each of these keys, he computes the MAC on the "Are you ready to receive a transaction?" message, and stores both the MAC result and the key in a table. Then he eavesdrops on each transaction and checks if the MAC of the first message appears in his table. If the MAC does appear in the table, then there is a very good chance that the authentication key for that transaction is the same key as the attacker used to compute that table entry, and that key value is stored right alongside the MAC value in the table. Now that the attacker knows the authentication key, he can insert arbitrary messages of his choosing into the transaction. (The birthday attack only allowed him to insert messages from an old transaction.)

How many transactions does the attacker need to listen to? Well, he has precomputed the MAC on 1 in 2^{32} of all the possible keys, so any time the system chooses a key, there is a 1 in 2^{32} chance of choosing one that he can recognize. So after about 2^{32} transactions, he can expect a transaction that uses a key he precomputed the MAC for. The total workload for the attacker is about 2^{32} steps in the precomputation plus listening in to 2^{32} transactions, which is a lot less work than trying all 2^{64} possible keys.

The difference between the birthday attack and the meet-in-the-middle attack is that in a birthday attack, you wait for a single value to occur twice within the same set of elements. In a meet-in-the-middle attack, you have two sets, and wait for an overlap between the two sets. In both cases you can expect to find the first result at around the same number of elements.

A meet-in-the-middle attack is more flexible than the birthday attack. Let's look at it in a more abstract way. Suppose we have N possible values. The first set has P elements, the second has Q elements. There are PQ pairs of elements, and each pair has a chance of $1/N$ of matching. We expect a collision as soon as PQ/N is close to 1. The most efficient choice is $P \approx Q \approx \sqrt{N}$. This is exactly the birthday bound again. The meet-in-the-middle attack provides extra flexibility. Sometimes it is easier to get elements for one of the sets than it is to get elements for the other set. The only requirement is that PQ is close to N. You could choose $P \approx N^{1/3}$ and $Q \approx N^{2/3}$. In the example above, the attacker might make a list of 2^{40} possible MAC values for the first message, and expect to find the first authentication key after listening to only 2^{24} transactions.

When we do a theoretical analysis of how easy a system is to attack, we often use the $\sqrt{N}$ size for both sets, because this generally minimizes the number of steps the attacker has to perform. It also requires a more detailed analysis to find out whether the elements of one set might be harder to get than the elements of the other set. If you ever want to perform a meet-in-the-middle attack in real life, you should carefully choose the sizes of the sets to ensure $PQ \approx N$ at the least possible cost.

3.6.8   Other Types of Attack

So far we have mostly talked about attacking encryption functions. You can also define attacks for other cryptographic functions, such as authentication, digital signatures, etc. We will discuss these as they arise.

3.7   Security Level

With enough effort, any cryptographic system can be attacked successfully. The real question is how much work it takes to break a system. An easy way to quantify the workload of an attack is to compare it to an exhaustive search. If an attack requires 2^{235} steps of work, then this corresponds to an exhaustive search for a 235-bit value.

We always talk about an attacker needing a certain number of steps, but haven't yet specified what a step is. This is partly laziness, but it also simplifies the analysis. When attacking an encryption function, computing a single encryption of a given message with a given key can be a single step. Sometimes a step is merely looking something up in a table. It varies. But in all situations, a step can be executed by a computer in a very short time. Sometimes it can be done in one clock cycle, sometimes it needs a million clock cycles, but in terms of the workloads that cryptographic attacks require, a single factor of a million is not terribly important. The ease of using a step-based analysis far outweighs the built-in inaccuracies. You can always do a more detailed analysis to find out how much work a step is. For a quick estimate we always assume that a single step requires a single clock cycle.

Any system designed today really needs a 128-bit security level. That means that any attack will require at least 2^{128} steps. A new system designed today is, if successful, quite likely to be in operation 30 years from now, and should provide at least 20 years of confidentiality for the data after the point at which it was last used. So we should aim to provide security for the next 50 years. That is a rather tall order, but there has been some work done to extrapolate Moore's law and apply it to cryptography. A security level of 128 bits is sufficient [63]. One could argue for 100 bits, or even 110 bits, but there are no cryptographic primitives with 110-bit keys around, so we'll use 128 bits.

This concept of security level is only approximate. We only measure the amount of work the attacker has to do, and ignore things like memory or interactions with the fielded system. Dealing only with the attacker's workload is hard enough; complicating the model would make the security analysis much harder still, and greatly increase the chance of overlooking a vital point. As the cost for using a simple and conservative approach is relatively low, we use the simple concept of security level.

3.8 Performance

Almost every time we design a system people complain about the cost in terms of speed and performance. Here are our thoughts on the subject.

First of all, security does not come for free. If you want security, you'll have to pay the price. If you can't afford it, then you won't get good security. It is as simple as that. Modern software expends a huge number of cycles to draw pretty three-dimensional windows with alpha-blending that provide little or no functional improvement at all. Security is one of the major problems in the industry, yet many are unwilling to spend as many cycles on the security as they spend on drawing their windows.

Every system we design we try to make as efficient as possible. However, after a certain point any performance increase becomes very expensive. As soon as you deviate from the beaten path in security, you have to do an enormous amount of analysis work to make sure you don't fool yourself into using a weak system. Such analysis requires experienced cryptographers, and they are expensive. For most systems, it is much cheaper to buy a faster computer than to go to the trouble and expense of designing and implementing a more efficient security system.

For most systems, the performance of the cryptography is not a problem. Modern CPUs are so fast that they can keep up with almost any data stream they handle. For example, encrypting a 100 Mb/s data link with the AES algorithm requires only 20% of the cycles on a 1 GHz Pentium III CPU. (Less in real life, as you never get to transfer 100 Mb/s over such a link due to the overhead of the communication protocol.) If you wait a few months to buy the machine, you get the 1.2 GHz CPU for the same price, and the overhead becomes zero compared to the 1 GHz CPU. One company once complained about the cost of encrypting a 1 Gb/s link. The machine that handled the data cost more than a half million dollars. You'd think they could afford to put in an extra CPU, or add a bit of hardware to a chip to handle the cryptography.

There are some situations in which cryptography creates a performance bottleneck. A good example is Web servers that use a very large number of SSL connections. The initialization of an SSL connection uses public-key cryptography and requires a large amount of computing power on the server side. Sure, we could develop an SSL-replacement that is more efficient for the server. You wouldn't want us to, though. It is far cheaper to buy some hardware accelerators to handle the existing SSL protocol than to pay an expert to develop a new protocol. And then pay people to standardize it. And then to implement it for both servers and browsers. And then to convince everybody to upgrade to a new browser version.

Recently we ran across a good argument to convince people to choose security over performance. "There are already enough insecure fast systems; we don't need another one." This is very true. Half-measures in security cost nearly as much as doing it well, but provide very little practical security. We firmly believe you should either do it well or not bother at all.

3.9   Complexity

There are no secure complex systems.

Design rule 1. *Complexity is the worst enemy of security.*

This is a simple rule, but it took us a while to really understand it. The IT industry is really pretty bad at building complex systems. They just plod along, implement something, and then beat it into working order ... well, sort of, at least. Something that works most of the time is the norm, and almost no software will stand up to intentional abuse.

This has to do with the test-and-fix development process used almost everywhere: build something, test for errors, go back and fix the errors, test to find more errors, etc. Test, fix, repeat. This goes on until company finances dictate that the product be shipped, or until the programmers get bored. Sure, the result is something that works reasonably well, as long as it is used only for the things it was tested for. This might be good enough for functionality, but it is wholly inadequate for security systems.

The problem with the test-and-fix method is that testing only shows the presence of errors, and really only those errors the testers were looking for. Security systems have to work even when under attack by clever, malicious people. The system cannot be tested for all the situations the attackers will expose the system to. The system has to be secure from the start.

Consider the following analogy. Suppose you write a medium-sized application in a popular programming language. You fix the syntax errors until it compiles the first time. Then, without further testing, you put it in a box and ship it to the customer. Nobody would expect to get a functional product that way.

Yet this is exactly what is normally done for security systems. They're impossible to test because nobody knows what to test for. And if there is any bug, the product is defective. So the only way to get a secure system is to build a very robust system from the ground up. This requires a simple system.

The only way we know of making a system simple is to modularize it. We all know this from software development. But this time we cannot afford any bug at all, so we have to be quite ruthless in the modularization. Here is our main rule:

Design rule 2. *Correctness must be a local property.*

In other words, one part of the system should behave correctly regardless of how the rest of the system works. No, we don't want to hear "this won't be a problem because this other part of the system will never let this happen." The other part may have a bug, or may change in some future version. Each part of the system is responsible for its own functionality.

You'll see this rule applied in many forms throughout this book. It is one of the reasons why many of our choices are so much more conservative than what is currently used in many other designs.

Part I

Message Security

Chapter 4

Block Ciphers

Block ciphers are one of the fundamental building blocks for cryptographic systems. There is a lot of literature on block ciphers, and they are among the best-understood parts of cryptography.

4.1   What Is a Block Cipher?

A *block cipher* is an encryption function for fix-sized blocks. The current generation of block ciphers has a block size of 128 bits (16 bytes). These block ciphers encrypt a 128-bit plaintext and generate a 128-bit ciphertext as the result. The block cipher is reversible; there is a decryption function that takes the 128-bit ciphertext and decrypts it to the original 128-bit plaintext. The plaintext and ciphertext are always the same size, and we call this the block size of the block cipher.

To encrypt, we need a secret key. Without secrets, there is no way to hide the message. Like the plaintext and ciphertext, the key is also a string of bits. Common key sizes are 128 and 256 bits. We often write $E(K, p)$ or $E_K(p)$ for the encryption of plaintext p with key K and $D(K, c)$ or $D_K(c)$ for the decryption of ciphertext c with key K.

Block ciphers are used mainly to encrypt information. For short messages you can use a block cipher directly. If the message is longer than the block length (which is more common) you need to use a block cipher mode, which we will discuss in chapter 5.

We always follow Kerckhoffs' principle, and assume that the algorithms for encryption and decryption are publicly known. Some people have a hard time accepting this, and they want to keep the algorithms secret. Don't ever trust a secret block cipher (or any other secret cryptographic primitive).

It is sometimes useful to look at a block cipher as a very big key-dependent table. For any fixed key, you could compute a lookup table that maps the plaintext to the ciphertext. This table would be huge. For a block cipher with 32-bit block size, the table would be 16 GB; for a 64-bit block size, it would be 150 million TB; and for a 128-bit block size it would be $5 \cdot 10^{39}$ bytes, a number so large there is not even a proper name for it. Of course, it is not practical to build such a table in reality, but this is a useful conceptual model. We also know that the block cipher is reversible. In other words, no two entries of the table are the same, or else the decryption function could not possibly decrypt the ciphertext to a unique plaintext. This big table will therefore contain every possible ciphertext value exactly once. This is what mathematicians call a permutation: the table is merely a list of all the possible elements where the order has been rearranged. A block cipher with a block size of k bits specifies a permutation on k-bit values for each of the key values.

4.2   Types of Attack

Given the definition of a block cipher, the definition of a secure block cipher seems simple enough: it is a block cipher that keeps the plaintext secret. Although this certainly is one of the requirements, it is not sufficient. This definition only requires that the block cipher is secure against ciphertext-only attacks, in which the attacker gets to see only the ciphertext of a message. There are a few published attacks of this type [54, 92], but they are rare. Most published attacks are of the chosen plaintext type. We gave an overview of general attack types in section 3.6. All of these attack types apply to block ciphers, and there are a few more that are specific to block ciphers.

The first one is the related-key attack. First introduced by Eli Biham in 1993 [7], a related-key attack assumes that the attacker has access to several encryption functions. These functions all have an unknown key, but their keys have a relationship that the attacker knows. This sounds very strange, but it turns out that this type of attack is useful against real systems [50]. There are real-world systems that use different keys with a known relationship. One proprietary system changes the key for every message by incrementing the key by one. Consecutive messages are therefore encrypted with consecutively numbered keys. It turns out that key relationships like this can be used to attack block ciphers.

There are even more esoteric attack types. The team that designed the Twofish block cipher introduced the concept of a chosen key attack in which the attacker specifies some part of the key and then performs a related-key attack on the rest of the key [86].[1]

Why would we even consider far-fetched attack types like related-key attacks and chosen-key attacks? We have several reasons. We have seen actual systems in which a related-key attack on the block cipher was possible, so these attacks are not that far-fetched at all. Block ciphers are very useful building blocks. They tend to get abused in every imaginable way. One standard technique of constructing a hash function from a block cipher is the Davies-Meyer construction [96]. In a Davies-Meyer hash function the attacker suddenly gets to choose the key of the block cipher, which allows related-key and chosen-key attacks. Any definition of block-cipher security that ignores these attack types, or any other attack type, is incomplete. The block cipher is a module that should have a simple interface. The simplest interface is to ensure that it has all the properties that anyone could reasonably expect the block cipher to have. Allowing imperfections in the block cipher just adds a lot of complexity, in the form of cross-dependencies, to any system using the cipher.

---

[1]Later analysis showed that this attack does not work on Twofish [32], but it might be successful against other block ciphers.

4.3   The Ideal Block Cipher

In order to define block cipher security, we first need to define the ideal block cipher. What would the ideal block cipher look like? It should be a random permutation. We should be more precise: for each key value we want the block cipher to be a random permutation, and the different permutations for the different key values should be chosen independently. As we mentioned before, you can think of a 128-bit block cipher (a single permutation on 128-bit values) as a huge lookup table of 2^{128} elements of 128 bits each. The ideal block cipher consists of one of these tables for each key value, with each table chosen randomly from the set of all possible permutations.

Strictly speaking, this definition of the ideal block cipher is incomplete, as the exact choice of the tables has not been specified. As soon as we specify the tables, however, the ideal cipher is fixed and no longer random. To formalize the definition we cannot talk about a single ideal block cipher, but we have to treat the ideal block cipher as a uniform probability distribution over the set of all possible block ciphers. Any time that you use the ideal block cipher you will have to talk in terms of probabilities. This is a mathematician's delight, but the added complexity would make our explanations far more complicated—so we will keep the informal but simpler concept of a randomly chosen block cipher.

4.4   Definition of Block Cipher Security

There are many definitions of security for block ciphers in the literature, for example [53]. These definitions are often fairly mathematical, and none of them capture all the aspects we have discussed. We prefer to use a simpler but informal definition.

Definition 1. *A secure block cipher is one for which no attack exists.*

This is a bit of a tautology. So now we have to define an attack on a block cipher.

Definition 2. *An attack on a block cipher is a nontrivial method of distinguishing the block cipher from an ideal block cipher.*

What do we mean by distinguishing a block cipher from an ideal block cipher? Given a block cipher X, we compare it to an ideal block cipher with the same block size and the same key size. A distinguisher is an algorithm that is given a black-box function which computes either the block cipher X or an ideal block cipher. (A black-box function is a function that can be evaluated, but the distinguisher algorithm does not know the internal workings of the function in the black box.) Both the encryption and decryption functions are available, and the distinguisher algorithm is free to choose any key for each of the encryptions and decryptions it performs. The distinguisher's task is to figure out whether the black-box function implements the block cipher X or the ideal cipher. It doesn't have to be a perfect distinguisher, as long as it provides the correct answer significantly more often than the wrong answer.

There are, of course, trivial solutions to this. We could encrypt the plaintext 0 with the key 0 and see if the result matches what we expect to get from block cipher X. This is a distinguisher, but to make it an attack, the distinguisher has to be nontrivial. This is where it becomes difficult to define block cipher security. We cannot formalize the notion of "trivial" and "nontrivial." It is a bit like obscenity: we know it when we see it.[2] A distinguisher is trivial if we can find a similar distinguisher for almost any block cipher. In the above case, the distinguisher is trivial because we can construct one just like it for any block cipher, even an ideal one.

We can also create a more advanced trivial distinguisher. Encrypt the plaintext 0 with all keys in the range $1, \ldots, 2^{32}$ and count how often each value for the first 32 bits of the ciphertext occurs. Suppose we find that for a cipher X the value t occurs 5 times instead of the expected one time. This is a property that is unlikely to hold for the ideal cipher. This is still a trivial distinguisher, as we can easily construct something similar for any cipher X. (It is in fact extremely unlikely that a cipher does not have a suitable value for t.)

Things become more complicated if we design a distinguisher as follows: We make a list of 1000 different statistics that we can compute about a cipher. We compute each of these for cipher X, and build the distinguisher from the

---

[2]In 1964, U.S. Supreme Court judge Potter Stewart used these words to define obscenity: "I shall not today attempt further to define the kinds of material ... but I know it when I see it."

statistic that gives the most significant result. We expect to find a statistic with a significance level of about 1 in 1000. We can of course apply the same technique to find distinguishers for any particular cipher, so this is a trivial attack, but the triviality now depends not only on the distinguisher itself, but also on how the distinguisher was found. That's why nobody has been able to formalize a definition of triviality and block cipher security. We would love to give you a clean definition of block cipher security, but the cryptographic community does not yet know enough about cryptography to be able to do this properly. Using a more formal definition that ignores certain types of attack is the wrong way to go about making secure systems.

We must not forget to limit the amount of computation allowed in the distinguisher. We could have done this explicitly in the definition, but that would have complicated it even further. If the block cipher has an explicit security level of n bits, then the distinguisher should be more efficient than an exhaustive search on n-bit values. If no explicit design strength is given, the design strength equals the key size. This formulation is rather roundabout for a reason. It is tempting to just say that the distinguisher has to work in less than 2^n steps. This is certainly true, but some types of distinguishers give you only a probabilistic result that is more like a partial key search. The attack could have a trade-off between the amount of work and the probability of distinguishing the cipher from the ideal cipher. For example: an exhaustive search of half the key space requires 2^{n-1} work and provides the right answer 75% of the time. (If the attacker finds the key, he knows the answer. If he doesn't find the key, he still has a 50% chance of guessing right. Overall, his chances of getting the right answer are therefore $0.5 + 0.5 \cdot 0.5 = 0.75$.) By comparing the distinguisher to such partial key-space searches we take this natural trade-off into account, and stop such partial key searches from being classified as an attack.

Our definition of block cipher security covers all possible forms of attack. Ciphertext only, known plaintext, (adaptively) chosen plaintext, related key, and all other types of attack all implement a nontrivial distinguisher. That is why we like our definition.

So why spend two pages on defining what a secure block cipher is? This definition is very important because it defines a simple and clean interface between the block cipher and the rest of the system. This sort of modularization is a hallmark of good design. In security systems, where complexity is one of our main enemies, good modularization is even more important than in most other areas. Once a block cipher satisfies our security definition, you can treat it as if it were an ideal cipher. After all, if it does not behave as an ideal cipher in the system, then you have found a distinguisher for the cipher, which means the cipher is not secure according to our definition. If you use a secure block cipher you no longer have to remember any particularities or imperfections; the cipher will have all the properties that you expect a block cipher to have. Because the ideal cipher is a rather simple concept to remember, the design work becomes much easier.

4.4.1   Parity of a Permutation

Unfortunately, we have one more complication. As we discussed, encryption under a single key corresponds to a lookup in a permutation table. Think about constructing this table in two steps. First you initialize the table with the identity mapping by giving the element at index i the value i. Then you create the permutation that you want by repeatedly swapping two elements in the table. It turns out that there are two types of permutations: those that can be constructed from an even number of swaps (called the even permutations) and those that can be constructed from an odd number of swaps (called the odd permutations). It should not surprise you that half of all permutations are even, and the other half are odd.

Most modern block ciphers have a 128-bit block size, but they operate on 32-bit words. They build the encryption function from many 32-bit operations. This has proved to be a very successful method, but it has one side-effect. It is rather hard to build an odd permutation from small operations; as a result virtually all block ciphers only generate even permutations.

This gives us a simple distinguisher for nearly any block cipher, one which we call the *parity attack*. For a given key, extract the permutation by encrypting all possible plaintexts. If the permutation is odd, we know that we have an ideal block cipher, because the real block cipher never generates an odd permutation. If the permutation is even, we claim to have a real block cipher. This distinguisher will be right 75% of the time. It will produce the wrong answer only if it is given an ideal cipher that produces an even permutation. The success rate can be improved by repeating the work for other key values.

This attack has no practical significance whatsoever. To find the parity of a permutation, you have to compute all but one of the plaintext/ciphertext pairs of the encryption function. (The last one is trivial to deduce: the sole remaining plaintext maps to the sole remaining ciphertext.) You should never allow that many plaintext/ciphertext queries to a block cipher in a real system, because other types of attacks start to hurt much sooner. In particular, once the attacker knows most of the plaintext/ciphertext pairs, he no longer needs a key to decrypt the message, but can simply use a lookup table created from those pairs.

We could declare the parity attack to be trivial by definition, but that seems disingenuous. Rather, we prefer to change the definition of the ideal block cipher, and limit it to randomly chosen *even* permutations.

Definition 3. *An ideal block cipher implements an independently chosen random even permutation for each of the key values.*

It is a pity to complicate our "ideal" cipher in this way, but the only alternative is to disqualify nearly all known block ciphers. For the overwhelming majority of applications, the restriction to even permutations is insignificant. As long as we never allow all plaintext/ciphertext pairs to be computed, even and odd permutations are indistinguishable.

If you ever have a block cipher that *can* generate odd permutations, you should revert to the original definition of the ideal cipher. In practice, parity attacks have more effect on the formal definition of security than on real-world systems, so you can probably forget about this whole issue of parity.

4.5   Real Block Ciphers

There are hundreds of block ciphers that have been proposed over the years. It is very easy to design a new block cipher. It is fiendishly hard to design a *good* new block cipher. We're not talking about security; that a block cipher has to be secure goes without saying. Boasting that your new cipher is secure is like boasting that your new roof keeps the rain out or that your new car has headlights. The difficult thing is to create a block cipher that is efficient in a wide variety of different applications.

Designing block ciphers can be fun and educational, but please, *please* don't use an unknown cipher in a real system. We don't trust a cipher until it has been reviewed thoroughly by other experts. A basic prerequisite is that the cipher has been published, but this is not enough. There are so many ciphers out there that few get any effective peer review. You are much better off using one of the well-known ciphers that already has been reviewed for you.

Virtually all block ciphers consist of several repetitions of a weak block cipher, known as a *round*. Several of these weak rounds in sequence make a strong block cipher. This structure is easy to design and implement, and is also a great help in the analysis. Most attacks on block ciphers begin by attacking versions with a reduced number of rounds. As the attacks improve, more and more rounds can be attacked.

We will discuss several block ciphers in more detail, but we won't define them exhaustively. The full specifications can be found in the references or on the Internet. We will instead concentrate on the overall structure and the properties of each cipher.

4.5.1   DES

The venerable working horse of cryptography, DES [70] has finally outlived its usefulness. Its restricted key size of 56 bits and small block size of 64 bits make it unsuitable for today's fast computers and large amounts of data. It survives in the form of 3DES [73], which is a block cipher built from three DES encryptions in sequence. This solves the most immediate problem of the small key size, but there is no known fix for the small block size. DES is not a particularly fast cipher by current standards, and 3DES is one-third the speed of DES. You will still find DES in many systems, but we do not recommend using either DES or 3DES in new designs.

Figure 4.1 gives an overview of a single round of DES. This is a line diagram of the DES computations; you will commonly find diagrams like this in cryptographic literature. Each box computes a particular function, and the lines show which value is used where. There are a few standard conventions. The XOR or exclusive-or operation, sometimes called bitwise addition or addition without carry, is shown in formulas as a $\oplus$ operator and in figures

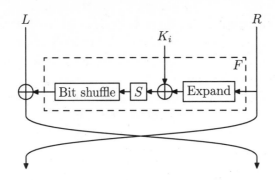

Figure 4.1: Structure of a single round of DES

as a large version of the $\oplus$ operator. You might also find drawings that include integer additions, which often are drawn to look like the $\boxplus$ operator.

DES has a 64-bit plaintext, which is split into two 32-bit halves L and R. This splitting is done by rearranging the bits in a semi-ordered fashion. Nobody seems to know why the designers bothered to rearrange the bits of the plaintext—it has no cryptographic effect—but that's how DES is defined. A similar swapping of bits is implemented at the end of the encryption to create the 64-bit ciphertext from the two halves L and R.

DES consists of 16 rounds numbered 1 through 16. Round i transforms the (L, R) pair into a new (L, R) pair under control of a round key K_i. Most of the work is done by the round function F, shown in the dashed box. As shown in the figure, the R value is first processed by an expand function, which duplicates a number of bits to produce 48 bits of output from the 32-bit input. The 48-bit result is XORed with the 48-bit round key K_i. The result of this is used in the S-box tables. An S-box (the term derives from *substitution box*) is basically just a lookup table that is publicly known. As you cannot build a lookup table with 48 input bits, the S-boxes consist of eight small lookup tables, each of which maps 6 bits to 4 bits. This brings the result size back to 32 bits. These 32 bits are then swapped around by the bit shuffle function before being XORed into the left value L. Finally, the values of L and R are swapped. This entire computation is repeated 16 times for a single DES encryption.

The basic structure of DES is called the Feistel construction [30]. It is a really elegant idea. Each round consists of XORing L with $F(K_i, R)$ for some function F, and then swapping L and R. The beauty of the construction is that decryption requires exactly the same set of operations as encryption. You need to swap L and R, and you need to XOR L with $F(K_i, R)$. This makes it much easier to implement the encryption and decryption functions together. It also means that you only have to analyze one of the two functions, as they are almost identical. A final trick used in most Feistel ciphers is to leave out the swap after the last round, which makes the encryption and decryption functions identical except for the order of the round keys. This is particularly nice for hardware implementations, as they can use the same circuit to compute both encryptions and decryptions.

DES needs 16 round keys of 48 bits each. Each round key is formed by selecting 48 bits from the 56-bit key, and this selection is different for each round key.[3]

The different parts of the DES cipher have different functions. The Feistel structure makes the cipher design simpler and ensures that the two halves L and R are mixed together. XORing the key material ensures that the key and data are mixed, which is the whole point of a cipher. The S-boxes provide nonlinearity. Without them, the cipher could be written as a bunch of binary additions, which would allow a very easy mathematical attack based on linear algebra. Finally, the combination of the S-box, expand, and bit shuffle functions provide diffusion. They ensure that if one bit is changed in the input of F, more than one bit is changed in the output. In the next round there will be more bit changes, and even more in the round after that, etc. Without good diffusion, a small change in the plaintext would lead to a small change in the ciphertext, which would be very easy to detect.

DES has a number of properties that disqualify it according to our security definition. Each of the round keys consists purely of some of the bits selected from the cipher key. If the cipher key is 0, then all the round keys are 0 as well. In particular, all the round keys are identical. Remember that the only difference between encryption and decryption is the order of the round keys. But all round keys are zero here. So encryption with the 0 key is the same function as decryption with the 0 key. This is a very easy property to

---

[3]There is some structure to this selection, which you can find in the DES specifications [70].

detect, and as an ideal block cipher does not have this property, it leads to an easy and efficient distinguishing attack.[4]

DES also has a complementation property that ensures that

$$E(\overline{K}, \overline{P}) = \overline{E(K, P)}$$

for all keys K and plaintexts P, where $\overline{X}$ is the value obtained by complementing all the bits in X. In other words, if you encrypt the complement of the plaintext with the complement of the key, you get the complement of the (original) ciphertext.

This is rather easy to see. Look at the figure and think about what happens if you flip all the bits in L, R, and K_i. The expand function merely copies bits around, so all the output bits are also flipped. The XOR with the key K_i has both inputs flipped, so the output remains the same. The input to the S-boxes remains the same, the output of the S-boxes remains the same, so the final XOR has one input that is flipped and one input that is the same. The new L value, soon to be swapped to the R position, is therefore also flipped. In other words, if you complement L and R at the beginning of the round and complement K_i as well, then the output is the complement of what you had originally. This property passes through the entire cipher.

The ideal block cipher would not have this curious property. More importantly, this particular property can lead to attacks on systems that use DES.

In short, DES does not pass muster anymore. The key length is wholly inadequate. There have already been several successful attempts to find a DES key by simple exhaustive search.

3DES has a larger key, but it inherits both the weak keys and the complementation property from DES, each of which is enough to disqualify the cipher by our standards. It is also severely limited by its 64-bit block size, which imposes severe restrictions on the amount of data we can encrypt with a single key. (See section 5.8 for details.) Sometimes you have to use 3DES in a design for legacy reasons, but be very careful with it because it does not behave like an ideal block cipher.

---

[4]There are three other keys that have this property too; together they are called the weak keys of DES.

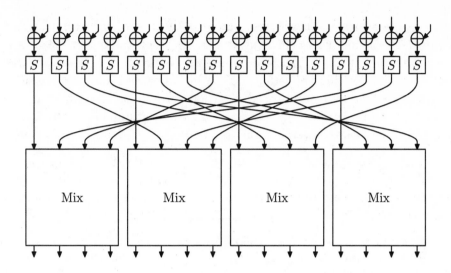

Figure 4.2: Structure of a single round of AES

4.5.2 AES

The Advanced Encryption Standard (AES) is a new U.S. government standard. Instead of designing or commissioning a cipher, NIST asked for proposals from the cryptographic community. A total of 15 proposals were submitted [72]. Five ciphers were selected as finalists [74], after which Rijndael was selected to become AES.[5] Overall, this process worked much better than we or anyone we know had expected. If any of you out there want to standardize a new cryptographic system, this is a lesson worth learning. If you get good proposals, an AES-style competition is far superior to a design by committee. If you don't have enough experts to get a good proposal, you probably shouldn't be standardizing anything at all.

AES uses a different structure than DES. It is not a Feistel cipher. Figure 4.2 shows a single round of AES. The subsequent rounds are similar. The plaintext comes in as 16 bytes at the very top. The first operation is to XOR the plaintext with 16 bytes (128 bits) of round key. This is shown

---

[5]There has been some confusion about the correct pronunciation of "Rijndael." Don't worry; unless you speak Dutch you will get it wrong, so just relax and pronounce it any way you like.

by the $\oplus$ operators; the key bytes come into the side of the XORs. Each of the 16 bytes is then used as an index into an S-box table that maps 8-bit inputs to 8-bit outputs. The S-boxes are all identical. The bytes are then rearranged in a specific order that looks a bit messy but has a simple structure. Finally, the bytes are mixed in groups of four using a linear mixing function. The term linear just means that each output bit of the mixing function is the XOR of several of the input bits.

This completes a single round. A full encryption consists of 10–14 rounds, depending on the size of the key. Like DES, there is a key schedule that generates the necessary round keys, but the key schedule uses a very different structure.

The AES structure has advantages and disadvantages. Each step consists of a number of operations that can be performed in parallel. This parallelism makes high-speed implementations easy. On the other hand, the decryption operation is significantly different from the encryption operation. You need the inverse lookup table of the S-box, and the inverse mixing operation is different from the original mixing operation.

We can recognize some of the same functional blocks as in DES. The XORs add key material to the data, the S-boxes provide nonlinearity, and the byte shuffle and mixing functions provide diffusion. AES is a very clean design with clearly separated tasks for each part of the cipher.

We have one criticism of AES: we don't quite trust the security. AES has always been a fairly aggressively designed cipher. In the original presentation the AES designers showed an attack on 6 rounds and chose 10–14 rounds for the full cipher, depending on the key size [18]. During the selection process, the attacks were improved to handle 7 rounds for 128-bit keys, 8 rounds for 192-bit keys, and even 9 rounds for 256-bit keys [31]. This still leaves a 3 to 5 round security margin. From a different perspective: for 128-bit keys, the best attack we know of covers 70% of the cipher. In other words, AES relies on the hope that future attacks will not give large improvements.

It is, as always, impossible to predict the future, but sometimes it helps to look at the past. Up to now the best-analyzed ciphers were DES, FEAL, and IDEA. In all cases, the attacks were significantly improved many years after the initial publication. Since then the field has progressed, but it still takes a leap of faith to think we know it all and that no significant improvements in attacks will be found.

By itself this is of some concern, but mostly to cryptographers. Even if current attacks were to be improved to the point of breaking AES, it would most likely be an attack that required something like 2^{120} steps and 2^{100} bytes of memory. This would be enough to consider the cipher "broken" by our standards, or rather, it would lead us to reduce the security level of the cipher to 120 bits. That would no longer satisfy our requirements, but if our money were at stake we would not lose any sleep over it. Such attacks are not practical yet, and are unlikely to become practical within our 50-year time frame (see section 3.7).

What concerns us the most about AES is its simple algebraic structure [34]. It is possible to write an AES encryption as a relatively simple closed algebraic formula over the finite field with 256 elements. This is not an attack, just a representation, but if anyone can ever solve those formulas, then AES will be broken. This opens up an entirely new avenue of attack. No other block cipher we know of has such a simple algebraic representation. We have no idea whether this leads to an attack or not, but not knowing is reason enough to be skeptical about the use of AES. We imagine this nightmare scenario in which five years from now, when AES is in widespread use, we will be sitting in a big room listening to a presentation from a PhD student from an entirely different branch of mathematics that begins: "I was bored one afternoon and I looked through this book that my friend had about cryptography. There were some formulas there that look just like the ones I had been studying for an unrelated project...." Twenty minutes later the presentation ends with "So it takes me about two hours on my PC to recover the key."

Let's be clear about this. This is an extremely unfair criticism of AES. We don't have an attack on AES. And every cipher, including AES, could be attacked in the future. Yet the simple algebraic structure of AES opens it up to an entirely different class of attacks. Cryptographers have no expertise in this area. No cryptographer we have spoken to knows anything about formulas like these. There might be people in this world who can handle this type of formula, but there is no reason to assume they know anything about cryptography. Let's be optimistic and assume there is only a 10% chance that this type of attack leads anywhere. And then there is only a 10%

chance that it leads to a practical attack on the full cipher. That translates to a 1% chance of a practical attack on AES—a risk we could avoid by using a more conventional cipher with a more complicated algebraic structure.

In the end, everybody will use AES because it is the U.S. government standard. We even advise people to use it, because it *is* the standard and using the standard avoids lots of discussions and problems. Even if AES is ever broken, nobody can fault you for having chosen the standard cipher. But the very aggressive design coupled with the clean algebraic structure just makes us feel uneasy.

4.5.3 Serpent

Serpent was another AES finalist [2]. It is built like a tank. Easily the most conservative of all the AES submissions, Serpent is in many ways the opposite of AES. Whereas AES puts emphasis on elegance and efficiency, Serpent is designed for security all the way. The best attack we know of covers only 10 of the 32 rounds [6]. The disadvantage of Serpent is that it is about one-third the speed of AES. It can also be difficult to implement efficiently, as the S-boxes have to be converted to a Boolean formula suitable for the underlying CPU.

In some ways Serpent has a similar structure to AES. It consists of 32 rounds. Each round consists of XORing in a 128-bit round key, applying a linear mixing function to the 128 bits, and then applying 32 four-bit S-boxes in parallel. In each round the 32 S-boxes are identical, but there are eight different S-boxes that are used each in turn in a round.

Serpent has an especially nice software implementation trick. A straightforward implementation would be very slow, as each round requires 32 S-box lookups and there are 32 rounds. In total there are 1024 S-box lookups, and doing those one by one would be very slow. The trick is to rewrite the S-boxes as Boolean formulas. Each of the four output bits is written as a Boolean formula of the four input bits. The CPU then evaluates this Boolean formula directly, using AND, OR, and XOR instructions. The trick is that a 32-bit CPU can evaluate 32 S-boxes in parallel, as each bit position in the registers computes the same function, albeit on different input data. This style of implementation is called a bitslice implementation. Serpent is specifically designed to be implemented in this way. The mixing phase is relatively easy to compute in a bitslice implementation.

If Serpent had been as fast as Rijndael (now AES), it would almost certainly have been chosen as AES because of its conservative design. But speed is always a relative thing. When measured per encrypted byte, Serpent is nearly as fast as DES and much faster than 3DES. It is only when Serpent is compared to the other AES finalists that it seems slow.

4.5.4 Twofish

Twofish was an AES finalist as well. It can be seen as a compromise between AES and Serpent. It is nearly as fast as AES, but it has a larger security margin. More importantly, it does not have a simple algebraic representation that we know of. The best attack we know of is on 8 of the 16 rounds. The biggest disadvantage of Twofish is that it can be rather expensive to change the encryption key, as Twofish is best implemented with a lot of precomputation on the key.

Twofish uses the same Feistel structure as DES. An overview is given in figure 4.3.[6] Twofish splits the 128-bit plaintext into four 32-bit values, and most operations are on 32-bit values. You can see the Feistel structure of Twofish, with F being the round function. The round function consists of two copies of the g function, a function called the PHT, and a key addition. The result of the F function is XORed into the right half (the two vertical lines on the right). The boxes with ≪ or ≫ symbols in them denote rotations of the 32-bit value by the specified number of bit positions.

Each g function consists of four S-boxes followed by a linear mixing function that is very similar to the AES mixing function. The S-boxes are somewhat different. In contrast to all the other block ciphers we have seen, these S-boxes are not constant; rather, their contents depends on the key. There is an algorithm that computes the S-box tables from the key material. The motivation for this design is that key-dependent S-boxes are much harder for an attacker to analyze. This is also why Twofish implementations often

---

[6]There is a reason why this figure is so much larger and detailed than the others. We are two of the Twofish designers, so we could lift this figure straight from our Twofish book [86].

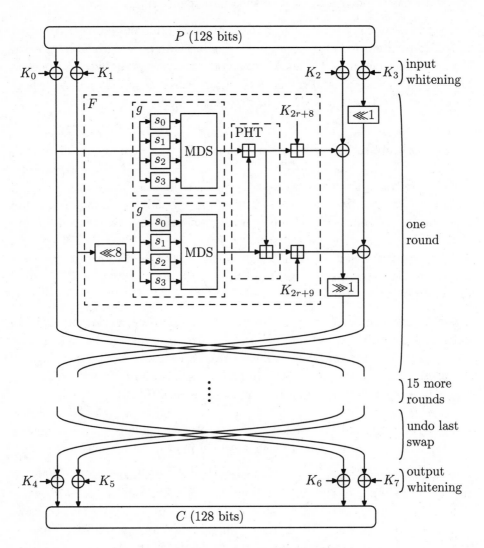

Figure 4.3: Structure of Twofish

do precomputations for each key. They precompute the S-boxes and store the result in memory.

The PHT function mixes the two results of the g functions using 32-bit addition operations. The last part of the F function is where the key material is added. Note that addition is shown as $\boxplus$ and exclusive or as $\oplus$.

Twofish also uses whitening. At both the start and the end of the cipher, additional key material is added to the data. This makes the cipher harder to attack for most types of attack, and it costs very little.

As with the other ciphers, Twofish has a key schedule to derive the round keys and the two additional keys at the start and end from the actual cipher key.

To be quite clear about things: we are biased in this matter. As two of the designers of Twofish, we still like our cipher. We have tried to be fair, but it is impossible to be unbiased. Twofish was designed in part to satisfy the requirements that we think should be imposed on a block cipher. AES and Serpent were designed to satisfy the requirements that their designers thought were most important. For example, in Twofish we deliberately added the two 1-bit rotations to the cipher. These rotations have two disadvantages. They make the encryption and decryption algorithms different, which makes implementations more expensive. They also slow the software implementations by about 5%. The only reason for adding the rotations was to break up the nice byte-aligned structure that we would have had otherwise. AES does not break up its byte-aligned structure. We think that AES is perhaps too neat and structured; the AES designers probably think that Twofish is unstructured and lacks elegance. This is a difference of opinion, and we certainly have the highest respect for the opinions of others in the field. But in this book our advice is driven by our opinion.

4.5.5   Other AES Finalists

We have discussed three of the five AES finalists in some detail. There are two more: RC6 [78] and MARS [13]. The reason why we don't discuss them in detail is because we don't like them quite as much as the three we have discussed.

RC6 is an interesting design that uses 32-bit multiplications in the cipher. During the AES competition, the best attack broke a 17-round version of RC6, compared to 20 rounds of the full RC6. This is too close for comfort for us.

MARS is a design with a nonuniform structure. It uses a large number of different operations and is therefore more expensive to implement than the other AES finalists. Apart from this disadvantage, we are troubled by two mistakes that were found. A software bug in the code which generated the S-box for MARS resulted in an S-box that did not satisfy the criteria the MARS team had set for the S-box. More seriously, the argument given by the MARS designers as to why the cipher was resistant to linear cryptanalysis (a specific way of attacking a cipher) turned out to contain a serious flaw. At this moment there is no good analysis of MARS's susceptibility to a linear attack. As linear attacks are quite powerful and widely known in the community, we expect any serious cipher to come with such an analysis.

Both RC6 and MARS are probably good block ciphers. We just think that AES, Serpent, and Twofish are better, and that you should choose from those three.

4.5.6   Equation-Solving Attacks

As we write this book, there is a new type of attack being developed. It has created quite a buzz in the community. The basic idea is to write a block cipher encryption as a group of linear and quadratic equations in some finite field, and then solve these equations using some newly developed techniques that go by names like XL, FXL, and XSL.

In 2002, Nicolas Courtois and Josef Pieprzyk claimed that they could use these techniques to attack Serpent and AES [17]. That sent quite a shock through the community. The claimed attack on AES got the most publicity. We were even more surprised by the claim of an attack on the full 32 rounds of Serpent, because we thought Serpent to be the most conservative of all AES candidates.

Since the publication of these results there have been several counterclaims that Courtois and Pieprzyk's attacks do not work. The problem is that it is all still theoretical. The XSL equation-solving algorithm is complicated, and it appears very sensitive to the exact form of the equations it is supposed to solve. The estimates of how much work is required to break AES and Serpent contain a fair amount of heuristics. So far, the estimates are still larger than 2^{128} steps, so the XSL attacks will have no effect on the systems we design, where we always use a 128-bit design strength. As long as the XSL attacks are not significantly improved, they pose no threat to any real system; but as with any new attack technique, we always expect improvements to be made in the future.

As far as we know, nobody has as yet implemented these techniques. We would love to see an actual computer program that uses these techniques to break reduced-round versions of both AES and Serpent. Some real-world experience on the actual ciphers would give us real data by which to judge the performance of the XSL algorithm on these ciphers. Without such experiments, we really don't know whether direct equation-solving attacks work.

Where is this going? We don't know. Ask us five years from now, and we will probably know more. At the moment it is more a matter of opinion than of science. This is an entirely new style of attack, and no cipher is designed to withstand it. If XSL-style techniques really work, then any cipher we currently use could be broken. A cipher could only survive by sheer luck. On the other hand, it is quite possible—even likely, in our opinion—that XSL-style techniques do not work in practice, or only work for a small number of highly structured designs.

So what about Twofish? Nobody has tried to apply these techniques to Twofish. This type of attack is more complex to perform on Twofish than on Serpent or AES, so nobody has tried. Thus, we don't know whether these techniques are effective against Twofish. If XSL turns out to be an effective attack against AES and Serpent, it will no doubt be applied against Twofish.

4.5.7 Which Block Cipher Should I Choose?

That is the question. Don't forget that we are biased because we were part of the team that designed Twofish. We also spent quite a lot of time attacking the other AES finalists, which further influences our point of view.

The XSL-style attack claims make choosing a block cipher an uncomfortable task. We simply don't know how XSL-style attacks affect block cipher security. We have very little information, and the few results that have been published are disputed. Because no block cipher has been designed to withstand these types of attacks, they could all be vulnerable. Therefore, we believe that, given the situation at the time of writing, you should not let your choice be influenced by the XSL attacks. There simply is not enough information to judge whether one cipher is more likely to be vulnerable than another cipher.

The safe choice for your career is AES. This is the official standard, sanctioned by the U.S. government. Everybody else will be using it, too. We do not think it is the absolute safest choice for your data, but if there is ever a successful attack on AES, it obviously won't be your fault. They used to say "Nobody gets fired for buying IBM." Similarly, nobody will fire you for choosing AES. As long as it isn't you who loses money and/or sleep if AES gets broken, choose AES.

AES has other advantages. It is relatively easy to use and implement. All cryptography libraries support it, and all customers like it as it is "the standard." In this sense, you cannot go wrong with AES.

If you are paranoid about the security of your data, and speed is not that important, then you should choose Serpent. During the AES process, every serious cryptographer agreed that Serpent was the most secure (or most conservative) of all the submissions.

That does not leave a lot of room for Twofish. You should only choose Twofish if you want the speed of AES without the security disadvantages listed above. Of course, all the institutional advantages of AES will now weigh against you. If Twofish is ever broken, you will be blamed for selecting it.

There are probably circumstances in which 3DES still is the best solution. If you have to be backward-compatible, or are locked into a 64-bit block size by other parts of the system, then 3DES is still your best choice. However, keep in mind that 3DES does not satisfy our security criteria, and be especially careful with the small 64-bit block size.

4.5.8 What Key Size Should I Use?

The three main candidates for your choice of block cipher (AES, Serpent, Twofish) all support keys of 128, 192, and 256 bits. For almost all applications, a 128-bit security level is enough. However, we don't like 128-bit keys at all.

A 128-bit key would be great except for one problem: collision attacks. Time and time again we find systems that can be attacked by a birthday attack or a meet-in-the-middle attack. We know these attacks exist. Sometimes designers just ignore them, and sometimes they think they are safe but somebody finds a new, clever way of using them. Most block cipher modes allow meet-in-the-middle attacks of some form. We've had enough of this race, so here is one of our design rules.

Design rule 3. *For a security level of n bits, every cryptographic value should be at least 2n bits long.*

This rule makes any type of collision attack useless, and it is relatively cheap to do. In real life it is hard to keep strictly to this rule. For 128-bit security we really want to use a block cipher with a block size of 256 bits, but all the common block ciphers have a block size of 128 bits. This is more serious than it sounds. There are quite a number of collision attacks on block cipher modes.

Still, at least we can use the large keys that all AES candidate block ciphers support. Therefore: use 256-bit keys!

Unfortunately, AES (Rijndael) is the one AES finalist that is slower for 256-bit keys than for 128-bit keys.[7] If you use AES, you might be pressured to use smaller keys for performance reasons. We are not saying that 128-bit keys are insecure per se; we are saying that you have to be very careful with them. It is possible to make a system with 128-bit security using 128-bit keys, but it is a difficult task. For example, you can't simply use one of the standard block cipher modes. You have to fix those up with some extra key material to stop collision attacks. This is exactly the kind of complexity that leads to weaknesses. So our advice is to stick to the 256-bit keys.

---

[7]Serpent is the same speed for any size of key. Twofish is slower in key setup for the larger keys, but in software the encryption speed is independent of the key size.

Note that we advocate the use of 256-bit keys for systems with a design strength of 128 bits. In other words, these systems are designed to withstand attackers that can perform 2^{128} operations in their attack. Just remember to use the design strength (128 bits), not the key length of 256 bits, for sizing the rest of the system.

One more complicating factor. We use a key of 256 bits to design a system with a design strength of 128 bits. The XSL-style attacks we talked about apply to the larger key sizes of AES and Serpent, and they are claimed to be more efficient than an exhaustive search *of the larger key size*. The claim is for a Serpent attack that requires more than 2^{128} steps. Even if XSL works as advertised against 256-bit Serpent, it would not be an attack against 256-bit Serpent if we set the design strength of Serpent to 128 bits, as we do in the rest of our system. After all, if the design strength is 128 bits, then the attack has to be more efficient than an exhaustive search over 2^{128} elements, and the current XSL attack on Serpent requires more work than that. The same holds for the XSL attack on AES.

Chapter 5

Block Cipher Modes

Block ciphers encrypt only fixed-size blocks. If you want to encrypt something that isn't exactly one block large, you have to use a block cipher mode. That's another name for an encryption function built using a block cipher.

Before proceeding with this chapter, we have one word of warning. Encryption modes stop an eavesdropper from reading the traffic. They do not provide any authentication, so an attacker can still change the message in any way she wants. Many people find this surprising, but this is simple to see. The decryption function of an encryption mode just decrypts the data. It might produce nonsense, but it still decrypts a (modified) ciphertext to some (modified and possibly nonsensical) plaintext. You should not rely on the fact that nonsensical messages do no harm. That involves relying on other parts of the system, which all too often leads to grief.

In almost all situations the damage that modified messages can do is far greater than the damage of leaking the plaintext. Therefore, you should always combine encryption with authentication. The modes we discuss here should be combined with a separate authentication function, which we discuss in chapter 7.

5.1 Padding

In general, a block cipher mode is a way to encrypt a plaintext P to a ciphertext C, where the plaintext and ciphertext are of an arbitrary length. Most modes require that the length of the plaintext P be an exact multiple of the block size. This requires some padding. There are many ways to pad the plaintext, but the most important rule is that the padding must be reversible. It must be possible to uniquely determine the original message from a padded message.

We sometimes see a very simple padding rule that consists of appending zeroes until the length is suitable. This is not a good idea. It is not reversible, as the plaintext p and $p\|0$ have the same padded form. (We use the operator $\|$ to denote concatenation.)

Throughout this book, we will restrict the discussions to sizes that are an integral number of bytes. Some cryptographic primitives are specified for odd sizes where the last byte is not fully used. We have never found this generalization useful, and it often is a hindrance. Many implementations do not allow for these odd sizes in any case, so all our sizes will be in bytes.

It would be nice to have a padding rule that does not make the plaintext any longer if it already has a suitable length. This is not possible to achieve for all situations. You can show that at least some messages that are already of a suitable length must be lengthened by any reversible padding scheme, and in practice all padding rules add a minimum of one byte to the length of the plaintext.

So how do we pad a plaintext? Let P be the plaintext and let $\ell(P)$ be the length of P in bytes. Let b be the block size of the block cipher in bytes. We suggest using one of two simple padding schemes:

1. Append a single byte with value 128, and then as many zero bytes as required to make the overall length a multiple of b. The number of zero bytes added is in the range $0, \ldots, b-1$.

2. Determine the number of padding bytes required. This is a number n which satisfies $1 \leq n \leq b$ and $n + \ell(P)$ is a multiple of b. Pad the plaintext by appending n bytes, each with value n.

Either padding scheme works just fine. There are no cryptographic ramifications to padding. Any padding scheme is acceptable, as long as it is reversible. The two we gave are just the simplest ones.

Once the padded length is a multiple of the block size, we cut the padded plaintext into blocks. The plaintext P is thereby turned into a sequence of blocks $P_1, \ldots, P_k$. The number of blocks k can be computed as $\lceil (\ell(P) + 1)/b \rceil$, where $\lceil \cdots \rceil$ denotes the ceiling function that rounds a number upward to the next integer. For most the rest of this chapter we will simply assume that the plaintext P consists of an integral number of blocks $P_1, \ldots, P_k$.

After decrypting the ciphertext using one of the block cipher modes we will discuss, the padding has to be removed. The code that removes the padding should also check that the padding was correctly applied. Each of the padding bytes has to be verified to ensure it has the correct value. An erroneous padding should be treated in the same manner as an authentication failure.

5.2   ECB

The simplest method to encrypt a longer plaintext is known as the *electronic codebook* mode, or ECB. This is defined by

$$C_i = E(K, P_i) \qquad \text{for } i = 1, \ldots, k$$

This is quite simple: you just encrypt each block of the message separately. Of course, things cannot be so simple, or we would not have allocated an entire chapter to the discussion of block cipher modes. Do not ever use ECB for anything. It has serious weaknesses, and is only included here so that we can warn you away from it.

What is the trouble with ECB? If two plaintext blocks are the same, then the corresponding ciphertext blocks will be identical, and that is visible to the attacker. Depending on the structure of the message, this can leak quite a lot of information to the attacker.

There are many situations in which large blocks of text are repeated. For example, this chapter contains the words "ciphertext block" many times.

If two of the occurrences happen to line up on a block boundary, then a plaintext block value will be repeated. In most Unicode strings, every other byte is a zero, which greatly increases the chance of a repeated block value. Many file formats will have large blocks of only zeroes, which result in repeated block values. In general, this weakness of ECB makes it too weak to use.

5.3 CBC

The *cipher block chaining* (CBC) mode is the most widely used block cipher mode. The problems of ECB are avoided by XORing each plaintext block with the previous ciphertext block. The standard formulation of CBC is as follows:

$$C_i = E(K, P_i \oplus C_{i-1}) \qquad \text{for } i = 1, \ldots, k$$

The problems of ECB are avoided by "randomizing" the plaintext using the previous ciphertext block. Equal plaintext blocks will typically encrypt to different ciphertext blocks, significantly reducing the information available to an attacker.

5.3.1 Fixed IV

We are still left with the question of which value to use for C_0. This value is called the *initialization vector*, or IV. You should not use a fixed IV, as that introduces the ECB problem for the first block of each message. If two different messages start with the same plaintext block, their encryptions will start with the same ciphertext blocks. In real life, messages often start with similar or identical blocks, and we do not want the attacker to be able to detect this.

5.3.2 Counter IV

An alternative idea we sometimes see is to use a counter for the IV. Use $IV = 0$ for the first message, $IV = 1$ for the second message, etc. Again, this is not a very good idea. As we mentioned, many real-life messages start in similar ways. If the first blocks of the messages have simple differences, then the simple IV counter could very well cancel the differences in the XOR, and generate identical ciphertext blocks again. For example: the values 0 and 1 differ in exactly one bit. If the leading plaintext blocks of the first two messages also differ in only this bit (which happens much more often than you might expect), then the leading ciphertext blocks of the two messages are identical. The attacker can promptly draw conclusions about the differences between the two messages, something a secure encryption scheme should not allow.

5.3.3   Random IV

The problems with ECB and fixed-IV or counter-IV CBC both stem from the fact that plaintext messages are highly nonrandom. Very often they have a fixed value header, or a very predictable structure. In CBC the ciphertext blocks are used to "randomize" the plaintext blocks, but for the first block we have to use the IV. This suggests that we should choose a random IV.

This leads to another problem. The recipient of the message needs to know the IV. The standard solution is to choose a random IV and to send it as a first block before the rest of the encrypted message. The resulting encryption procedure is as follows:

$$C_0 := \text{random block value}$$
$$C_i := E(K, P_i \oplus C_{i-1}) \qquad \text{for } i = 1, \ldots, k$$

with the understanding that the (padded) plaintext $P_1, \ldots, P_k$ is encrypted as $C_0, \ldots, C_k$. Note that the ciphertext starts at C_0 and not C_1; the ciphertext is one block longer than the plaintext. The corresponding decryption procedure is easy to derive:

$$P_i := D(K, C_i) \oplus C_{i-1} \qquad \text{for } i = 1, \ldots, k$$

Using a random IV has two disadvantages. First of all, the encryption algorithm must have access to a source of randomness. Implementing a good random generator is quite a lot of work, and it would be nice to avoid this requirement. Furthermore, the ciphertext is one block longer than the plaintext. For short messages, this results in a significant message expansion, which is always undesirable.

5.3.4   Nonce-Generated IV

This is often the best solution to the IV problem. The solution consists of two steps. First of all, each message that is to be encrypted with this key is given a unique number called a *nonce*. The term is a contraction of number used <u>once</u>. The critical property of a nonce is that it is unique. You should never use the same nonce twice with the same key. Typically, the nonce is a message number of some sort, possibly combined with some other information. Message numbers are already available in most systems, as they are used to keep the messages in their correct order, detect duplicate messages, etc. The nonce does not have to be secret, but it can be used only once. This is especially important for the recipient of the messages, who receives the nonce along with each message and still has to ensure that the same nonce value is not used twice.

The IV necessary for CBC encryption is generated by encrypting the nonce with the block cipher.

In a typical scenario, the sender numbers the messages consecutively and includes the message number in each transmission. The following steps should be used to send a message:

1. Assign a message number to this message. Typically, the message number is provided by a counter that starts at 0. Note that the counter should never be allowed to wrap around back to 0, as that would destroy the uniqueness property.

2. Use the message number to construct a unique nonce. For a given key, the nonce should be unique in the entire system, not just on this computer. For example, if the same key is used to encrypt traffic in two directions, then the nonce should consist of the message number plus an indication of which direction this message is being sent in. The nonce should be as large as a single block of the block cipher.

3. Encrypt the nonce with the block cipher to generate the IV.

4. Encrypt the message in CBC mode using this IV.

5. Add enough information to the ciphertext to ensure that the receiver can reconstruct the nonce. Typically this involves adding the message

number just in front of the ciphertext. The IV value itself (C_0 in our equations) does not have to be sent.

6. Make sure that the receiver will accept any one message number only once. The typical way to do this is for the receiver to reject message numbers that are less than or equal to the message number of the last received message.

The extra information that needs to be included in the message is usually much smaller than in the random IV case. For most systems, a message counter of 32–48 bits is sufficient, compared to a 128-bit random IV overhead for the random IV solution. Most practical communications systems need a message counter anyway, so the generated IV solution adds no message overhead.

5.4   OFB

So far the modes have all taken the message and encrypted it by applying the block cipher to the message blocks in some way. *Output feedback* mode, or OFB, is different in that the message itself is never used as an input to the block cipher. Instead, the block cipher is used to generate a pseudorandom stream of bytes (called the key stream), which in turn is XORed with the plaintext to generate the ciphertext. An encryption scheme that generates such a random key stream is called a stream cipher. Some people seem to think that stream ciphers are bad in some way. Not at all! Stream ciphers are extremely useful, and do their work very well. They just require a bit of care in their use. Abuse of a stream cipher, mostly in the form of reusing a nonce, can very easily lead to a very insecure system. A mode like CBC is more robust in the sense that even when abused it still does a pretty good job. Still, the advantages of stream ciphers often outweigh this disadvantage.

OFB is defined by:

$$K_0 := \text{IV}$$
$$K_i := E(K, K_{i-1}) \qquad \text{for } i = 1, \ldots, k$$
$$C_i := P_i \oplus K_i$$

Here too, there is an IV K_0 which is used to generate the key stream $K_1, \ldots, K_k$ by repeatedly encrypting the value. The key stream is then XORed with the plaintext to generate the ciphertext.

The IV value has to be random, and as with CBC it can either be chosen randomly and transmitted with the ciphertext (see section 5.3.3), or it can be generated from a nonce (see section 5.3.4).

One advantage of OFB is that decryption is exactly the same operation as encryption, which saves on implementation effort. Especially useful is that you only need to use the encryption function of the block cipher, so you don't even have to implement the decryption function.

A second advantage is that you don't need any padding. If you think of the key stream as a sequence of bytes, then you can use as many bytes as your message is long. In other words, if the last plaintext block is only partially full, then you only send the ciphertext bytes that correspond to actual plaintext bytes. The lack of padding reduces the overhead, which is especially important with small messages.

OFB also demonstrates the one danger of using a stream cipher. If you *ever* use the same IV for two different messages, then they will be encrypted with the same key stream. This is very bad indeed. Let us suppose that two messages are the plaintexts P and P', and they have been encrypted using the same key stream to the ciphertexts C and C' respectively. The attacker can now compute $C_i \oplus C'_i = P_i \oplus K_i \oplus P'_i \oplus K_i = P_i \oplus P'_i$. In other words, the attacker can compute the difference between the two plaintexts. Suppose the attacker already knows one of the plaintexts. (This does happens very often in real life.) Then it is trivial for him to compute the other plaintext. There are even well-known attacks that recover information about two unknown plaintexts from the difference between them [45].

OFB has one further problem: if you are unlucky you will repeat a key block value, after which the sequence of key blocks simply repeats. In a single large message you might be unlucky and get into a cycle of key block values. Or the IV for one message might be the same as a key block halfway through the second message, in which case the two messages use the same key stream for part of their plaintexts. In either case you end up encrypting different message blocks with the same key block, which is not a secure encryption scheme.

You need to encrypt quite a lot of data before this becomes plausible. It is basically a collision attack between the key stream blocks and the initial starting points, so you are talking about encrypting at least 2^{64} blocks of data before you expect such a collision. If you limit the amount of data that you encrypt with each key, you can limit the probability of repeating a key block value. Unfortunately, the risk always remains, and if you are unlucky you could lose the confidentiality of an entire message.

5.5 CTR

Our favorite mode for encryption using block ciphers is *counter* mode, also known by its three-letter abbreviation CTR. Although it has been around for ages, it was not standardized as an official DES mode [69], and therefore has often been overlooked in textbooks. It has recently been standardized by NIST [27]. Like OFB, counter mode is a stream cipher mode. It is defined by:

$$K_i := E(K, \text{Nonce} \parallel i) \qquad \text{for } i = 1, \ldots, k$$
$$C_i := P_i \oplus K_i$$

Like any stream cipher, you must supply a unique nonce of some form. Most systems build the nonce from a message number and some additional data to ensure the nonce's uniqueness.

CTR uses a remarkably simple method to generate the key stream. It concatenates the nonce with the counter value, and encrypts it to form a single block of the key stream. This requires that the counter and the nonce fit in a single block, but with the modern 128-bit block sizes, this is rarely a problem. Obviously, the nonce must be smaller than a single block, as there needs to be room for the counter value i. A typical setup might use a 48-bit message number, 16 bits of additional nonce data, and 64 bits for the counter i. This limits the system to encrypting 2^{48} different messages using a single key, and limits each message to 2^{68} bytes.

As with OFB mode, you must make absolutely sure never to reuse a single key/nonce combination. This is a disadvantage that is often mentioned for CTR, but CBC has exactly the same problem. If you use the same IV twice, you start leaking data about the plaintexts. CBC is a bit more robust as it is more likely to limit the amount of information leaked. But any leakage of information violates the requirements, and in a modularized design you cannot count on the rest of the system to limit the damage if you only leak a little bit of information. So both in the case of CBC and CTR you have to ensure that the nonce or IV is unique.

Other than this, CTR mode is very easy to use. You only need to implement the encryption function of the block cipher, and the CTR encryption and decryption functions are identical. It is very easy to access arbitrary parts of the plaintext, as any block of the key stream can be computed immediately. For high-speed applications, the computation of the key stream can be parallelized to an arbitrary degree. Furthermore, the security of CTR mode is trivially linked to the security of the block cipher. Any weakness of CTR encryption mode immediately implies a chosen plaintext attack on the block cipher. The logical converse of this is that if there is no attack on the block cipher, then there is no attack on CTR mode (other than the information leakage we will discuss shortly).

5.6   Newer Modes

All of the modes we have discussed so far date back to the 1970s and early 1980s. In the last few years some new block cipher modes have been proposed. OCB is probably the most publicized one [83, 84]. These modes provide both authentication and encryption. Although these modes are very attractive, we cannot recommend them for two main reasons.

First of all, they are very new, and new things are always suspect in this field. Many of the new modes, including OCB, have a proof of security. But we don't trust proofs any more than we trust any product of human effort. Security proofs have been wrong in the past. They will be wrong in the future. Proofs like these are often quite complex, and it is very optimistic to think that the proofs themselves are without flaw. (We have not seen any attempts to prove the correctness of the proofs.)

Security proofs do not prove that the system is secure. They provide a *security reduction*. The proof might, for example, say that if you can break

OCB encryption in X amount of time, then you can break the underlying block cipher in Y amount of time. This is a very valuable result, and neatly fits into our modularization of cryptographic design. However, it proves the security of the block cipher mode, not the security of encryption using the block cipher mode. There is nothing bad about a security proof, and having one is certainly preferable to not having one, but it is not such an absolute proof as some would like us to believe.

Second, the current patent licensing status of these modes is very unclear, as different parties are claiming patent coverage of various modes. As we write this the patents have not even issued, so the exact coverage of each patent is unknown. Using any one of these modes is a liability minefield. You have been warned.

5.7 Which Mode Should I Use?

We have discussed several modes, but there are really only two modes we would consider using: CBC and CTR. We've already explained that ECB is not secure enough. OFB is a good mode, but CTR is better in some respects and doesn't suffer from the short cycle problem. There is no reason to choose OFB over CTR.

So, should you use CBC or CTR? Let us compare the two.

Padding CBC requires message padding, CTR does not.

Speed Both modes require the same amount of computation, but CTR allows you to parallelize the computations arbitrarily, therefore allowing implementations to reach higher speeds.

Implementation CTR only requires the block cipher encryption function; CBC requires both the encryption and decryption function to be implemented.

Robustness If you ever reuse the same nonce, CBC might leak some information about the initial plaintext block. CTR will leak information about the entire message.

Nonce CBC can use a random IV or a nonce. CTR requires a unique
nonce. In practice, CBC encryption almost always uses a nonce, so
CBC and CTR are equivalent in this respect.

CTR is superior on every point, except robustness. If you ever happen
to reuse the same nonce, then CTR leaks more data than CBC. In most
systems you (as the designer) get to specify the nonce system yourself, so it
is easy to do things right. In our view, the advantages of CTR are sufficient
to choose it over CBC, except for situations where you cannot control the
way in which the encryption function is used.

Earlier we said that each part of a system should secure itself, and not
depend on other parts. But here we're recommending CTR mode, which
depends on the rest of the system to provide a unique nonce. Are we con-
tradicting ourselves? Yes and no. We would prefer a block cipher mode
that does not depend on the rest of the system. But none of the encryption
modes we discussed have that property. They all depend to some extent
on the rest of the system. That is because a block cipher mode is not a
complete encryption system, nor is it an independent design module. The
block cipher is a module, which you can replace with another suitable block
cipher. The block cipher *mode* is just a method we use in our next level
module: the encrypt-and-authenticate-a-message module, which we will discuss in chapter 8. As it is not an independent module we cannot expect the
block cipher mode to be secure independent of the rest of the system.

Always keep in mind that an encryption mode only provides confidentiality.
That is, the attacker cannot find any information about the data you are
communicating, other than the fact *that* you are communicating, *when* you
are communicating, *how much* you are communicating, and *whom* you are
communicating with.[1] Encrypting data does nothing to stop the attacker
from changing the data.

---

[1] This kind of analysis is called *traffic analysis*. It can provide very useful information
to an attacker. Preventing traffic analysis is possible, but generally too expensive in terms
of bandwidth for anyone but the military.

5.8   Information Leakage

We now come to the dark secret of block cipher modes. All block cipher modes leak information. None of them are perfect. You rarely see an analysis of this in the literature, so we will include one here.

For this discussion, we will assume that we have a perfect block cipher. But even with a perfect block cipher, the ciphertexts that the encryption modes produce reveal information about the plaintexts. This has to do with equalities and inequalities of ciphertext and plaintext blocks.

Let's start with ECB. If two plaintext blocks are equal to $P_i = P_j$, then the two ciphertext blocks are equal to $C_i = C_j$. For random plaintexts this will happen very rarely, but most plaintext is not random but highly structured. Thus equal plaintext blocks occur far more frequently, and the equal ciphertext blocks reveal this structure. That is why we dismissed ECB.

What about CBC mode? Equal plaintext blocks do not lead to equal ciphertext blocks, as each plaintext block is first XORed with the previous ciphertext block before it is encrypted. Think of all the ciphertext blocks as random values; after all, they were produced by a block cipher that produces a random output for any given input. But what if we have two ciphertext blocks that are equal? We have

$$
\begin{aligned}
C_i &= C_j \\
E(K, P_i \oplus C_{i-1}) &= E(K, P_j \oplus C_{j-1}) \qquad \text{from the CBC specifications} \\
P_i \oplus C_{i-1} &= P_j \oplus C_{j-1} \qquad \text{decrypt both sides} \\
P_i \oplus P_j &= C_{i-1} \oplus C_{j-1} \qquad \text{basic algebra}
\end{aligned}
$$

The last equation gives the difference between two plaintext blocks as the XOR of two ciphertext blocks, which we assume the attacker knows. This is certainly not something you would expect from a perfect message encryption system. And if the plaintext is something with a lot of redundancy, such as plain English text, it probably contains enough information to recover both plaintext blocks.

A similar situation occurs when two ciphertexts are unequal. Knowing that $C_i \neq C_j$ implies that $P_i \oplus P_j \neq C_{i-1} \oplus C_{j-1}$, so each unequal pair of ciphertexts leads to an inequality formula between the plaintext blocks.

CTR has similar properties. With this encryption mode we know that the K_i blocks are all different, because they are encryptions of a nonce and counter value. All the plaintext values of the encryption are different, so all the ciphertext values (which form the key blocks) are different. Given two ciphertexts C_i and C_j, you know that $P_i \oplus P_j \neq C_i \oplus C_j$ because otherwise the two key stream blocks would have had to been equal. In other words, CTR mode provides a plaintext inequality for each pair of ciphertext blocks.

There are no problems with collisions in CTR. Two key blocks are never equal, and equal plaintext blocks or equal ciphertext blocks lead to nothing. The only thing that makes CTR deviate from the absolute ideal stream cipher is the absence of key block collisions.

OFB is worse than either CBC or CTR. As long as there are no collisions on the key stream blocks, OFB leaks the same amount of information as CTR. But if there is ever a collision of two key stream blocks, then all subsequent key stream blocks also produce a collision. This is a disaster from a security point of view, and the main reason why CTR is preferable to OFB.

5.8.1 Chances of a Collision

So what are the chances that two ciphertext blocks are equal? Let's say we encrypt M blocks in total. It doesn't matter whether this is done in a few large messages, or in a large number of small messages. All that counts is the total number of blocks. A good rough estimate is that there are $M(M - 1)/2$ pairs of blocks, and each pair has a chance of 2^{-n} of being equal, where n is the block size of the block cipher. So the expected number of equal ciphertext blocks is $M(M - 1)/2^{n+1}$, which gets close to unity when $M \approx 2^{n/2}$. In other words, when you encrypt about $2^{n/2}$ blocks, you can expect to get two ciphertext blocks that are equal.[2] With a block size of $n = 128$ bits, we can expect the first duplicate ciphertext block value after about 2^{64} blocks. This is the birthday paradox we explained in section 3.6.6. Now, 2^{64} blocks is a lot of data, but don't forget that we are designing systems with a lifetime of 30 years. Maybe people will want to process something close to 2^{64} blocks of data in the future.

---

[2]The actual number of blocks you can encrypt before you expect the first duplicate is close to $\sqrt{\pi 2^{n-1}} = 2^{n/2}\sqrt{\pi/2}$, but the theory behind the analysis is much harder and we don't need that level of precision here.

Smaller data sets are also at risk. If we process 2^{40} blocks (about 16 TB of data) then there is a 2^{-48} chance of having a ciphertext block collision. That is a really small probability. But look at it from the attacker's point of view. For a particular key that is being used, he collects 2^{40} blocks and checks for duplicate blocks. Because the chance of finding one is small, he has to repeat this whole job for about 2^{48} different keys. The total amount of work before he finds a collision is $2^{40} \cdot 2^{48} = 2^{88}$, which is much less than our design strength of 128 bits.

Let's concentrate on CBC and CTR. In CTR you get a plaintext inequality for every pair of blocks. In CBC you get an inequality if the two ciphertext blocks are unequal, and an equality if the blocks are equal. Obviously an equality provides much more information about the plaintext to the attacker than an inequality does, so CTR leaks less information.

5.8.2   How to Deal With Leakage

So how do we achieve our goal of a 128-bit security level? Basically, we don't. There is no easy way of achieving a 128-bit security level with a block cipher whose block size is 128 bits. This is why we want to have block ciphers with 256-bit blocks, but there are no widely studied proposals of such a block cipher out there, so that is a dead end. What we can do is get close to our design security level, and limit the damage.

CTR leaks very little data. Suppose we encrypt 2^{64} blocks of data and produce a ciphertext C. For any possible plaintext P that is 2^{64} blocks long, the attacker can compute the key stream that would have to be used for this P to be encrypted to C. There is roughly a 50% chance that the resulting key stream will contain a collision. We know that CTR mode never produces collisions, so if a collision occurs, that particular plaintext P can be ruled out. This means that the attacker can rule out approximately half of all possible plaintexts. This corresponds to leaking a single bit of information to the attacker, which is not much at all. If we restrict ourselves to encrypting only 2^{48} blocks, then the attacker can rule out approximately 2^{-32} of all plaintexts, which provides almost no information at all. In a practical setting, such a small leakage is insignificant. So although CTR encryption is not perfect, we can limit the damage to an extremely small leak by not encrypting too much information with a single key. It would be reasonable to limit the cipher mode to 2^{60} blocks, which allows you to encrypt 2^{64} bytes but restricts the leakage to a small fraction of a bit.

When using CBC mode you should be a bit more restrictive. If a collision occurs in CBC mode, you leak 128 bits of information about the plaintext. It is a good policy to keep the probability of such a collision low. We suggest limiting CBC encryption to 2^{32} blocks or so. That leaves a residual risk of 2^{-64} that you will leak 128 bits, which is probably harmless for most applications, but certainly far from our desired security level.

Just a reminder; these limits are on the total amount of information encrypted using a single key. It does not matter whether the data is encrypted in one very large message, or as a large number of smaller messages.

This is not a satisfactory state of affairs, but it is the situation we face. The best you can do at this point is to use CTR or CBC and limit the amount of data you process with any one key. We will talk later about key negotiation protocols. It is quite easy to set up a fresh key when the old key is nearing its usage limit. Assuming you already use a key negotiation protocol to set up the encryption key, having to refresh a key is not particularly difficult; it is just a complication. And we don't like those. But at the moment, it is the best solution available.

5.8.3   About Our Math

Readers with a mathematical background may be horrified at our easy use of probabilities without checking whether the probabilities are independent. They are right, of course, when arguing from a purely mathematical standpoint. But just like the physicists, cryptographers use math in a way that they have found useful. Cryptographic values typically behave very randomly. After all, cryptographers go to great length to absolutely destroy all patterns, as any pattern leads to an attack. Experience shows that this style of dealing with probabilities leads to quite accurate results. Mathematicians are welcome to work through the details and figure out the exact results for themselves, but we prefer the rougher approximations for their simplicity.

Chapter 6

Hash Functions

Of all the cryptographic primitives, hash functions are the most versatile. You can use a hash function for encryption, authentication, and even for a simple digital signature scheme.[1]

A hash function is a function that takes as input an arbitrarily long string of bits (or bytes) and produces a fixed-size result. A typical use of a hash function is digital signatures. Given a message m, you could sign the message itself. However, the public-key operations of most digital signature schemes are fairly expensive in computational terms. So instead of signing m itself, you apply a hash function h and sign $h(m)$ instead. The result of h is typically between 128 and 512 bits, compared to thousands or millions of bits for the message m itself. Signing $h(m)$ is therefore much faster than signing m directly. For this construction to be secure, it must be impossible to construct two messages m_1 and m_2 that hash to the same value. We'll discuss the details of the security properties of hash functions below.

Hash functions are sometimes called *message digest* functions, and the hash result is also known as the *digest*, or the *fingerprint*. We prefer the more common name *hash function*, as hash functions have many other uses besides digesting messages. We must warn you about one possible confusion: the term "hash function" is also used for the mapping function used in accessing hash tables, a data structure used in many algorithms. These so-called hash

---

[1]The very first digital signature scheme, by Leslie Lamport, is of this type [21].

functions have similar properties to cryptographic hash functions, but there is a huge difference between the two. The cryptographic hash functions we use in cryptography have specific security properties. The hash-table mapping-function has far weaker requirements. Don't ever confuse the two. When we talk about hash functions in this book, we always mean cryptographic hash functions.

Hash functions have many applications in cryptography. They make great glue between different parts of a cryptographic system. Any time you have a variable-sized value, you can use a hash function to map it to a fixed-size value. Hash functions can be used as cryptographic pseudorandom generators to generate several keys from a single shared secret. And they have a one-way property that isolates different parts of a system, ensuring that even if an attacker learns one value, he doesn't learn the others.

Even though hash functions are used in almost every system, we know far less about hash functions than we do about block ciphers. This is one of the failures of the cryptographic community. Compared to block ciphers, very little research has been done on hash functions, and there are not very many practical proposals to choose from.

6.1   Security of Hash Functions

As we mentioned above, a hash function maps an arbitrarily long input m to a fixed-size output $h(m)$. Typical output sizes are 128–512 bits. There are several requirements for a hash function. The simplest one is that it must be a one-way function: given a message m it is easy to compute $h(m)$, but given a value x it is not possible to find an m such that $h(m) = x$. In other words, a one-way function is a function that can be computed but that cannot be inverted—hence its name.

Of the many properties that a good hash function should have, the one that is mentioned most often is collision resistance. This is a somewhat stronger requirement than the one-way property. A collision is two different inputs m_1 and m_2 for which $h(m_1) = h(m_2)$. Of course, every hash function has an infinite number of these collisions. (There are an infinite number of possible input values, and only a finite number of possible output values.) Thus, a hash function is never collision-free. The collision-resistance requirement merely states that, although collisions exist, they cannot be found.

Collision resistance is the property that makes hash functions suitable for use in signature schemes. However, there are collision-resistant hash functions that are utterly unsuitable for many other applications, such as key derivation, one-way functions, etc. In practice, cryptographic designers expect a hash function to be a random mapping. Therefore, we require that a hash function be indistinguishable from a random mapping. Any other definition leads to a situation in which the designer can no longer treat the hash function as an idealized black-box, but instead has to consider how the hash function properties interact with the system around it.

Definition 4. *The ideal hash function is a random mapping from all possible input values to the set of possible output values.*

Like our definition of the ideal block cipher (in section 4.3), this is an incomplete definition. Strictly speaking, there is no such thing as a random mapping; you can only talk about a probability distribution over all possible mappings. However, for our purposes this definition is good enough.

We can now define what an attack on a hash function is.

Definition 5. *An attack on a hash function is a nontrivial method of distinguishing the hash function from an ideal hash function.*

Here the ideal hash function must obviously have the same output size as the hash function we are attacking. As with the block ciphers, the "nontrivial" requirement takes care of all the generic attacks. Our remarks about trivial attacks on block ciphers carry over to this situation.

The one remaining question is how much work the distinguisher is allowed to perform. Unlike the block cipher, the hash function has no key, and there is no generic attack like the exhaustive key search. The one interesting parameter is the size of the output. One generic attack on a hash function is the birthday attack, which generates collisions. For a hash function with an n-bit output, this requires about $2^{n/2}$ steps. But collisions are only relevant for certain uses of hash functions. In other situations, the goal is to find a pre-image (given x, find an m with $h(m) = x$), or to find some kind of structure in the hash outputs. The generic pre-image attack requires about 2^n steps. We're not going to discuss at length here which attacks are relevant and how much work would be reasonable for the distinguisher to use for a particular style of attack. To be sensible, a distinguisher has to be more efficient than a generic attack that yields similar results. We know this is not an exact definition, but we don't know how to create an exact definition. If somebody claims an attack, simply ask yourself if you could get a similar or better result from a generic attack that does not rely on the specifics of the hash function. If the answer is yes, the distinguisher is useless. If the answer is no, then the distinguisher is real.

As with the block ciphers, we allow a reduced security level if it is specified. We can imagine a 512-bit hash function that specifies a security level of 128 bits. In that case, distinguishers are limited to 2^{128} steps.

6.2   Real Hash Functions

Here is our first practical problem. There are very few good hash functions out there. At this moment you are really stuck with the SHA family, or possibly MD5. There are other published proposals, but none of them have received enough attention for us to trust them. Even the SHA family has not been analyzed nearly enough, but at least they have been standardized by NIST, and they were developed by NSA.[2]

Almost all real-life hash functions, and all the ones we will discuss, are iterative hash functions. Iterative hash functions split the input into a sequence of fixed-size blocks $m_1, \ldots, m_k$, using a padding rule to fill out the last block. (A typical block length is 512 bits.) The message blocks are then processed in order, using a compression function and a fixed-size intermediate state. This process starts with a fixed value H_0, and defines $H_i = h'(H_{i-1}, m_i)$. The final value H_k is the result of the hash function.

Such an iterative design has significant practical advantages. First of all, it is easy to specify and implement, compared to a function that handles variable-length inputs directly. Furthermore, this structure allows you to

---

[2]Whatever you may think about the NSA, so far the cryptography they have published has been quite decent.

start computing the hash of a message as soon as you have the first part of it. So in applications where a stream of data is to be hashed, the message can be hashed on the fly without ever storing the data.

As with the block ciphers, we will not spend our time explaining the various hash functions in great detail. Implementers can find the full specifications in the literature we cite, or on the Internet. For everybody else, the full specifications are needless details that only distract from the main line of this book.

6.2.1   MD5

MD5 is a 128-bit hash function developed by Ron Rivest [82]. It is a further development of MD4 [79] with additional strengthening against attacks.[3]

The first step in computing MD5 is to split the message into blocks of 512 bits. The last block is padded and the length of the message is included as well. MD5 has a 128-bit state that is split into four words of 32 bits each. The compression function h' has four rounds, and in each round the message block and the state are mixed. The mixing consists of a combination of addition, XOR, AND, OR, and rotation operations on 32-bit words. (For details, see [82].) Each round mixes the entire message block into the state, so each message word is in fact used four times. After the four rounds of the h' function, the input state and result are added together to produce the output of h'.

This structure of operating on 32-bit words is very efficient on 32-bit CPUs. It was pioneered by MD4, and is now a general feature of many cryptographic primitives.

One of the basic ideas behind the iterative hash function design is that if h' is collision-resistant, then the hash function h built from h' is also collision-resistant. After all, any collision in h can only occur due to a collision in h'. The problem with MD5 is that the compression function h' is known to have collisions [20]. At the moment, there are no known attacks on MD5 itself, but the presence of collisions in the compression function makes us wary of using MD5.

---

[3]MD4 is very fast, but also very broken [25]. Don't use it.

For most applications the 128-bit hash size of MD5 is insufficient. Using the birthday paradox, we can find a real MD5 collision in about 2^{64} evaluations of the hash function, which is insufficient for modern systems. Our advice: don't use MD5.

6.2.2   SHA-1

The Secure Hash Algorithm was designed by the NSA and standardized by NIST [71]. The first version was just called SHA (now often called SHA-0), but it contained a weakness. The NSA found this weakness, and developed a fix which NIST published as an improved version, called SHA-1. However, they did not release any details about the weakness. Three years later, Chabaud and Joux published a weakness of SHA-0 [16]. This is a weakness that is fixed by the improved SHA-1, so it is reasonable to assume that we now know what the problem was.

SHA-1 is a 160-bit hash function based on MD4. Because of its shared parentage it has a lot of features in common with MD5, but it is a far more conservative design. It is also two to three times slower than MD5. Still, thus far we know of no security problems with SHA-1, and it is widely used.

SHA-1 has a 160-bit state consisting of five 32-bit words. Like MD5, it has four rounds that consist of a mixture of elementary 32-bit operations. Instead of processing each message block four times, SHA-1 uses a linear recurrence to "stretch" the 16 words of a message block to the 80 words it needs. This is a generalization of the MD4 technique. In MD5, each bit of the message is used four times in the mixing function. In SHA-1, the linear recurrence ensures that each message bit affects the mixing function at least a dozen times. Interestingly enough, the only change from SHA-0 to SHA-1 was the addition of a one-bit rotation to this linear recurrence.

The main problem with SHA-1 is the 160-bit result size. Collisions can be generated in only 2^{80} steps, well below the security level of modern block ciphers with key sizes from 128 to 256 bits. It is also insufficient for our design security level of 128 bits.

6.2.3   SHA-256, SHA-384, and SHA-512

Recently, NIST published a draft standard containing three new hash functions [75]. These have 256-, 384-, and 512-bit outputs respectively. They are designed to be used with the 128-, 196-, and 256-bit key sizes of AES. Their structure is very similar to SHA-1.

These hash functions are very new. We don't want to recommend them, but we don't have much choice. If you want more security than SHA-1 can give you, you need a hash function with a larger result. None of the published designs for larger hash functions has received a lot of public analysis; at least the SHA family has been vetted by the NSA, who seems to generally know what it is doing.

SHA-256 is much slower than SHA-1. For long messages, computing a hash with SHA-256 takes about as much time as encrypting the message with AES or Twofish, or maybe a little bit more. This is not necessarily bad. Because we feel that hashing is a more difficult problem than encryption, we are not surprised that a hash function would be slower than an encryption function. We are, instead, surprised at the speed of SHA-1 and MD5. But then, relatively little research has been done on attacking these fast hash functions; certainly nowhere near the amount of work that has gone into attacking block ciphers.

SHA-384 is relatively useless. To compute it, you do all the work that is required for SHA-512, and then throw away some of the bits. We don't need a separate function for that, and we recommend sticking with SHA-256 and SHA-512.

6.3   Weaknesses of Hash Functions

Unfortunately, all of these hash functions have some properties that disqualify them according to our security definition.

6.3.1   Length Extensions

Our greatest peeve about all these hash functions is that they have a length-extension bug that leads to real problems and that could easily have been avoided. Here is the problem. A message m is split into blocks $m_1, \ldots, m_k$ and hashed to a value H. Let's now choose a message m' that splits into the block $m_1, \ldots, m_k, m_{k+1}$. Because the first k blocks of m' are identical to the k blocks of message m, the hash value $h(m)$ is merely the intermediate hash value after k blocks in the computation of $h(m')$. We get $h(m') = h'(h(m), m_{k+1})$. When using MD5 or any cipher from the SHA family, you have to choose m' carefully to include the padding and length field, but this is not a problem as the method of constructing these fields is known.

The length extension problem exists because there is no special processing at the end of the hash function computation. The result is that $h(m)$ provides direct information about the intermediate state after the first k blocks of m'.

This is certainly a surprising property for a function we want to think of as a random mapping. In fact, this property immediately disqualifies all of the mentioned hash functions, according to our security definition. All a distinguisher has to do is to construct a few suitable pairs (m, m') and check for this relationship. You certainly wouldn't find this relationship in an ideal hash function, so this is a valid attack. The attack itself takes only a few hash computations, so it is very quick.

How could this property be harmful? Imagine a system where Alice sends a message to Bob and wants to authenticate it by sending $h(X \parallel m)$, where X is a secret known only to Bob and Alice, and m is the message. If h were an ideal hash function, this would make a decent authentication system. But with length extensions, Eve can now append text to the message m, and update the authentication code to match the new message. An authentication system which allows Eve to modify the message is, of course, of no use to us.

6.3.2 Partial-Message Collision

A second problem is inherent in the iterative structure of most hash functions. We'll explain the problem with a specific distinguisher.

The first step of any distinguisher is to specify the setting in which it will differentiate between the hash function and the ideal hash function. Sometimes this setting can be very simple: given the hash function, find a collision. Here we use a slightly more complicated setting. Suppose we have a system that authenticates a message m with $h(m \parallel X)$, where X is the authentication key. The attacker can choose the message m, but the system will only authenticate a single message.[4]

For a perfect hash function of size n, we expect that this construction has a security level of n bits. The attacker cannot do any better than to choose an m, get the system to authenticate it as $h(m \parallel X)$, and then search for X by exhaustive search. The attacker can do much better with an iterative hash function. She finds two strings m and m' that lead to a collision when hashed by h. This can be done using the birthday attack in only $2^{n/2}$ steps or so. She then gets the system to authenticate m, and replaces the message with m'. Remember that h is computed iteratively, so once there is a collision and the rest of the hash inputs are the same, the hash value stays the same too. Because hashing m and m' leads to the same value, $h(m \parallel X) = h(m' \parallel X)$ for every X.

This is a typical example of a distinguisher. The distinguisher sets its own "game" (a setting in which it attempts an attack), and then attacks the system. The object is still to distinguish between the hash function and the ideal hash function, but that is easy to do here. If the attack succeeds, it is an iterative hash function; if the attack fails, it is the ideal hash function.

---

[4]Most systems will only allow a limited number of messages to be authenticated; this is just an extreme case. In real life, many systems include a message number with each message, which has the same effect on this attack as allowing only a single message to be chosen.

6.4   Fixing the Weaknesses

We want a hash function that we can treat as a random mapping, but all well-known hash functions fail this property. Will we have to check for length-extension problems in every place we use a hash function? Do we check for partial-message collisions everywhere? Are there any other weaknesses we need to check for?

Leaving weaknesses in the hash function is a very bad idea. We can guarantee that it will be used somewhere in a way that exposes the weakness. Even if you document the known weaknesses they will not be checked for in real systems. Even if you could control the design process that well, you would run into a complexity problem. Suppose the hash function has three weaknesses, the block cipher two, the signature scheme four, etc. Before you know it you will have to check hundreds of interactions among these weaknesses: a practical impossibility. We have to fix the hash function.

We should point out that this is a somewhat unorthodox point of view. Most cryptographers are happy with iterative hash functions; even new designs do not fix the problems we mentioned. Sometimes users of hash functions take great care to avoid the problems. Most of the time users don't even think about them, and have enough luck to avoid any problems. But often enough real problems appear. These problems can be fixed on an ad hoc basis, but we think that is the wrong way around; we should fix the hash function.

6.4.1   A Thorough Fix

We do not know of any literature about how to fix the hash functions, but here is what we came up with while writing this book. These problems can be avoided by using the hash function twice. We believe that this solution solves all the problems we mentioned. But designing cryptographic functions is tricky and we're not quite sure. Our solution has not been reviewed by our peers, which would take years and years anyway, assuming we could interest anyone into looking at hash functions. That's life.

Let h be one of the hash functions mentioned above. Instead of $m \mapsto h(m)$, we use $m \mapsto h(h(m) \,\|\, m)$ as hash function.[5] Effectively we put $h(m)$ before the message we are hashing. This ensures that the iterative hash computations immediately depend on all the bits of the message, and no partial-message or length extension attacks can work.

Definition 6. *Let h be an iterative hash function. The hash function h_{DBL} is defined by $h_{\mathrm{DBL}}(m) := h(h(m) \,\|\, m)$.*

We believe that if h is any of the hash functions mentioned above, then this construction has a security level of n bits, where n is the size of the hash result.

The disadvantage with this approach is that it is slow. You have to hash the entire message twice, which takes twice as long. Personally, we don't mind because we firmly believe that security is far more important than speed. There are enough fast insecure systems out there, and we don't need to design another one. Yet hashing speed is the performance bottleneck in some applications, so we'd like to find something better.

Another disadvantage is that this approach requires the whole message m to be buffered. You can no longer compute the hash of a stream of data as it passes by. Some applications depend on this ability, and using h_{DBL} would simply not work.

6.4.2   A More Efficient Fix

So how do we keep the full speed of the original hash function? We cheat, kind of. Instead of $h(m)$, we can use $h(h(m))$ as a hash function, and claim a security level of only $n/2$ bits. The cheat is that we normally expect an n-bit hash function to provide a security level of n bits for those situations in which a collision attack is not possible.[6] The partial-message collision attacks all rely on birthday attacks, so if we reduce the security level to $n/2$ bits, these attacks no longer fall within the claimed security level.

---

[5]The notation $x \mapsto f(x)$ is a way of writing down a function without having to give it a name. For example: $x \mapsto x^2$ is a function that squares its input.

[6]Even the SHA-256 documentation claims that an n-bit hash function should require 2^n steps to find a pre-image of a given value.

In most situations, reducing the security level in this way would be unacceptable, but we are lucky here. Hash functions are already designed to be used in situations where collision attacks are possible, so the hash function sizes are suitably large. If we apply this construction to SHA-256, we get a hash function with a 128-bit security level, which is exactly what we need.

Some might argue that all n-bit hash functions provide only $n/2$ bits of security. That is a valid point of view. Unfortunately, unless you are very specific about these things, people will abuse the hash function and assume it provides n bits of security. For example, people want to use SHA-256 to hash a 256-bit key for AES, assuming that it will provide a security level of 256 bits. As we explained earlier, we use 256-bit keys to achieve a 128-bit security level, so this matches perfectly with the reduced security level of our fixed version of SHA-256. This is not accidental. In both cases the gap between the size of the cryptographic value and the claimed security level is due to collision attacks. As we assume collision attacks are always possible, the different sizes and security levels will fit together nicely.

Here is a more formal definition of this fix.

Definition 7. *Let h be an iterative hash function. The hash function h_d is defined by $h_d := h(h(m))$, and has a claimed security level of $\min(k, n/2)$ where k is the security level of h and n is the size of the hash result.*

We will use this construction mostly in combination with hash functions from the SHA family. For any hash function SHA-X, where X is 1, 256, 384, or 512, we define SHA$_d$-X as the function that maps m to SHA-X(SHA-$X(m)$). In particular, SHA$_d$-256 is just the function $m \mapsto$ SHA-256(SHA-256(m)).

Again, these are new constructions, and they should therefore be distrusted. Fortunately, it can be demonstrated that our fixed hash function h_d is at least as strong as the underlying hash function h.[7] HMAC uses a similar hash-it-again approach to protect against length-extension attacks. Both h_{DBL} and h_d eliminate the length extension bug that poses the most danger to real systems. Whether h_{DBL} in fact has a security level of n bits remains to be seen. We would trust both of them up to $n/2$ bits of security, so in practice we would use the more efficient h_d construction.

---

[7]We're cheating a little bit here. By hashing twice, the range of the function is reduced, and birthday attacks are a little bit easier. This is a small effect, and it falls well within the margin of approximation we've used elsewhere.

6.5   Which Hash Function Should I Choose?

There's not a lot of choice. As far as we are concerned, you should choose one from the SHA_d family. The only choice there is the size of the hash function and the associated performance.

As we mentioned, the cryptographic community has done only a little work on hash functions. Unlike block ciphers, where distinguisher attacks are often used, attacks on hash functions have mostly been of the collision type. So for all practical purposes, nobody has ever analyzed the hash functions using our security definition. By some stroke of fortune, the h_d construction already makes us use the reduced $n/2$-bit security level, so this is not a real problem. The SHA family was designed to withstand collision attacks, so they should have at least that security level.

This clearly points to not using SHA_d-1, as the 80-bit security level is not sufficient for any long-term use. That leaves SHA_d-256 and SHA_d-512. (There is no point in using SHA_d-384, as you can get SHA_d-512 for the same amount of work.)

We've set our design standard at a security level of 128 bits, so the obvious choice for the hash function is SHA_d-256. For higher security levels you should use SHA_d-512, but you are probably fooling yourself if you think that you can actually achieve a higher security level; without a good block cipher that takes a key larger than 256 bits, this is very hard to achieve. And of course, the performance penalty of SHA_d-512 over SHA_d-256 might be too large to accept, in which case you will have to accept the 128-bit security limit of SHA_d-256.

6.6   Future Work

There is an enormous amount of work to be done on hash functions. Basically, we think that the public cryptographic community is as good at designing and attacking hash functions as we were at designing and attacking block ciphers in the mid-1980s. We need to learn a lot more about making and breaking hash functions. A good start would be to attack reduced-round versions of the SHA family. We have yet to see any progress in this area.

Chapter 7

Message Authentication Codes

A *message authentication code*, or MAC, is a construction that prevents tampering with messages. Encryption prevents Eve from reading the messages but does not prevent her from manipulating the messages. This is where the MAC comes in. Like encryption, MACs use a secret key, K, known to both Alice and Bob but not to Eve. Alice sends not just the message m, but also a MAC value computed by a MAC function. Bob checks that the MAC value of the message received equals the MAC value received. If they do not match, he discards the message as unauthenticated. Eve cannot manipulate the message because without K she cannot find the correct MAC value to send with the manipulated message.

In this chapter we will only consider authentication. The mechanisms for combining encryption and authentication will be dealt with in chapter 8.

7.1   What a MAC Does

A MAC is a function that takes two arguments, a fixed size key K and an arbitrarily sized message m, and produces a fixed size MAC value. We'll write the MAC function as MAC(K, m). To authenticate a message, Alice sends not only the message m but also the MAC code MAC(K, m).

We start with a look at the MAC function in isolation. Be warned that using a MAC function properly is more complicated than just applying it to the message. We'll get to those problems later on, in section 7.8.

7.2   The Ideal MAC

First we define an ideal MAC function. Then, we define a secure MAC as one that cannot be distinguished from the ideal one. The ideal MAC is, not surprisingly, a random mapping. Let n be the number of bits in the result of MAC.

Definition 8. *An ideal MAC function is a random mapping from all possible inputs to n-bit outputs.*

The ideal MAC is quite similar to the ideal hash function. Both are random mappings. The main difference is the MAC security definition, which is more lenient and allows a MAC to be more efficient than a hash.

7.3   MAC Security

As mentioned, the MAC has two inputs, a key K and a message m. The key K is not known to the attacker or, more precisely, it is not fully known. There could be a weakness in the rest of the system that provides partial information about K to the attacker. Let k be the uncertainty that the attacker has about the value of K. Here, "uncertainty" is the number of bits of K that the attacker does not know. More generally, if the uncertainty is k, then there are about 2^k possible values that K could have, from the attacker's point of view, of course.[1]

Definition 9. *Let n be the size of the MAC result, and k be the uncertainty, in bits, that the attacker has about the key K. An attack on a MAC function is a nontrivial way of distinguishing the MAC function from the ideal MAC function in less than $2^{\min(n,k)}$ steps.*

---

[1]This notion of uncertainty can be made precise by using the definition of entropy, but that detracts from our current discussion. For those who like these details: the value k is the entropy, in bits, of K, given the knowledge of the attacker.

In other words, a MAC function is a random mapping with the security level limited to k bits. This is very different from a general random mapping. In a random mapping, the attacker knows everything; here the attacker is uncertain about the value of K. (If he is certain, then $k = 0$ and the security level is 0, so we have nothing to discuss.)

Of course, a particular MAC function can also claim a lower security level than the output size it provides. The attacker is then limited to $2^{\min(s,k)}$ steps where s is the claimed security level. The uncertainty about K can be used to make MAC functions that are more efficient than a hash function.

We should mention that nobody else defines MAC security this way. Most researchers define MAC security in a more limited way. Very roughly, the attack model used is one in which the attacker selects n different messages of his choosing, and is given the MAC value for each of these messages. The attacker then has to come up with $n + 1$ messages, each with a valid MAC value. This attack model excludes some form of attack, such as related-key attacks and attacks that assume that the attacker has partial knowledge about the key. That is why we prefer our style of security definitions, which are robust even if the function is abused or used in an unusual environment.

7.4   CBC-MAC

This is a method of turning a block cipher into a MAC. The key K is used as the block cipher key. The idea behind CBC-MAC is to encrypt the message m using CBC mode and then throw away all but the last block of ciphertext. For a message $P_1, \ldots, P_k$, the MAC is computed as:

$$H_0 := \text{IV}$$
$$H_i := E_K(P_i \oplus H_{i-1})$$
$$\text{MAC} := H_k$$

Sometimes the output of the CBC-MAC function is taken to be half of the last block, but that depends on the details.

The classical definition of CBC-MAC requires the IV to be fixed at 0. This is what you will see in some textbooks. It is possible to use CBC-MAC with any of the other IV constructions we talked about with CBC encryption, but this does not seem to provide any real advantage.

Don't ever use the same key for both the encryption and authentication unless you know what you are doing. It is especially dangerous to use CBC encryption and CBC-MAC authentication with the same key. The MAC ends up being equal to the last ciphertext block.

Using CBC-MAC is a bit tricky, but it is generally considered secure if the underlying cipher is secure. There are a number of different collision attacks on CBC-MAC that effectively limit the security to half the length of the block size [12]. Here is a simple collision attack: let M be a CBC-MAC function. If we know that $M(a) = M(b)$ then we also know that $M(a \parallel c) = M(b \parallel c)$. This is due to the structure of CBC-MAC. Let's illustrate this with a simple case: c consists of a single block. We have

$$M(a \parallel c) = E_K(c \oplus M(a))$$
$$M(b \parallel c) = E_K(c \oplus M(b))$$

and these two must be equal, because $M(a) = M(b)$.

The attack proceeds in two stages. In the first stage the attacker collects the MAC values of a large number of messages until a collision occurs. This provides the a and b for which $M(a) = M(b)$. If the attacker can now get the sender to authenticate $a \parallel c$, he can replace the message with $b \parallel c$ without changing the MAC value. The receiver will check the MAC and accept the bogus message $b \parallel c$. (Remember, we work in the paranoia model. It is quite acceptable for the attacker to create a message and get it authenticated by the sender. There are many situations in which this is possible.) There are many extensions to this attack that work even with the addition of length fields and padding rules [12].

This is not a trivial attack, as it does not work on an ideal MAC function. Finding the collision is not the problem. That can be done for an ideal MAC function in exactly the same way. But once you have two messages a and b, for which $M(a) = M(b)$, you cannot use them to forge a MAC on a new message, whereas you can do that with CBC-MAC.

There are some nice theoretical results which argue that, in the particular proof model used, CBC-MAC provides 64 bits of security when the block size is 128 bits [4]. Unfortunately, this is not good enough for our design strength. CBC-MAC would be fine if we could use a block cipher with a 256-bit block size.

You have to be careful with how you use CBC-MAC. You cannot just CBC-MAC the message itself, as that leads to simple attacks. Instead, you should do the following:

1. Construct a string s from the concatenation of l and m, where l is the length of m encoded in a fixed-length format.

2. Pad s until the length is a multiple of the block size. (See section 5.1 for details.)

3. Apply CBC-MAC to the padded string s.

4. Output the last ciphertext block, or part of that block. Do not output any of the intermediate values.

The advantage of CBC-MAC is that it uses the same type of computations as the block cipher encryption modes. Encryption and MAC are the only two functions which are ever applied to the bulk data, so these are two speed-critical areas. Having them use the same primitive functions makes efficient implementations easier, especially in hardware.

Still, we would rather not use CBC-MAC because it is so difficult to use correctly.

7.5   HMAC

Given that the ideal MAC is a random mapping and that we already have hash functions which behave like random mappings, it is an obvious idea to use a hash function to build a MAC. This is exactly what HMAC is [3, 59]. The designers of HMAC were of course aware of the problems with hash functions, which we discussed in chapter 6. Whereas hash functions provide only $n/2$ bits of security against some attacks, a MAC function is expected to provide n bits of security. Defining $\text{MAC}(K, m)$ as $h(K \,\|\, m)$, $h(m \,\|\, K)$, or even $h(K \,\|\, m \,\|\, K)$ is not secure if you use one of the standard iterative hash functions [77]. Having the key at the front allows length extension attacks. Having a key at the end allows a clever key-recovery attack in about $2^{n/2}$ steps.

The HMAC designers carefully crafted HMAC to resist these attacks, and provided security bounds on the resulting construction. They avoid the key recovery attack that reveals K to the attacker, and avoid attacks that can be done by the attacker without interaction with the system. However, HMAC is still limited to $n/2$ bits of security, as there are birthday attacks against the function that make use of the internal collisions of the iterated hash function. The HMAC construction ensures that these require $2^{n/2}$ interactions with the system under attack, which is more difficult to do than performing $2^{n/2}$ computations on your own computer.

To keep things simple, we don't make the distinction between online attacks and offline attacks. Rather, we only look at the amount of work the attacker has to do. So even with all its careful design, HMAC is still limited to a security level of $n/2$ bits for an n-bit hash function.

The HMAC paper [3] presents several good examples of the problems that arise when the primitives (in this case the hash function) have unexpected properties. This is why we are so compulsive about providing simple behavioral specifications for our cryptographic primitives.

HMAC computes $h(K \oplus a \,\|\, h(K \oplus b \,\|\, m))$, where a and b are specified constants. The message itself is only hashed once, and the output is hashed again with the key. For details, see the specifications in [3, 59]. HMAC works with any of the iterative hash functions we discussed in chapter 6. This is the one exception where you can use the SHA family directly without using SHA_d; HMAC already takes care of the problems that SHA_d solves.

We like the HMAC construction. It is neat, efficient, and easy to implement. It is widely used with both MD5 and SHA-1 as hash functions, and by now you will find it in a lot of libraries. Still, to achieve our 128-bit security level, we would only use it with a 256-bit hash function such as SHA-256. As HMAC takes care of the SHA-256 weaknesses itself you don't need to use SHA_d-256 to build HMAC from.

7.5.1 HMAC versus SHA$_d$

Earlier we mentioned that using $h(K \parallel m)$ makes a good MAC function as long as h is a good hash function. And we said that SHA$_d$-256 was a good hash function. If we write this out, we get the function

$$(K, m) \mapsto \text{SHA-256}(\text{SHA-256}(K \parallel m))$$

as a good MAC function. But now we recommend HMAC with SHA-256 as hash function, which expands to

$$(K, m) \mapsto \text{SHA-256}((K \oplus a) \parallel \text{SHA-256}((K \oplus b) \parallel m))$$

Why are we recommending HMAC when the first construction is simpler?

This is a very good question. The answer is a subtle one. HMAC was designed for a slightly different attacking cost model. Suppose Alice is using the MAC function for authentication purposes. We only count the number of steps an attacker has to perform, and ignore things like whether each step requires interaction with Alice or not. HMAC considers offline attacks (which do not require any interaction) to be easier to perform than online attacks (which use interaction) and takes special care to protect against them. This is the reason that HMAC uses the key in the second hash computation as well.

The HMAC designers are right, of course. Offline attacks are easier to perform than online attacks. But we don't feel that this justifies having different security levels for online and offline attacks. The problem is that we don't want to give a fixed cost factor, such as "Each step in an online attack is equivalent to S steps in an offline attack." We have no idea what value to assign to S, especially since we have no information about the application the MAC will be used in. Therefore, we stick to our uniform 128-bit security level. This is not a criticism of the HMAC designers. When they designed HMAC, most hash functions had a 128-bit result. An offline collision attack would require only 2^{64} steps, something that you definitely have to protect against. With the larger hash functions, these attacks are insignificant.

So which of these two should you choose? Choose HMAC. The extra cost compared to SHA$_d$-256$(K \parallel m)$ is insignificant, and HMAC has been around for a while. It has received a lot more cryptanalytical attention. We always try to be conservative, and HMAC is definitely the more conservative choice.

7.6   UMAC

The UMAC family of MAC functions is a good example of how you can use the uncertainty about K to make a much faster MAC than you can make from a hash function [8, 60].[2] UMAC can be an order of magnitude faster than HMAC, and there are proofs of security for UMAC.

Unfortunately, UMAC has a few problems that prevent it from being the ideal MAC.

7.6.1   Size of MAC

The UMAC publications suggest using a 64-bit result for most applications. This is fairly standard practice, and until a year or two ago we would have written the same. The reason the MAC result can be smaller is that there is no such thing as an offline exhaustive search on MAC results. If you search for MAC values, you have to interact with the system to verify if the MAC value is correct. As long as the system does not allow the attacker to forge an extremely large number of messages, a smaller MAC result is still secure.

We have changed our position and now consider a 64-bit result too small. The security of the MAC should not depend on other parts of "the system." As MAC designers, we don't know how the MAC will be used—or abused.[3] Some systems allow attackers to try many forged messages. Other systems abuse the MAC function in different modes, and wind up with real weaknesses. We don't want this type of complication in our designs. Cryptographic design is already too difficult, and complicating the system with extra cross-dependencies is a recipe for disaster. Therefore, we want a MAC

---

[2]The UMAC documentation uses the word "hash" to refer to a *universal hash function*. This is a completely different beast than the hash functions we have been talking about. Don't confuse them.

[3]Abuse is common. For example, in the IKE protocol of IPsec [41] the MAC function is sometimes used in situations in which the message is secret but the key is known!

with 128 bits of output. Well, actually, going by our own design rule 3 (see page 65), we want one with 256 bits of output to be sure that a birthday attack still leaves us with 128 bits of security. If you can get away with it, use a 256-bit MAC value. But as most systems currently use 64- or 96-bit MAC values, it could be hard to argue that you need 256 bits. Especially since the MAC value is sent with each message, and therefore directly affects the message overhead. If you use a good MAC function, and you don't introduce a way for an attacker to perform a collision attack on your MAC values, then you can get away with using only a 128-bit MAC value.

7.6.2   Which UMAC?

This is a more important question: which UMAC should you use? The original paper [8] defined four different ones: UMAC-STD-30, UMAC-STD-60, UMAC-MMX-30, and UMAC-MMX-60. The newer draft RFC [60] proposes a significantly different construction, and defines two more: UMAC16 and UMAC32. In fact, the draft RFC specifies a UMAC with six parameters, and UMAC16 and UMAC32 are just recommended parameter value sets.

We could just choose one of the parameter sets, but which one? The parameters have a significant effect on the efficiency of UMAC. Some are faster on little-endian machines, others on big-endian machines; some are suitable for use with the MMX instructions of the Pentium, others are more suitable for 32-bit multiplies on other CPUs; some use unsigned multiply instructions, others use signed multiply instructions. The list goes on and on. Any one choice is bound to get you into a nasty discussion with those whose hardware you disadvantaged, as the penalty can be significant. On any one platform, UMAC performance can easily differ by a factor of three to five depending on exactly which parameter set you choose, and different platforms prefer different parameter sets.

This plethora of UMAC functions is a result of the extreme optimizations that the designers applied. In their quest for speed the designers created different versions for different situations, as each situation allows specific optimizations to be performed.

We disagree with this approach. Although it has advantages in the short term, it has significant disadvantages in the longer term. There is no UMAC standard, such as there is with HMAC or SHA-1. Different designers will choose different UMAC versions. If you have to interface between those two systems, you will need to implement several UMAC versions. Libraries will often allow the UMAC parameter set to be selected only at compile time, which creates a host of problems if your application needs two or more different UMAC versions. And CPU architectures are going to change enormously over the 20–30 year life of a system. Micro-optimizing for current architectures is a bad idea in the long run.

7.6.3   Platform Flexibility

As we mentioned above, various UMAC versions are optimized for specific platforms. What's more, UMAC poses fairly stringent requirements on the platform. As long as you have a fast multiply instruction and a reasonable amount of memory, UMAC can achieve good speeds. However, we don't think UMAC has an acceptable performance on smart cards or other small memory-limited 8-bit CPU devices. The temporary storage requirements are quite high, and smart cards always have a very limited amount of memory.

All of this implies that UMAC is suitable for current desktop machines, but not for small CPUs.[4] Off the cuff we'd guess that it is also fairly expensive to implement efficiently in hardware, certainly when compared to alternatives like HMAC. As such we don't think that UMAC makes a good standard. It is more like a race-horse than a working horse. It is fast, but only useful in special circumstances.

7.6.4   Amount of Analysis

Our final problem with UMAC is the lack of cryptanalysis on the design. As previously mentioned, there is a proof of security, but that is not a substitute for hostile analysis. It wouldn't be the first time that a provably secure system has been broken. This is, of course, a disadvantage of any new

---

[4]There is an old debate in which some people claim that small CPUs are irrelevant, as they will all be replaced by big CPUs within the next few years. We disagree. The small CPUs have been around for decades, and will just migrate to even smaller applications. The 8-bit CPUs designed in the early 1970s are still in widespread use, despite at least a decade of predictions of their demise.

design, such as AES, SHA-256, and several of the constructions we propose
in this book. Of these, AES has probably received the most cryptanalytical
attention. (We should know; we did some of that analysis.) SHA-256 was
designed by NSA, and so far its designs have been pretty good. NSA also
employs a large number of experts, some of which undoubtedly reviewed
SHA-256 internally before its release. The new constructions we propose
in this book have not received any hostile analysis, but they are all very
conservative, and for many it is easy to see that they are at least as good as
the standard construction that everybody has used for many years. UMAC
is a very aggressive design that relies very heavily on the proof of security.
Let's be optimistic and assume that there is a 95% chance that the proof
is actually complete and correct. That leaves a 5% chance of UMAC being
a very aggressive design without a proof of security—a chance we'd rather
not take.

7.6.5 Why Mention UMAC at All?

If we don't like UMAC, why did we spend so much time discussing it? Well,
we think the direction that UMAC takes is very important. The idea of using
the uncertainty in K to speed up the MAC are very valuable. We'd love to
do more research into this area. There must be a MAC that is much faster
than a hash function, yet as robust and flexible as modern block ciphers.

7.7 Which MAC to Choose?

As you may have gathered from the discussion, we would choose HMAC-
SHA-256: the HMAC construction using SHA-256 as a hash function. We
really want to use the full 256 bits of the result. Most systems use 64-
or 96-bit MAC values, and even then people complain about the overhead.
Adding 32 bytes (256 bits) to each message is not going to make you popular
in whatever project you are working on. As far as we know, there is no
collision attack on the MAC value if it is used in the traditional manner, so
truncating the results from HMAC-SHA-256 to 128 bits should be safe. We
hope.

We reiterate that there is no reason to use SHA_d-256 as the hash function for HMAC, as HMAC already stops the length extension bug. But to achieve 128 bits of security, we need to use a 256-bit hash function internally, which is why HMAC-SHA-1 is not good enough.

We are not particularly happy with this situation, as we believe that it should be possible to create faster MAC functions. But until suitable functions are published and analyzed, there is not a whole lot we can do about it.

7.8   Using a MAC

Using a MAC properly is much more complicated than it seems. We'll discuss the major problems here.

When Bob receives the value $\text{MAC}(K, m)$, he knows that somebody who knew the key K approved the message m. When using a MAC you have to be very careful that this statement implies all security properties that you need. Eve could record a message from Alice to Bob, and then send a copy to Bob at a later time. Without some kind of special protection against these sorts of attacks, Bob would accept it as a valid message from Alice. Similar problems arise if Alice and Bob use the same key K for traffic in two directions. Eve could send the message back to Alice, who would believe that it came from Bob.

In many situations, Alice and Bob want to authenticate not only the message m, but also additional data d. This additional data includes things like the message number used to prevent replay attacks, the source and destination of the message, and so on. Mostly these fields are part of the header of the authenticated (and often encrypted) message. The MAC has to authenticate d as well as m. The general solution is to apply MAC to $d \parallel m$ instead of just to m.

The next issue is best captured in a design rule:

Design rule 4. *The Horton Principle: Authenticate what is being meant, not what is being said.*

A MAC only authenticates a string of bytes, whereas Alice and Bob want to authenticate a message with a specific meaning. The gap between what is being said (i.e., the bytes being sent) and what is meant (i.e., the interpretation of the message) is important.

Suppose Alice uses the MAC to authenticate $m := a \,\|\, b \,\|\, c$, where a, b, and c are some data fields. Bob receives m, and splits it into a, b, and c. But how does Bob split m into fields? Bob must have some rules, and if those rules are not compatible with the way Alice constructed the message, Bob will get the wrong field values. This would be bad, as Bob would have received authenticated bogus data. Therefore it is vital that Bob split m into the fields that Alice put in.

This is easy to do in simple systems. Fields have a fixed size. But soon you will find a situation in which some fields need to be variable in length, or a newer version of the software will use larger fields. Of course, a new version will need a backward compatibility mode to talk to the old software. And here is the problem. Once the field length is no longer constant, Bob is deriving it from some context, and that context could be manipulated by the attacker. For example, Alice uses the old software and the old, short field sizes. Bob uses the new software. Eve, the attacker, manipulates the communications between Alice and Bob to make Bob believe that the new protocol is in use. (Details of how this works are not important; the MAC system shouldn't depend on other parts of the system being secure.) Bob happily splits the message using the larger field sizes, and gets bogus data.

This is where the Horton Principle [93] comes in.[5] You should authenticate the meaning, not the message. This means that the MAC should authenticate not only m, but also all of the information that Bob uses in parsing m into its meaning. This would typically include data like protocol identifier, protocol version number, protocol message identifier, sizes for various fields, etc. One partial solution is to not just concatenate the fields but use a data structure like XML that can be parsed without further information.

The Horton Principle is one of the reasons why authentication at lower protocol levels does not provide adequate authentication for higher-level protocols. An authentication system at the IP packet level cannot know how the e-mail program is going to interpret the data. This precludes it from checking that the context in which the message is interpreted is the

---

[5]For readers who did not grow up in the U.S.: this is named after one of the characters of Dr. Seuss, a writer of children's books [90].

same as the context in which the message was sent.   The only solution is to have the e-mail program provide its own authentication of the data exchanged. In addition to the authentication on the lower levels, of course.

To recap: whenever you do authentication, always think carefully about what other information should be included in the authentication. Be sure that you code all of this information, including the message, into a string of bytes in a way that can be parsed back into the fields in a unique manner. Do not forget to apply this to the concatenation of the additional data and the message we discussed at the start of this section. If you authenticate $d \parallel m$, you had better have a fixed rule on how to split the concatenation back into d and m.

Chapter 8

The Secure Channel

Finally we come to the first of the real-world problems we will solve. The secure channel is probably the most common of all practical problems.

8.1 Problem Statement

Informally, we can define the problem as creating a secure connection between Alice and Bob. We'll have to formalize this a bit before it becomes clear what we are talking about.

8.1.1 Roles

First of all, most connections are bi-directional. Alice sends messages to Bob, and Bob sends messages to Alice. You don't want to confuse the two streams of message, so there must be some kind of asymmetry in the protocol. In real systems, maybe one party is the client and the other the server, or maybe it is easier to speak of the initiator (the party that initiated the secure connection) and the responder. It doesn't matter how you do it, but you have to assign the Alice and Bob roles to the two parties in question in such a way that each of them knows who is playing which role.

Of course, there is always Eve, who tries to attack the secure channel in any way possible. Eve can read all of the communications between Alice and

Bob and arbitrarily manipulate these communications. In particular, Eve can delete, insert, or modify data that is being transmitted.

We always talk about transmitting messages from Alice to Bob, and most of the time our mental image is of two separate computers sending messages to each other over a network of some sort. Another very interesting application is storing data securely. If you think of storing data as transmitting it to the future, then all the discussions make sense. Alice and Bob might be the same person, and the transmission medium could be a tape. You still want to protect the medium from outside eavesdroppers and manipulations. Of course, when you send data to the future, you cannot have an interactive protocol, since the future cannot send a message back to the past.

8.1.2   Key

To implement a secure channel, we need a shared secret. In this case we will assume that Alice and Bob share a secret key K, but that nobody else knows this key. This is an essential property. The cryptographic primitives can never identify Alice as a person. They can at most identify the key. Thus Bob's verification algorithm will tell him something like: "This message was sent by somebody who knows the key K and who played the role of Alice." This statement is only useful if Bob knows that knowledge of K is restricted, preferably to himself and Alice.

How the key is established is not our business here. We just assume the key is there. We will talk about key management in great detail in chapter 15. The requirements for the key are as follows:

- The key K is known only to Alice and Bob.

- Every time the secure channel is initialized a new value is generated for the key K.

The second item is also important. If the same key is used over and over again, then messages from older sessions can be replayed to Alice or Bob, and lead to much confusion. Therefore, even in situations where you have a fixed password as key, you need a key negotiation protocol between Alice and

Bob to set up a suitable unique key K, and you must re-run this protocol every time a secure channel is established. A key such as K that is used for a single communication session is called a *session key*. Again, how K is generated will be discussed in chapter 15.

The secure channel is designed to achieve a security level of 128 bits. Following our design rule (see page 65), we will use a 256-bit key. Thus, K is a 256-bit value.

8.1.3 Messages or Stream

The next question is whether we look at the communications between Alice and Bob as a sequence of discrete messages (such as e-mails) or as a continuous stream of bytes (such as streaming media). We will only consider systems that handle discrete messages. These can trivially be converted to handle a stream of bytes by cutting the data stream into separate messages and reassembling the stream at the receiver's end. In practice, almost all systems use a discrete message system at the cryptographic layer.

We also assume that the underlying transport system that conveys the messages between Alice and Bob is not reliable. Even a reliable communication protocol like TCP/IP does not form a reliable communication channel from a cryptographic point of view. After all, the attacker can easily change, remove, or insert data in a TCP stream without interrupting the flow of data. TCP is only reliable with respect to random events such as loss of packet. It does not protect against an active adversary. From our adversarial point of view, there is no such thing as a reliable communication protocol. (This is a good example of how cryptographers see the world differently.)

8.1.4 Security Properties

We can now formulate the security properties of the channel. Alice sends a sequence of messages $m_1, m_2, \ldots$ that are processed by the secure channel algorithms and then sent to Bob. Bob processes the received messages through the secure channel algorithms, and ends up with a sequence of messages $m'_1, m'_2, \ldots$.

The following properties must hold:

- Eve does not learn anything about the messages m_i except for their timing and size.

- Even when Eve attacks the channel by manipulating the data that is being communicated, the sequence $m'_1, m'_2, \ldots$ of messages that Bob receives is a subsequence of $m_1, m_2, \ldots$, and Bob learns exactly which subsequence he received. (A subsequence is best defined by saying that it can be constructed from the original sequence by the removal of zero or more elements.)

The first property is secrecy. Ideally, Eve should not learn *anything* about the messages. In real life this is very hard to achieve. It is extremely hard to hide information such as the size or the timing of the messages. The known solutions require Alice to send a continuous stream of messages at the maximum bandwidth that she will ever use. If she doesn't have any messages to send, she should invent some trivial ones and send those. This might be acceptable for military applications, but it is not acceptable for most civilian applications. Given that Eve can see the size and timing of messages on a communication channel, she can find out who is communicating with whom, how much, and when. This is called *traffic analysis*. It yields a host of information, and is extremely hard to prevent. We will not solve it in this book, so Eve will be able to perform traffic analysis on our secure channel.

The second property ensures that Bob only gets proper messages, and that he gets them in their correct order. Ideally, we would want Bob to receive the exact sequence of messages that Alice sent. But none of the real-world communications protocols are reliable in a cryptographic sense. Eve can always delete a message in transit. As we cannot prevent the loss of messages, Bob will necessarily have to make do with getting only a subsequence of the messages. Note that the remaining messages that he does receive are in order. There are no duplicates, no modified messages, and no bogus messages sent by someone other than Alice. As a further requirement, Bob learns exactly which messages he has missed. This can be important in some applications where the interpretation of the message depends on the order in which they are received.

In most situations, Alice wants to ensure that Bob gets all the information that she sent him. Most systems implement a scheme whereby Bob sends acknowledgments (either explicit or implicit) to Alice, and Alice resends any information for which she didn't receive an acknowledgment from Bob. Note that our secure channel never takes the initiative in resending a message. Alice will have to do that herself, or at least the protocol layer that makes use of the secure channel will have to do that.

So why not make the secure channel reliable by implementing the resend functionality inside the secure channel? Because that would complicate the secure channel description. We like to keep the security-critical modules simple. Message acknowledgments and resends are standard communication protocol techniques, and they can be implemented on top of our secure channel. This is a book about cryptography, not about basic communication protocol techniques.

8.2   Order of Authentication and Encryption

Obviously we will apply both encryption and authentication to the message. There are two approaches: we can either encrypt first and then authenticate the ciphertext, or we authenticate first and then encrypt both the message and the MAC value.

There are two main arguments in favor of encrypting first. There are theoretical results that show that given certain specific definitions of secure encryption and authentication, the encrypt-first solution is secure, whereas the authenticate-first solution is insecure. If you look at the details, it turns out that authenticate-first is only insecure if the encryption scheme has a specific type of weakness. In practical systems we never use encryption schemes with such weaknesses. However, these weak encryption schemes satisfy a particular formal security definition. (This is a good example of the gap between practical security work and provable security results.) Applying the MAC to the ciphertext of such a weak encryption scheme fixes it and makes it secure. For any real-life encryption scheme, these theoretical results have little meaning. In fact, there are similar proofs that these problems do not occur at all for stream ciphers (such as CTR mode) and CBC-mode encryption.

The second argument in favor of encrypting first is that it is more efficient in discarding bogus messages. For normal messages, Bob has to both decrypt

the message and check the authentication, irrespective of the order they
were applied in. If the message is bogus (i.e., has a wrong MAC field) then
Bob will discard it. With encrypt-first, the decryption is done last on the
receiver side, and Bob never has to decrypt bogus messages, since he can
identify and discard them before decryption. With authenticate-first, Bob
has to first decrypt the message before he can check the authentication. This
is more work for bogus messages. The situation in which this is relevant is
when Eve sends Bob a very large number of bogus messages. With encrypt-
first Bob saves the work of decrypting them, which reduces the CPU load.
Under some very special circumstances this makes a denial-of-service (DOS)
attack a little bit harder. In most real-life situations a DOS attack works by
saturating the communication channel rather than by bogging down Bob's
CPU. We do not find this argument compelling, because we are willing to
sacrifice efficiency for security.

There are two main arguments in favor of authenticating first. In the
encrypt-first configuration, the MAC input and MAC value are both visible to Eve. In the authenticate-first configuration, Eve only gets to see the
ciphertext and the encrypted MAC value; the MAC input (i.e., the plaintext) and actual MAC value are hidden. This makes it much harder to
attack the MAC than in the encrypt-first situation. The real choice is which
of the two functions is applied last. If encryption is applied last, then Eve
gets to attack the encryption function without further hindrance. If the
authentication function is applied last, she gets to attack the authentication function without further hindrance. In general, authentication is more
important than encryption. We therefore prefer to expose the encryption
function to Eve's direct attacks, and protect the MAC as much as possible.

That's right: authentication is more important than encryption. This is
contrary to what most people think. But imagine a situation in which a
secure channel is being used. Consider how much damage Eve could do if
she could read all the traffic. Then think about how much damage Eve could
do if she could modify the data being communicated. In most situations,
modifying data is a devastating attack, and does far more damage than
merely reading it.

The second argument in favor of authenticating first is the Horton Principle.
You should authenticate what you mean, not what you say. Authenticating
the ciphertext breaks this rule, and creates a vulnerability. The danger is

that Bob might check that the ciphertext is correctly authenticated, but then decrypt the ciphertext with a different key than what Alice used to encrypt the message. Bob will get a different plaintext than Alice sent, even though the authentication checked out. There is a particular (unusual) configuration of IPsec that has this problem [33]. This vulnerability has to be fixed. You could include the encryption key in the additional data being authenticated, but we don't like using keys for anything but their normal use. It introduces extra risks; you don't want a faulty MAC function leaking information about the encryption key. The standard solution is to derive both the encryption key and the authentication key for the secure channel from a single secure channel key, as we will be doing in section 8.4.1. This removes the vulnerability, but it also introduces a cross-dependency. The authentication suddenly depends on the key derivation system.

You can argue for hours which order of operations is better. Both solutions can result in good systems, both can result in bad systems. Each has its own advantages and disadvantages. In the end it comes down to what you think is more important. We choose to authenticate first, because we find the security and simplicity advantages more important than saving CPU time during an attack.

8.3 Outline

The solution consists of three components: message numbering, authentication, and encryption.

8.3.1 Message Numbers

Message numbers are vital for various reasons. They provide a source for IVs for the encryption algorithm; they allow Bob to reject replayed messages without the necessity of keeping a large database; they tell Bob which messages were lost in transit; and they ensure that Bob receives the messages in their correct order. For these reasons, the message number must increase monotonically (i.e., later messages have larger message numbers) and must be unique (no two messages may have the same message number).

Assigning message numbers is easy. Alice numbers the first message as 1, the second message as 2, etc. Bob keeps track of the message number of the last message he received. Any new message must have a message number that is larger than the message number of the previous message. By accepting only increasing message numbers, Bob ensures that Eve cannot replay him an old message.

For our secure channel design, we will use a 32-bit number for the message number. The first message is numbered 1. The number of messages is limited to $2^{32} - 1$. If the message number overflows, then Alice will have to stop using this key and rerun the key negotiation protocol to generate a new key. The message number *must* be unique, so we cannot allow it to wrap back to 0.

We could have used a 64-bit message number, but that has a higher overhead. (We would have to include 8 bytes of message number with each message, instead of only 4 bytes.) 32 bits is enough for most applications. Besides, the key should be changed regularly anyway.[1] You can, of course, use 40 or 48 bits if you want to; it doesn't matter much.

Why start numbering at 1 when most C programmers like to start at 0? A small implementation trick. If there are N numbers that could be assigned, then both Alice and Bob need to be able to keep track of $N + 1$ states. After all, the number of messages sent so far could be any of the set $\{0, \ldots, N\}$. By restricting ourselves to $2^{32} - 1$ messages, this state can be encoded in a single 32-bit number. Had we started numbering the messages at 0, then each implementation would require an additional flag to indicate that either no messages had been sent so far, or that the message number space was exhausted. Extra flags add a lot of tricky extra code that is executed very rarely. If it is rarely used, it will have been tested only a few times, and therefore it will probably not work. In essence, it is another area of easy mistakes that we can eliminate by starting our numbering at 1.

Throughout the rest of this chapter we'll write i for the message number.

---

[1] All keys should be updated at reasonable intervals. Heavily used keys should be updated more often. Restricting a key to $2^{32} - 1$ messages is quite reasonable.

8.3.2 Authentication

We need a MAC for the authentication function. As you might expect, we will use HMAC-SHA-256 with the full 256-bit result. The input to the MAC consists of the message m_i and the extra authentication data x_i. As we explained in chapter 7, there is often some contextual data that has to be included in the authentication. This is the context data that Bob will use to interpret what the message means; it typically includes the protocol version number, negotiated field sizes, and the fact that this is the third message from the Foobar Secure Transaction Protocol login sequence. We are just specifying the secure channel here, so the actual value for x_i will have to be provided by the rest of the application. From our point of view, each x_i is a string and both Alice and Bob have the same value for x_i.

Let $\ell(\cdot)$ be the function that returns the length (in bytes) of a string of data. The MAC value a is computed as

$$a_i := \text{MAC}(i \,\|\, \ell(x_i) \,\|\, x_i \,\|\, m_i)$$

where i and $\ell(x_i)$ are both 32-bit unsigned integers in least-significant-byte-first format. The $\ell(x_i)$ ensures that the string $i \,\|\, \ell(x_i) \,\|\, x_i \,\|\, m_i$ uniquely parses into its fields. Without $\ell(x_i)$, there would be many ways to split it into i, x_i, and m_i, and as a result, the authentication would not be unambiguous. Of course, x_i should be encoded in such a way that it can be parsed into its different fields without further context information, but that is not something we can ensure at this level. The application using this secure channel will have to guarantee that.

8.3.3 Encryption

For encryption, we will use AES in CTR mode. This is made easy by the message number that provides the unique nonce value that CTR mode needs.

We limit the size of each message to $16 \cdot 2^{32}$ bytes, which limits the block counter to 32 bits. Of course we could use a 64-bit counter, but 32 bits is easier to implement on many platforms, and most applications don't need to process such huge messages.

The key stream consists of the byte $k_0, k_1, \ldots$. For a message with nonce i, the key stream is defined by

$$k_0, \ldots, k_{2^{36}-1} :=$$
$$E(K, 0 \parallel i \parallel 0) \parallel E(K, 1 \parallel i \parallel 0) \parallel \cdots \parallel E(K, 2^{32} - 1 \parallel i \parallel 0)$$

where each plaintext block of the cipher is built from a 32-bit block number, the 32-bit message number, and 64 bits of zeroes. The key stream is a very long string. We will only use the first $\ell(m_i) + 32$ bytes of the key stream. (We shouldn't have to mention that you don't have to compute the rest of the key stream...) We concatenate m_i and a_i, and XOR these bytes with $k_0, \ldots, k_{\ell(m_i)+15}$.

8.3.4 Frame Format

We cannot just send the encrypted $m_i \parallel a_i$, because Bob needs to know the message number. The final message sent will consist of i coded as a 32-bit integer, least significant byte first, followed by the encrypted m_i and a_i.

8.4 Details

We can now discuss the details of the secure channel. For convenience we've defined the channel to be bi-directional, so that the same key can be used for both directions. If we define the channel to be one-directional, then you can bet on it that somebody will use the same key for both directions and utterly destroy the security. Making the channel bi-directional reduces this risk.

We describe all our algorithms using a pseudocode notation that should be easy to read for anyone familiar with the conventions of programming. Program blocks are denoted both by the indent level and by paired key words such as if/fi and do/od.

8.4.1 Initialization

The first algorithm we show is the initialization of the channel data. This has two main functions: setting up the keys and setting up the message numbers. We derive four subsidiary keys from the channel key: an encryption key and an authentication key to send messages from Alice to Bob, and an encryption key and an authentication key to send messages from Bob to Alice.

function INITIALIZESECURECHANNEL

input: K Key of the channel, 256 bits.

             R Role. Specifies if this party is Alice or Bob.

output: S State for the secure channel.

First compute the four keys that are needed. The four strings are ASCII strings without any length or zero-termination.

KEYSENDENC $\leftarrow$ SHA$_d$-256$(K \parallel$ "Enc Alice to Bob")

KEYRECENC $\leftarrow$ SHA$_d$-256$(K \parallel$ "Enc Bob to Alice")

KEYSENDAUTH $\leftarrow$ SHA$_d$-256$(K \parallel$ "Auth Alice to Bob")

KEYRECAUTH $\leftarrow$ SHA$_d$-256$(K \parallel$ "Auth Bob to Alice")

Swap the encryption and decryption keys if this party is Bob.

if $R = $ "Bob" **then**

     SWAP(KEYSENDENC, KEYRECENC)

     SWAP(KEYSENDAUTH, KEYRECAUTH)

fi

Set the send and receive counters to zero. The send counter is the number of the last sent message. The receive counter is the number of the last received message.

(MSGCNTSEND, MSGCNTREC) $\leftarrow (0, 0)$

Package the state.

$S \leftarrow$ (KEYSENDENC,

        KEYRECENC,

        KEYSENDAUTH,

        KEYRECAUTH,

        MSGCNTSEND,

        MSGCNTREC)

return S

There is also a function to wipe the state information $\mathcal{S}$. We will not specify this in any detail. All it does is wipe the memory that $\mathcal{S}$ used to store information. It is vital that this information be wiped because the keys were stored in that area. On many systems, just deallocating the memory doesn't necessarily wipe it, so you must erase $\mathcal{S}$ when you are done with it.

8.4.2   Sending a Message

We now turn to the processing required to send a message. This algorithm takes the session state, a message to send, and additional data to be authenticated, and produces the encrypted and authenticated message ready for transmission. The recipient must have the same additional data at hand to check the authentication.

function SendMessage
input: $\mathcal{S}$ Secure session state.
             m Message to be sent.
             x Additional data to be authenticated.
output: t Data to be transmitted to the receiver.

First check the message number and update it.
assert MsgCntSend $< 2^{32} - 1$
MsgCntSend $\leftarrow$ MsgCntSend $+ 1$
$i \leftarrow$ MsgCntSend

Compute the authentication. The values $\ell(x)$ and i are encoded in four bytes, least significant byte first.
$a \leftarrow$ HMAC-SHA-256(KeySendAuth, $i \parallel \ell(x) \parallel x \parallel m$)
$t \leftarrow m \parallel a$

Generate the key stream. Each plaintext block of the block cipher consists of a four-byte counter, four bytes of i, and eight zero bytes. Integers are LSByte first, E is AES encryption with a 256-bit key.
$K \leftarrow$ KeySendEnc
$k \leftarrow E_K(0 \parallel i \parallel 0) \parallel E_K(1 \parallel i \parallel 0) \parallel \cdots$

Form the final text. Again, i is encoded as four bytes, LSByte first.
$t \leftarrow i \parallel (t \oplus$ First-$\ell(t)$-bytes$(k))$
return t

Given our earlier discussions, this is relatively straightforward. We check for exhaustion of the message counter. We cannot stress enough how important this check is. If the counter ever wraps, the entire security falls apart—and this is a mistake we've seen often. The authentication and encryption are as described in our previous discussion. Finally, we send i with the encrypted and authenticated message so that the receiver will know the message number.

Note that the session state is updated because the MsgCntSend value is modified. Again, this is vital, as the message number must be unique. In fact, almost everything in these algorithms is vital for the security.

8.4.3   Receiving a Message

The receiving algorithm requires the encrypted and authenticated message that SendMessage produced and the same additional data x to be authenticated.

function ReceiveMessage
input: S Secure session state.
              t Text received from the transmitter.
              x Additional data to be authenticated.
output: m Message that was sent.

The received message must contain at least a 4-byte message number and a 32-byte MAC field. This check ensures that all the future splitting operations will work.
assert $\ell(t) \geq 36$

Split t into i and the encrypted message plus authenticator. The split is well-defined because i is always 4 bytes long.
$i \parallel t \leftarrow t$

Generate the key stream, just as the sender did.
$K \leftarrow$ KeyRecEnc
$k \leftarrow E_K(0 \parallel i \parallel 0) \parallel E_K(1 \parallel i \parallel 0) \parallel \cdots$

Decrypt the message and MAC field, and split. The split is well-defined because a is always 32 bytes long.
$m \parallel a \leftarrow t \oplus$ First-$\ell(t)$-bytes(k)

Recompute the authentication. The values $\ell(x)$ and i are encoded in four
      bytes, least significant byte first.
$a' \leftarrow$ HMAC-SHA-256(KeyRecAuth, $i \parallel \ell(x) \parallel x \parallel m$)
if $a' \neq a$ **then**
    destroy k, m
    return AuthenticationFailure
else if $i \leq$ MsgCntRec **then**
    destroy k, m
    return MessageOrderError
fi
MsgCntRec $\leftarrow i$
return m

We have used the canonical order for the operations here. You could put the
check on the message number before the decryption, but then this function
would report the wrong error if i were mangled during transmission. Instead
of notifying the caller that the message was mangled, it would notify the
caller that the message is in the wrong order. As the caller might wish to
handle the two situations differently, this routine should not give the wrong
information. The reason some people like to put the check earlier is that
it allows false messages to be discarded more quickly. We don't consider
this to be of great importance; if you receive so many false packets that the
speed of discarding them becomes significant, you already have much bigger
problems.

There is one very important issue for the receiver. The RECEIVEMESSAGE
function may not release any information about the key stream or the plaintext message until the authentication has been verified. If the authentication fails, a failure indication is returned, but neither the key stream nor
the plaintext may be revealed. An actual implementation should wipe the
memory areas used to store these elements. So why is this so important?
The plaintext message reveals the key stream, because it is assumed that
every attacker knows the ciphertext. The danger is that the attacker will
send a fake message (with an incorrect MAC value) but still learn the key
stream from the data released by the receiver. This is the paranoia model
at work again. Any data released or leaked by this routine is automatically
assumed to end up in possession of the attacker. By destroying the data

held in k and m before returning with an error, this routine ensures that this data can never be leaked.

8.4.4 Message Order

Like the transmitter, the receiver updates the state S by modifying the MSGCNTREC variable. The receiver ensures that the message numbers of the messages it accepts are strictly increasing. This certainly ensures that no message is accepted twice, but if the stream of messages is reordered during transmission, otherwise perfectly valid messages will be lost.

It is relatively easy to fix this, but at a cost. If you let the receiver accept messages out of order, then the application which uses the secure channel must be able to handle these out-of-order messages. Many applications cannot deal with this. Some applications are designed to handle it, but have subtle bugs (often security-relevant) when messages are reordered. In most situations we prefer to fix the underlying transport layer and prevent accidental reordering of messages, so that the secure channel does not have to deal with this problem.

There is one situation that we know of in which the receiver allows messages to arrive out of order, and for a very good reason. This is IPsec, the IP security protocol [51] that encrypts and authenticates IP packets. As IP packets can be reordered during transport, and as all applications that use IP are very well aware of this property, IPsec maintains a replay protection window rather than just remembering the counter value of the last received message. If c is the message number of the last received message, then IPsec maintains a bitmap for the message numbers $c - 31, c - 30, c - 29, \ldots, c - 1, c$. Each bit indicates whether a message with the corresponding message number has been received. Messages with numbers smaller than $c - 31$ are always refused. Messages in the range $c - 31$ to $c - 1$ are only accepted if the corresponding bit is 0 (and this bit is then set, of course). If the new message has a message number larger than c, then c is updated and the bitmap is shifted to maintain the invariant. Such a bitmap construction allows some limited reordering of the messages without adding too much state to the receiver.

8.5   Alternatives

The secure channel definition we have given is not always practical; especially when implementing a secure channel in embedded hardware, it becomes relatively costly to implement SHA-256. What are the alternatives?

While we were writing this book, Niels had a customer with exactly this problem. The initial plan was to use OCB [83, 84]. This mode has the advantage that both encryption and authentication are done using a block cipher, and no extra cryptographic primitive is needed. Unfortunately, the problems surrounding OCB's patent licenses make it a costly and high-risk solution. There are other recently proposed block cipher modes that provide the same authenticate-and-encrypt functionality, but they are subject to similar patent problems.

To resolve this problem, Doug Whiting, Russ Housley, and Niels developed a straightforward combination of CTR mode encryption and CBC-MAC authentication. This block cipher mode was dubbed CCM [94]. Compared to OCB, it requires twice as many computations to encrypt and authenticate a message, but as far as we know there are no patent issues at all with CCM. The designers know of no patents that cover CCM, and they have not applied, nor will they apply, for a patent. Jakob Jonsson provided a proof of security for CCM [44], and NIST is considering whether to standardize CCM as a block cipher mode.

So should you use OCB or CCM? Both are fairly new modes (CCM is the newest), which makes them a bit suspect. Both have proofs of security which we don't trust completely. CCM is a combination of well-established techniques, whereas OCB is a completely new construction. OCB is twice as efficient, but is covered by various patents.

One significant difference is how these two modes behave under collision attacks. CCM uses CTR encryption, and as we saw earlier, CTR starts to leak information when it is used to encrypt more than 2^{64} blocks of information (assuming a block size of 128 bits). For this reason, the CCM specifications limit the number of blocks encrypted with a single key to 2^{60} blocks, which reduces the leakage to insignificant levels (a fraction of a bit). There are no known collision attacks on the authentication portion of CCM.

So although CCM cannot fully achieve a 128-bit security level, it gets pretty close and does at least as well as any other block cipher mode.

OCB, on the other hand, has a collision attack on the authentication. If a collision occurs, the authentication property is lost completely [35]. This means that OCB cannot achieve a 128-bit security level. If you encrypt 2^{48} blocks per key, it achieves a security level of only 81 bits or so. We don't think that is good enough in the long run, although many real-world systems are using similar security levels today.

It shouldn't surprise you that we prefer CCM. We think it is a reasonable alternative to the secure channel defined in this chapter. But of course we are biased, as we have been involved in the design of CCM.

One more point: CCM, OCB, and similar modes do not provide the full secure channel. They provide the encryption/authentication functionality, and require a key and a unique nonce for each packet. It is easy to adapt our secure channel algorithms to use one of these block cipher modes rather than the separate MAC and encryption functions. Instead of the four subsidiary keys generated in INITIALIZESECURECHANNEL, you will need two keys, one for each direction of traffic. The nonce can be constructed by padding the message number to the correct size.

8.6   Conclusion

The secure channel is one of the most useful applications of cryptography, and it is used in almost all cryptographic systems. Given good encryption and authentication primitives, constructing a secure channel is not too difficult. There are a lot of small details to pay attention to, and all the details must of course be done correctly, but that is the usual situation in cryptography. In the real world implementing a secure channel system is not the main difficulty; rather, it is convincing people that they need it, and establishing a key.

Chapter 9

Implementation Issues (I)

Now that we have come this far, we would like to talk a bit about implementation issues. Implementing cryptographic systems is sufficiently different from implementing normal programs to deserve its own treatment.

The big problem is, as always, the weakest-link property (see section 2.2). It is very easy to screw up the security at the implementation level. In fact, implementation errors (most commonly in the form of buffer overflows) are by far the biggest security problem in real-world systems. If you have been paying any attention to computer security problems over the last few years, you know what we mean. You rarely hear about cryptography systems that are broken in practice. This is not because the cryptography in most systems is any good; we've reviewed enough of them to know this is not the case. It is just easier to find an implementation-related hole than it is to find a cryptographic vulnerability, and attackers are smart enough not to bother with the cryptography when there is this much easier route.

So far in this book we have restricted our discussion to cryptography, but in this chapter we will focus more on the environment in which the cryptography operates. Every part of the system affects security, and to do a really good job the entire system must be designed from the ground up not just with security in mind, but with security as one of the primary goals. The "system" we're talking about is very big. It includes everything that could damage the security properties if it were to misbehave.

One major part is, as always, the operating system. But none of the operating systems in widespread use is designed with security as a primary goal. The logical conclusion to draw from this is that it is impossible to implement a secure system. We don't know how to do it, and we don't know anyone else who knows how to do it, either. Real-life systems include many components that were never designed for security, and that makes it impossible to achieve the level of security that we really need. So should we just give up? Of course not. When we design a cryptographic system, we do our very best to make sure that at least our part is secure. This might sound like a civil-servant mentality: all we care about is our little domain. But we *do* care about the other parts of the system; we just can't do anything about them. That is one of the reasons for writing this book: to get other people to understand the insidious nature of security, and how important it is to do it right.

Another important reason to get at least the cryptography right is one we mentioned before: attacks on the cryptography are especially damaging because they can be invisible. If the attacker succeeds in breaking your cryptography, you are unlikely to notice. This can be compared to a burglar who has a set of keys to your house. If the burglar exercises reasonable caution, how would you ever find out?

Our long-term goal is to make secure computer systems. To achieve that goal, everybody will have to do their part. Our work, and the work this book is about, is making the cryptography secure. Other parts of the system will have to be made secure, too. We don't know how to do this, but maybe other people do, or maybe we will learn in future. Until then, the overall security of the system is going to be limited by the weakest link, and we will do our utmost to ensure that the weakest link will never be the cryptography.

Another important reason to do the cryptography right is that it is very difficult to switch cryptographic systems once they've been implemented. An operating system runs on a single computer. Cryptographic systems are often used in communication protocols to let many computers communicate with each other. Upgrading the operating system of a single computer is feasible, and in practice it is done relatively often. Modifying the communication protocols in a network is a nightmare, and as a result many networks still use the designs of the 1970s and 1980s. We must keep in mind that any new cryptographic system we design today, if adopted widely, is quite likely to still be used 30 or 50 years from now. We hope that by that time the other parts of the system will have achieved a much higher level of security.

9.1 Creating Correct Programs

The core of the implementation problem is that we in the IT industry don't know how to write a correct program or module. (A "correct" program is one that behaves exactly according to its specifications.) There are several reasons for the difficulty that we seem to have in writing correct programs.

9.1.1 Specifications

The first problem is that for most programs, there is no clear description of what they are supposed to do. If there are no specifications, then you cannot even check whether a program is correct or not. For such programs the whole concept of correctness is undefined.

Many software projects have a document called the functional specification. In theory, this should be the specification of the program. But in practice this document either does not exist, is incomplete, or specifies things that are irrelevant for the behavior of the program. Without clear specifications there is no hope of getting a correct program.

There are really three stages in the specification process:

Requirements Requirements are an informal description of what the program is supposed to achieve. It is really a *"what* can I do with it" document, rather than a "how exactly do I do something with it" document. Requirements are often a bit vague and leave details out in order to concentrate on the larger picture.

Functional specification The functional specifications give a detailed and exhaustive definition of the behavior of the program. The functional specification can only specify things that you can measure on the outside of the program.

For each item in the functional specifications, ask yourself whether you could create a test on the finished program that would determine whether that item was adhered to or not. The test can only use the external behavior of the program, not anything from the inside. If you can't create a test for an item, it does not belong in the functional specification.

The functional specifications should be complete. That is, every piece of functionality should be specified. Anything not in the functional specification does not have to be implemented.

Another way to think of the functional specification is as the basis for testing the finished program. Any item can, and should, be tested.

Implementation design This document has many names, but it specifies how the program works internally. It contains all of the things that cannot be tested from the outside. A good implementation design will often split the program into several modules, and describe their functionality. In turn, these module descriptions can be seen as the requirements for the module, and the whole cycle starts all over again for the module.

Of these three, the functional specification is without a doubt the most important one. This is the document against which the program will be tested when it is finished. You can sometimes get by with informal requirements, or an implementation design that is nothing but a few sketches on a whiteboard. But without functional specifications, there is no way to even describe what you have achieved in the end when the program is finished.

9.1.2   Test and Fix

The second problem in writing correct programs is the test-and-fix development method that is in almost universal use. Programmers write a program, and then test whether it behaves correctly. If it doesn't, they fix the bugs and test again. As we all know, this does not lead to a correct program. It results in a program that kind of works in the most common situations.

Back in 1972, Edsger Dijkstra commented in his Turing Award lecture that testing can only show the presence of bugs, never the absence of bugs [23].

This is very true, and ideally we would like to write programs that we can demonstrate to be correct. Unfortunately, current techniques in proving the correctness of programs are nowhere good enough to handle day-to-day programming tasks, let alone a whole project.

Computer scientists do not know how to solve this. Maybe it will be possible in the future to prove that a program is correct. Maybe we just need a far more extensive and thorough testing infrastructure and methodology. But even without having a full solution, we can certainly do our very best with the tools we do have.

There are some childishly simple rules about bugs that any good software engineering book includes:

- If you find a bug, first implement a test that detects the bug. Check that the bug is detected. Then fix the bug, and check that the test no longer finds the bug. And then keep running that test on every future version to make sure the bug does not reappear.

- Whenever you find a bug, think about what caused it. Are there any other places in the program where a similar bug might reside? Go check them all.

- Keep track of every bug you find. Simple statistical analysis of the bugs you have found can show you which part of the program is especially buggy, or what type of error is made most frequently, etc. Such feedback is necessary for a quality control system.

This is not even a bare minimum, but there is not a lot of methodology to draw from. There are quite a few books that discuss software quality. They don't all agree with each other. Many of them present a particular software development methodology as *the* solution, and we are always suspicious of such one-cure-does-it-all schemes. The truth is almost always somewhere in the middle.

9.1.3 Lax Attitude

The third problem is the incredibly lax attitude of most people in the computer industry. Errors in programs are just accepted as a matter of course.

If your word processor crashes and destroys a day's worth of work, everybody seems to think this is quite normal and acceptable. Often they blame the user: "You should have saved your work more often." Software companies routinely ship products with many known bugs in them. This wouldn't be so bad if they only sold computer games, but nowadays our work, our economy, and—more and more—our lives depend on software. If a car manufacturer finds a defect (bug) in a car after it was sold, they will recall the car and fix it. Software companies get away with disclaiming any and all liability in their software license, something they wouldn't be allowed to do if they produced any other product. This lax attitude means that no serious attempts are being made at producing correct software.

9.1.4   So How Do We Proceed?

Don't ever think that all you need is a good programmer or code reviews or an ISO 9001–certified development process or extensive testing or even a combination of all of them. Reality is much more difficult. Software is too complex to be tamed by a few rules and procedures. We find it instructive to look at the best engineering quality control system in the world: the airline industry. Everybody in that industry is involved in the safety system. There are very strict rules and procedures for almost every operation. There are multiple backups in case of failures. Every nut and bolt of the airplane has to be flight-qualified before it can ever be used. Anytime a mechanic takes a screwdriver to the plane, his work is checked and signed off by a supervisor. Every modification is carefully recorded. Any accident is meticulously investigated to find all the underlying causes, which are then fixed. This fanatical pursuit of quality has a very high cost. An airplane is probably an order of magnitude more expensive than it would be if you just sent the drawings to an ordinary engineering firm. But the pursuit of quality has also been amazingly effective. Flying is an entirely routine operation today, in a machine where every failure is potentially fatal. A machine where you cannot just hit the brakes and stop when something goes wrong. One where the only safe way back to the ground is the quite delicate operation of landing on one of the rare specially prepared spots in the world. The airline industry has been amazingly effective at making flying secure. We would do well to learn all we can from them. Maybe writing correct software *does* cost an order of magnitude more than what we are used to now. But given the cost to society of the bugs in software that we see today, we are sure that it would be cost-effective in the long run.

9.2   Creating Secure Software

So far we have only talked about correct software. Just writing correct software is not good enough for a security system. The software must be secure as well.

What is the difference? Correct software has a specified functionality. If you hit button A, then B will happen. Secure software has an additional requirement: a *lack* of functionality. No matter what the attacker does, she cannot do X. This is a very fundamental difference; you can test for functionality, but not for lack of functionality. The security aspects of the software cannot be tested in any effective way, which makes writing secure software much more difficult than writing correct software. The inevitable conclusion is:

Standard implementation techniques are entirely inadequate to create secure code.

We actually don't know how to create secure code. Software quality is a vast area that would take several books to cover. We don't know enough about it to write those books, but we *do* know the cryptography-specific issues and the problems that we see most frequently, and that is what we will discuss in the rest of this chapter.

Before we start, let us make our point of view clear: unless you are willing to put real effort into developing a secure implementation, there is no point in bothering with the cryptography at all. Designing cryptographic systems might be fun, but it is a waste of time if you implement them badly.

9.3   Keeping Secrets

Anytime you work with cryptography, you are dealing with secrets. And secrets have to be kept. This means that the software that deals with the secrets has to ensure that they don't leak out.

For the secure channel we have two types of secrets: the keys and the data. Both of these secrets are transient secrets; we don't have to store them for a long time. The data is only stored while we process each message. The keys are only stored for the duration of the secure channel. Here we will only discuss keeping transient secrets. For a discussion on storing secrets long-term, see chapter 22.

Transient secrets are kept in memory. Unfortunately, the memory on most computers is not very secure. We will discuss each of the typical problems in turn.

9.3.1   Wiping State

A basic rule of writing security software: wipe any information as soon as you no longer need it. The longer you keep it, the higher the chance that someone will be able to access it. What's more, you should definitely wipe the data before you lose control over the underlying storage medium. For transient secrets, this involves wiping the memory locations.

This sounds easy to do, but it leads to a surprising number of problems. If you write the entire program in C, you can take care of the wiping yourself. If you write a library for others to use, then you have to depend on the main program to inform you that the state is no longer needed. For example, when the communication connection is closed, the crypto library should be informed so that it can wipe the secure channel session state. The library can contain a function for this, but we all know that the programmer of the application is probably not going to bother calling this function. After all, the program works perfectly well without calling this function.

In some object-oriented languages, things are a bit easier. In C++, there is a destructor function for each object, and the destructor can wipe the state. This is certainly standard practice for security-relevant code in C++. As long as the main program behaves properly and destroys all objects it no longer needs, the memory state will be wiped. The C++ language ensures that all stack-allocated objects are properly destroyed when the stack is unwound during exception handling, but the program has to ensure that all heap-allocated objects are destroyed. Calling an operating system function to exit the program might not even unwind the call stack. And you have to ensure that all sensitive data is wiped even if the program is about to exit. After all, the operating system gives no guarantees that it will wipe the data soon, and some operating systems don't even bother wiping the memory before they give it to the next application.

Even if you do all this, the computer might still frustrate your attempts. Some compilers try too hard to optimize. A typical security-relevant function performs some computations in local variables, and then tries to wipe them. You can do this in C with a call to the `memset` function. Good compilers will optimize the `memset` function to in-line code, which is more efficient. But some of them are too clever by half. They detect that the variable or array that is being wiped will never be used again, and "optimize" the `memset` away. It's faster, but suddenly the program does not behave the same way anymore. It is not uncommon to see code that reveals data that it happens to find in memory. If the memory is given to some library without having been wiped first, the library might leak the data to an attacker. So check the code that your compiler produces, and make sure the secrets are actually being wiped.

In a language like Java, the situation is even more complicated. All objects live on the heap, and the heap is garbage-collected. This means that the finalization function (similar to the C++ destructor) is not called until the garbage collector figures out that the object is no longer in use. There are no specifications about how often the garbage collector is run, and it is quite conceivable that secret data remains in memory for a very long time. The use of exception handling makes it hard to do the wiping by hand. If an exception is thrown, then the call-stack unwinds without any way for the programmer to insert his own code, except by writing *every* function as a big try clause. The latter solution is so ugly that it is impractical. It also has to be applied throughout the program, making it impossible to create a security library for Java that behaves properly. During exception handling, Java happily unwinds the stack, throwing away the references to the objects without cleaning up the objects themselves. Java is really bad in this respect. The best solution we've been able to come up with is to at least ensure that the finalization routines are run at program exit. The `main` method of the program uses a `try-finally` statement. The finally block contains some code to force a garbage collect, and to instruct the garbage collector to attempt to complete all the finalization methods. (See the functions `System.gc()` and `System.runFinalization()` for more details.) There is still no guarantee that the finalization methods will be run, but it is the best we've been able to find.

What we really need is support from the programming language itself. In C++ it is at least theoretically possible to write a program that wipes all states as soon as they are no longer needed, but many other features of the language make it a poor choice for security software. Java makes it very difficult to wipe the state. One improvement would be to declare variables as "sensitive," and have the implementation guarantee that they will be wiped. Even better would be a language that always wipes all data that is no longer needed. That would avoid a lot of errors without significantly affecting efficiency.

There are other places where secret data can end up. All data is eventually loaded into a CPU register. Wiping registers is not possible in most programming languages, but on register-starved CPUs like the Pentium, it is very unlikely that any data will survive for any reasonable amount of time.

During a context-switch (when the operating system switches from running one program to running the next program) the values in the registers of the CPU are stored in memory where their values might linger for a long time. As far as we know, there is nothing you can do about this, apart from fixing the operating system to ensure the confidentiality of that data.

9.3.2 Swap File

Most operating systems (including all current Windows versions and all UNIX versions) use a virtual memory system to increase the number of programs that can be run in parallel. While a program is running, not all of its data is kept in memory. Some is stored in a swap file. When the program tries to access data that is not in memory, the program is interrupted. The virtual memory system reads the required data from the swap file into a piece of memory, and the program is allowed to continue. What's more, when the virtual memory system decides that it needs more free memory, it will take an arbitrary piece of memory from a program and write it to the swap file.

Of course, most virtual memory systems do not make any serious attempt to keep the data secret, or to encrypt it before it is written to the disk. Most software is designed for a cooperative environment, not the adversarial environment that cryptographers work in. So our problem is the following: the virtual memory system could just take some of the memory of our program and write it to the swap file on disk. The program never gets told, and does not notice. Suppose this happens to the memory in which the keys are stored. If the computer crashes—or is switched off—the data remains on the disk. Most operating systems leave the data on disk even when you shut them down properly. Typically there is no mechanism to wipe the swap file, so the data could linger indefinitely on disk. Who knows who will have access to this swap file in future? We really cannot afford the risk of having our secrets written to the swap file.[1]

So how do we stop the virtual memory system from writing our data to disk? On some operating systems there are system calls that you can use to inform the virtual memory system that specified parts of memory are not to be swapped out. Rarely do we find an operating system that supports a secure swap system where the swapped-out data is cryptographically protected. If neither of these options is available, you are out of luck. Complain loudly about the operating system, and do the best you can.

Assuming you can lock the memory and prevent it from being swapped out, which memory should be locked? All the memory that can ever hold secrets, of course. This brings up a secondary problem. Many programming environments make it very hard to know where exactly your data is being stored. Objects are often allocated on a heap, data can be statically allocated, and many local variables end up on the stack. Figuring out the details is complicated and very error-prone. Probably the best solution is to simply lock all the memory of your application. Even that is not quite as easy as it

---

[1]In fact, we should never write secrets to any permanent media without encrypting them, but that is an issue we will discuss later.

sounds, because you could lose a number of operating system services such as the automatically allocated stack. And locking all the memory makes the virtual memory system ineffective.

It shouldn't be this difficult. The proper solution is, of course, to make a virtual memory system that protects the confidentiality of the data. This is an operating system change, and beyond our control. Even if the next version of your operating system were to have this feature, you should carefully check that the virtual memory system does a good job of keeping secrets.

9.3.3   Caches

Modern computers don't just have a single type of memory. They have a hierarchy of memories. At the bottom is the main memory—often hundreds of megabytes large. But because the main memory is relatively slow, there is also a cache. This is a smaller but faster memory. The cache keeps a copy of the most recently used data from the main memory. If the CPU wants to access the data, it first checks the cache. If the data is in the cache, the CPU gets the data relatively quickly. If the data is not in the cache, it is read (relatively slowly) from main memory, and a copy is stored in the cache for future use. To make room in the cache, a copy of some other piece of data is thrown away.

This is important because caches keep copies of data, including copies of our secret data. The problem is that when we try to wipe our secrets, this wiping might not take place properly. In some systems, the modifications are only written to the cache and not to the main memory. The data will eventually be written to main memory, but only when the cache needs more room to store other data. We don't know all the details of these systems, and they change with every CPU. There is no way to know if there is some interaction between the memory allocation unit and the cache system that might result in some wipe operations escaping the write-to-main-memory part when the memory is deallocated before the cache is flushed. Manufacturers never specify how to wipe data in a guaranteed manner. At least, we have never seen any specifications like that, and as long as it is not specified, we can't trust it.

A secondary danger of caches is that under some circumstances a cache learns that a particular memory location has been modified, perhaps by the other CPU in a multi-CPU system. The cache then marks the data it has for that location as "invalid," but typically the actual data is not wiped. Again, there might exist a copy of our secrets that has not been wiped.

There is very little you can do about this. It is not a great danger, because in most systems only the OS code can access the cache mechanisms directly. And we have to trust the operating system anyway, so we could trust it with this as well. We are nevertheless concerned about these designs, because they clearly do not provide the functionality that is required to implement security systems properly.

9.3.4   Data Retention by Memory

Something that surprises many people is that simply overwriting data in memory does not delete the data. The details depend to some extent on the exact type of memory involved, but basically if you store data in a memory location, that location slowly starts to "learn" the data. When you overwrite or switch off the computer, the old value is not completely lost. Depending on the circumstances, just powering the memory off and back on again can recover some or all of the old data. Other memories can "remember" old data if you access them using (often undocumented) test modes [39].

Several mechanisms cause this phenomenon. If the same data is stored for a time in the same location in SRAM (Static RAM), then this data becomes the preferred power-up state of that memory. A friend of ours encountered this problem with his home-built computer long ago [9]. He wrote a BIOS that used a magic value in a particular memory location to determine whether a reset was a cold reboot or a warm reboot.[2] After a while the machine refused to boot after power-up because the memory had learned the magic value, and the boot process therefore treated every reset as a warm reboot. As this did not initialize the proper variables, the boot

---

[2]In those days home-built machines were programmed by entering the binary form of machine language directly. This led to many errors, and the one sure way to recover from a program that crashed was to reset the machine. A cold reboot is one after power-up. A warm reboot is the sort performed when the user presses the reset button. A warm reboot does not reinitialize all the state, and therefore does not wipe the settings the user made.

process failed. The solution in his case was to swap some memory chips around, scrambling the magic value that the SRAM had learned. For us it was a lesson to remember: memory retains more data than you think.

Similar processes happen in DRAM, although they are somewhat more complicated. DRAM works by storing a small charge on a very small capacitor. The insulating material around the capacitor is stressed by the resulting field. The stress results in changes to the material, specifically causing the migration of impurities [39]. An attacker with physical control over the memory can potentially recover this data.

It is arguable whether this is a significant threat, but we think it is important. If your computer is ever compromised (e.g., stolen) you do not want the data that you had and then wiped to be compromised as well. To achieve this goal, we have to make the computer forget information.

We can only give a partial solution, which works if we make some reasonable assumptions about the memory. This solution, which we call a Boojum,[3] works for relatively small amounts of data, such as keys. Let m be the data we want to store. Instead of storing m, we generate a random string R and store both R and $R \oplus m$. These two values are stored in different memory locations, preferably not too close together. The trick is to change R regularly. At regular intervals, say every 100 ms, we generate a new random R', and update the memory to store $R \oplus R'$ and $R \oplus R' \oplus m$. This ensures that each bit of the memory is written with a sequence of random bits. To wipe the memory, you simply write a new m with the value zero, which results in the two storage locations getting the same (random) data.

To read information from this storage you read both halves and XOR them together to get m. Writing is done by XORing the new data with R and storing it in the second location.

Care should be taken that the bits of R and $R \oplus m$ are not adjacent on the RAM chip. Without information about how the RAM chip works, this can be difficult, but most memories store bits in a rectangular matrix of bits, with some address bits selecting the row and other address bits selecting the column. If the two pieces are stored at addresses that differ by 0x5555, then it is highly unlikely that the two will be stored adjacent on the chip.

---

[3]After Lewis Carroll's *The Hunting of the Snark* [15].

(This assumes that the memory does not use the even-indexed address bits as row number and the odd-indexed address bits as column number, but we have never seen a design like that.) An even better solution might be to choose two random addresses in a very large address space. This makes the probability that the two locations are adjacent very small, independent of the actual chip layouts of the memory.

This is only a partial solution, and a rather cumbersome one at that. It is limited to small amounts of data, as the update function would otherwise be too expensive. But using this solution ensures that there is no physical point on the memory chip that is continually stressed or unstressed depending on the secret data.

There is still no guarantee that the memory will be wiped. If you read the documentation of a memory chip, there are no specifications that prevent the chip from retaining all data ever stored in it. No chip does that, of course, but it shows that we can at most achieve a heuristic security.

We have concentrated on the main memory here. The same solution will work for the cache memory, except that you cannot control the position on the chip where the data will be stored. This solution does not work for the CPU registers, but they are used so often for so much different data that we doubt they will pose a data retention problem. On the other hand, extension registers, such as floating point registers or MMX-style registers, are used far less frequently, so they could pose a problem.

If you have large amounts of data that need to be kept secret, then the solution of storing two copies and XORing new random strings into both copies regularly becomes too expensive. A better solution is to encrypt a large block of data and store the ciphertext in memory that potentially retains information. Only the key needs to be stored in a way that avoids data retention, for example, using a Boojum. For details, see [24].

9.3.5 Access by Others

There's yet another problem with keeping secrets on a computer: other programs on the same machine might access the data. Some operating systems allow different programs to share memory. If the other program can read your secret keys, you have a serious problem. Often the shared memory has to be set up by both programs, which reduces the risk. In other situations, the shared memory might be set up automatically as a result of loading a shared library.

Debuggers are especially dangerous. Modern operating systems often contain features designed to be used by debuggers. Various Windows versions allow you to attach a debugger to an already running process. The debugger can do many things, including reading the memory. Under UNIX it is sometimes possible to force a core-dump of a program. The core-dump is a file that contains a memory image of the program data, including all of your secrets.

Another danger comes from especially powerful users. Called *superusers*, or *administrators*, these users can access things on the machine that normal users cannot. Under UNIX, for example, the superuser can read any part of the memory.

In general, your program cannot effectively defend itself against these types of attacks. If you are careful you may be able to eliminate some of these problems, but often you'll find yourself limited in what can be achieved. Still, you should consider these issues on the particular platform you are working on.

9.3.6   Data Integrity

In addition to keeping secrets, we should protect the integrity of the data we are storing. We use the MAC to protect the integrity of the data during transit, but if the data can be modified in memory, we still have problems.

In this discussion, we will assume that the hardware is reliable. If the hardware is unreliable, there is very little you can do. If you are unsure about the hardware reliability, perhaps you should spend part of your time and memory simply to verify it, although that is really the operating system's job. One thing we try to do is to make sure the main memory on our machines is ECC (error-correcting code) memory.[4] If there is a single bit failure, then

---

[4]You have to make sure that all components of the computer support ECC memory. Beware of slightly cheaper memory modules that do not store the extra information but instead recompute it on the fly. This defeats the whole purpose of ECC memory.

the error-correcting code will detect and correct the error. Without ECC memory, any bit error leads to the CPU reading the wrong data.

Why is this important? There is an enormous number of bits in a modern computer. Suppose the engineering is done really well, and each bit has only a 10^{-15} chance of failing in each second. If you have 128 MB of memory, then you have about 10^{12} bits of memory, and you can expect one bit failure every 1000 seconds, or about every 17 minutes. This is an unacceptable error rate to us. The error rate increases with the amount of memory in the machine, so it is even worse if you have 1 GB of memory. Servers typically use ECC memory because they have more memory and run for longer periods of time. We like to have the same stability in all machines.

Of course, this is a hardware issue, and you typically don't get to specify the type of memory on the machine that will run the final application.

Some of the dangers that threaten data confidentiality also endanger the data integrity. Debuggers can sometimes modify your program's memory. Superusers can directly modify memory, too. Again, there is nothing you can do about it, but it is useful to be aware of the situation.

9.3.7   What to Do

Keeping a secret on a modern computer is not as easy as it sounds. There are many ways in which the secret can leak out. To be fully effective, you have to stop all of them. Unfortunately, current operating systems and programming languages do not provide the required support to stop the leakage completely. You have to do the best you can. This involves a lot of work, all of it specific to the environment you work in.

These problems also make it very difficult to create a library with the cryptographic functions in it. Keeping the secrets safe often involves modifications to the main program. And of course, the main program also handles data that should be kept confidential; otherwise, it wouldn't need the cryptography library in the first place. This is the familiar issue of security considerations affecting every part of the system.

9.4   Quality of Code

If you create an implementation for a cryptographic system, you will have to
spend a great deal of time on the quality of the code. This book is not about
programming, but as quality of code is typically left out of programming
books, we will say a few words here.

9.4.1   Simplicity

Complexity is the main enemy of security. Therefore, any security design
should strive for simplicity. We are quite ruthless about this, even though
this does not make us popular. Eliminate all the options that you can.
Get rid of all those baroque features that few people use. Stay away from
committee designs, because the committee process always leads to extra
features or options in order to achieve compromise. In security, simplicity
is king.

A typical example is our secure channel. It has no options. It doesn't allow
you to encrypt the data without authenticating it, or to authenticate the
data without encrypting it. People always ask for these features, but typically they do not know the consequences of using partial security features.
Most users do not understand enough about security to be able to select the
correct security options. The best solution is to have no options and make it
secure by default. If you absolutely have to, provide a single option: secure
or insecure.

Many systems also have multiple cipher suites, where the user (or someone
else) can choose which cipher and which authentication function to use. If
at all possible, eliminate this complexity. Choose a single mode that is
secure enough for all possible applications. The computational difference
between the various encryption modes is not that large, and cryptography
is rarely the bottleneck for modern computers. Apart from getting rid of
the complexity, it also gets rid of the danger that users might configure their
application to use weak cipher suites. After all, if choosing an encryption
and authentication mode is so difficult that the designer can't do it, what
makes you think the user understands enough to make an informed decision?

9.4.2   Modularization

Even after you have eliminated a lot of options and features, the resulting system will still be quite complex. There is one main technique of making the complexity manageable: modularization. You divide the system into separate modules, and design, analyze, and implement each module separately.

You should already be familiar with modularization; in cryptography it becomes even more important to do it right. Earlier we talked about cryptographic primitives as modules. The module interface should be simple and straightforward. It should behave according to the reasonable expectations of a user of the module. Look closely at the interface of your modules. Often there are features or options that exist to solve some other module's problems. If possible, rip them out. Each module should solve its own problems. We have found that when module interfaces start to develop weird features, it is time to redesign the software because they are almost always a result of design deficiencies.

Modularization is so important because it is the only efficient way we have of dealing with complexity. If a particular option is restricted to a single module, it can be analyzed within the context of this module. However, if the option changes the external behavior of one module, it can affect other modules as well. If you have 20 modules, each with a single binary option that changes the module behavior, there are over a million possible configurations. You would have to analyze each of these configurations for security—an impossible task.

We have found that many options are created in the quest for efficiency. This is a well-known problem in software engineering. Many systems contain so-called optimizations that are useless, counterproductive, or insignificant because they do not optimize those parts of the system that form the bottleneck. We have become quite conservative about optimizations. Usually we don't bother with them. We do create a careful design, and try to ensure that work can be done in large "chunks." A typical example is the old IBM PC BIOS. The routine to print a character on the screen took a single character as an argument. This routine spent almost all of its time on overhead, and only a very small fraction on actually putting the character on the screen. If the interface of the routine had allowed a string as argument, then the entire string could have been printed in only slightly more time than it took to print a single character. The result of this bad design was that all DOS machines had a terribly slow display. This same principle applies to cryptographic designs. Make sure that work can be done in large enough chunks. Then only optimize those parts of your program that you can *measure* as having a significant effect on the performance.

9.4.3 Assertions

Assertions are a good tool to help improve the quality of your code.[5]

When implementing cryptographic code, adopt an attitude of professional paranoia. Each module distrusts the other modules, and always checks parameter validity, enforces calling sequence restrictions, and refuses unsafe operations. Most of the times these are straightforward assertions. If the module specifications state that you have to initialize the object before you use it, then using an object before initialization will result in an assertion error. Assertion failures should always lead to an abort of the program with ample documentation of which assertion failed, and for what reason.

The general rule is: any time you can make a meaningful check on the internal consistency of the system, you should add an assertion. Catch as many errors as you can, both your own and those of other programmers. An error caught by an assertion will not lead to a security breach.

There are some programmers who implement assertion checking in development, but switch it off when they ship the product. Who thought that up? What would you think of a nuclear power station where the operators train with all the safety systems in place, but switch them off when they go to work on the real reactor? Or a parachutist who wears his emergency parachute while training on the ground, but leaves it off when he jumps out of the airplane? Why would anyone ever switch off the assertion checking on production code? That is the only place where you really need it! If an assertion fails in production code, then you have just encountered a programming error. Ignoring the error will most likely result in some kind of

---

[5]We know that this is starting to sound like a programming lesson, but we find we have to repeat these things time and time again to the programmers we work with.

wrong answer, because at least one assumption the code makes is wrong. Generating wrong answers is probably the worst thing a program can do. It is much better to at least inform the user that a programming error has occurred, so that he does not trust the erroneous results of the program. Leave all your error checking on.

9.4.4   Buffer Overflows

It is an embarrassment for the IT industry that we need a section with this title. Buffer overflow problems have been known for 40 years. Perfectly good solutions to avoid them have been available for the same amount of time. Some of the earliest higher-level programming languages, such as Algol 60, completely solved the problem by introducing mandatory array bounds checking. Even so, buffer overflows cause about half of the security problems on the Internet. And still people refuse to banish them by using better tools. We consider this criminal negligence. It is comparable to a car manufacturer making the gas tank out of waxed paper. Sure, if everything goes right, there's no problem, but we'd throw the CEO into jail all the same. For some reason, large parts of our IT industry act as if they were not responsible for the consequences of their actions. (Maybe because our lawmakers let them get away with disclaimers that would be unconscionable in any other industry.) With this prevailing attitude, we sometimes wonder whether it's worth attempting something as advanced as cryptography at all.

But those are all things we cannot change. We can give you advice on how to write good cryptographic code. Avoid any programming language that allows buffer overflows. Specifically: don't use C or C++. And don't ever switch off the array bounds checking of whichever language you use instead. It is such a simple rule, and it will probably solves half of all your security bugs.

9.4.5   Testing

Extensive testing is always part of any good development process. Testing can help find bugs in programs, but it is useless to find security holes. Never confuse testing with security analysis. The two are complementary, but different.

There are two types of tests that should be implemented. The first is a generic set of tests developed from the module's functional specifications. Ideally, one programmer implements the module and a second programmer implements the tests. Both work from the functional specifications. Any misunderstanding between the two is a clear indication that the specifications have to be clarified. The generic tests should attempt to cover the entire operational spectrum of the module. For some modules, this is simple; for others, the test program will have to simulate an entire environment. In much of our own code the test code is about as big as the operational code, and we have not found a way of significantly improving that.

A second set of tests are developed by the programmer of the module itself. These are designed to test any implementation limits. For example, if a module uses a 4 KB buffer internally, then extra tests of the boundary conditions at the start and end of the buffer will help to catch any buffer-management errors. Sometimes it requires knowledge of the internals of a module to devise specific tests.

We frequently write test sequences that are driven by a random generator. We will discuss PRNGs extensively in chapter 10. Using a PRNG makes it very easy to run a very large number of tests. If we save the seed we used for the PRNG we can repeat the same test sequence, which is very useful for testing and debugging. Details depend on the module in question.

Finally, we have found it useful to have some "quick test" code that can run every time the program starts up. In one of Niels's recent projects, he had to implement AES. The initialization code runs AES on a few test cases and checks the output against the known correct answers. If the AES code is ever destabilized during the further development of the application, this quick test is very likely to detect the problem.

9.5   Side-Channel Attacks

There is a whole class of attacks that we call side-channel attacks [49]. These are possible when an attacker has an additional channel of information about the system. For example, an attacker could make detailed measurements of the time it takes to encrypt a message. If the cryptography is embedded in a smart card, then the attacker can measure how much current the card draws over time. Magnetic fields, RF emissions, power consumption, timing, and interference on other data channels can all be used for side-channel attacks.

Not surprisingly, side-channel attacks can be remarkably successful against systems that are not designed with these attacks in mind. Power analysis of smart cards is extremely successful [57].

It is very difficult, if not impossible, to protect against all forms of side-channel attacks, but there are some simple precautions you can take. Years ago, when Niels worked on implementing cryptographic systems in smart cards, one of the design rules was that the sequence of instructions that the CPU executed could only depend on information already available to the attacker. This stops timing attacks, and makes power analysis attacks more complicated because the sequence of instructions that is being executed can no longer leak any information. It is not a full solution, and modern power analysis techniques would have no problem breaking the smart cards that were fielded in those days. Still, what we did was about the best that could be done with the smart cards of the day. Resistance against side-channel attacks will always come from a combination of countermeasures—some of them in the software that implements the cryptographic system, and some of them in the actual hardware.

Preventing side-channel attacks is a rat race. You try to protect yourself against the known side channels, and then a smart person somewhere discovers a new side channel, so then you have to go back and take that one into account as well. In real life, the situation is not that bad, because most side-channel attacks are difficult to perform. Side channels are a real danger to smart cards because the card is under full control of the adversary, but only a few types of side channels are practical against most other computers. In practice, the most important side channels are timing and RF emissions. (Smart cards are particularly vulnerable to measuring the power consumption.)

9.6   Conclusion

We hope this chapter has made it clear that security does not start or stop with the cryptographic design. All aspects of the system have to do their part to achieve security. This is why security people are universally hated; they stick their noses into absolutely everything, go around telling people how to do their work, and then forbid a lot of very useful features just because they are insecure.

Implementing cryptographic systems is an art in itself. The most important aspect is the quality of the code. Low-quality code is the most common cause of real-world attacks, and it is rather easy to avoid. In our experience, writing high-quality code takes about as long as writing low-quality code, if you count the time from start to finished product, rather than from start to first buggy version. Be fanatical about the quality of your code. It can be done, and it needs to be done, so go do it!

Ideally we would redesign our entire environment, including our programming language and operating system, with security as a primary goal. We'd love to work on this project, so contact us if you are willing to spend a few million dollars on a computer you can *really* trust.

Part II

Key Negotiation

Chapter 10

Generating Randomness

To generate key material, we need a random number generator, or RNG. Generating good randomness is a vital part of many cryptographic operations, and it is one of the most difficult ones.

We won't go into a detailed discussion of what randomness really is. There are nice mathematical definitions, but they are too complicated to discuss here. A good informal definition is that random data is unpredictable to the attacker, even if he is taking active steps to defeat our randomness.

Good random number generators are necessary for many cryptographic functions. Part I discussed the secure channel and its components. We assumed that there is a key known to both Alice and Bob. That key has to be generated somewhere. Key management systems use random number generators to choose keys. If you get the RNG wrong, you end up with a weak key. This is exactly what happened to one of the early versions of the Netscape browser [38].

The measure for randomness is called *entropy* [91]. We won't go into all the mathematical details, but we want to at least give you an idea of what it is. If you have a 32-bit word that is completely random, then it has 32 bits of entropy. If the 32-bit word takes on only four different values, and each value has a 25% chance of occurring, then the word has 2 bits of entropy. Entropy does not measure how many bits are in a value, but how *uncertain* you are about the value. You can think of entropy as the average

155

number of bits you would need to specify the value if you could use an ideal compression algorithm. Note that the entropy of a value depends on how much you know. A random 32-bit word has 32 bits of entropy. Now suppose you happen to know that the value has exactly 18 bits that are 0 and 14 bits that are 1. There are about $2^{28.8}$ values that satisfy these requirements, and the entropy is also limited to 28.8 bits. In other words, the more you know about a value, the smaller its entropy is.

It is a bit more complicated to compute the entropy for values that have a nonuniform probability distribution. The most common definition of entropy for a variable X is

$$H(X) := -\sum_x P(X = x) \log_2 P(X = x)$$

where $P(X = x)$ is the probability that the variable X takes on the value x. We won't use this formula, so you don't need to remember it. This definition is what most mathematicians refer to when they talk about entropy. There are a few other definitions of entropy that mathematicians use as well; which one they use depends on what they are working on. And don't confuse our entropy definition with the entropy that physicists talk about. They use the word for a concept from thermodynamics that is only tangentially related.

10.1   Real Random

In an ideal world we would use "real random" data. The world is not ideal, and real random data is extremely hard to find.

Typical computers have a number of sources of entropy. The exact timing of keystrokes and the exact movements of a mouse are well-known examples. There has even been research into using the random fluctuations in hard-disk access time caused by turbulence inside the enclosure [19]. All of these sources are somewhat suspect because there are situations in which the attacker can perform measurements on the random source, or can influence the random source.

Many implementers seem quite optimistic about the amount of entropy that can be extracted from various sources. We've seen software that will gener-ate 1 or 2 bytes of random data from the timing of a single keystroke. We are far more pessimistic about the amount of entropy in a single keystroke. A good typist can keep the time between consecutive keystrokes predictable to within a dozen milliseconds. And the keyboard scan frequency limits the resolution with which keystroke timings can be measured. The data being typed is not very random either, even if you ask the user just to hit some keys to generate random data. Furthermore, there is always a risk that the attacker has additional information about the "random" events. A microphone can pick up the sounds of the keyboard, which helps to determine the timing of keystrokes. Be very careful in estimating how much entropy you think a particular piece of data contains. We are, after all, dealing with a very clever and active adversary.

There are many physical processes that behave randomly. For example, the laws of quantum physics force certain behavior to be perfectly random. It would be very nice if we could measure such random behavior and use it. Technically, this is certainly possible. However, the attacker has a few lines of attack on this type of solution. First of all, the attacker can try to influence the behavior of the quantum particles in question to make them behave predictably. The attacker can also try to eavesdrop on the measurements we make; if he gets a copy of our measurements, then the data might still be random, but it won't have any entropy from the attacker's point of view. (If he knows the value, then it has no entropy for him.) Maybe the attacker can set up a strong RF field in an attempt to bias our detector. There are even some quantum physics–based attacks that can be contemplated. The Einstein-Podolsky-Rosen paradox could be used to subvert the randomness we are trying to measure [5, 11]. Similar comments apply to other sources of entropy, such as thermal noise of a resistor and tunneling and breakdown noise of a Zener diode.

Some modern computers have a built-in real random number generator [42]. This is a significant improvement over a separate real random generator, as it makes some of the attacks more difficult. The random number generator is still only accessible to the operating system, so an application has to trust the operating system to handle the random data in a secure manner.

10.1.1   Problems With Using Real Random Data

Aside from the difficulty of collecting real random data, there are several other problems with its practical use. First of all, it is not always available. If you have to wait for keystroke timings, then you cannot get any random data unless the user is typing. That can be a real problem when your application is a Web server on a machine with no keyboard connected to it. A related problem is that the amount of real random data is always limited. If you need a lot of random data, then you have to wait; something that is unacceptable for many applications.

A second problem is that real random sources, such as a physical random number generator, can break. Maybe the generator will become predictable in some way. Because real random generators are fairly intricate things in the very noisy environment of a computer, they are much more likely to break than the traditional parts of the computer. If you rely on the real random generator directly, then you're out of luck when it breaks.

A third problem is judging how much entropy you can extract from any specific physical event. Unless you have specially designed dedicated hardware for the random generator it is extremely difficult to know how much entropy you are getting. We'll discuss this in greater detail later.

10.1.2   Pseudorandom Data

An alternative to using real random data is to use pseudorandom data. Pseudorandom data is not really random at all. It is generated from a seed by a deterministic algorithm. If you know the seed, you can predict the pseudorandom data. Traditional pseudorandom number generators, or PRNGs, are not secure against a clever adversary. They are designed to eliminate statistical artifacts, not to withstand an intelligent attacker. The second volume of Knuth's *The Art of Computer Programming* contains an extensive discussion of random number generators, but all generators are analyzed for statistical randomness only [55]. We have to assume that our adversary knows the algorithm that is used to generate the random data. Given some of the pseudorandom outputs, is it possible for him to predict some future (or past) random bits? For many traditional PRNGs the answer might be yes. For a proper cryptographical PRNG the answer is no.

In the context of a cryptographic system, we have more stringent requirements. Even if the attacker sees a lot of the random data generated by the PRNG, she should not be able to predict anything about the rest of the output of the PRNG. We call such a PRNG cryptographically strong. As we have no need for a traditional PRNG, we will only talk about cryptographically strong PRNGs.

Forget about the normal random function in your programming library, because it is almost certainly not a cryptographic PRNG. Many libraries ship with a PRNG that fails even simple statistical tests. Unless the cryptographic strength is explicitly documented, you should never use a library PRNG.

10.1.3   Real Random Data and PRNGs

We only use real random data for a single thing: to seed a PRNG. This construction resolves some of the problems of using real random data. Once the PRNG is seeded, random data is always available. You can keep adding the real random data that you receive to the PRNG seed, thereby ensuring that it never becomes fully predictable even if the seed were to become known.

There is a theoretical argument that real random data is better than pseudorandom data from a PRNG. In certain cryptographic protocols you can prove that certain attacks are impossible if you use real random data. The protocol is unconditionally secure. If you use a PRNG, then the protocol is only secure as long as the attacker cannot break the PRNG; the protocol is computationally secure. This distinction, however, is only relevant for people in ivory towers. All cryptographic protocols use computational assumptions for almost everything. Removing the computational assumption for one particular type of attack is an insignificant improvement, and generating real random data, which you need for the unconditional security, is so difficult that you are far more likely to reduce the system security by trying to use real random data. Any weakness in the real random generator immediately leads to a loss of security. However, if you use the real random data to seed a PRNG, you can afford to be far more conservative in your assumptions about the entropy sources, which makes it much more likely that you will end up with a secure system in the end.

10.2   Attack Models for a PRNG

There has been comparatively little research into PRNGs. The task of generating (pseudo)random numbers from a seed is fairly simple. The problem is how to get a random seed, and how to keep it secret in a real-world situation [48]. The best design up to now that we know of is called Yarrow [47], a design we created a few years ago together with John Kelsey. Yarrow tries to prevent all the known attacks.

At any point in time the PRNG has an internal state. Requests for random data are honored by using a cryptographic algorithm to generate pseudo-random data. This algorithm also updates the internal state to ensure that the next request does not return the same random data. This process is easy; any hash function or block cipher can be used for this step.

There are various forms of attack on a PRNG. There is a straightforward attack where the attacker attempts to reconstruct the internal state from the output. This is a classical cryptographic attack, and rather easy to counter using cryptographic techniques.

Things become more difficult if the attacker is at some point able to acquire the internal state. For the purposes of this discussion, it is unimportant how that happens. Maybe there is a flaw in the implementation, or maybe the computer was just booted for the first time and has had no random seed yet, or maybe the attacker managed to read the seed file from disk. Bad things happen, and you have to be able to handle them. In a traditional PRNG, if the attacker acquires the internal state, he can follow all the outputs and all the updates of the internal state. This means that if the PRNG is ever attacked successfully, then it can never recover to a secure state.

Recovering a PRNG whose state has been compromised is difficult. We will need some source of entropy from a real random number generator. To keep this discussion simple, we will assume that we have one or more sources that provide some amount of entropy (typically in small chunks that we call events) at unpredictable times.

Even if we mix in the small amounts of entropy from an event into the internal state, this still leaves an avenue of attack. The attacker simply makes frequent requests for random data from the PRNG. As long as the total amount of entropy added between two such requests is limited to say, 30 bits, then the attacker can simply try all possibilities for the random inputs and recover the new internal state after the mixing. This would require about 2^{30} tries, which is quite practical to do.[1] The random data generated by the PRNG provides the necessary verification when the attacker hits upon the right solution.

The best defense against this particular attack is to pool the incoming events that contain entropy. You collect entropy until you have enough to mix into the internal state without the attacker being able to guess the pooled data. How much is enough? Well, we want the attacker to spend at least 2^{128} steps on any attack, so you want to have 128 bits of entropy. But here is the real problem: making any kind of estimate of the amount of entropy is extremely difficult, if not impossible. It depends heavily on how much the attacker knows or can know, but that information is not available to the developers during the design phase. This is Yarrow's main problem. It tries to measure the entropy of a source using an entropy estimator, and such an estimator is impossible to get right for all situations.

10.3   Fortuna

While writing this chapter we came up with an improvement on Yarrow that we've dubbed Fortuna, after the Roman goddess of chance.[2] Fortuna solves the problem of having to define entropy estimators by getting rid of them. The rest of this chapter is mostly about the details of Fortuna.

There are three parts to the Fortuna. The generator takes a fixed-size seed and generates arbitrary amounts of pseudorandom data. The accumulator collects and pools entropy from various sources, and occasionally reseeds the generator. Finally, the seed file control ensures that the PRNG can generate random data even when the computer has just booted.

---

[1]We are being sloppy with our math here. In this instance we should use guessing entropy, rather than the standard Shannon entropy. For extensive details on entropy measures, see [14].

[2]We thought about calling it Tyche, after the Greek goddess of chance, but nobody would know how to pronounce it.

10.4   The Generator

The generator is the part that converts a fixed-size state to arbitrarily long outputs. We'll use an AES-like block cipher for the generator; feel free to choose AES (Rijndael), Serpent, or Twofish for this function (see section 4.5.7). The internal state of the generator consists of a 256-bit block cipher key and a 128-bit counter.

The generator is basically just a block cipher in counter mode. CTR mode generates a random stream of data, which will be our output. There are a few refinements.

If a user or application asks for random data, the generator runs its algorithm and generates pseudorandom data. Now suppose an attacker manages to compromise the generator's state after the completion of the request. It would be nice if this would not compromise the previous results the generator gave. Therefore, after every request we generate an extra 256 bits of pseudorandom data and use that as the new key for the block cipher. We can then forget the old key, thereby eliminating any possibility of leaking information about old requests.

To ensure that the data we generate will be statistically random, we cannot generate too much data at one time. After all, in purely random data there can be repeated block values, but the output of counter mode never contains repeated block values. (See section 5.8.2 for details.) There are various solutions; we could use only half of each ciphertext block, which would hide most of the statistical deviation. We could use a different building block called a *pseudorandom function*, rather than a block cipher, but there are no well-analyzed and efficient proposals that we know of. The simplest solution is to limit the number of bytes of random data in a single request, which makes the statistical deviation much harder to detect.

If we were to generate 2^{64} blocks of output from a single key, we would expect close to one collision on the block values. A few repeated requests of this size would quickly show that the output is not perfectly random; it lacks the expected block collisions. We limit the maximum size of any one request to 2^{16} blocks (that is, 2^{20} bytes). For an ideal random generator, the probability of finding a block value collision in 2^{16} output blocks is about 2^{-97}, so the complete absence of collisions would not be detectable until about 2^{97} requests had been made. The total workload for the attacker ends up being 2^{113} steps. Not quite the 2^{128} steps that we're aiming for, but reasonably close.

We know we are being lax here and accepting a (slightly) reduced security level. There seems to be no good alternative. We don't have any suitable cryptographic building blocks that give us a PRNG with a full 128-bit security level. We could use SHA-256, but that would be much slower. We've found that people will argue endlessly not to use a good cryptographic PRNG, and speed has always been one of the arguments. Slowing down the PRNG by a perceptible factor to get a few bits more security is counterproductive. Too many people will simply switch to a really bad PRNG, so the overall system security will drop.

If we had had a block cipher with a 256-bit block size, then the collisions would not have been an issue at all. This particular attack is not such a great threat. Not only does the attacker have to perform 2^{113} steps, but the computer that is being attacked has to perform 2^{113} block cipher encryptions. So this attack depends on the speed of the user's computer, rather than on the speed of the attacker's computer. Most users don't add huge amounts of extra computing power just to help an attacker. We don't like these types of security arguments. They are more complicated, and if the PRNG is ever used in an unusual setting this argument might no longer apply. Still, given the situation, our solution is the best compromise we can find.

When we rekey the block cipher at the end of each request, we do not reset the counter. This is a minor issue, but it avoids problems with short cycles. Suppose we were to reset the counter every time. If the key value ever repeats, and all requests are of a fixed size, then the next key value will also be a repeated key value. We could end up in a short cycle of key values. This is an unlikely situation, but by not resetting the counter we can avoid it entirely. As the counter is 128 bits, we will never repeat a counter value (2^{128} blocks is beyond the computational capabilities of our computers), and this automatically breaks any cycles. Furthermore, we use a counter value of 0 to indicate that the generator has not yet been keyed, and therefore cannot generate any output.

Note that the restriction that limits each request to at most 1 MB of data is not an inflexible restriction. If you need more than 1 MB of random data, just do repeated requests. In fact, the implementation could provide an interface that automatically performs such repeated requests.

The generator by itself is an extremely useful module. We expect that most implementations will make it available as part of the interface, not just as a component, of Fortuna. Take a program that performs a Monte Carlo simulation.[3] You really want the simulation to be random, but you also want to be able to repeat the exact same computation, if only for debugging and verification purposes. A good solution is to call the operating system's random generator once at the start of the program to get a random seed. This seed can be logged as part of the simulator output, and from this seed our generator can generate all the random data needed for the simulation. Knowing the original seed of the generator also allows all the computations to be verified by running the program again using the same input data and seed. And for debugging, the same simulation can be run again and again, and it will behave exactly the same every time, as long as the starting seed is kept constant.

We can now specify the operations of the generator in detail.

10.4.1   Initialization

This is rather simple. We set the key and the counter to zero to indicate that the generator has not been seeded yet.

function INITIALIZEGENERATOR
output: $\mathcal{G}$ Generator state.

 Set the key K and counter C to zero.
 $(K, C) \leftarrow (0, 0)$
 Package up the state.
 $\mathcal{G} \leftarrow (K, C)$
 return $\mathcal{G}$

---

[3]A Monte Carlo simulation is a simulation that is driven by random choices.

10.4.2 Reseed

The reseed operation updates the state with an arbitrary input string. At this level we do not care what this input string contains. To ensure a thorough mixing of the input with the existing key, we use a hash function.

function RESEED
input: $\mathcal{G}$ Generator state; modified by this function.
         s New or additional seed.

Compute the new key using a hash function.
$K \leftarrow \text{SHA}_d\text{-256}(K \parallel s)$

Increment the counter to make it nonzero and mark the generator as seeded. Throughout this generator, C is a 16-byte value treated as an integer using the LSByte first convention.
$C \leftarrow C + 1$

The counter C is used here as an integer. Later it will be used as a plaintext block. To convert between the two we use the least-significant-byte-first convention. The plaintext block is a block of 16 bytes $p_0, \ldots, p_{15}$ which corresponds to the integer value

$$\sum_{i=0}^{15} p_i 2^{8i}$$

By using this convention throughout, we can treat C both as a 16-byte string and as an integer.

10.4.3 Generate Blocks

This function generates a number of blocks of random output. This is an internal function used only by the generator. Any entity outside the PRNG should not be able to call this function.

function GENERATEBLOCKS
input: $\mathcal{G}$ Generator state; modified by this function.
         k Number of blocks to generate.
output: r Pseudorandom string of $16k$ bytes.

assert $C \neq 0$
Start with the empty string.
$r \leftarrow \epsilon$
Append the necessary blocks.
for $i = 1, \ldots, k$ **do**
    $r \leftarrow r \parallel E(K, C)$
    $C \leftarrow C + 1$
od
return r

Of course, the $E(K, C)$ function is the block cipher encryption function with key K and plaintext C. The GENERATEBLOCKS function first checks that C is not zero, as that is the indication that this generator has never been seeded. The loop starts with an empty string in r, and appends each newly computed block to r to build the output value.

10.4.4   Generate Random Data

This function generates random data at the request of the user of the generator. It allows for output of up to 2^{20} bytes, and ensures that the generator forgets any information about the result it generated.

function PSEUDORANDOMDATA
input: $\mathcal{G}$ Generator state; modified by this function.
          n Number of bytes of random data to generate.
output: r Pseudorandom string of n bytes.

    Limit the output length to reduce the statistical deviation from perfectly random outputs. Also ensure that the length is not negative.
    assert $0 \leq n \leq 2^{20}$
    Compute the output.
    $r \leftarrow$ *first-n-bytes*(GENERATEBLOCKS($\mathcal{G}, \lceil n/16 \rceil$))
    Switch to a new key to avoid later compromises of this output.
    $K \leftarrow$ GENERATEBLOCKS($\mathcal{G}, 2$)
    return r

The output is generated by a call to GENERATEBLOCKS, and the only change is that the result is truncated to the correct number of bytes. (The $\lceil \cdot \rceil$

operator is the round-upwards operator.) We then generate two more blocks to get a new key. Once the old K has been forgotten, there is no way to recompute the result r. As long as PSEUDORANDOMDATA does not keep a copy of r, or forget to wipe the memory r was stored in, then the generator has no way of leaking any data about r once the function completes. This is exactly why any future compromise of the generator cannot endanger the secrecy of earlier outputs. It does endanger the secrecy of future outputs, a problem that the accumulator will address.

The function PSEUDORANDOMDATA is limited in the amount of data it can return. We won't bother specifying a wrapper around this that can return larger random strings by repeated calls to PSEUDORANDOMDATA. Note that you should not increase the maximum output size per call, as that increases the statistical deviation from pure random. Doing repeated calls to PSEUDORANDOMDATA is quite efficient. The only real overhead is that for every 1 MB of random data produced, you have to generate 32 extra random bytes (for the new key) and run the key schedule of the block cipher again. This overhead is insignificant for all of the block ciphers we suggest.

10.4.5   Generator Speed

The generator for Fortuna that we just described is a cryptographically strong PRNG in the sense that it converts a seed into an arbitrarily long pseudorandom output. It is about as fast as the underlying block cipher; on a PC-type CPU it should run in less than 20 clock cycles per generated byte for large requests. It can be used as a drop-in replacement for most PRNG library functions.

10.5   Accumulator

The accumulator collects real random data from various sources and uses it to reseed the generator.

10.5.1   Entropy Sources

We assume that there are several sources of entropy in the environment. Each source can produce events containing entropy at any point in time. It does not matter exactly what you use as your sources, as long as there is at least one source that generates data that is unpredictable to the attacker. As you cannot know how the attacker will attack, the best bet is to turn anything that looks like unpredictable data into a random source. In particular, keystrokes and mouse movements make reasonable sources. In addition, you should add as many timing sources as practical. You could use accurate timing of keystrokes, mouse movements and clicks, and responses from the disk drives and printers, preferably all at the same time. Again, it is not a problem if the attacker can predict or copy the data from some of the sources, as long as he cannot do it for all of them.

Implementing sources can be a lot of work. The sources typically have to be built into the various hardware drivers of the operating system. This is almost impossible to do at the user level.

We identify each source by a unique source number in the range $0 \ldots 255$. Implementors can choose whether to allocate the source numbers statically or dynamically. The data in each event is a short sequence of bytes. Sources should only include the unpredictable data in each event. For example, timing information can be represented by the two or four least significant bytes of an accurate timer. There is no point including the day, month, and year. It is safe to assume that the attacker knows those.

We will be concatenating various events from different sources. To ensure that a string constructed from such a concatenation uniquely encodes the events, we have to make sure the string is parsable. Each event is encoded as three or more bytes of data. The first byte contains the random source number. The second byte contains the number of additional bytes of data. The subsequent bytes contain whatever data the source provided.

Of course, the attacker will know the events generated by some of the sources. To model this, we assume that some of the sources are completely under the attacker's control. The attacker chooses which events these sources generate at which times. And like any other user, the attacker can ask for random data from the PRNG at any point in time.

10.5.2 Pools

To reseed the generator, we need to pool events in a pool large enough that the attacker can no longer enumerate the possible values for the events in the pool. A reseed with a "large enough" pool of random events destroys the information the attacker might have had about the generator state. Unfortunately, we don't know how many events to collect in a pool before using it to reseed the generator. This is the problem Yarrow tried to solve by using entropy estimators and various heuristic rules. Fortuna solves it in a much better way.

There are 32 pools: $P_0, P_1, \ldots, P_{31}$. Each pool conceptually contains a string of bytes of unbounded length. In practice, the only way that string is used is as the input to a hash function. Implementations do not need to store the unbounded string, but can compute the hash of the string incrementally as it is assembled in the pool.

Each source distributes its random events over the pools in a cyclical fashion. This ensures that the entropy from each source is distributed more or less evenly over the pools. Each random event is appended to the string in the pool in question.

We reseed the generator every time pool P_0 is long enough. Reseeds are numbered $1, 2, 3, \ldots$. Depending on the reseed number r, one or more pools are included in the reseed. Pool P_i is included if 2^i is a divisor of r. Thus P_0 is used every reseed, P_1 every other reseed, P_2 every fourth reseed, etc. After a pool is used in a reseed, it is reset to the empty string.

This system automatically adapts to the situation. If the attacker knows very little about the random sources, then he will not be able to predict P_0 at the next reseed. But the attacker might know a lot more about the random sources, or he might be (falsely) generating a lot of the events. In that case he probably knows enough of P_0 so that he can reconstruct the new generator state from the old generator state and the generator outputs. But when P_1 is used in a reseed, it contains twice as much data that is unpredictable to him; and P_2 will contain four times as much. Irrespective of how many fake random events the attacker generates, or how many of the events he knows, as long as there is at least one source of random events he can't predict, there will always be a pool that collects enough entropy to defeat him.

The speed at which the system recovers from a compromised state depends on the rate at which entropy (with respect to the attacker) flows into the pools. If we assume that this is a fixed rate ρ, then after t seconds we have in total ρt bits of entropy. Each pool receives about $\rho t/32$ bits in this time period. The attacker can no longer keep track of the state if the generator is reseeded with a pool with more than 128 bits of entropy in it. There are two cases. If P_0 collects 128 bits of entropy before the next reseed operation, then we have recovered from the compromise. How fast this happens depends on how large we let P_0 grow before we reseed. The second case is when P_0 is reseeding too fast, due to random events known to (or generated by) the attacker. Let t be the time between reseeds. Then pool P_i collects $2^i \rho t/32$ bits of entropy between reseeds, and is used in a reseed every $2^i t$ seconds. The recovery from the compromise happens the first time we reseed with pool P_i where $128 \leq 2^i \rho t/32 < 256$. (The upper bound derives from the fact that otherwise pool P_{i-1} would contain 128 bits of entropy between reseeds.) This inequality gives us

$$\frac{2^i \rho t}{32} < 256$$

and thus

$$2^i t < \frac{8192}{\rho}$$

In other words, the time between recovery points ($2^i t$) is bounded by the time it takes to collect 2^{13} bits of entropy ($8192/\rho$). The number 2^{13} seems a bit large, but it can be explained in the following way. We need at least 2^7 bits to recover from a compromise. We might be unlucky if the system reseeds just before we have collected 2^7 bits in a particular pool, and then we have to use the next pool, which will collect close to 2^8 bits before the reseed. Finally, we divide our data over 32 pools, which accounts for another factor of 2^5.

This is a very good result. This solution is within a factor of 64 of an ideal solution (it needs at most 64 times as much randomness as an ideal solution would need). This is a constant factor and it ensures that we can never do terribly badly, and will always recover eventually. Furthermore, we do not need to know how much entropy our events have or how much the attacker knows. That is the real advantage Fortuna has over Yarrow. The impossible-to-construct entropy estimators are gone for good. Everything is fully automatic; if there is a good flow of random data, the PRNG will recover quickly. If there is only a trickle of random data, it takes a long time to recover.

So far we've ignored the fact that we only have 32 pools, and that maybe even pool P_{31} does not collect enough randomness between reseeds to recover from a compromise. This could happen if the attacker injected so many random events that 2^{32} reseeds would occur before the random sources that the attacker has no knowledge about have generated 2^{13} bits of entropy. This is unlikely, but to stop the attacker from even trying, we will limit the speed of the reseeds. A reseed will only be performed if the previous reseed was more than 100 ms ago. This limits the reseed rate to 10 reseeds per second, so it will take more than 13 years before P_{32} would ever have been used, had it existed. Given that the economic and technical lifetime of most computer equipment is considerably less than ten years, it seems a reasonable solution to limit ourselves to 32 pools.

10.5.3   Implementation Considerations

There are a couple of implementation considerations in the design of the accumulator.

Distribution of Events Over Pools

The incoming events have to be distributed over the pools. The simplest solution would be for the accumulator to take on that role. However, this is dangerous. There will be some kind of function call to pass an event to the accumulator. It is quite possible that the attacker could make arbitrary calls to this function, too. The attacker could make extra calls to this function every time a "real" event was generated, and thereby influence the pool the next "real" event would go to. If the attacker manages to get all "real" events into pool P_0, then the whole multi-pool system is ineffective and the single-pool attacks apply. If the attacker gets all "real" events into P_{31}, then they essentially never get used.

Our solution is to let every event generator pass the proper pool number with each event. This requires the attacker to have access to the memory of the program that generates the event if he wants to influence the pool choice. If the attacker has that much access, then the entire source is probably compromised as well.

The accumulator could check that each source routes its events to the pools in the correct order. It is a good idea for a function to check that its inputs are properly formed, so this would be a good idea in principle. But in this situation, it is not always clear what the accumulator should do if the verification fails. If the whole PRNG runs as a user process, the PRNG could throw a fatal error and exit the program. That would deprive the system of the PRNG just because a single source misbehaved. If the PRNG is part of the operating system kernel, it is much harder. Let's assume a particular driver generates random events, but the driver cannot keep track of a simple 5-bit cyclical counter. What should the accumulator do? Return an error code? Chances are that a programmer who makes such simple mistakes doesn't check the return codes. Should the accumulator halt the kernel? A bit drastic, and it crashes the whole machine because of a single faulty driver. The best idea we've come up with is to penalize the driver in CPU time. If the verification fails, the accumulator can delay the driver in question by a second or so.

This idea is not terribly useful, because the reason why we let the caller determine the pool number is that we assume the attacker might make false calls to the accumulator with fake events. If this happens and the accumulator checks the pool ordering, the real event generator will be penalized for the misbehavior of the attacker. Our conclusion: the accumulator should not check the pool ordering, because there isn't anything useful the accumulator can do if it detects something is wrong. Each random source is responsible for distributing its events in cyclical order over the pools. If a random source screws up, we might lose the entropy from that source (which we expect), but no other harm will be done.

Running Time of Event Passing

We want to limit the amount of computation necessary when an event is passed to the accumulator. Many of the events are timing events, and they are generated by real-time drivers. These drivers do not want to call an accumulator if once in a while the call takes a long time to complete.

There is a certain minimum amount of computations that we will need to do. We have to append the event data to the selected pool. Of course, we are not going to store the entire pool string in memory, because the length of a pool string is potentially unbounded. For each pool we will have a short buffer and compute a partial hash as soon as that buffer is full. This is the minimum amount of computation required per event.

We do not want to do the whole reseeding operation, which uses one or more pools to reseed the generator. This takes an order of magnitude more time than just adding an event to a pool. Instead, this work will be delayed until the next user asks for random data, when it will be performed before the random data is generated. This shifts some of the computational burden from the event generators to the users of random data. Not only are the users less likely to be in a real hurry, but they are also the ones who are benefiting from the PRNG service. After all, most event generators are not benefiting from the random data they help to produce.

To allow the reseed to be done just before the request for random data is processed, we must encapsulate the generator. In other words, the generator will be hidden so that it cannot be called directly. The accumulator will provide a RANDOMDATA function with the same interface as PSEUDORANDOMDATA. This avoids problems with certain users calling the generator directly and bypassing the reseeding process that we worked so hard to perfect. Of course, users can still create their own instance of the generator for their own use.

A typical hash function like SHA_d-256 processes message inputs in fixed-size blocks. If we process each block of the pool string as soon as it is complete, then each event will lead to at most a single hash block computation. However, this also has a disadvantage. Modern computers use a hierarchy of caches to keep the CPU busy. One of the effects of the caches is that it is more efficient to keep the CPU working on the same thing for a while. If you process a single hash code block, then the CPU must read the hash function code into the fastest cache before it can be run. If you process several blocks in sequence, then the first block forces the code into the fastest cache, and the subsequent blocks take advantage of this. In general, performance on modern CPUs can be significantly increased by keeping the CPU working within a small loop, and not letting it switch between different pieces of code all the time.

Considering the above, one option is to increase the buffer size per pool and collect more data in each buffer before computing the hash. The advantage is a reduction in the total amount of CPU time needed. The disadvantage is that the maximum time it takes to add a new event to a pool increases. This is an implementation trade-off that we cannot resolve here. It depends too much on the details of the environment.

10.5.4   Initialization

Initialization is, as always, a simple function. So far we've only talked about the generator and the accumulator, but the functions we are about to define are part of the external interface of Fortuna. Their names reflect the fact that they operate on the whole PRNG.

function INITIALIZEPRNG
output: $\mathcal{R}$ PRNG state.

> *Set the 32 pools to the empty string.*
> **for** $i = 0, \ldots, 31$ **do**
> > $P_i \leftarrow \epsilon$
>
> **od**
> *Set the reseed counter to zero.*
> RESEEDCNT $\leftarrow 0$
> *And initialize the generator.*
> $\mathcal{G} \leftarrow$ INITIALIZEGENERATOR()
> *Package up the state.*
> $\mathcal{R} \leftarrow (\mathcal{G}, \text{RESEEDCNT}, P_0, \ldots, P_{31})$
> **return** $\mathcal{R}$

10.5.5   Getting Random Data

This is not quite a simple wrapper around the generator component of the PRNG because we have to handle the reseeds here.

function RANDOMDATA
input: $\mathcal{R}$ PRNG state, modified by this function.
                n Number of bytes of random data to generate.
output: r Pseudorandom string of bytes.
    if $length(P_0) \geq$ MINPOOLSIZE $\wedge$ last reseed > 100 ms ago **then**
        We need to reseed.
        RESEEDCNT $\leftarrow$ RESEEDCNT $+ 1$
        Append the hashes of all the pools we will use.
        $s \leftarrow \epsilon$
        for $i \in 0, \ldots, 31$ **do**
            if $2^i \mid$ RESEEDCNT **then**
                $s \leftarrow s \parallel \text{SHA}_d\text{-}256(P_i)$
                $P_i \leftarrow \epsilon$
            fi
        od
        Got the data, now do the reseed.
        RESEED$(\mathcal{G}, s)$
    fi
    Reseeds (if needed) are done. Let the generator that is part of $\mathcal{R}$ do the
        work.
    return PSEUDORANDOMDATA$(\mathcal{G}, n)$

This function starts by checking the size of pool P_0 against the parameter MINPOOLSIZE to see if it should do a reseed. You can use a very optimistic estimate of how large the pool size has to be before it can contain 128 bits of entropy. Assuming that each event contains 8 bits of entropy and takes 4 bytes in the pool (this corresponds to 2 bytes of event data), then a suitable value for MINPOOLSIZE would be 64 bytes. It doesn't matter much, although choosing a value smaller than 32 seems inadvisable. Choosing a much larger value is not good either, because that will delay the reseed even if there are very good random sources available.

The next step is to increment the reseed count. The count was initialized to 0, so the very first reseed uses the value 1. This automatically ensures that the first reseed uses only P_0, which is what we want.

The loop appends the hashes of the pools. We could also have appended the pools themselves, but then every implementation would have to store entire pool strings, not just the running hash-computation of each pool. The notation $2^i \mid \text{RESEEDCNT}$ is a divisor test. It is true if 2^i is a divisor of the value RESEEDCNT. Astute readers will notice that once an i value fails this test, all tests of the subsequent loop iterations will also fail, which suggests an optimization.

10.5.6   Add an Event

Random sources call this routine when they have another random event. Note that the random sources are each uniquely identified by a source number. We will not specify how to allocate the source numbers because the solution depends on the local situation.

function ADDRANDOMEVENT

input: $\mathcal{R}$ PRNG state, modified by this function.

          s Source number in range $0, \ldots, 255$.

          i Pool number in range $0, \ldots, 31$. Each source must distribute its events over all the pools in a round-robin fashion.

          e Event data. String of bytes; length in range $1, \ldots, 32$.

Check the parameters first.
assert $1 \leq length(e) \leq 32 \wedge 0 \leq s \leq 255 \wedge 0 \leq i \leq 31$

Add the data to the pool.
$P_i \leftarrow P_i \parallel s \parallel length(e) \parallel e$

The event is encoded in $2 + length(e)$ bytes, with both s and $length(e)$ being encoded as a single byte. This concatenation is then appended to the pool. Note that our specifications just append data to the pool, but do not mention any hash computation. We only specify the hashing of the pool at the point in time where we use it. A real implementation should compute the hashes on the fly. That is functionally equivalent and easier to implement, but specifying it directly would be far more complicated.

We have limited the length of the event data to 32 bytes. Larger events are fairly useless; random sources should not pass large amounts of data but rather only those few bytes that contain unpredictable random data. If a source has a large amount of data that contains some entropy spread throughout it, the source should hash the data first. The ADDRANDOM-EVENT function should always return quickly. This is especially important because many sources—by their very nature—perform real-time services. These sources cannot spend too much time calling ADDRANDOMEVENT. Even if a source produces small events, it should not have to wait on other callers whose events are large. Most implementations will need to serialize the calls to ADDRANDOMEVENT by using a mutex of some sort to ensure that only one event is being added at the same time.[4]

Some random sources might not have the time to call ADDRANDOMEVENT. In this case it might be necessary to store the events in a buffer, and have a separate process pick the events from the buffer and feed them to the accumulator.

An alternative architecture allows the sources to simply pass the events to the accumulator process, and has a separate thread in the accumulator perform all the hash computations. This is a more complex design, but it does have advantages for the entropy sources. The choice depends very much on the actual situation.

10.6   Seed File Management

Our PRNG so far will collect entropy and generate random data after the first reseed. However, if we reboot a machine we have to wait for the random sources to produce enough events to trigger the first reseed before any random data is available. In addition, there is no guarantee that the state after the first reseed is, in fact, unpredictable to the attacker.

The solution is to use a seed file. The PRNG keeps a separate file full of entropy, called the seed file. This seed is not made available to anyone else. After a reboot the PRNG reads the seed file and uses it as entropy to get into an unknown state. Of course, once the seed file has been used in this manner, it needs to be rewritten with new data.

---

[4]In a multithreaded environment, you should always be very careful to ensure that different threads do not interfere with each other.

We will describe seed file management, first under the assumption that the file system supports atomic operations; later we will discuss the issues involved with implementing seed file management on real systems.

10.6.1   Write Seed File

The first thing to do is generate a seed file. This is done with a simple function.

function WriteSeedFile
input: $\mathcal{R}$ PRNG state, modified by this function.
             f File to write to.

$\quad write(f, \text{RandomData}(\mathcal{R}, 64))$

This function simply generates 64 bytes of random data and writes it to the file. This is slightly more data than absolutely needed, but there is little reason to be parsimonious with the bytes here.

10.6.2   Update Seed File

Obviously we need to be able to read a seed file too. For reasons explained below we always update the seed file in the same operation.

function UpdateSeedFile
input: $\mathcal{R}$ PRNG state, modified by this function.
             f File to be updated.

$\quad s \leftarrow read(f)$
$\quad \textbf{assert } length(s) = 64$
$\quad \text{Reseed}(\mathcal{G}, s)$
$\quad write(f, \text{RandomData}(\mathcal{R}, 64))$

This function reads the seed file, checks its length, and reseeds the generator. It then rewrites the seed file with new random data.

This routine must ensure that no other use is made of the PRNG between the reseed it causes and the writing of the new data to the seed file. Here is the problem: after a reboot, the seed file is read by this function, and the data is used in a reseed. Suppose the attacker asks for random data before the seed file has been updated. As soon as this random data is returned, but before the seed file is updated, the attacker resets the machine. At the next reboot the same seed file data will be read and used to reseed the generator. This time an innocent user asks for random data before the seed file has been rewritten. He will get the same random data that the attacker got earlier. This violates the secrecy of the random data. As we often use random data to generate cryptographic keys, this is a rather serious problem.

The implementation should ensure that the seed file is kept secret. Also, all updates to the seed file must be atomic (see section 10.6.5).

10.6.3 When to Read and Write the Seed File

When the computer is rebooted, the PRNG does not have any entropy to generate random data from. This is why the seed file is there. Thus, the seed file should be read and updated after every reboot.

As the computer runs, it collects entropy from various sources. We eventually want this entropy to affect the seed file as well. One obvious solution is to rewrite the seed file just as the machine is shutting down. As some computers will never be shut down in an orderly fashion, the PRNG should also rewrite the seed file at regular intervals. We won't spell out the details here as they are quite uninteresting, and often depend on the platform. It is important to ensure that the seed file is updated regularly from the PRNG after it has collected a fair amount of entropy. A reasonable solution would be to rewrite the seed file at every shutdown and every 10 minutes or so.

10.6.4 Backups

Trying to do the reseeding right opens a can of worms. We cannot allow the same state of the PRNG to be repeated twice. We use the file system to store a seed file to prevent this. But most file systems are not designed to avoid repeating the same state twice, and this causes us a lot of trouble.

First of all, there are backups. If you make a backup of the entire file system and then reboot the computer, the PRNG will be reseeded from the seed file.

If you later restore the entire file system from the backup and reboot the computer, the PRNG will be reseeded from the very same seed file. In other words, until the accumulator has collected enough entropy, the PRNG will produce the same output after the two reboots. This is a serious problem, as an attacker can do this to retrieve the random data that another user got from the PRNG.

There is no direct defense against this attack. If the backup system is capable of recreating the entire permanent state of the computer, there is nothing that we can do to prevent the PRNG state from repeating itself. Ideally we would fix the backup system to be PRNG-aware, but that is probably too much to ask. Hashing the seed file together with the current time would solve the problem as long as the attacker does not reset the clock to the same time. The same solution can be used if the backup system were guaranteed to keep a counter of how many restore-operations it had done. We could hash the seed file with the restore counter. This issue deserves further study, but because it is highly platform-dependent, we cannot give a general treatment here.

10.6.5   Atomicity of File System Updates

Another important problem associated with the seed file is the atomicity of file system updates. On most computers, if you write a seed file, all that happens is that a few memory buffers get updated. The data is not actually written to disk until much later. Even if you instruct the operating system to write the data to the disk (assuming this is possible at all), there are many disk drives that will simply buffer the data without any guarantee as to how long it will take before the data is written to the magnetic media.

Whenever we reseed from our seed file we must update it before allowing any user to ask for random data. In other words, we must be absolutely sure that the data has been modified on the magnetic media. Things become even more complicated when you consider that many file systems treat file data and file administration information separately. So rewriting the seed file might make the file administration data temporarily inconsistent. If the power fails during that time we could get a corrupted seed file or even lose the seed file entirely. Not a good idea for a security system.

Some file systems use a journal to solve some of these problems. This is a technique originally developed for large database systems. The journal is a sequential list of all the updates that have been done to the file system. When properly used, a journal can ensure that updates are always consistent. Such a file system is always preferable from a reliability point of view. Unfortunately, we do not know of any file system in common use that provides full guarantees as to when an update has been written to permanent storage.

As long as the hardware and operating system do not support fully atomic and permanent file updates, we cannot create a perfect seed file solution. You will need to investigate the particular platform that you work on, and do the best you can to reliably update the seed file.

10.6.6 First Boot

When we start the PRNG for the very first time, there is no seed file to use for a reseed. Take, for example, a new PC which had its OS installed in the factory. The OS is now generating some administrative cryptographic keys for the installation, for which it needs the PRNG. For ease of production, all machines are identical and loaded with identical data. There is no initial seed file, so we cannot use that. We could wait for enough random events to trigger one or more reseeds, but that takes a long time and we'd never know when we had collected enough entropy to be able to generate good cryptographic keys.

A good idea would be for the installation procedure to generate a random seed file for the PRNG right during the configuration. It could, for example, use a PRNG on a separate computer to generate a new seed file for each machine. Or maybe the installation software could ask the tester to wiggle the mouse to collect some initial entropy. The choice of solution depends on the details of the environment, but somehow initial entropy has to be provided. Not providing initial entropy is not an option. The entropy accumulator can take quite a while to seed the PRNG properly, and it is quite likely that some very important cryptographic keys will be generated by the PRNG shortly after the installation of the machine.

Keep in mind that the Fortuna accumulator will seed the generator as soon as it *might* have enough entropy to be really random. Depending on how much entropy the sources actually deliver—something that Fortuna has no knowledge about—it could take quite a while before enough entropy has been gathered to properly reseed the generator. Having an outside source of randomness to create the first seed file is probably the best solution.

10.7   So What Should I Do?

First of all, don't trust any of the random number generators provided with your programming language or your operating system. Most of them fail virtually all requirements for a cryptographically strong PRNG. What we've described in this chapter is a significant improvement in the state of the art, so we'd go for a Fortuna PRNG. But as usual, we are biased for the obvious reasons.

It is always difficult to collect entropy. Get as many sources as you can. The big advantage of Fortuna is that low-quality sources cannot harm the system, so there is little reason not to add them. Still, getting to the entropy sources might involve modifying operating system drivers and such, which is not an easy thing to do.

The seed file is an easy concept to understand but fiendishly difficult to implement properly. We gave you some practical advice here, but much of it depends on the detailed circumstances. You might have to alter parts of the operating system or even the hardware to do it right. This is one more example of security influencing other parts of the system. Do the best you can. Good luck!

10.8   Choosing Random Elements

Our PRNG produces sequences of random bytes. Sometimes this is exactly what you need. In other situations you try to pick a random element from a set. This requires some care to do right.

Whenever we choose a random element, we implicitly assume that the element is chosen uniformly at random from the specified set (unless we specify another distribution). This means that each element should have exactly the same probability of being chosen.[5] This is harder than you'd think, and many programs get it wrong.

Let n be the number of elements in the set we are choosing from. We will only discuss how to choose a random element from the set $0, 1, \ldots, n-1$. Once you can do this, you can choose elements from any set of size n.

If $n = 0$, there are no elements to choose from, so this is a simple error. If $n = 1$ you have no choice; again a simple case. If $n = 2^k$, then you just get k bits of random data from the PRNG, and interpret them as a number in the range $0, \ldots, n-1$. This number is uniformly random. (You might have to get a whole number of bytes from the PRNG and throw away a few bits of the last byte until you're left with k bits, but this is easy.)

What if n is not a power of two? Well, some programs choose a random 32-bit integer and take it modulo n. But that algorithm introduces a bias in the resulting probability distribution. Let's take $n = 5$ as an example, and define $m := \lfloor 2^{32}/5 \rfloor$. If we take a uniformly random 32-bit number and reduce it modulo 5, then the results 1, 2, 3, and 4 each occur with a probability of $m/2^{32}$, while the result 0 occurs with a probability of $(m+1)/2^{32}$. The deviation in probability is small, but could very well be significant. It would certainly be easy to detect the deviation within the 2^{128} steps we allow the attacker.

The proper way to select a random number in an arbitrary range is to use a trial-and-error approach. To generate a random value in the range $0, \ldots, 4$, we first generate a random value in the range $0, \ldots, 7$, which we can do since 8 is a power of 2. If the result is 5 or larger, we throw it away and choose a new random number in the range $0, \ldots, 7$. We keep doing this until the result is in the desired range. In other words, we generate a random number with the right number of bits in it, and throw away all the improper ones.

Here is a more formal specification for how to choose a random number in the range $0, \ldots, n-1$ for $n \geq 2$.

---

[5]If we are designing for a 128-bit security level, we could afford a deviation from the uniform probability of 2^{-128}, but it is easier to do it perfectly.

1. Let k be the smallest integer such that $2^k \geq n$.

2. Use the PRNG to generate a k-bit random number K. This number will be in the range $0, \ldots, 2^k - 1$. You might have to generate a whole number of bytes and throw away part of the last byte, but that's easy.

3. If $K \geq n$ go back to step 2.

4. The number K is the result.

This can be a bit of a wasteful process. In the worst case we throw away half our attempts on average. Here is an improvement. As $2^{32} - 1$ is a multiple of 5, we could choose a random number in the range $0, \ldots, 2^{32} - 2$ and take the result modulo 5 for our answer. To choose a value in the range $0, \ldots, 2^{32} - 2$, we use the "inefficient" try-and-throw-away algorithm, but now the probability of having to throw the intermediate result away is very low.

The general formulation is to choose a convenient k such that $2^k \geq n$. Define $q := \lfloor 2^k / n \rfloor$. First choose a random number r in the range $0, \ldots, nq - 1$ using the try-and-throw-away rules. Once a suitable r has been generated, the final result is given by $(r \bmod n)$.

We don't know of any way to generate uniformly random numbers on sizes that are not a power of two without having to throw away some random bits now and again. That is not a problem. Given a decent PRNG, there is no shortage of random bits.

Chapter 11

Primes

The following two chapters explain public-key cryptographic systems; unfortunately, this requires quite a bit of mathematics. It is always tempting to dispense with the understanding and only present the formulas and equations, but we feel very strongly that this is a dangerous thing to do. To use a tool, you must understand the properties of that tool. This is easy with something like a hash function. We have an "ideal" model of a hash function, and we require that the actual hash function behave like the ideal model. This is not so easy to do with public-key systems because there are no "ideal" models to work with. In practice, you have to deal with the mathematical properties of the public-key systems, and to do that safely you must understand these properties. There is no shortcut here; you must understand the mathematics. It's not that difficult; the only background knowledge required is high school math. More specifically: the type of math the authors were taught in high school.

This chapter is about prime numbers. Prime numbers play an important role in mathematics, but we are interested in them because the most important public-key crypto systems are based on prime numbers.

11.1   Divisibility and Primes

A number a is a divisor of b (notation $a \mid b$, pronounced "a divides b") if you can divide b by a without leaving a remainder. For example, 7 is a divisor of 35 so we write $7 \mid 35$. We call a number a *prime* number if it has exactly two divisors, namely 1 and itself. For example, 13 is a prime; the two divisors are 1 and 13. The first few primes are easy to find: 2, 3, 5, 7, 11, 13, ... Any integer greater than 1 that is not prime is called a composite. The number 1 is neither prime nor composite.

We will use the proper mathematical notation and terminology in the chapters ahead. This will make it much easier to read other texts on this subject. The notation might look difficult and complicated at first, but this part of mathematics is really easy.

Here is a simple lemma about divisibility:

Lemma 1. *If $a \mid b$ and $b \mid c$ then $a \mid c$.*

Proof. If $a \mid b$, then there is an integer s such that $as = b$. (After all, b is divisible by a so it must be a multiple of a.) And if $b \mid c$ then there is an integer t such that $bt = c$. But this implies that $c = bt = (as)t = a(st)$ and therefore a is a divisor of c. (To follow this argument, just verify that each of the equal signs is correct. The conclusion is that the first item c must be equal to the last item $a(st)$.)   □

The lemma is a statement of fact. The proof argues why the lemma is true. The little square box signals the end of the proof. Mathematicians love to use lots of symbols.[1] This is a very simple lemma, and the proof should be easy to follow, as long as you remember what the notation $a \mid b$ means.

Prime numbers have been studied by mathematicians throughout the ages. Even today, if you want to generate all primes below one million, you should use an algorithm developed just over 2000 years ago by Eratosthenes, a friend of Archimedes. (Eratosthenes was also the first person to accurately measure the diameter of the earth. A mere 1700 years later Columbus allegedly used

---

[1] Using symbols has advantages and disadvantages. We'll use whatever we think is most appropriate for this book.

a much smaller—and wrong—estimate for the size of the earth when he planned to sail to India by going due west.) Euclid, another great Greek mathematician, gave a beautiful proof that showed there are an infinite number of primes. This is such a beautiful proof that we'll include it here. Reading through it will help you reacquaint yourself with the math.

Before we start with the real proof we will give a simple lemma.

Lemma 2. *Let n be a positive number greater than 1. Let d be the smallest divisor of n that is greater than 1. Then d is prime.*

Proof. First of all, we have to check that d is well defined. (If there is a number n which has no smallest divisor, then d is not properly defined and the lemma is nonsensical.) We know that n is a divisor of n, and $n > 1$, so there is at least one divisor of n that is greater than 1. Therefore, there must also be a smallest divisor greater than 1.

To prove that d is prime we use a standard mathematician's trick called *reductio ad absurdum* or *proof by contradiction*. To prove a statement X we first assume that X is not true, and show that this assumption leads to a contradiction. If assuming that X is not true leads to a contradiction, then obviously X must be true.

In our case we will assume that d is not a prime. If d is not a prime, it has a divisor e such that $1 < e < d$. But we know from Lemma 1 that if $e \mid d$ and $d \mid n$ then $e \mid n$, so e is a divisor of n and is smaller than d. But this is a contradiction, because d was defined as the smallest divisor of n. Because a contradiction cannot be true, our assumption must be false, and therefore d must be prime. □

Don't worry if you find this type of proof a bit confusing; it takes some getting used to.

We can now prove that there are an infinite number of primes.

Theorem 3 (Euclid). *There are an infinite number of primes.*

Proof. We again assume the opposite of what we try to prove. Here we assume that the number of primes is finite, and therefore that the list of primes is finite. Let's call them $p_1, p_2, p_3, \ldots, p_k$, where k is the number of primes. We define the number $n := p_1 p_2 p_3 \cdots p_k + 1$, which is the product of all our primes plus one.

Consider the smallest divisor greater than 1 of n; we'll call it d again. Now d is prime (by Lemma 2) and $d \mid n$. But none of the primes in our finite list of primes is a divisor of n. After all, they are all divisors of $n - 1$, so if you divide n by one of the p_i's in the list you are always left with a remainder of 1. So d is a prime and it is not in the list. But this is a contradiction, as the list is defined to contain all the primes. Thus, assuming that the number of primes is finite leads to a contradiction. We are left to conclude that the number of primes is infinite.   □

This is basically the proof that Euclid gave over 2000 years ago.

There are many more results on the distribution of primes, but interestingly enough there is no easy formula for the number of primes in a specific interval. Primes seem to occur fairly randomly. There are even very simple conjectures which have never been proven. For example, the Goldbach conjecture is that every even number greater than 2 is the sum of two primes. This is easy to verify with a computer for relatively small even numbers, but mathematicians still don't know whether it is true for all even numbers.

The *fundamental theorem of arithmetic* is also useful to know: any integer greater than 1 can be written in exactly one way as the product of primes (if you disregard the order in which you write the primes). For example, $15 = 3 \cdot 5$; $255 = 3 \cdot 5 \cdot 17$; and $60 = 2 \cdot 2 \cdot 3 \cdot 5$. We won't try to prove this here. Check any textbook on number theory if you want to know the details.

11.2   Generating Small Primes

Sometimes it is useful to have a list of small primes, so here is the Sieve of Eratosthenes, which is still the best algorithm to generate small primes with.

function SMALLPRIMELIST
input: n Limit on primes to generate. Must satisfy $2 \le n \le 2^{20}$.
output: P List of all primes $\le n$.

   Limit the size of n. If n is too large we run out of memory.

assert $2 \leq n \leq 2^{20}$

Initialize a list of flags all set to one.
$(b_2, b_3, \ldots, b_n) \leftarrow (1, 1, \ldots, 1)$
$i \leftarrow 2$
while $i^2 \leq n$ **do**

> *We have found a prime i. Mark all multiples of i composite.*
> **for** $j \in 2i, 3i, 4i, \ldots, \lfloor n/i \rfloor i$ **do**
> > $b_j \leftarrow 0$
>
> **od**
>
> *Look for the next prime in our list. It can be shown that this loop*
> *never results in the condition $i > n$, which would access a*
> *nonexistent b_i.*
> **repeat**
> > $i \leftarrow i + 1$
>
> **until** $b_i = 1$

od

All our primes are now marked with a one. Collect them in a list.
$P \leftarrow [\,]$
for $k \in 2, 3, 4, \ldots, n$ **do**
> **if** $b_k = 1$ **then**
> > $P \leftarrow P \parallel k$
>
> **fi**

od
return P

The algorithm is based on a simple idea. Any composite number c is divisible by a prime that is smaller than c. We keep a list of flags, one for each of the numbers up to n. Each flag indicates whether the corresponding number could be prime. Initially all numbers are marked as potential primes by setting the flag to 1. We start with i being the first prime 2. Of course, none of the multiples of i can be prime so we mark $2i$, $3i$, $4i$, etc. as being composite by setting their flag to 0. We then increment i until we have another candidate prime. Now this candidate is not divisible by any smaller prime, or it would have been marked as a composite already. So the new i must be the next prime. We keep marking the composite numbers and finding the next prime until $i^2 > n$.

It is clear that no prime will ever be marked as a composite, since we only mark a number as a composite when we know a factor of it. (The loop that marks them as composite loops over $2i, 3i, \ldots$. Each of these terms has a factor i and therefore cannot be prime.)

Why can we stop when $i^2 > n$? Well, suppose a number k is composite, and let p be its smallest divisor greater than 1. We already know that p is prime (see Lemma 2). Let $q := k/p$. We now have $p \leq q$; otherwise, q would be a divisor of k smaller than p, which contradicts the definition of p. The crucial observation is that $p \leq \sqrt{k}$, because if p were larger than $\sqrt{k}$ we would have $k = p \cdot q > \sqrt{k} \cdot q \geq \sqrt{k} \cdot p > \sqrt{k} \cdot \sqrt{k} = k$. This last inequality would show that $k > k$ which is an obvious fallacy. So $p \leq \sqrt{k}$.

We have shown that any composite k is divisible by a prime $\leq \sqrt{k}$. So any composite $\leq n$ is divisible by a prime $\leq \sqrt{n}$. When $i^2 > n$ then $i > \sqrt{n}$. But we have already marked the multiples of all the primes less than i as composite in the list, so every composite $< n$ has already been marked as such. The numbers in the list that are still marked as primes are really prime.

The final part of the algorithm simply collects them in a list to be returned.

There are several optimizations you can make to this algorithm, but we have left them out to make things simpler. Properly implemented, this algorithm is very fast.

You might wonder why we need the small primes. It turns out that small primes are useful to generate large primes with, something we will get to soon.

11.3   Computations Modulo a Prime

The main reason why primes are so useful in cryptography is that you can compute modulo a prime.

Let p be a prime. When we compute modulo a prime we only use the numbers $0, 1, \ldots, p - 1$. The basic rule for computations modulo a prime is to do the computations using the numbers as integers, just as you normally would, but every time you get a result r you take it modulo p. Taking a modulo is easy: just divide the result r by p, throw away the quotient, and keep the remainder as the answer. For example, if you take 25 modulo 7 you divide 25 by 7, which gives us a quotient of 3 with a remainder of 4. The remainder is the answer, so $(25 \bmod 7) = 4$. The notation $(a \bmod b)$ is used to denote an explicit modulo operation, but as modulo computations are used very often, and mathematicians are rather lazy, there are several other notations in general use as well. Often the entire equation will be written without any modulo operations, and then $(\bmod\ p)$ will be added at the end of the equation to remind you that the whole thing is to be taken modulo p. When the situation is clear from the context even this is left out, and you have to remember the modulo yourself.

You don't need to write parentheses around a modulo computation. We could just as well have written $a \bmod b$, but as the modulo operator looks very much like normal text this can be a bit confusing for people who are not used to it. To avoid confusion we tend to put $(a \bmod b)$ in parentheses.

One word of warning: Any integer taken modulo p is always in the range $0, \ldots, p - 1$, even if the original integer is negative. Some programming languages have the (for mathematicians very irritating) property that they allow negative results from a modulo operation. If you want to take -1 modulo p, then the answer is $p - 1$. More generally: to compute $(a \bmod p)$, find integers q and r such that $a = qp + r$ and $0 \leq r < p$. The value of $(a \bmod p)$ is defined to be r. If you fill in $a = -1$ then you find that $q = -1$ and $r = p - 1$.

11.3.1 Addition and Subtraction

Addition modulo p is easy. Just add the two numbers, and subtract p if the result is greater than or equal to p. As both inputs are in the range $0, \ldots, p - 1$, the sum cannot exceed $2p - 1$, so you have to subtract p at most once to get the result back in the proper range.

Subtraction is similar to addition. Subtract the numbers, and add p if the result is negative.

These rules only work when the two inputs are both modulo p numbers already. If they are outside the range, you have to do a full reduction modulo p.

It takes a while to get used to modulo computations. You get equations like $5 + 3 = 1 \pmod 7$. This looks odd at first. You know that 5 plus 3 is not 1. But while $5 + 3 = 8$ is true in the integer numbers, working modulo 7 we have 8 mod 7 = 1, so $5 + 3 = 1 \pmod 7$.

We use modulo arithmetic in real life quite often without realizing it. When computing the time of day, we take the hours modulo 12 (or modulo 24). A bus schedule might state that the bus leaves at 55 minutes past the hour and takes 15 minutes. To find out when the bus arrives, we compute $55 + 15 = 10 \pmod{60}$, and determine it arrives at 10 minutes past the hour. For now we will restrict ourselves to computing modulo a prime, but you can do computations modulo any number you like.

11.3.2 Multiplication

Multiplication is, as always, more work than addition. To compute (ab mod p) you first compute ab as an integer, and then take the result modulo p. Now ab can be as large as $(p-1)^2 = p^2 - 2p + 1$. Here you have to perform a long division to find (q, r) such that $ab = qp + r$ and $0 \leq r < p$. Throw away the q; the r is the answer.

Let's give you an example: Let $p = 5$. When we compute $3 \cdot 4 \pmod p$ the result is 2. After all, $3 \cdot 4 = 12$, and $(12 \bmod 5) = 2$. So we get $3 \cdot 4 = 2 \pmod p$.

11.3.3 Groups and Finite Fields

Mathematicians call the set of numbers modulo a prime p a *finite field*, and often refer to it as the "mod p" field, or simply "mod p." Here are some useful reminders about computations in a mod p field:

- You can always add or subtract any multiple of p from your numbers without changing the result.

- All results are always in the range $0, 1, \ldots, p - 1$.

- You can think of it as doing your entire computation in the integers and only taking the modulo at the very last moment. So all the algebraic rules you learned about the integers (such as $a(b + c) = ab + ac$) still apply.

The finite field of the integers modulo p is referred to using different notations in different books. We will use the notation $\mathbb{Z}_p$ to refer to the finite field modulo p. In other texts you might see $\mathrm{GF}(p)$ or even $\mathbb{Z}/p\mathbb{Z}$.

We also have to introduce the concept of a *group*—another mathematical term, but a simple one. A group is simply a set of numbers together with an operation, such as addition or multiplication.[2] The numbers in $\mathbb{Z}_p$ form a group together with addition. You can add any two numbers and get a third number in the group. If you want to use multiplication in a group you cannot use the 0. (This has to do with the fact that multiplying by 0 is not very interesting, and that you cannot divide by 0.) However, the numbers $1, \ldots, p-1$ together with multiplication modulo p form a group. This group is called the *multiplicative group modulo p*, and is written in various ways; we will use the notation $\mathbb{Z}_p^*$. A finite field consists of two groups: the addition group and the multiplication group. In the case of $\mathbb{Z}_p$ the finite field consists of the addition group, defined by addition modulo p, and the multiplication group $\mathbb{Z}_p^*$.

A group can contain a *subgroup*. A subgroup consists of some of the elements of the full group. If you apply the group operation to two elements of the subgroup, you again get an element of the subgroup. That sounds complicated, so here is an example. The numbers modulo 8 together with addition (modulo 8) form a group. The numbers $\{0, 2, 4, 6\}$ form a subgroup. You can add any two of these numbers modulo 8 and get another element of the subgroup. The same goes for multiplicative groups. The multiplicative subgroup modulo 7 consists of the numbers $1, \ldots, 6$, and the operation is multiplication modulo 7. The set $\{1, 6\}$ forms a subgroup, as does the set $\{1, 2, 4\}$. You can check that if you multiply any two elements from the same subgroup modulo 7, you get another element from that subgroup.

We use subgroups to speed up certain cryptographic operations. They can also be used to attack systems, which is why you need to know about them.

---

[2]There are a couple of further requirements, but they are all met by the groups we will be talking about.

So far we've only talked about addition, subtraction, and multiplication modulo a prime. To fully define a multiplicative group you also need the inverse operation of multiplication: division. It turns out that you can define division on the numbers modulo p. The simple definition is that a/b (mod p) is a number c such that $c \cdot b = a$ (mod p). You cannot divide by zero, but it turns out that the division a/b (mod p) is always well defined as long as $b \neq 0$.

So how do you compute the quotient of two numbers modulo p? This is more complicated and it will take a few pages to explain. We first have to go back more than 2000 years to Euclid again, and to his algorithm for the GCD.

11.3.4 The GCD Algorithm

Another high-school math refresher course: The *greatest common divisor* (or GCD) of two numbers a and b is the largest k such that $k \mid a$ and $k \mid b$. In other words, $\gcd(a, b)$ is the largest number that divides both a and b.

Euclid gave an algorithm for computing the GCD of two numbers which is still in use today, thousands of years later. For a detailed discussion of this algorithm see Knuth [55].

function GCD
input: a Positive integer.
            b Positive integer.
output: k The greatest common divisor of a and b.

    assert $a \geq 0 \wedge b \geq 0$
    while $a \neq 0$ **do**
        $(a, b) \leftarrow (b \bmod a, a)$
    od
    return b

Why would this work? The first observation is that the assignment does not change the set of common divisors of a and b. After all, ($b \bmod a$) is just $b - sa$ for some integer s. Any number k that divides both a and b will also divide both a and ($b \bmod a$). (The converse is also true.) And when $a = 0$, then b is a common divisor of a and b, and b is obviously the largest such common divisor. You can check for yourself that the loop must terminate because a and b keep getting smaller and smaller until they reach zero.

Let's compute the GCD of 21 and 30 as an example. We start with $(a, b) = (21, 30)$. In the first iteration we compute $(30 \bmod 21) = 9$, so we get $(a, b) = (9, 21)$. In the next iteration we compute $(21 \bmod 9) = 3$, so we get $(a, b) = (3, 9)$. In the final iteration we compute $(9 \bmod 3) = 0$ and get $(a, b) = (0, 3)$. The algorithm will return 3, which is indeed the greatest common divisor of 21 and 30.

The GCD has a cousin: the LCM or *least common multiple*. The LCM of a and b is the smallest number that is both a multiple of a and a multiple of b. For example, $\mathrm{lcm}(6, 8) = 24$. The GCD and LCM are tightly related by the equation

$$\mathrm{lcm}(a, b) = \frac{ab}{\gcd(a, b)}$$

which we won't prove here but just state as a fact.

11.3.5   The Extended Euclidean Algorithm

This still does not help us to compute division modulo p. For that we need what is called the extended Euclidean algorithm. The idea is that while computing $\gcd(a, b)$ we can also find two integers u and v such that $\gcd(a, b) = ua + vb$. This will allow us to compute $a/b \pmod{p}$.

function EXTENDEDGCD
input: a Positive integer argument.
             b Positive integer argument.
output: k The greatest common divisor of a and b.
            (u, v) Integers such that $ua + vb = k$.
    assert $a \geq 0 \wedge b \geq 0$
    $(c, d) \leftarrow (a, b)$
    $(u_c, v_c, u_d, v_d) \leftarrow (1, 0, 0, 1)$
    while $c \neq 0$ **do**
        Invariant: $u_c a + v_c b = c \wedge u_d a + v_d b = d$
        $q \leftarrow \lfloor d/c \rfloor$
        $(c, d) \leftarrow (d - qc, c)$

$$(u_c, v_c, u_d, v_d) \leftarrow (u_d - qu_c, v_d - qv_c, u_c, v_c)$$
od
return $d, (u_d, v_d)$

This algorithm is very much like the GCD algorithm. We introduce new variables c and d instead of using a and b because we need to refer to the original a and b in our invariant. If you only look at c and d, this is exactly the GCD algorithm. (We've rewritten the $d \bmod c$ formula slightly, but this gives the same result.) We have added four variables that maintain the given invariant; for each value of c or d that we generate, we keep track of how to express that value as a linear combination of a and b. For the initialization this is easy, as c is initialized to a and d to b. When we modify c and d in the loop it is not terribly difficult to update the u and v variables.

Why bother with the extended Euclidean algorithm? Well, suppose we want to compute $1/b \bmod p$ where $1 \le b < p$. We use the extended Euclidean algorithm to compute EXTENDEDGCD(b, p). Now, we know that the GCD of b and p is 1, because p is prime and it therefore has no other suitable divisors. But the EXTENDEDGCD function also provides two numbers u and v such that $ub + vp = \gcd(b, p) = 1$. In other words, $ub = 1 - vp$ or $ub = 1 \pmod{p}$. This is the same as saying that $u = 1/b \pmod{p}$, the inverse of b modulo p. The division a/b can now be computed by multiplying a by u, so we get $a/b = au \pmod{p}$, and this last formula is something that we know how to compute.

The extended Euclidean algorithm allows us to compute an inverse modulo a prime, which in turn allows us to compute a division modulo p. Together with the addition, subtraction, and multiplication modulo p, this allows us to compute all four elementary operations in the finite field modulo p.

Note that u could be negative, so it is probably a good idea to reduce u modulo p before using it as the inverse of b.

If you look carefully at the EXTENDEDGCD algorithm, you'll see that if you only want u as output, you can leave out the v_c and v_d variables, as they do not affect the computation of u. This slightly reduces the amount of work needed to compute a division modulo p.

+	0	1
0	0	1
1	1	0

·	0	1
0	0	0
1	0	1

Figure 11.1: Addition and multiplication modulo 2

11.3.6 Working Modulo 2

An interesting special case is computation modulo 2. After all, 2 is a prime, so we should be able to compute modulo it. If you've done any programming this might look familiar to you. The addition and multiplication tables modulo 2 are shown in figure 11.1. Addition modulo 2 is exactly the exclusive-or (XOR) function you find in programming languages. Multiplication is just a simple AND operation. In the field modulo 2 there is only one inversion possible $(1/1 = 1)$ so division is the same operation as multiplication. It shouldn't surprise you that the field $\mathbb{Z}_2$ is an important tool to analyze certain algorithms used by computers.

11.4 Large Primes

Several cryptographic primitives use very large primes, and we're talking about many hundreds of digits here. Don't worry, you won't have to compute with these primes by hand. That's what the computer is for.

To do any computations at all with numbers this large, you need a multi-precision library. You cannot use floating-point numbers, because they do not have several hundred digits of precision. You cannot use normal integers, because in most programming languages they are limited to a dozen digits or so. Few programming languages provide native support for arbitrary precision integers. Writing routines to perform computations with large integers is fascinating. For a good overview, see Knuth [55, section 4.3]. However, implementing a multiprecision library is far more work than you might expect. Not only do you have to get the right answer, but you always strive to compute it as quickly as possible. There are quite a number of special situations you have to deal with carefully. Save your time for more important things, and download one of the many free libraries from the Internet, or use a language like Python that has built-in large integer support.

For public-key cryptography, the primes we want to generate are 2000–4000 bits long. The basic method of generating a prime that large is surprisingly simple: take a random number and check whether it is prime. There are very good algorithms to determine whether a large number is prime or not. There are also very many primes. In the neighborhood of a number n, approximately one in every $\ln n$ numbers is prime. (The natural logarithm of n, or $\ln n$ for short, is one of the standard functions on any scientific calculator. To give you an idea of how slowly the logarithm grows when applied to large inputs: the natural logarithm of 2^k is slightly less than $0.7 \cdot k$.) A number that is 2000 bits long falls between 2^{1999} and 2^{2000}. In that range about one in every 1386 of the numbers is prime. And this includes a lot of numbers that are trivially composite, such as the even numbers.

Generating a large prime looks something like this:

function GENERATELARGEPRIME
input: l Lower bound of range in which prime should lie.
         u Upper bound of range in which prime should lie.
output: p A random prime in the interval $l, \ldots, u$

> *Check for a sensible range.*
> **assert** $2 < l \leq u$
>
> *Compute maximum number of attempts*
> $r \leftarrow 100(\lfloor \log_2 u \rfloor + 1)$
> **repeat**
> > $r \leftarrow r - 1$
> > **assert** $r > 0$
> > *Choose n randomly in the right interval*
> > $n \in_R l, \ldots, u$
> > *Continue trying until we find a prime.*
>
> **until** ISPRIME(n)
> **return** n

We use the operator $\in_{\mathcal{R}}$ to indicate a random selection from a set. Of course, this requires some output from the PRNG.

The algorithm is relatively straightforward. We first check that we get a sensible interval. The cases $l \leq 2$ and $l \geq u$ are not useful and lead to problems. Note the boundary condition: the case $l = 2$ is not allowed.[3] Next we compute how many attempts we are going to make to find a prime. There are intervals that do not contain a prime. For example, the interval $90, \ldots, 96$ is prime-free. A proper program should never hang, independent of its inputs, so we limit the number of tries and generate a failure if we exceed this number. How many times should we try? As stated before, in the neighborhood of u about one in every $0.7 \log_2 u$ numbers is prime. (The function $\log_2$ is the logarithm to the base 2. The simplest definition is that $\log_2(x) := \ln x / \ln 2$. The number $\log_2 u$ is difficult to compute but $\lfloor \log_2 u \rfloor + 1$ is much easier; it is the number of bits necessary to represent u as a binary number. So if u is an integer that is 2017 bits long, then $\lfloor \log_2 u \rfloor + 1 = 2017$. The factor 100 ensures that it is extremely unlikely that we will not find a prime. For large enough intervals, the probability of a failure due to bad luck is less than 2^{-128}, so we can ignore this risk. At the same time, this limit does ensure that the GENERATELARGEPRIME function will terminate. We've been a bit sloppy in our use of an assertion to generate the failure; a proper implementation would generate an error with explanations of what went wrong.

The main loop is simple. After the check that limits the number of tries, we choose a random number and check whether it is prime using the ISPRIME function. We will define this function shortly.

Make sure that the number n you choose is uniformly randomly in the range $l, \ldots, u$. Also make sure that the range is not too small if you want your prime to be a secret. If the attacker knows the interval you use, and there are fewer than 2^{128} primes in that interval, the attacker could potentially try them all.

If you wish, you can make sure the random number you generate is odd by setting the least significant bit just after you generate a candidate n.

---

[3]The Rabin-Miller algorithm we use below does not work well when it gets 2 as an argument. That's okay, we already know that 2 is prime so we don't have to generate it here.

As 2 is not in your interval, this will not affect the probability distribution of primes you are choosing, and it will halve the number of attempts you have to make. But this is only safe if u is odd, otherwise setting the least significant bit might bump n just outside the allowed range.

The ISPRIME function is a two-step filter. The first phase is a simple test where we try to divide n by all the small primes. This will quickly weed out the great majority of numbers which are composite and divisible by a small prime. If we find no divisors, we employ a heavyweight test called the Rabin-Miller test.

function ISPRIME
input: n Integer ≥ 3.
output: b Boolean whether n is prime.
    assert $n \geq 3$
    for $p \in \{$ all primes $\leq 1000 \}$ **do**
        if p is a divisor of n **then**
            return $p = n$
        fi
    od
    return RABIN-MILLER(n)

If you are lazy and don't want to generate the small primes, you can cheat a bit. Instead of trying all the primes, you can try 2 and all odd numbers $3, 5, 7, \ldots, 999$, in that order. This sequence contains all the primes below 1000, but it also contains a lot of useless composite numbers. The order is important to ensure that a small composite number like 9 is properly detected as being composite. The bound of 1000 is arbitrary, and can be chosen for optimal performance.

All that remains to explain is the mysterious Rabin-Miller test that does the hard work.

11.4.1   Primality Testing

It turns out to be remarkably easy to test whether a number is prime. At least, it is remarkably easy compared to factoring a number and finding its prime divisors. These easy tests are not perfect. They are all probabilistic.

There is a certain chance they give the wrong answer. By repeatedly running the same test we can reduce the probability of error to an acceptable level.

The primality test of choice is the Rabin-Miller test. The mathematical basis for this test is well beyond the scope of this book, although the outline is fairly simple. The purpose of this test is to determine whether an odd integer n is prime. We choose a random value a less than n, called the *basis*, and check a certain property of a modulo n that always hold when n is prime. However, you can prove that when n is not a prime, this property holds for at most 25% of all possible basis values. By repeating this test for different random values of a, you build your confidence in the final result. If n is a prime, it will always test as a prime. If n is not a prime, then at least 75% of the possible values for a will show so, and the chance that n will pass multiple tests can be made as small as you want. We limit the probability of a false result to 2^{-128} to achieve our required security level.

Here is how it goes:

function RABIN-MILLER
input: n An odd number ≥ 3.
output: b Boolean indicating whether n is prime or not.
   assert $n \geq 3 \wedge n \bmod 2 = 1$
   First we compute (s, t) such that s is odd and $2^t s = n - 1$.
   $(s, t) \leftarrow (n - 1, 0)$
   while $s \bmod 2 = 0$ **do**
       $(s, t) \leftarrow (s/2, t + 1)$
   od
   We keep track of the probability of a false result in k. The probability is at most 2^{-k}. We loop until the probability of a false result is small enough.
   $k \leftarrow 0$
   while $k < 128$ **do**
       Choose a random a such that $2 \leq a \leq n - 1$.
       $a \in_{\mathcal{R}} 2, \ldots, n - 1$
       The expensive operation: a modular exponentiation.
       $v \leftarrow a^s \bmod n$
       When $v = 1$, the number n passes the test for basis a.
       if $v \neq 1$ **then**

The sequence $v, v^2, \ldots, v^{2^t}$ must finish on the value 1, and the last value not equal to 1 must be $n-1$ if n is a prime.

$i \leftarrow 0$

while $v \neq n - 1$ **do**

    if $i = t - 1$ **then**

        return false

    else

        $(v, i) \leftarrow (v^2 \bmod n, i + 1)$

    fi

    od

fi

When we get to this point, n has passed the primality test for the basis a. We have therefore reduced the probability of a false result by a factor of 2^2, so we can add 2 to k.

    $k \leftarrow k + 2$

od

return true

This algorithm only works for an odd n greater or equal to 3, so we test that first. The ISPRIME function should only call this function with a suitable argument, but each function is responsible for checking its own inputs and outputs. You never know how the software will be changed in future.

The basic idea behind the test is known as Fermat's little theorem.[4] For any prime n and for all $1 \leq a < n$, the relation $a^{n-1} \bmod n = 1$ holds. To fully understand the reasons for this requires more math than we will explain here. A simple test (also called the Fermat primality test) verifies this relation for a number of randomly chosen a values. Unfortunately, there are some obnoxious numbers called the Carmichael numbers. These are composite but they pass the Fermat test for (almost) all basis a.

The Rabin-Miller test is a variation of the Fermat test. First we write $n-1$ as $2^t s$, where s is an odd number. If you want to compute a^{n-1} you can first compute a^s and then square the result t times to get $a^{s \cdot 2^t} = a^{n-1}$. Now if $a^s = 1 \pmod{n}$ then repeated squaring will not change the result so we

---

[4]There are several theorems named after Fermat. Fermat's last Theorem is the most famous one, involving the equation $a^n + b^n = c^n$ and a proof too small to fit in the margin of the page.

have $a^{n-1} = 1 \pmod{n}$. If $a^s \neq 1 \pmod{n}$, then we look at the numbers $a^s, a^{s \cdot 2}, a^{s \cdot 2^2}, a^{s \cdot 2^3}, \ldots, a^{s \cdot 2^t}$ (all modulo n, of course). If n is a prime, then we know that the last number must be 1. If n is a prime, then the only numbers that satisfy $x^2 = 1 \pmod{n}$ are 1 and $n - 1$.[5] So if n is prime, then one of the numbers in the sequence must be $n - 1$, or we could never have the last number be equal to 1. This is really all the Rabin-Miller test checks. If any choice of a demonstrates that n is composite, we return immediately. If n continues to test as a prime, we repeat the test for different a values until the probability that we have generated a wrong answer and claimed that a composite number is actually prime is less than 2^{-128}.

If you apply this test to a random number, the probability of failure of this test is much, much smaller than the bound we use. For almost all composite numbers n, almost all basis values will show that n is composite. You will find a lot of libraries that depend on this and perform the test for only 5 or 10 bases or so. This idea is fine, though we would have to investigate how many attempts are needed to reach an error level of 2^{-128} or less. But it only holds as long as you apply the ISPRIME test to *randomly* chosen numbers. Later on we will encounter situations where we apply the primality test to numbers that we received from someone else. These might be maliciously chosen, so the ISPRIME function must achieve a 2^{-128} error bound all by itself.

Doing the full 64 Rabin-Miller tests is necessary when we receive the number to be tested from someone else. It is overkill when we try to generate a prime randomly. But when generating a prime, you spend most of your time rejecting composite numbers. (Almost all composite numbers are rejected by the very first Rabin-Miller test that you do.) As you might have to try hundreds of numbers before you find a prime, doing 64 tests on the final prime is only marginally slower than doing 10 of them.

In an earlier version of this chapter, the Rabin-Miller routine had a second argument that could be used to select the maximum error probability. But it was a perfect example of a needless option, so we removed it. Always doing a good test to a 2^{-128} bound is simpler, and much less likely to be improperly used.

---

[5]It is easy to check that $(n - 1)^2 = 1 \pmod{n}$.

There is still a chance of 2^{-128} that our ISPRIME function will give you the wrong answer. To give you an idea of how small this chance actually is, the chance that you will be killed by a meteorite while you read this sentence is far larger. Still alive? Okay, so don't worry about it.

11.4.2   Evaluating Powers

The Rabin-Miller test spends most of its time computing $a^s \bmod n$. You cannot compute a^s first and then take it modulo n. No computer in the world has enough memory to even store a^s, much less the computing power to compute it; both a and s can be thousands of bits long. But we only need $a^s \bmod n$; we can apply the mod n to all the intermediate results, which stops the numbers from growing too large.

There are several ways of computing $a^s \bmod n$, but here is a simple description. To compute $a^s \bmod n$ use the following rules:

- If $s = 0$ the answer is 1.

- If $s > 0$ and s is even, then first compute $y := a^{s/2} \bmod n$ using these very same rules. The answer is given by $a^s \bmod n = y^2 \bmod n$.

- If $s > 0$ and s is odd, then first compute $y := a^{(s-1)/2} \bmod n$ using these very same rules. The answer is given by $a^s \bmod n = a \cdot y^2 \bmod n$.

This is a recursive formulation of the so-called binary algorithm. If you look at the operations performed, it builds up the desired exponent bit by bit from the most significant part of the exponent down to the least significant part. It is also possible to convert this from a recursive algorithm to a loop.

How many multiplications are required to compute $a^s \bmod n$? Let k be the number of bits of s; i.e., $2^{k-1} \le s < 2^k$. Then this algorithm requires at most $2k$ multiplications modulo n. This is not too bad. If we are testing a 2000-bit number for primality, then s will also be about 2000 bits long and we only need 4000 multiplications. That is still a lot of work, but certainly within the capabilities of most desktop computers.

Many public-key cryptographic systems make use of modular exponentiations like this. Any good multiprecision library will have an optimized routine for evaluating modular exponentiations. A special type of multiplication called Montgomery multiplication is well suited for this task. There are also ways of computing a^s using fewer multiplications [10, Ch. 4]. Each of these tricks can save 10%–30% of the time it takes to compute a modular exponentiation, so used in combination they can be important.

Straightforward implementations of modular exponentiation are often vulnerable to timing attacks. See section 16.3 for details and possible remedies.

Chapter 12

Diffie-Hellman

For the presentation of public-key cryptography we're going to follow the historical path. Public-key cryptography was really started by Whitfield Diffie and Martin Hellman when they published their "New Directions in Cryptography" article in 1976 [22].

So far in this book we've only talked about encryption and authentication with shared secret keys. But where do we get those shared secret keys from? If you have 10 friends you want to communicate with, you can meet them all and exchange a secret key with each of these friends for future use. But like all keys, these keys should be refreshed regularly, so then you have to meet and exchange keys all over again. A total of 45 keys are needed for a group of 10 friends. But as the group gets larger, the number of keys grows quadratically. For 100 people all communicating with each other, you need 4950 keys. This quickly becomes unmanageable.

Diffie and Hellman posed the question of whether it would be possible to do this more efficiently. Suppose you have an encryption algorithm where the encryption and decryption keys are different. You can publish your encryption key and keep your decryption key secret. Anyone can now send you an encrypted message, and only you can decrypt it. This would solve the problem of having to distribute so many different keys.

Diffie and Hellman posed the question, but they could only provide a partial answer. Their partial solution is today known as the Diffie-Hellman key exchange protocol, often shortened to DH protocol [22].

The DH protocol is a really nifty idea. It turns out that two people communicating over an insecure line can agree on a secret key in such a way that both of them receive the same key without divulging it to someone who is listening in on their conversation.

12.1   Groups

If you've read the last chapter, it won't surprise you that primes are involved. For the rest of this chapter, p is a large prime. Think of p as being 2000 to 4000 bits long. Most of our computations in this chapter will be modulo p— in many places we will not specify this again explicitly. The DH protocol uses $\mathbb{Z}_p^*$, the multiplicative group modulo p that we discussed in section 11.3.3.

Choose any g in the group and consider the numbers $1, g, g^2, g^3, \ldots$, all modulo p, of course. This is an infinite sequence of numbers, but there is only a finite set of numbers in $\mathbb{Z}_p^*$. (Remember, $\mathbb{Z}_p^*$ is the numbers $1, \ldots, p-1$ together with the operation of multiplication modulo p.) At some point the numbers must start to repeat. Let us assume this happens at $g^i = g^j$ with $i < j$. As we can do divisions modulo p, we can divide each side by g^i and get $1 = g^{j-i}$. In other words, there is a number $q := j - i$ such that $g^q = 1$ (mod p). We call the smallest positive value q for which $g^q = 1$ (mod p) the *order* of g. (Unfortunately, there is quite a bit of terminology associated with this stuff. We feel it is better to use the standard terminology than to invent our own words; otherwise readers will be confused later on when they read other books.)

If we keep on multiplying gs we can reach the numbers $1, g, g^2, \ldots, g^{q-1}$. After that, the sequence repeats as $g^q = 1$. We say that g is a generator and that it generates the set $1, g, g^2, \ldots, g^{q-1}$. The number of elements that can be written as a power of g is exactly q, the order of g.

One property of multiplication modulo p is that there is at least one g that generates the entire group. That is, there is at least one g value for which $q = p - 1$. So instead of thinking of $\mathbb{Z}_p^*$ as the numbers $1, \ldots, p-1$, we can also think of them as $1, g, g^2, \ldots, g^{p-2}$. A g that generates the whole group is called a *primitive element* of the group.

Other values of g can generate smaller sets. Observe that if we multiply two numbers from the set generated by g, then we get another power of g, and therefore another element from the set. If you go through all the math, it turns out that the set generated by g is another group. That is, you can multiply and divide in this group just as you can in the large group modulo p. These smaller groups are called subgroups (see section 11.3.3). They will be important in various attacks.

There is one last thing to explain. For any element g, the order of g is a divisor of $p-1$. This isn't too hard to see. Choose g to be a primitive element. Let h be any other element. As g generates the whole group, there is an x such that $h = g^x$. Now consider the elements generated by h. These are $1, h, h^2, h^3, \ldots$ which are equal to $1, g^x, g^{2x}, g^{3x}, \ldots$. (All our computations are still modulo p, of course.) The order of h is the smallest q at which $h^q = 1$, which is the same as saying that it is the smallest q such that $g^{xq} = 1$. For any t, $g^t = 1$ is the same as saying $t = 0 \pmod{p-1}$. So q is the smallest q such that $xq = 0 \pmod{p-1}$. This happens when $q = (p-1)/\gcd(x, p-1)$. So q is obviously a factor of $p-1$.

Here's a simple example. Let's choose $p = 7$. If we choose $g = 3$ then g is a generator because $1, g, g^2, \ldots, g^6 = 1, 3, 2, 6, 4, 5$. (Again, all computations modulo p.) The element $h = 2$ generates the subgroup $1, h, h^2 = 1, 2, 4$ because $h^3 = 2^3 \bmod 7 = 1$. The element $h = 6$ generates the subgroup $1, 6$. These subgroups have sizes 3 and 2 respectively, which are both divisors of $p-1$.

This also explains parts of the Fermat test we talked about in section 11.4.1. Fermat's test is based on the fact that for any a we have $a^{p-1} = 1$. This is easy to check. Let g be a generator of $\mathbb{Z}_p^*$, and let x be such that $g^x = a$. As g is a generator of the whole group, there is always such an x. But now $a^{p-1} = g^{x(p-1)} = (g^{p-1})^x = 1^x = 1$.

$$\textbf{Alice} \hspace{8cm} \textbf{Bob}$$

$$x \in_{\mathcal{R}} \mathbb{Z}_p^*$$

$$\xrightarrow{\hspace{3cm} g^x \hspace{3cm}}$$

$$y \in_{\mathcal{R}} \mathbb{Z}_p^*$$

$$\xleftarrow{\hspace{3cm} g^y \hspace{3cm}}$$

$$k \leftarrow (g^y)^x \hspace{6cm} k \leftarrow (g^x)^y$$

Figure 12.1: The original Diffie-Hellman protocol.

12.2   Basic DH

For the original DH protocol, we first choose a large prime p, and a primitive element g which generates the whole group $\mathbb{Z}_p^*$. Both p and g are public constants in this protocol, and we assume that all parties, including the attackers, know them. The protocol is shown in figure 12.1. This is one of the usual ways in which we write cryptographic protocols. There are two parties involved: Alice and Bob. Time progresses from the top to the bottom. First Alice chooses a random x in $\mathbb{Z}_p^*$, which is the same as choosing a random number in $1, \ldots, p-1$. She computes $g^x \bmod p$ and sends the result to Bob. Bob in turn chooses a random y in $\mathbb{Z}_p^*$. He computes $g^y \bmod p$ and sends the result to Alice. The final result k is defined as g^{xy}. Alice can compute this by raising the g^y she got from Bob to the power x that she knows. (High-school math: $(g^y)^x = g^{xy}$.) Similarly, Bob can compute k as $(g^x)^y$. They both end up with the same value k which they can use as a secret key.

But what about an attacker? The attacker gets to see g^x and g^y, but not x or y. The problem of computing g^{xy} given g^x and g^y is known as the Diffie-Hellman problem, or DH problem for short. As long as p and g are chosen correctly, there is no efficient algorithm to compute this—at least, there is none that we know of. The best method known is to first compute x from g^x, after which the attacker can compute k as $(g^y)^x$ just like Alice did. In the real numbers, computing x from g^x is called the logarithm function, which you find on any scientific calculator. In the finite field $\mathbb{Z}_p^*$, it is called a *discrete logarithm*, and in general the problem of computing x from g^x in a finite group is known as the discrete logarithm problem, or DL problem.

The original DH protocol can be used in many ways. We've written it as an exchange of messages between two parties. Another way of using it is to let everybody choose a random x, and publish $g^x \pmod p$ in the digital equivalent of a phone book. If Alice now wants to communicate with Bob securely, she gets g^y from the phone book, and using her x, computes g^{xy}. Bob can similarly compute g^{xy} without any interaction with Alice. This makes the system usable in settings such as e-mail where there is no direct interaction.

12.3   Man in the Middle

The one thing that DH does not protect against is the man in the middle. Look back at the protocol. Alice knows she is communicating with somebody, but she does not know whom she is communicating with. Eve can sit in the middle of the protocol and pretend to be Bob when speaking to Alice, and pretend to be Alice when speaking to Bob. This is shown in figure 12.2. To Alice, this protocol looks just like the original DH protocol. There is no way in which Alice can detect she is talking to Eve, not Bob. The same holds for Bob. Eve can keep up these pretenses for as long as she likes. Suppose Alice and Bob start to communicate using the secret key they think they have set up. All Eve needs to do is forward all the communications between Alice and Bob. Of course, Eve has to decrypt all the data she gets from Alice that was encrypted with key k, and then encrypt it again with key k' to send to Bob. She has to do the same with the traffic in the other direction, but that is not a lot of work.

With a digital phone book this attack is harder. As long as the publisher of the book verifies the identity of everybody when they send in their g^x, Alice knows she is using Bob's g^x. We'll discuss other solutions when we talk about digital signatures and PKIs later on in this book.

There is one setting where the man-in-the-middle attack can be addressed without further infrastructure. If the key k is used to encrypt a phone conversation (or a video link), Alice can talk to Bob and recognize him by

Alice	**Eve**	**Bob**
$x \in_{\mathcal{R}} \mathbb{Z}_p^*$		

$$\xrightarrow{\quad g^x \quad}$$

$v \in_{\mathcal{R}} \mathbb{Z}_p^*$

$$\xrightarrow{\quad g^v \quad}$$

$y \in_{\mathcal{R}} \mathbb{Z}_p^*$

$$\xleftarrow{\quad g^y \quad}$$

$w \in_{\mathcal{R}} \mathbb{Z}_p^*$

$$\xleftarrow{\quad g^w \quad}$$

$k \leftarrow (g^w)^x$	$k \leftarrow (g^x)^w$	
	$k' \leftarrow (g^y)^v$	$k' \leftarrow (g^v)^y$

Figure 12.2: Diffie-Hellman protocol with a man in the middle.

his voice. Let h be a hash function of some sort. If Bob reads the first few digits of $h(k)$ to Alice, then Alice can verify that Bob is using the same key as she is. Alice can read the next few digits of $h(k)$ to Bob to allow Bob to do the same verification. This works, but only in situations where you can tie knowledge of the key k to the actual person on the other side. In most computer communications, this solution is not possible. And if Eve ever succeeds in building a speech synthesizer that can emulate Bob, it all falls apart. Finally, the biggest problem with this solution is that it requires discipline from the users. But users regularly ignore security procedures.

12.4   Pitfalls

Implementing the DH protocol can be a bit tricky. For example, if Eve intercepts the communications and replaces both g^x and g^y with the number 1, then both Alice and Bob will end up with $k = 1$. The result is a key negotiation protocol that looks as if it completed successfully, except that

Eve knows the resulting key. That is bad, and we will have to prevent this attack in some way.

A second problem is if the generator g is not a primitive element of $\mathbb{Z}_p^*$ but rather generates only a small subgroup. Maybe g has an order of one million. In that case the set $\{\, 1, g, g^2, \ldots, g^{q-1} \,\}$ only contains a million elements. As k is in this set, Eve can easily search for the correct key. Obviously, one of the requirements is that g must have a high order. But who chooses p and g? All users are using the same values, so most of them get these values from someone else. To be safe, they have to verify that p and g are chosen properly. Alice and Bob should each check that p is prime, and that g is a primitive element modulo p.

The subgroups modulo p form a separate problem. Eve's attack of replacing g^x with the number 1 is easy to counter by having Bob check for this. But Eve could also replace g^x with the number h, where h has a small order. The key that Bob derives now comes from the small set generated by h, and Eve can try all possible values to find k. (Of course, Eve can play the same attack against Alice.) What both Alice and Bob have to do is verify that the numbers they receive do not generate small subgroups.

Let's have a look at the subgroups. Working modulo a prime, all (multiplicative) subgroups can be generated from a single element. The entire group $\mathbb{Z}_p^*$ consists of the elements $1, \ldots, p-1$ for a total of $p-1$ elements. Each subgroup is of the form $1, h, h^2, h^3, \ldots, h^{q-1}$ for some h and where q is the order of h. As we discussed earlier, it turns out that q must be a divisor of $p-1$. In other words: the size of any subgroup is a divisor of $p-1$. The converse also holds: for any divisor d of $p-1$ there is a single subgroup of size d. If we don't want any small subgroups, then we must avoid small divisors of $p-1$.

This is a problem. If p is a large prime, then $p-1$ is always even, and therefore divisible by 2. Thus there is a subgroup with two elements; it consists of the elements 1 and $p-1$. But apart from this subgroup that is always present, we could avoid other small subgroups by insisting that $p-1$ has no other small factors.

12.5   Safe Primes

One solution is to use a *safe prime* for p. A safe prime is a (large enough) prime p of the form $2q + 1$ where q is also prime. The multiplicative group $\mathbb{Z}_p^*$ now has the following subgroups:

- The trivial subgroup consisting only of the number 1.

- The subgroup of size 2, consisting of 1 and $p - 1$.

- The subgroup of size q.

- The full group of size $2q$.

The first two are trivial to avoid. The third is the group we want to use. The full group has one remaining problem. Consider the set of all numbers modulo p that can be written as a square of some other number (modulo p, of course). It turns out that exactly half the numbers in $1, \ldots, p - 1$ are squares, and the other half are non-squares. Any generator of the entire group is a non-square. (If it were a square, then raising it to some power could never generate a non-square, so it does not generate the whole group.)

There is a mathematical function called the Legendre symbol that determines whether a number modulo p is a square or not, without ever needing to find the root. There are efficient algorithms for computing the Legendre symbol. So if g is a non-square and you send out g^x, then any observer, such as Eve, can immediately determine whether x is even or odd. If x is even, then g^x is a square. If x is odd, then g^x is a non-square. As Eve can determine the square-ness of a number using the Legendre symbol function, she can determine whether x is odd or even. This is exceptional behavior; Eve cannot learn the value x, except for the least significant bit. The solution to avoid this problem is to use only the squares modulo p. This is exactly the subgroup of order q. Another nice property is that q is prime, so there are no further subgroups we have to worry about.

Here is how to use a safe prime. Choose (p, q) such that $p = 2q + 1$ and both p and q are prime. (You can use the ISPRIME function to do this on a trial-and-error basis.) Choose a random number α in the range $2, \ldots, p - 2$ and set $g = \alpha^2 \pmod{p}$. Check that $g \neq 1$ and $g \neq p - 1$. (If g is one of these forbidden values, choose another α and try again.) The resulting parameter set (p, q, g) is suitable for use in the Diffie-Hellman protocol.

Every time Alice (or Bob) receives a value that is supposed to be a power of g, she (or he) must check that the value received is indeed in the subgroup generated by g. When you use a safe prime as described above, you can use the Legendre symbol function to check for proper subgroup membership. There is also a simpler but slower method. A number r is a square if and only if $r^q = 1 \pmod p$. You also want to forbid the value 1, as its use always leads to problems. So the full test is: $r \neq 1 \wedge r^q \bmod p = 1$.

12.6   Using a Smaller Subgroup

The disadvantage of using the safe prime approach is that it is inefficient. If the prime p is n bits long, then q is $n-1$ bits long and so all exponents are $n-1$ bits long. The average exponentiation will take about $3n/2$ multiplications of numbers modulo p. For large primes p, this is quite a lot of work.

The standard solution is to use a smaller subgroup. Here is how that is done. We start by choosing q as a 256-bit prime. (In other words: $2^{255} < q < 2^{256}$). Next we find a (much) larger prime p such that $p = Nq+1$ for some arbitrary value N. To do this, we choose N randomly in the suitable range, compute p as $Nq + 1$, and check whether p is prime. As p must be odd, it is easy to see that N must be even. The prime p will be thousands of bits long.

Next we have to find an element of order q. We do that in a similar fashion to the safe prime case. Choose a random α in $\mathbb{Z}_p^*$ and set $g := \alpha^N$. Now verify that $g \neq 1$ and $g^q = 1$. (The case $g = p - 1$ is covered by the second test, as q is odd.) If g is not satisfactory, choose a different α and try again. The resulting parameter set (p, q, g) is suitable for use in the Diffie-Hellman protocol.

When we use this smaller subgroup, the values that Alice and Bob will exchange are all in the subgroup generated by g. But Eve could interfere and substitute a completely different value. Therefore, every time Alice or Bob receives a value that is supposed to be in the subgroup generated by g, they should check that it actually is. This check is the same as in the safe prime case. A number r is in the proper subgroup if $r \neq 1 \wedge r^q \bmod p = 1$.

Of course, they should also check that r is not outside the set of modulo-p numbers, so the full check becomes $1 < r < p \wedge r^q = 1$.

For all numbers r in the subgroup generated by g we have that $r^q = 1$. So if you ever need to raise number r to a power e, you only have to compute $r^{e \bmod q}$, which can be considerably less work if e is much larger than q.

How much more efficient is the subgroup case? The large prime p is at least 2000 bits long. In the safe-prime situation, computing a general g^x takes about 3000 multiplications. In our subgroup case, g^x takes about 384 multiplies because x can be reduced modulo q and is therefore only 256 bits long. This is a savings of a factor of nearly eight. When p grows larger, the savings increase further. This is the reason that subgroups are widely used.

12.7   The Size of p

Choosing the right sizes for the parameters of a DH system is difficult. Up to now, we have been using the requirement that an attacker has to spend 2^{128} steps to attack the system. That was an easy target for all the symmetric key primitives. Public-key operations like the DH system are far more expensive to start with, and the computational cost grows much more quickly with the desired security level.

If we keep to our requirement of forcing the attacker to use 2^{128} steps to attack the system, the prime p should be about 6800 bits long. In practical systems today that will be a real problem from a performance point of view.

There is a big difference between key sizes for symmetric primitives and key sizes for public-key primitives like DH. Never, ever fall into the trap of comparing a symmetric key size (such as 128 or 256 bits) to the size of a public key that can be thousands of bits. The public-key sizes are always much larger than the symmetric key sizes.[1]

The public-key operations are far slower than encryption and authentication functions we presented earlier. In most systems, the symmetric-key operations are insignificant, whereas the public-key operations can have a real

---

[1]This holds for the public-key schemes we discuss in this book. Other public-key schemes, such as those based on elliptic curves, can have completely different key size parameters.

effect on performance. We must therefore look much more closely at the performance aspects of public-key operations.

Symmetric key sizes are typically fixed in a system. Once you design your system to use a particular block cipher and hash function, you also fix the key size. That means that the symmetric key size is fixed for the life of the system. Public-key sizes, on the other hand, are almost always variable. This makes it much easier to change the key size. We set out to design a system that will be used for 30 years, and the data must be kept secure for 20 years after it was first processed. The symmetric key size must be chosen large enough to protect the data up to 50 years from now. But the variable-sized public keys only have to protect the data for the next 20 years. After all, all keys have a limited lifetime. A public key might be valid for one year, and should protect data for 20 more years. This means that the public key only needs to protect data 21 years, rather than the 50 years needed for symmetric keys. Each year you generate a new public key, and you can choose larger public keys as progress in computing technology requires.

The best estimates of how large your prime p needs to be can be found in [63]. A prime of 2048 bits can be expected to secure data until around 2022; 3072 bits is secure until 2038; and 4096 bits until 2050. The 6800 bits we mentioned above are derived from the same formulas used in [63]. That is the size of p if you want to force the attacker to perform 2^{128} steps in an attack.

Be very careful with these types of predictions. There is some reasonable basis for these numbers, but predicting the future is always dangerous. We might be able to make some sensible predictions about key sizes for the next 10 years, but making predictions about what things will be like 50 years from now is really rather silly. Just compare the current state of the art in computers and cryptography with the situation 50 years ago. The predictions in [63] are by far the best estimates we have, but don't put too much faith in them.

So what are we to do? As cryptographic designers, we have to choose a key size which will be secure for at least the next 20 years. Obviously 2048 bits is a lower bound. Larger is better, but larger keys have a significant extra cost. In the face of so much uncertainty, we would like to be conservative. So here is our advice: use 2048 bits as an absolute minimum. (And don't forget that as time passes this minimum will grow.) If at all possible from a performance point of view, use 4096 bits, or as close to 4096 bits as you can afford. Furthermore, make absolutely sure that your system can handle sizes up to 8192 bits. This will save the day if there are unexpected developments in attacking public-key systems. Improvements in cryptanalysis will most likely lead to attacks on the smaller key sizes. Switching to a very much larger key size can be done while the system is in the field. It will cost some performance, but the basic operation of the system will be preserved. This is far better than losing all security and having to reengineer the system, which is what you would have to do if the system cannot use larger keys.

Some applications require data to be kept secret for much longer than 20 years. In these cases you need to use the larger keys now.

12.8   Practical Rules

Here are our practical rules for setting up a subgroup that you can use for the DH protocol.

Choose q as a 256-bit prime. (There are collision-style attacks on the exponent in DH, so all our exponents should be 256 bits long to force the attacker to use at least 2^{128} operations.) Choose p as a large prime of the form $Nq + 1$ for some integer N. (See section 12.7 for a discussion of how large p should be. Computing the corresponding range for N is trivial.) Choose a random g such that $g \neq 1$ and $g^q = 1$. (The easy way to do this is to choose a random α, set $g = \alpha^N$, and check g for suitability. Try another α if g fails the criteria.)

Any party receiving the subgroup description (p, q, g) should verify that:

- Both p and q are prime, q is 256 bits long, and p is sufficiently large. (Don't trust keys that are too small.)

- q is a divisor of $(p - 1)$.

- $g \neq 1$ and $g^q = 1$.

Alice
known: (p, q, g)

check (p, q, g) parameters

$x \in_{\mathcal{R}} \{\, 1, \ldots, q - 1 \,\}$

$$\xrightarrow{\quad X := g^x \quad}$$

Bob
known: (p, q, g)

check (p, q, g) parameters

$1 \overset{?}{<} X \overset{?}{<} p,\ X^q \overset{?}{=} 1$

$y \in_{\mathcal{R}} \{\, 1, \ldots, q - 1 \,\}$

$$\xleftarrow{\quad Y := g^y \quad}$$

$1 \overset{?}{<} Y \overset{?}{<} p,\ Y^q \overset{?}{=} 1$

$k \leftarrow (Y)^x$

$k \leftarrow (X)^y$

Figure 12.3: Diffie-Hellman in a subgroup.

This should be done even if the description is provided by a trusted source. You would be amazed at how often systems fail in some interesting way, especially when they are under attack. Checking a set (p, q, g) takes a little time, but in most systems the same subgroup is used for a long time, so these checks need only be performed once.

Any time a party receives a number r that is supposed to be in the subgroup, it should be verified that $1 < r < p$ and $r^q = 1$. Note that $r = 1$ is *not* allowed.

Using these rules, we get the version of the Diffie-Hellman protocol shown in figure 12.3. Both parties start by checking the group parameters. Each of them only has to do this once at start-up, not every time they run a DH protocol. (They should do it after every reboot or reinitialization, however, because the parameters could have changed.)

The rest of the protocol is very much the same as the original DH protocol in figure 12.1. Alice and Bob now use the subgroup, so the two exponents x and y are in the range $1, \ldots, q - 1$. Both Alice and Bob check that the number they receive is in the proper subgroup to avoid any small-subgroup attacks by Eve.

The notation that we use for the checks is a relational operator (such as $=$ or $<$) with a question mark above it. This means that Alice (or Bob) should check that the relation holds. If it does, then everything is all right. If the relation is not correct, then Alice has to assume that she is under attack. The standard behavior is to stop the execution of the protocol, not send any other messages, and destroy all protocol-specific data. For example, in this protocol Alice should destroy x and Y if the last set of checks fails. See section 14.5.5 for a detailed discussion of how to handle these failures.

This protocol describes a secure variant of DH, but it should not be used in exactly this form. The result k has to be hashed before it is used by the rest of the system. See section 15.6 for a more detailed discussion.

12.9 What Could Go Wrong

Very few books or articles talk about the importance of checking that the numbers you receive are in the correct subgroup. Niels first found this problem in the Internet Key Exchange (IKE) protocol of IPsec [41]. Some of the IKE protocols include a DH exchange. As IKE has to operate in the real world, it has to deal with lost messages. So IKE specifies that if Bob receives no answer, he should resend his last message. IKE does not specify how Alice should process the message that Bob sent again. And it is easy for Alice to make a serious mistake.

For simplicity, let us suppose Alice and Bob use the DH protocol in the subgroup illustrated in figure 12.3 without checking that X and Y are proper values. Furthermore, after this exchange Alice starts using the new key k to send an encrypted and authenticated message to Bob which contains some further protocol data. (This is a very usual situation, and similar situations can occur in IKE.)

Here is the dangerous behavior by Alice: when she receives a resend of the second message containing Y, she simply recomputes the key k and sends the appropriate reply to Bob. Sounds entirely harmless, right? But the attacker Eve can now start to play games. Let d be a small divisor of $(p - 1)$. Eve can replace Y by an element of order d. Alice's key k is now limited to d possible values, and is completely determined by Y and $(x \bmod d)$. Eve tries all possible values for $(x \bmod d)$, computes the key k that Alice would have gotten, and tries to decrypt the next message that Alice sends. If Eve guesses $(x \bmod d)$ correctly, this message will decrypt properly, and Eve has learned $(x \bmod d)$.

But what if $p - 1$ contains a number of small factors $(d_1, d_2, \ldots, d_k)$? Then Eve can run this attack repeatedly for each of these factors and learn $(x \bmod d_1), \ldots, (x \bmod d_k)$. Using the general form of the Chinese Remainder Theorem (see section 13.2) she can combine this knowledge to $(x \bmod d_1 d_2 d_3 \cdots d_k)$. So if the product of all small divisors of $p - 1$ is large, Eve can get a significant amount of information about x. As x is supposed to be secret, this is always a bad development. In this particular case, Eve can finish by forwarding the original Y to Alice and letting Alice and Bob complete the protocol. But Eve has collected enough information about x that she can now find the key k that Alice and Bob use.

To be quite clear: this is not an attack on IKE. It is an attack on an implementation of IKE that is allowed by the standard. Still, in our opinion the protocol should include enough information for a competent programmer to create a secure implementation. Leaving this type of information out is dangerous, as somebody somewhere will implement it the wrong way.

Eve has to be lucky that $p - 1$ has enough small divisors. We are designing against an adversary that can perform 2^{128} steps of computing. This allows Eve to take advantage of all divisors of $p - 1$ up to about 2^{128} or so. We've never seen a good analysis of the probabilities of how much information Eve could get, but a quick estimate indicates that on average Eve will be able to get about 128 bits of information about x from the factors smaller than 2^{128}. She can then attack the unknown part of x using a collision-style attack, and as x is only 256 bits long, this leads to a real attack. At least, it would if we didn't check that X and Y were in the proper subgroup.

The attack becomes even easier if Eve was the person selecting the subgroup (p, q, g). She may have put the small divisors into $p - 1$ herself when she selected p in the first place. Or maybe she sat on the committee that recommended certain parameters for a standard. This isn't as crazy as it seems. The U.S. government, in the form of NIST, helpfully provides primes that can be used with DSA, a signature scheme that uses subgroups like this. Other parts of that same U.S. government (e.g., NSA, CIA, FBI) have a vested interest in being able to break into private communications. We certainly don't want to imply that these primes are bad, but it is something that you would want to check before you use them. This is easy to do; in fact, NIST published an algorithm for choosing parameters that does not insert additional small factors, and you can check whether the algorithm was indeed followed. But few people ever do.

In the end, the simplest solution is to check that every value you receive is in the proper subgroup. All other ways of stopping small subgroup attacks are much more complicated. You could try to detect the small factors of $p - 1$ directly, but that is way too complicated. You could require the person who generated the parameter set to provide the factorization of $p - 1$, but that adds lots of complexity to the whole system. Verifying that the received values are in the right subgroup is a bit of work, but it is by far the simplest and most robust solution.

Chapter 13

RSA

The RSA system is probably the most widely used public-key cryptosystem in the world. It is certainly the best known. It provides both digital signatures and public-key encryption, which makes it a very versatile tool, and it is based on the difficulty of factoring large numbers, a problem that has fascinated many people over the last few millennia and has been studied extensively.

13.1   Introduction

RSA is similar to, yet very different from, Diffie-Hellman (see chapter 12). Diffie-Hellman (or DH for short) is based on a one-way function: assuming p and g are publicly known, you can compute $(g^x \pmod p)$ from x, but you cannot compute x given $g^x \bmod p$. RSA is based on a trapdoor one-way function. Given the publicly known information n and e, it is easy to compute $m^e \pmod n$ from m, but not the other way around. However, if you know the factorization of n, then it is easy to do the inverse computation. The factorization of n is the trapdoor information. If you know it, you can invert the function; if you do not know it, you cannot invert the function. This trapdoor functionality allows RSA to be used both for encryption and digital signatures. RSA was invented by Ronald Rivest, Adi Shamir, and Leonard Adleman, and first published in 1978 [81].

Throughout this chapter we will use the values p, q, and n. The values p and q are different large primes, each on the order of a thousand bits long or more. The value n is defined by $n := pq$. (An ordinary product, that is, not modulo something.)

13.2   The Chinese Remainder Theorem

Instead of doing computations modulo a prime p as in the DH system, we will be doing computations modulo the composite number n. To explain what is going on, we will need a little more number theory about computations modulo n. A very useful tool is the *Chinese Remainder Theorem*, or CRT. It is named so because the basic version was first stated by the first-century Chinese mathematician Sun Tsu. (Most of the math you need for DH and RSA dates back thousands of years, so it can't be too difficult, right?)

The numbers modulo n are $0, 1, \ldots, n-1$. These numbers do not form a finite field as they would if n were a prime. Mathematicians still write $\mathbb{Z}_n$ for these numbers and call this a ring, but that is a term that we won't need. For each x in $\mathbb{Z}_n$, we can compute the pair $(x \bmod p, x \bmod q)$. The Chinese Remainder Theorem states that you can compute the inverse function: if you know $(x \bmod p, x \bmod q)$ you can reconstruct x.

For ease of notation we will define $(a, b) := (x \bmod p, x \bmod q)$.

First we show that reconstruction is possible at all, and then we'll give an algorithm to compute the original x. To be able to compute x given (a, b), we must be sure there is not a second number x' in $\mathbb{Z}_n$ such that $x' \bmod p = a$ and $x' \bmod p = b$. If this were the case, then both x' and x would result in the same (a, b) pair, and no algorithm could figure out which of these two numbers was the original input.

Let $d := x - x'$, the difference between the numbers that lead to the same (a, b) pair. We have $(d \bmod p) = (x - x') \bmod p = (x \bmod p) - (x' \bmod p) = a - a = 0$; thus d is a multiple of p. For much the same reason, d is a multiple of q. This implies that d is a multiple of $\mathrm{lcm}(p, q)$ because lcm is, after all, the *least* common multiple. As p and q are different primes, $\mathrm{lcm}(p, q) = pq = n$, and thus $x - x'$ is a multiple of n. But both x and x' are in the range $0, \ldots, n-1$, so $x - x'$ must be a multiple of n in the range

$-n + 1, \ldots, n - 1$. The only valid solution is $x - x' = 0$, or $x = x'$. This proves that for any given pair (a, b), there is at most one solution for x. All we have to do now is find that solution.

13.2.1 Garner's Formula

The most practical way of computing the solution is *Garner's formula*.

$$x = (((a - b)(q^{-1} \bmod p)) \bmod p) \cdot q + b$$

Here the $(q^{-1} \bmod p)$ term is a constant that depends only on p and q. Remember that we can divide modulo p, and therefore we can compute $(1/q \bmod p)$, which is just a different way of writing $(q^{-1} \bmod p)$.

We don't need to understand Garner's formula. All we need to do is prove that the result x is correct.

First of all, we show that x is in the right range $0, \ldots, n - 1$. Obviously $x \geq 0$. The part $t := (((a - b)(q^{-1} \bmod p)) \bmod p)$ must be in the range $0, \ldots, p - 1$ because it is a modulo p result. If $t \leq p - 1$, then $tq \leq (p - 1)q$ and $x = tq + b \leq (p - 1)q + (q - 1) = pq - 1 = n - 1$. This shows that x is in the range $0, \ldots, n - 1$.

The result should also be correct modulo both p and q.

$$
\begin{aligned}
x \bmod q &= ((((a - b)(q^{-1} \bmod p)) \bmod p) \cdot q + b) \bmod q \\
&= (K \cdot q + b) \bmod q \qquad\qquad\qquad \text{for some } K \\
&= b \bmod q \\
&= b
\end{aligned}
$$

The whole thing in front of the multiplication by q is some integer K, but any multiple of q is irrelevant when computing modulo q. Modulo p is a bit more complicated:

$$
\begin{aligned}
x \bmod p &= ((((a - b)(q^{-1} \bmod p)) \bmod p) \cdot q + b) \bmod p \\
&= (((a - b)q^{-1}) \cdot q + b) \bmod p \\
&= ((a - b)(q^{-1}q) + b) \bmod p \\
&= ((a - b) + b) \bmod p \\
&= a \bmod p \\
&= a
\end{aligned}
$$

In the first line we simply expand $(x \bmod p)$. In the next line we eliminate a couple of redundant $\bmod\, p$ operators. We then change the order of the multiplications, which does not change the result. (You might remember from school that multiplication is associative, so $(ab)c = a(bc)$.) The next step is to observe that $q^{-1}q = 1 \pmod p$, so we can remove this term altogether. The rest is trivial.

This derivation is a bit more complicated than the ones we have seen so far, especially as we use more of the algebraic properties. Don't worry if you can't follow it.

We can conclude that Garner's formula gives a result x that is in the right range and for which $(a, b) = (x \bmod p, x \bmod q)$. As we already know that there can only be one such solution, Garner's formula solves the CRT problem completely.

In real systems, you typically precompute the value $q^{-1} \bmod p$, so Garner's formula requires one subtraction modulo p, one multiplication modulo p, one full multiplication, and an addition.

13.2.2   Generalizations

The CRT also works when n is the product of multiple primes that are all different.[1] Garner's formula can be generalized to these situations, but we won't need that in this book.

---

[1] There are versions that work when n is divisible by the square or higher power of some primes, but those are even more complicated.

13.2.3   Uses

So what is the CRT good for? If you ever have to do a lot of computations modulo n, then using the CRT saves a lot of time. For a number $0 \leq x < n$, we call the pair $(x \bmod p, x \bmod q)$ the CRT representation of x. If we have x and y in CRT representation, then the CRT representation of $x + y$ is $((x + y) \bmod p, (x + y) \bmod q)$ which is easy to compute from the CRT representations of x and y. The first component $(x + y) \bmod p$ can be computed as $((x \bmod p) + (y \bmod p) \bmod p)$. This is just the sum (modulo p) of the first half of each of the CRT representations. The second component of the result can be computed in a similar manner.

You can compute a multiplication in much the same way. The CRT representation of xy is $(xy \bmod p, xy \bmod q)$, which is easy to compute from the CRT representations. The first part $(xy \bmod p)$ is computed by multiplying $(x \bmod p)$ and $(y \bmod p)$ and taking the result modulo p again. The second part is computed in the same manner modulo q.

Let k be the number of bits of n. Each of the primes p and q is about $k/2$ bits long. One addition modulo n would require one k-bit addition, perhaps followed by a k-bit subtraction if the result exceeded n. In the CRT representation you have to do two modulo additions on numbers half the size. This is approximately the same amount of work.

For multiplication, the CRT saves a lot of time. Multiplying two k-bit numbers requires far more work than twice multiplying two $k/2$-bit numbers. For most implementations, CRT multiplication is twice as fast as a full multiplication. That is a significant savings.

For exponentiations, the CRT saves even more. Suppose you have to compute $x^s \bmod n$. The exponent s can be up to k bits long. This requires about $3k/2$ multiplications modulo n. Using the CRT representation, each multiplication is less work, but there is also a second savings. We want to compute $(x^s \bmod p, x^s \bmod q)$. When computing modulo p, we can reduce the exponent s modulo $(p - 1)$, and similarly modulo q. So we only have to compute $(x^{s \bmod (p-1)} \bmod p, x^{s \bmod (q-1)} \bmod q)$. Each of the exponents is only $k/2$ bits long and requires only $3k/4$ multiplications. Instead of $3k/2$ multiplications modulo n, we now do $2 \cdot 3k/4 = 3k/2$ multiplications modulo one of the primes. This saves a factor of 3–4 in computing time in a typical implementation.

The only costs of using the CRT are the additional software complexity and the necessary conversions. If you do more than a few multiplications in one computation, the overhead of these conversions is worthwhile. Most textbooks only talk about the CRT as an implementation technique for RSA. We find that the CRT representation makes it much easier to understand the RSA system. This is why we explained the CRT first. We'll soon use it to explain the behavior of the RSA system.

13.2.4   Conclusion

In conclusion: a number x modulo n can be represented as a pair (x mod p, x mod q) when $n = pq$. Conversion between the two representations is fairly straightforward. The CRT representation is useful if you have to do many multiplies modulo a composite number that you know the factorization of. (You cannot use it to speed up your computations if you don't know the factorization of n.)

13.3   Multiplication Modulo n

Before we delve into the details of RSA, we must look at how numbers modulo n behave under multiplication. This is somewhat different from the modulo p case we discussed before.

For any prime p, we know that for all $0 < x < p$ the equation $x^{p-1} = 1$ (mod p) holds. This is not true modulo a composite number n. For RSA to work, we need to find an exponent t such that $x^t = 1$ mod n for (almost) all x. Most textbooks just give the answer, which does not help the reader understand why the answer is true. It is actually relatively easy to find the correct answer by using the CRT.

We want a t such that, for almost all x, $x^t = 1$ (mod n). This last equation implies that $x^t = 1$ (mod p) and $x^t = 1$ (mod q). As both p and q are prime, this only holds if $p - 1$ is a divisor of t, and $q - 1$ is a divisor of t. The smallest t that has this property is therefore $\text{lcm}(p - 1, q - 1) =$

$(p-1)(q-1)/\gcd(p-1, q-1)$. For the rest of this chapter we will use the convention that $t = \text{lcm}(p-1, q-1)$.

The letters p, q, and n are used by everybody, although some use capital letters. Most books don't use our t, but instead use the Euler totient function $\phi(n)$. For an n of the form $n = pq$, the Euler totient function can be computed as $\phi(n) = (p-1)(q-1)$, which is a multiple of our t. It is certainly true that $x^{\phi(n)} = 1$, and that using $\phi(n)$ instead of t gives correct answers, but using t is more precise.

We've skipped over one small issue in our discussion: $x^t \bmod p$ cannot be equal to 1 if $x \bmod p = 0$. So the equation $x^t \bmod n = 1$ cannot hold for *all* values x. There are not many numbers that suffer from this deficiency; there are q numbers with $x \bmod p = 0$ and p numbers with $x \bmod q = 0$, so the total number of values that have this problem is $p+q$. Or $p+q-1$ to be more precise, because we counted the value 0 twice. This is an insignificant fraction of the total number of values $n = pq$. Even better, the actual property used by RSA is that $x^{t+1} = x \pmod{n}$, and this still holds even for these special numbers. Again, this is easy to see when using the CRT representation. If $x = 0 \pmod{p}$, then $x^{t+1} = 0 = x \pmod{p}$, and similarly modulo q. The fundamental property $x^{t+1} = x \pmod{n}$ is preserved, and holds for all numbers in $\mathbb{Z}_n$.

13.4 RSA Defined

We can now define the RSA system. Start by randomly choosing two different large primes p and q, and compute $n = pq$. The primes p and q should be of (almost) equal size, and the modulus n ends up being twice as long as p and q are.

We use two different exponents, traditionally called e and d. The requirement for e and d is that $ed = 1 \pmod{t}$ where $t := \text{lcm}(p-1, q-1)$ as before. We choose the public exponent e to be some small odd value and use the EXTENDEDGCD function from section 11.3.5 to compute d as the inverse of e modulo t. This ensures that $ed = 1 \pmod{t}$.

To encrypt a message m, the sender computes the ciphertext $c := m^e$ $\pmod{n}$. To decrypt a ciphertext c, the receiver computes $c^d \pmod{n}$.

This is equal to $(m^e)^d = m^{ed} = m^{kt+1} = (m^t)^k \cdot m = (1)^k \cdot m = m \pmod{n}$, where k is some value that exists. So the receiver can decrypt the ciphertext m^e to get the plaintext m.

The pair (n, e) forms the public key. These are typically distributed to many different parties. The values (p, q, t, d) are the private key and are kept secret by the person who generated the RSA key.

For convenience we often write $c^{1/e} \bmod n$ instead of $c^d \bmod n$. The exponents of a modulo n computation are all taken modulo t, because $x^t = 1 \pmod{n}$, so multiples of t in the exponent do not affect the result. And we computed d as the inverse of e modulo t, so writing d as $1/e$ is natural. The notation $c^{1/e}$ is often easier to follow, especially when multiple RSA keys are in use. That is why we also talk about taking the e'th root of a number. Just remember that computations of any roots modulo n require knowledge of the private key.

13.4.1   Digital Signatures with RSA

So far we've only talked about encrypting messages with RSA. One of the great advantages of RSA is that it can be used for both encrypting messages and signing messages. These two operations use the same computations. To sign a message m, the owner of the private key computes $s := m^{1/e} \bmod n$. The pair (m, s) is now a signed message. To verify the signature, anyone who knows the public key can verify that $s^e = m \pmod{n}$.

As with encryption, the security of the signature is based on the fact that the e'th root on m can only be computed by someone who knows the private key.

13.4.2   Public Exponents

The procedure described so far has one problem. If e has a common factor with $t = \text{lcm}(p-1, q-1)$, there is no solution for d. So we have to choose p, q, and e such that this situation does not occur. This is more of a nuisance than a problem, but it has to be dealt with.

Choosing a short public exponent makes RSA more efficient, as fewer computations are needed to raise a number to the power e. We therefore try to choose a small value for e. In this book we will choose a fixed value for e, and choose p and q to satisfy the conditions above.

You have to be careful that the encryption functions and digital signature functions don't interact in undesirable ways. You don't want it to be possible for an attacker to decrypt a message c by convincing the owner of the private key to sign c. After all, signing the "message" c is the same operation as decrypting the ciphertext c. The encoding functions presented later in this book will prevent this, but we still don't want to use the same RSA operation for both functions. We could use different RSA keys for encryption and authentication, but that would increase complexity and double the amount of key material.

Our solution is to use two different public exponents on the same n. We will use $e = 3$ for signatures and $e = 5$ for encryption. This decouples the systems because cube roots and fifth roots modulo n are independent of each other. Knowing one does not help the attacker to compute the other [29].

Choosing fixed values for e simplifies the system and also gives predictable performance. It does impose a restriction on the primes that you can use, as both $p - 1$ and $q - 1$ cannot be multiples of 3 or 5. It is easy to check for this when you generate the primes in the first place.

The rationale for using 3 and 5 is simple. These are the smallest suitable values.[2] We choose the smaller public exponent for signatures, because signatures are often verified multiple times, whereas any piece of data is only encrypted once. It therefore makes more sense to let the signature verification be the more efficient operation.

Other common values used for e are 17 and 65537. We prefer the smaller values as they are more efficient. There are some minor potential problems with the small public exponents, but we will eliminate them with our encoding functions further on.

It would also be nice to have a small value for d, but we have to disappoint you here. Although it is possible to find a pair (e, d) with a small d, using a

---

[2]You could in principle use $e = 2$, but that would introduce a lot of extra complexities.

small d is insecure [95]. So don't play any games by choosing a convenient value for d.

13.4.3   The Private Key

It is extremely difficult for the attacker to find any of the values of the private key p, q, t, or d if he knows only the public key (n, e). As long as n is large enough, there is no known algorithm that will do this in an acceptable time. The best solution we know of is to factor n into p and q, and then compute t and d from that. This is why you often hear about factoring being so important for cryptography.

We've been talking about the private key consisting of the values p, q, t, and d. It turns out that knowledge of any one of these values is sufficient to compute all the other three. This is quite instructive to see.

We assume that the attacker knows the public key (n, e), as that is typically public information. If he knows p or q, things are easy. Given p he can compute $q = n/p$, and then he can compute t and d just as we did above.

What if the attacker knows (n, e, t)? First of all, $t = (p-1)(q-1)/\gcd(p-1, q-1)$, but as $(p-1)(q-1)$ is very close to n, it is easy to find $\gcd(p-1, q-1)$ as it is the closest integer to n/t. (The value $\gcd(p-1, q-1)$ is never very large because it is very unlikely that two random numbers share a large factor.) This allows the attacker to compute $(p-1)(q-1)$. He can also compute $n - (p-1)(q-1) + 1 = pq - (pq - p - q + 1) + 1 = p + q$. So now he has both $n = pq$ and $s := p + q$. He can now derive the following equations:

$$s = p + q$$
$$s = p + n/p$$
$$ps = p^2 + n$$
$$0 = p^2 - ps + n$$

The last is just a quadratic equation in p that he can solve with high-school math. Of course, once the attacker has p he can compute all the other private key values as well.

Something similar happens if the attacker knows d. In all our systems, e will be very small. As $d < t$, the number $ed - 1$ is only a small factor times

t. The attacker can just guess this factor, compute t, and then try to find p and q as above. If he fails he just tries the other possibilities. (There are faster techniques, but this one is easy to understand.)

In short, knowing any one of the values p, q, t, or d lets the attacker compute all the other ones. It is therefore safe to assume that the owner of the private key has all four values. Implementations only need to store one of these values, but often store several of the values they need to perform the RSA decryption operation. This is implementation dependent, and is not relevant from a cryptographic point of view.

If Alice wants to decrypt or sign a message, she must obviously know d. As knowing d is equivalent to knowing p and q, we can safely assume that she knows the factors of n and can therefore use the CRT representation for her computations. This is nice, because raising a number to the power d is the most expensive operation in RSA, and using the CRT representation saves a factor of 3–4 work.

13.4.4   The Size of n

The modulus n should be the same size as the modulus p that you would use in the DH case. See section 12.7 for the detailed discussion. To reiterate: the absolute minimum size for n is 2048 bits or so if you want to protect your data for 20 years. This minimum slowly increases as computers get faster. If you can afford it in your application, let n be 4096 bits long, or as close to this size as you can get it. Furthermore, make sure that your software supports values of n up to 8192 bits long. You never know what the future will bring, and it can be a lifesaver if you can switch to using larger keys without replacing software or hardware.

The two primes p and q should be of equal size. For a k-bit modulus n you can just generate two random $k/2$-bit primes and multiply them. You might end up with a $k - 1$-bit modulus n, but that doesn't matter much.

13.4.5   Generating RSA Keys

To pull everything together, we present two routines that generate RSA keys with the desired properties. The first one is a modification of the GENER-

ATELARGEPRIME function of section 11.4. The only functional change is that we require that the prime satisfies $p \bmod 3 \neq 1$ and $p \bmod 5 \neq 1$ to ensure that we can use the public exponents 3 and 5. Of course, if you want to use a different fixed value for e, you have to modify this routine accordingly.

function GENERATERSAPRIME
input: k Size of the desired prime, in number of bits.
output: p A random prime in the interval $2^{k-1}, \ldots, 2^k - 1$ subject to
                      $p \bmod 3 \neq 1 \wedge p \bmod 5 \neq 1$.

    Check for a sensible range.
    assert $1024 \leq k \leq 4096$

    Compute maximum number of attempts.
    $r \leftarrow 100k$
    repeat
        $r \leftarrow r - 1$
        assert $r > 0$

        Choose n as a random k-bit number.
        $n \in_{\mathcal{R}} 2^{k-1}, \ldots, 2^k - 1$

        Keep on trying until we find a prime.
    until $n \bmod 3 \neq 1 \wedge n \bmod 5 \neq 1 \wedge$ ISPRIME(n)
    return n

Instead of specifying a full range in which the prime should fall, we only specify the size of the prime. This is a less-flexible definition, but somewhat simpler, and it is sufficient for RSA. The extra requirements are in the loop condition. A clever implementation will not even call ISPRIME(n) if n is not suitable modulo 3 or 5, as ISPRIME can take a significant amount of computations.

So why do we still include the loop counter with the error condition? Surely, now that the range is large enough, we will always find a suitable prime? We'd hope so, but stranger things have happened. We are not worried about getting a range with no primes in it—we're worried about a broken PRNG that always returns the same composite result. This is, unfortunately, a common failure mode of random number generators, and this simple check makes GENERATERSAPRIME safe from misbehaving PRNGs. Another possible failure mode is a broken ISPRIME function that always claims that the number is composite.

The next function generates all the key parameters.

function GENERATERSAKEY
input: k Size of the modulus, in number of bits.
output: p, q Factors of the modulus.
            n Modulus of about k bits.
            d_3 Signing exponent.
            d_5 Decryption exponent.

Check for a sensible range.
assert $2048 \leq k \leq 8192$

Generate the primes.
$p \leftarrow$ GENERATERSAPRIME($\lfloor k/2 \rfloor$)
$q \leftarrow$ GENERATERSAPRIME($\lfloor k/2 \rfloor$)

A little test just in case our PRNG *is bad...*
assert $p \neq q$

Compute t as $\mathrm{lcm}(p-1, q-1)$.
$t \leftarrow (p-1)(q-1)/\mathrm{GCD}(p-1, q-1)$

Compute the secret exponents using the modular inversion feature of the extended GCD algorithm.
$g, (u, v) \leftarrow$ EXTENDEDGCD($t, 3$)

Check that the GCD is correct, or we don't get an inverse at all.
assert $g = 1$

Reduce u modulo t, as u could be negative and d_3 shouldn't be.
$d_3 \leftarrow u \bmod t$

And now for d_5.
$g, (u, v) \leftarrow$ EXTENDEDGCD($t, 5$)
assert $g = 1$
$d_5 \leftarrow u \bmod t$
return p, q, pq, d_3, d_5

Note that we've used the fixed choices for the public exponents, and that we generate a key that can be used both for signing ($e = 3$) and for encryption ($e = 5$).

13.5   Pitfalls Using RSA

Using RSA as presented so far is very dangerous. The problem is the mathematical structure. For example, if Alice digitally signs two messages m_1 and m_2, then Bob can compute Alice's signature on $m_3 := m_1 m_2 \bmod n$. After all, Alice has computed $m_1^{1/e}$ and $m_2^{1/e}$ and Bob can multiply the two results to get $(m_1 m_2)^{1/e}$.

Another problem arises if Bob encrypts a very small message m with Alice's public key. If $e = 5$ and $m < \sqrt[5]{n}$, then $m^e = m^5 < n$, so no modular reduction ever takes place. The attacker Eve can recover m by simply taking the fifth root of m^5, which is easy to do because there are no modulo reductions involved. A typical situation in which this goes wrong is if Bob tries to send an AES key to Alice. If he just takes the 256-bit value as an integer, then the encrypted key is less than $2^{256 \cdot 5} = 2^{1280}$ which is much smaller than our n. There is never a modulo reduction, and Eve can compute the key by simply computing the fifth root of the encrypted key value.

One of the reasons we have explained the theory behind RSA in such detail is to teach you some of the mathematical structure that we encounter. This very same structure invites many types of attack. The simple ones we've mentioned in the previous paragraph. There are far more advanced attacks, based on techniques for solving polynomial equations modulo n. All of them come down to a single thing: it is very bad to have *any* kind of structure in the numbers that RSA operates on.

The solution is to use a function that destroys any available structure. Sometimes this is called a padding function, but this is a misnomer. The word padding is normally used for adding additional bytes to get a result of the right length. People have used various forms of padding for RSA encryption and signatures, and quite a few times this has resulted in attacks on their designs. What you need is a function that removes as much structure as possible. We'll call this the encoding function.

There are standards for this, most notably PKCS #1 v2.1 [85]. As usual, this is not a single standard. There are two RSA encryption schemes and two RSA signature schemes, each of which can take a variety of hash functions. This is not necessarily bad, but we don't like the extra complexity. We'll therefore present some simpler methods, even though they might not have all the features of some of the PKCS methods.

The PKCS #1 v2.1 standard also demonstrates a common problem in technical documentation: it mixes specification with implementation. The RSA decryption function is specified twice; once using the equation $m = c^d \bmod n$ and once using the CRT equations. These two computations have the same result: one is merely an optimized implementation of the other. Such implementation descriptions should not be part of the standard, as they do not produce different behavior. They should be discussed separately. We don't want to criticize this PKCS standard in particular; it is a very widespread problem that you find throughout the computer industry.

13.6   Encryption

Encrypting a message is the canonical application of RSA, yet it is almost never used in practice. The reason is simple: the size of the message that can be encrypted using RSA is limited by the size of n. In real systems you cannot even use all the bits because the encoding function has an overhead. This limited message size is too impractical for most applications, and because the RSA operation is quite expensive in computational terms, you don't want to split a message into smaller blocks and encrypt each of them with a separate RSA operation.

The solution used almost everywhere is to choose a random secret key K, and encrypt K with the RSA keys. The actual message m is then encrypted with key K using a block cipher or stream cipher. So instead of sending something like $E_{\text{RSA}}(m)$ you send $E_{\text{RSA}}(K), E_K(m)$. The size of the message is no longer limited, and only a single RSA operation is required, even for large messages. You have to transmit a little bit of extra data, but this is usually a small price to pay for the advantages you get.

We will use an even simpler method of encryption. Instead of choosing a K and encrypting K, we choose a random $r \in \mathbb{Z}_n$ and define the bulk encryption key as $K := h(r)$ for some hash function h. Encrypting r is done by simply raising it to the fifth power modulo n. (Remember, we use $e = 5$ for encryption.) This solution is simple and secure. As r is chosen randomly, there is no structure in r that can be used to attack the RSA part of the encryption. The hash function in turn ensures that no structure between different r's propagates to structure in the K's, except for the obvious requirement that equal inputs must yield equal outputs.

For simplicity of implementation, we choose our r's in the range $0, \ldots, 2^k - 1$, where k is the largest number such that $2^k < n$. It is easier to generate a random k-bit number than to generate a random number in $\mathbb{Z}_n$, and this small deviation from the uniform distribution is harmless in this situation.

Here is a more formal definition:

function ENCRYPTRANDOMKEYWITHRSA
input: (n, e) RSA public key, in our case $e = 5$.
output: K Symmetric key that was encrypted.
            c RSA ciphertext.

> *Compute k.*
> $k \leftarrow \lfloor \log_2 n \rfloor$
> *Choose a random r such that $0 \le r < 2^k - 1$.*
> $r \in_\mathcal{R} \left\{ 0, \ldots, 2^k - 1 \right\}$
> $K \leftarrow \mathrm{SHA}_d\text{-}256(r)$
> $c \leftarrow r^e \bmod n$
> **return** (K, c)

The receiver computes $K = h(c^{1/e} \bmod n)$ and gets the same key K.

function DECRYPTRANDOMKEYWITHRSA
input: (n, d) RSA private key with $e = 5$.
            c Ciphertext.
output: K Symmetric key that was encrypted.

> **assert** $0 \le c < n$
> *This is trivial.*
> $K \leftarrow \mathrm{SHA}_d\text{-}256(c^{1/e} \bmod n)$
> **return** K

We've just extensively discussed how to compute $c^{1/e}$ given the private key, so we won't discuss that here again. Just don't forget to use the CRT for a factor of 3–4 speed-up.

Here is a good way to look at the security. Let's assume that Bob encrypts a key K for Alice, and Eve wants to know more about this key. Bob's message depends only on some random data and on Alice's public key. So at worst this message could leak data to Eve about K, but it cannot leak any data about any other secret, such as Alice's private key. The key K is computed using a hash function, and we can pretend that the hash function is a random mapping. (If we cannot treat the hash function as a random mapping, it doesn't satisfy our security requirement for hash functions.) The only way to get information about the output of a hash function is to know most of the input. That means having information about r. But if RSA is secure—and we have to assume that since we have chosen to use it—then it is impossible to get any significant amount of information about a randomly chosen r given just $(r^e \bmod n)$. This leaves the attacker with a lot of uncertainty about r, and consequently, no knowledge about K.

Suppose the key K is later revealed to Eve, maybe due to a failure of another component of the system. Does this reveal anything about Alice's private key? No. K is the output of a hash function, and it is impossible for Eve to derive any information about the inputs to the hash function. So even if Eve chose c in some special way, the K she acquires does not reveal anything about r. Alice's private key was only used to compute r, so Eve cannot learn anything about Alice's private key either.

This is one of the advantages of having a hash function in the DECRYPT-RANDOMKEYWITHRSA function. Suppose it just returned $c^{1/e} \bmod n$. This routine can now be used to play all kinds of games. Suppose some other part of the system has a weakness and Eve learns the least significant bit of the output. Eve could now send specially chosen values $c_1, c_2, c_3, \ldots$ to Alice and get the least significant bits of $c_1^{1/e}, c_2^{1/e}, c_3^{1/e}, \ldots$. These answers have all kinds of algebraic properties, and it is quite conceivable that Eve could learn something useful from a situation like this. The hash function h in DECRYPTRANDOMKEYWITHRSA destroys all mathematical structure. Learning one bit from the output K gives Eve almost no information about $c^{1/e}$. Even the full result K divulges very little useful information; the hash function is not invertible. Adding the hash function here makes the RSA routines more secure against failures in the rest of the system.

This is also the reason why DECRYPTRANDOMKEYWITHRSA does *not* check that the r we compute from c falls in the range $0, \ldots, 2^k - 1$. If we checked this condition, we would have to handle the error that could result. As error handling always leads to different behavior, it is quite probable that Eve could detect whether this error occurred. This would provide Eve with a function that reveals information: Eve could choose any value c and learn whether $c^{1/e} \bmod n < 2^k$. Eve cannot compute this property without Alice's help, and we don't want to help Eve if we can avoid it. By not checking the condition, we at most generate a nonsense output, and that is something that can happen in any case, as c might have been corrupted without resulting in an invalid r value.[3]

An aside: there is a big difference between revealing a random pair $(c, c^{1/e})$, and computing $c^{1/e}$ for a c chosen by someone else. Anybody can produce pairs of the form $(c, c^{1/e})$. All you do is choose a random r, compute the pair (r^e, r), and then set $c := r^e$. There is nothing secret about pairs like that. But if Alice is kind enough to compute $c^{1/e}$ for a c she receives from Eve, Eve can choose c values with some special properties; something she couldn't do for the $(c, c^{1/e})$ pairs she generates herself. Don't provide this extra service for your attacker.

13.7   Signatures

For signatures, we have to do a bit more work. The problem is that the message m that we want to sign can have a lot of structure to it, and we do not want any structure in the number we compute the RSA root on. We have to destroy the structure.

The first step is to hash the message. So instead of a variable-length message m, we deal with a fixed-size value $h(m)$ where h is a hash function. If we use $\text{SHA}_d\text{-}256$, we get a 256-bit result. But n is much bigger than that, so we cannot use $h(m)$ directly.

The simple solution is to use a pseudorandom mapping to expand $h(m)$ to a random number s in the range $0, \ldots, n-1$. The signature on m is then computed as $s^{1/e} \pmod{n}$. Mapping $h(m)$ to a modulo n value is a bit

---

[3]Placing more restrictions on r does not stop the problem of nonsensical outputs. Eve can always use Alice's public key and a modified ENCRYPTRANDOMKEYWITHRSA function to send Alice encryptions of nonsensical keys.

of work (see the discussion in section 10.8). In this particular situation, we can safely simplify our problem by mapping $h(m)$ to a random element in the range $0, \ldots, 2^k - 1$, where k is the largest number such that $2^k < n$. Numbers in the range $0, \ldots, 2^k - 1$ are easy to generate because we only need to generate k random bits. In this particular situation this is a safe solution, but don't use it just anywhere. There are many situations in cryptography where this will break your entire system.

We will use the generator from our Fortuna PRNG from chapter 10. Many systems use the hash function h to build a special little random generator for this purpose, but we've already defined a good generator. Besides, you need the PRNG to choose the primes to generate the RSA keys, so you have the PRNG in the software already.

This results in three functions—one to map the message to s, one to sign the message, and one to verify the signature.

function MsgToRSANumber
input: n RSA public key, modulus.
       m Message to be converted to a value modulo n.
output: s A number modulo n.

  Create a new PRNG generator.
  $\mathcal{G} \leftarrow$ InitialiseGenerator()
  Seed it with the hash of the message.
  ReSeed($\mathcal{G}$, SHA$_d$-256(m))

  Compute k.
  $k \leftarrow \lfloor \log_2 n \rfloor$
  $x \leftarrow$ GenerateRandomData($\mathcal{G}$, $\lceil k/8 \rceil$)

  As usual, we treat the byte-string x as an integer using the LSByte first convention. The modulo reduction can be implemented with a simple AND on the last byte of x.
  $s \leftarrow x \bmod 2^k$
  return s

function SignWithRSA
input: (n, d) RSA private key with $e = 3$.
       m Message to be signed.
output: σ Signature on m.

$s \leftarrow \text{MSGToRSANUMBER}(n, m)$
$\sigma \leftarrow s^{1/e} \bmod n$
return σ

The letter σ, or sigma, is often used for signatures because it is the Greek equivalent of our letter s. By now you should now how to compute $s^{1/e} \bmod n$, given the private key.

function VERIFYRSASIGNATURE
input: (n, e) RSA public key with $e = 3$.
                m Message that is supposed to be signed.
                σ Signature on the message.
$s \leftarrow \text{MSGToRSANUMBER}(n, m)$
assert $s = \sigma^e \bmod n$

Of course, in a real application there will be some action to take if the signature verification fails. We've just written an assertion here to indicate that normal operations should not proceed. A signature failure should be taken like any other failure in a cryptographic protocol: as a clear signal that you are under active attack. Don't send any replies unless you absolutely have to, and destroy all the material you are working on. The more information you send out, the more information you give the attacker.

The security arguments for our RSA signatures is similar to that of the RSA encryptions. If you ask Alice to sign a bunch of messages $m_1, m_2, \ldots, m_i$, then you are getting pairs of the form $(s, s^{1/e})$ but the s values are effectively random. As long as the hash function is secure, you can only affect $h(m)$ by trial and error. The random generator is again a random mapping. Anyone can create pairs of the form $(s, s^{1/e})$ for random s values, so this provides no new information that helps the attacker forge a signature. However, for any particular message m, only someone who knows the private key can compute the corresponding $(s, s^{1/e})$ pair, because s must be computed from $h(m)$, and then $s^{1/e}$ must be computed from s. This requires the private key. Therefore, anyone who verifies the signature knows that Alice must have signed it.

This brings us to the end of our treatment of RSA, and to the end of the math-heavy part of this book. We will be using DH and RSA for our key

negotiation protocol and the PKI, but that only uses the math we have
already explained. No new mathematics will be introduced.

Chapter 14

Introduction to Cryptographic Protocols

Cryptographic protocols consist of an exchange of messages between participants. We've already seen a simple cryptographic protocol in chapter 12.

Protocols are probably the most difficult part of cryptography. The main problem is that as a designer or implementer, you are not in control. Up to now we have been designing a system and have had control over the behavior of various parts. Once you start communicating with other parties, you have no control over their behavior. The other party has a different set of interests than you do, and he could deviate from the rules to try to get an advantage. When working on protocols, you must assume that you are dealing with the enemy.

14.1 Roles

Protocols are typically described as being executed by Alice and Bob, or between a customer and a merchant. Names like "Alice," "Bob," "customer," and "merchant" are not really meant to identify a particular individual or organization. They identify a role within the protocol. If Mr. Smith wants to communicate with Mr. Jones, he might run a key agreement protocol. Mr. Smith could take the role of Alice, and Mr. Jones the role of Bob. The

next day the roles might be reversed. It is important to keep in mind that
a single entity can take on any of the roles.[1] This is especially important to
remember when you analyze the protocol for security. We've already seen
the man-in-the-middle attack on the DH protocol. In that attack, Eve takes
on the roles of both Alice and of Bob. (Of course, Eve is just another role,
too.)

14.2   Trust

Trust is the ultimate basis for all dealings that we have with other people.
If you don't trust anybody with anything at all, why bother interacting
with them? For example, buying a candy bar requires a basic level of trust.
The customer has to trust the merchant to provide the candy and give
proper change. The merchant has to trust the customer to pay. Both have
recourse if the other party misbehaves. Shoplifters are prosecuted. Cheating
merchants risk bad publicity, lawsuits, and getting punched in the nose.

There are several sources of trust:

Ethics Ethics has a large influence in our society. Although very few, if any,
people behave ethically all the time, most people behave ethically most
of the time. Attackers are few. Most people pay for their purchases,
even when it would be laughably easy to steal them.

Reputation Having a "good name" is very important in our society. People
and companies want to protect their reputation. Often the threat of
bad publicity gives them an incentive to behave properly.

Law In civilized societies there is a legal infrastructure that supports lawsuits and prosecution of people who misbehave. This gives people an
incentive to behave properly.

Physical Threat Another incentive to behave properly is the fear of harm
if you cheat and are caught. This is one of the sources of trust for drugs
deals and other illegal trades. The threat can be physical violence, or
other actions.

---

[1]In protocols with three or more participants, it is even possible for a single person to
take on more than one role at the same time.

MAD A cold war term: Mutually Assured Destruction. In milder forms, it is the threat to do harm to both yourself and the other party. If you cheat your friend, she might break off the friendship, doing you both harm. Sometimes you see two companies in a MAD situation, especially when they file patent infringement lawsuits against each other.

All of these sources are mechanisms whereby a party has an incentive not to cheat. The other party knows this incentive, and therefore feels he can trust his opponent to some extent. This is why these incentives all fail when you deal with completely irrational people: you can't trust them to act in their own best interest, which undermines all these mechanisms.

It is hard to develop trust over the Internet. Suppose Alice lives abroad and connects to the ACME Web site. ACME has almost no reason to trust Alice; of the mechanisms of trust we mentioned, only ethics remains. Legal recourse against private individuals abroad is almost impossible, and certainly prohibitively expensive. You can't effectively harm their reputation, threaten them, or even threaten them with MAD.

There is still a basis of trust between Alice and ACME, because ACME has a reputation to protect. This is important to remember when you design a protocol for e-commerce. If there are any failure modes (and there always are), the failure should be to ACME's advantage, because ACME has an incentive to settle the matter properly by manual intervention.[2] If the failure is to Alice's advantage, the issue is less likely to be settled properly. Furthermore, ACME will be vulnerable to attackers who try to induce the failure mode and then profit by it.

Trust is not a black-and-white issue. It is not that you either trust someone or you don't trust him. You trust different people to different degrees. You might trust a friend with $100 but not with your lottery ticket that just won a $5,000,000 prize. We trust the bank to keep our money safe, but we get receipts and copies of canceled checks because we don't fully trust their administration. The question "Do you trust him?" in incomplete. It should be "Do you trust him with X?"

---

[2]Almost all telephone, mail, and electronic commerce to individuals follows this rule by having the customer pay for the order before it is shipped.

14.2.1 Risk

Trust is fundamental to business, but it is usually expressed as risk rather than trust. Risk can be seen as the converse of trust. Risks are evaluated, compared, and traded in many forms.

When working on cryptographic protocols it is easier to talk in terms of trust than in terms of risks. But a lack of trust is simply a risk, and that can sometimes be handled by standard risk-management techniques such as insurance. We talk about trust when we design protocols. Always keep in mind that business people think and talk in terms of risks. You'll have to convert between the two perspectives if you want to be able to talk to them.

14.3 Incentive

The incentive structure is another fundamental component of any analysis of a protocol. What are the goals of the different participants? What would they like to achieve? Even in real life, analyzing the incentive structure gives insightful conclusions.

Several times every week we get press reports that announce things like, "New research has shown that ... " Our first reaction is always to ask: who paid for the research? Research whose results are advantageous to the party who paid for it is always suspect. Several factors are at play here. First, the researchers know what their customer wants to hear, and know they can get repeat contracts if they produce "good" results. This introduces a bias. Secondly, the sponsor of the research is not going to publish any negative reports. Publishing only the positive reports introduces another bias. Tobacco companies published "scientific" reports that nicotine was not addictive. Microsoft pays for research that "proves" that open source software is bad in some way. Don't ever trust research that supports the company that paid for it.

The authors are personally quite familiar with these pressures. During our many years as consultants, we performed many security evaluations for paying customers. We were often harsh—the average product we evaluated was quite bad—and we rarely wrote positive evaluations for components. That didn't always make us popular with our customers. One of them even called Bruce and said: "Stop your work and send me your bill. I've found someone who is cheaper and who writes better reports." Guess which meaning of 'better' was intended here? The only reason we could be unbiased was that we had enough work. If work is scarce and you have to put food on the table, the temptation is great to bite your tongue and say whatever your client wants to hear.

We see exactly the same problem in other areas. As we write this book, the press is filled with stories about the accounting and banking industries. Analysts and accountants were writing reports favorable for their clients rather than unbiased evaluations. We blame the incentive structure that gave these people a reason to bias their reports. Looking at the incentives is quite instructive, and something we've both done for years. With a bit of practice it is surprisingly easy, and it yields valuable insights. And yes, it makes you more cynical of people's motives.

If you pay your management in stock options, you give them the following incentive structure: increase the share price over the next three years and make a fortune; decrease the share price, and get a golden handshake. It is a "Heads I win a lot, tails I win a little" incentive, so guess what some managers do? They go for a high-risk short-term strategy. If they get the opportunity to double the amount they gamble they will always take it, because they will only collect the winnings and never pay the loss. If they can inflate the share price for a few years with bookkeeping tricks they will, because they can cash out before they are found out. Some of the gambles fail, but others pay the bills.

A similar thing happened with the savings and loans industry in the United States in the 1980s. The federal government liberalized the rules, allowing S&Ls to invest their money more freely. At the same time, the government guaranteed the deposits. Now look at the incentive structure. If the investments pay off, the S&L makes a profit, and no doubt management gets a nice bonus. If the investments lose money, the federal government pays off the depositors. Not surprisingly, a bunch of S&Ls lost a lot of money on high-risk investments—and the federal government picked up the bill.

Fixing the incentive structure is often relatively easy. For example, instead of the company itself paying for the audit, the stock exchange can arrange and pay for the audit of the books. Give the auditors a significant bonus for every error they find and you'll get a much more accurate report.

Examples of undesirable incentive structures abound. Divorce lawyers have an incentive to make the divorce very acrimonious, as they are paid for every hour spent fighting over the estate. It is a safe bet that they will advise you to settle as soon as the legal fees exceed the value of the estate.

In American society, lawsuits are common. If an accident happens, every participant has a great incentive to hide, deny, or otherwise avoid the blame. Strict liability laws and huge damage awards might seem good for society at first, but it greatly hinders our ability to figure out why the accident happened, and how we can avoid it in future. Liability laws that are supposed to protect consumers make it all but impossible for a company like Firestone to admit that there is a problem with their product so we can all learn how to build better tires.

Cryptographic protocols interact in two ways with incentive structures. First of all, they rely on incentive structures. Some electronic payment protocols do not stop the merchant from cheating the customer, but provide the customer with proof of the cheating. This works because the merchant has an incentive not to have people out there with proofs that they were cheated. The proof could be used either in a court case or just to damage the reputation of the merchant.

Cryptographic protocols also change the incentive structure. They make certain things impossible, removing them from the incentive structure. They can also open up new possibilities and new incentives. Once you have online banking, you create an incentive for a thief to break into your computer and steal your money.

At first, incentives look like they are mostly materialistic, but that is only part of it. Many people have nonmaterialistic motives. Most computer break-ins are not done for any material gain, but just for fun, status, or bragging rights. In personal relationships, the most fundamental incentives have little to do with money. Keep an open mind, and try to understand what drives people. Then create your protocols accordingly.

14.4   Trust in Cryptographic Protocols

The function of cryptographic protocols is to minimize the amount of trust required. Let's repeat that. The function of cryptographic protocols is to minimize the amount of trust required. This means minimizing both the number of people who need to trust each other and the amount of trust they need to have.

One powerful tool for designing cryptographic protocols is the paranoia model. When Alice takes part in a protocol, she assumes that all other participants are conspiring together to cheat her. This is really the ultimate conspiracy theory. Of course, each of the other participants is making the same assumption. This is the default model in which all cryptographic protocols are designed.

Any deviations from this default model must be explicitly documented. It is surprising how often this step is overlooked. We sometimes see protocols used in situations where the required trust is not present. For example, most secure Web sites use the SSL protocol. The SSL protocol requires trusted certificates. Browsers will often accept any certificate, and a certificate is easy to get. The result is that the user is communicating securely with a Web site, but she doesn't know which Web site she is communicating with. Numerous scams against PayPal users have exploited this vulnerability.

It is very tempting not to document the trust that is required for a particular protocol, as it is often "obvious." That might be true to the designer of the protocol, but like any module in the system, the protocol should have a clearly specified interface, for all the usual reasons.

From a business point of view, the documented trust requirements also list the risks. Each point of required trust implies a risk that has to be dealt with.

14.5   Messages and Steps

A typical protocol description consists of a number of messages that are sent between the participants of the protocol and a description of the computations that each participant has to do.

Almost all protocol descriptions are done at a very high level. Most of the details are not described. This allows you to focus on the core functionality of the protocol, but it creates a great danger. Without careful specifications of all the actions that each participant should take, it is extremely difficult to create a safe implementation of the protocol.

Sometimes you see protocols specified with all the minor details and checks. Such specifications are often so complicated that nobody fully understands them. This might help an implementer, but anything that is too complicated cannot be secure.

The solution is, as always, a modularization. With cryptographic protocols, as with communication protocols, we can split the required functionality into several protocol layers. Each layer works on top of the previous layer. All the layers are important, but most of the layers are the same for all protocols. Only the topmost layer is highly variable, and that is the one you always find documented.

14.5.1   The Transport Layer

Network specialists must forgive us for reusing one of their terms here. For us cryptographers, the transport layer is the underlying communication system that allows parties to communicate. This consists of sending strings of bytes from one participant to another. How this is done is irrelevant for our purposes. What we as cryptographers care about is that we can send a string of bytes from one participant to the other. You can use UDP packets, a TCP data stream, e-mail, or any other method. In many cases, the transport layer needs some additional encoding. For example, if a program executes multiple protocols simultaneously, the transport layer must deliver the message to the right protocol execution. This might require an extra destination field of some sort. When using TCP, the length of the message needs to be included to provide message-oriented services over the stream-oriented TCP protocol.

To be quite clear, we expect that the transport layer transmits arbitrary strings of bytes. Any byte value could occur in the message. The length of the string is variable. The string received should of course be identical to the string that was sent; deleting trailing zero bytes, or any other modification, is not allowed.

Some transport layers include things like magic constants to provide an early detection of errors or to check the synchronization of the TCP stream. If the magic constant is not correct on a received message, the rest of the message should be discarded.

There is one important special case. Sometimes we run a cryptographic protocol over a cryptographically secured channel like the one we designed in chapter 8. In cases like that, the transport layer also provides confidentiality, authentication, and replay protection. That makes the protocol much easier to design, because there are far fewer types of attacks to worry about.

14.5.2 Protocol and Message Identity

The next layer up provides protocol and message identifiers. When you receive a message, you want to know which protocol it belongs to and which message within that protocol it is.

The protocol identifier typically contains two parts. The first part is the version information which provides room for future upgrades. The second part identifies which particular cryptographic protocol the message belongs to. In an electronic payment system there might be protocols for withdrawal, payment, deposit, refund, etc. The protocol identifier avoids confusion among messages of different protocols.

The message identifier indicates which of the messages of the protocol in question this is. If there are four messages in a protocol you don't want there to be any confusion about which message is which.

Why do we include so much identifying information? Can't an attacker forge all of this? Of course he can. This layer doesn't provide any protection against active forgery; rather, it detects accidental errors. It is important to have good detection of accidental errors. Suppose you are responsible for maintaining a system, and you suddenly get a large number of error messages. Differentiating between active attacks and accidental errors such as configuration and version problems is a valuable service.

Protocol and message identifiers also make the message more self-contained, which makes much of the maintenance and debugging easier. Cars and airplanes are designed to be easy to maintain. Software is even more complex— all the more reason why it should be designed for ease of maintenance.

Probably the most important reason to include message identifying information has to do with the Horton Principle. When we use authentication (or a digital signature) in a protocol, we typically authenticate several messages and data fields. By including the message identifying information we never run the risk that a message will be interpreted in the wrong context.

14.5.3   Message Encoding and Parsing

The next layer is the encoding layer. Each data element of the message has to be converted to a sequence of bytes. This is a standard programming problem and we won't go into too much detail about that here.

One very important point is the parsing. The receiver must be able to parse the message, which looks like a sequence of bytes, back into its constituent fields. This parsing must not depend on contextual information.

A fixed-length field that is the same in all versions of the protocol is easy to parse. You know exactly how long it is. The problems begin when the size or meaning of a field depends on some context information, such as earlier messages in the protocol. This is an invitation to trouble.

Many messages in cryptographic protocols end up being signed or otherwise authenticated. The authentication function authenticates a string of bytes, and usually it is the simplest solution to authenticate the message at the level of the transport layer. If the interpretation of a message depends on some contextual information, the signature or authentication is ambiguous. We've broken several protocols due to this type of failure.

A good way to encode fields is to use Tag-Length-Value or TLV encoding. Each field is encoded as three data elements. The tag identifies the field in question. The length is the length of the value encoding, and the value is the actual data to be encoded. The best-known TLV encoding is ASN.1 [43], but it is so incredibly complex and badly specified that we shy away from it. A subset of ASN.1 could be very useful.

A newer alternative is XML. Forget the XML hype; we're only using XML as a data encoding system. As long as you use a fixed Document Template Definition (DTD), the parsing is not context-dependent, and you won't have any problems.

14.5.4   Protocol Execution States

In many implementations, it is possible for a single computer to take part in several protocol executions at the same time. To keep track of all the protocols requires some form of protocol execution state. The state contains all the information necessary to complete the protocol.

Implementing protocols requires some kind of event-driven programming, as the execution has to wait for external messages to arrive before it can proceed. This can be implemented in various ways, such as using one thread or process per protocol execution, or using some kind of event dispatch system.

Given an infrastructure for event-driven programming, implementing a protocol is relatively straightforward. The protocol state contains a state machine that indicates the type of message expected next. As a general rule, no other type of message is acceptable. If the expected type of message arrives, then it is parsed and processed according to the rules.

14.5.5   Errors

Protocols always contain a multitude of checks. These include verifying the protocol type and message type, checking that it is the expected type of message for the protocol execution state, parsing the message, and performing the cryptographic verifications specified. If any of these checks fail, we have encountered an error.

Errors need very careful handling, as they are a potential avenue of attack. The safest procedure is not to send any reply to an error and immediately delete the protocol state. This minimizes the amount of information the attacker can get about the protocol. Unfortunately, it makes for an unfriendly system, as there is no indication of the error.

To make systems usable, you often need to add error messages of some sort. If you can get away with it, don't send an error message to the other parties in the protocol. Log an error message on a secure log so that the system administrator can diagnose the problem. If you *must* send an error message, make it as uninformative as possible. A simple "There was an error" message is often sufficient.

One dangerous interaction is between errors and timing attacks. The attacker Eve can send a bogus message to Alice and wait for her error reply. The time it takes Alice to detect the error and send the reply often contains detailed information about what was wrong and exactly where it went wrong.

Here is a good illustration of the dangers of these interactions. Years ago, Niels worked with a commercially available smart card system. One of the features was a PIN code that was needed to enable the card. The four-digit PIN code was sent to the card, and the card responded with a message indicating whether the card was now enabled or not. Had this been implemented well, it would have taken 10,000 tries to exhaust all the possible PIN codes. The smart card allowed five failed PIN attempts before it locked up, after which it would require special unlocking by other means. The idea was that an attacker who didn't know the PIN code could make five attempts to guess the four-digit PIN code, which gave her a 1 in 2000 probability of guessing the PIN code before the card locked up.

The design was good, and similar designs are widely used today. A 1 in 2000 chance is good enough for many applications. But unfortunately the programmer of that particular smart card system was a bit careless. To verify the four-digit PIN code, the program first checked the first digit, then the second, etc. The card reported the PIN code failure as soon as it detected that one of the digits was wrong. The weakness was that the time it took the smart card to send the "wrong PIN" error depended on how many of the digits of the PIN were correct. A smart attacker could measure this time and learn a lot of information. In particular, the attacker could find out at which position the first wrong digit was. Armed with that knowledge, it would take the attacker only 40 attempts to exhaustively search the PIN space. (After 10 attempts the first digit would have to be right, after another 10 attempts the second, etc.) After five tries her chances of finding the correct PIN code rose to 1 in 143. That is much better than the 1 in 2000 chance she should have had. If she got 20 tries, her chances rose to 60%, which is a lot more than the 0.2% she should have had.

Even worse, there are certain situations where having 20 or 40 tries is not infeasible. Smart cards that lock up after a number of failed PIN tries always reset the counter once the correct PIN has been used, so that the user gets another five tries to type the correct PIN the next time. Suppose your roommate has a smart card like the one described above. If you can get at your roommate's smart card, you can run one or two tries before putting the smart card back. Wait for him to use the card for real somewhere, using the correct PIN and resetting the failed-PIN attempt counter in the smart card. Now you can do one or two more tries. Soon you'll have the whole PIN code because it takes at most 40 tries to find it.

Error handling is too complex to give you a simple set of rules. This is something we as a community do not know enough about yet. At the moment, the best we can say is: be very careful.

14.5.6   Replay and Retries

A replay attack occurs when the attacker records a message and then later sends that same message again. Message replays have to be protected against. They can be a bit tricky to detect, as the message looks exactly like a proper one. After all, it *is* a proper one.

Closely related to the replay attack is the retry. Suppose Alice is performing a protocol with Bob, and she doesn't get a response. There could be many reasons for this, but one common one is that Bob didn't receive Alice's last message and is still waiting for it. This happens in real life all the time, and we solve this by sending another letter or e-mail, or repeating our last remark. In automated systems this is called a retry. Alice retries her last message to Bob and again waits for a reply.

So, Bob can receive replays of messages sent by the attacker and retries sent by Alice. Somehow Bob has to deal properly with them and ensure correct behavior without introducing a security weakness.

Sending retries is relatively simple. Each participant has a protocol execution state of some form. All you need to do is keep a timer and send the last message again if you do not receive an answer within a reasonable time. The exact time limit depends on the underlying communication infrastructure. If you use UDP packets (a protocol that uses IP packets directly), there is a reasonable probability that the message will get lost, and you want a short retry time, on the order of a few seconds. If you send your messages over TCP, then TCP retries any data that was not received properly using its own time-outs. There is little reason to do a retry at the cryptographic protocol level, and most systems that use TCP do not do this. Nevertheless, for the rest of this discussion we are going to assume that retries are being used, as the general techniques of handling received retries also work even if you never send them.

When you receive a message you have to figure out what to do with it. We assume that each message is recognizable so that you know which message in the protocol it is supposed to be. If it is the message that you expect, then there is nothing out of the ordinary and you just follow the protocol rules. Suppose it is a message from the "future" of the protocol, i.e., one that you only expect at a later point in time. This is easy; ignore it. Don't change your state, don't send a reply, just drop it and do nothing. It is probably part of an attack. Even in weird protocols where it could be part of a sequence of errors induced by lost messages, ignoring a message has the same effect as the message being lost in transit. As the protocol is supposed to recover from lost messages, ignoring a message is always a safe solution.

That leaves the case of "old" messages; messages that you already processed in the protocol you are running. There are three situations in which this could occur. In the first one, the message you receive is the previous one you responded to, and it is identical to the message you responded to. In this case, the message is probably a retry, so you send exactly the same reply you sent the first time. Note that the reply should be the same. Don't recompute the reply with a different random value, and don't just assume that the message you get is identical to the first one you replied to. You have to check.

The second case is when you receive a message that has the same message identification as the message you last responded to, but the message contents are different. For example, suppose in the DH protocol Bob receives the first message from Alice, and then later receives another message that claims to be the first message in the protocol, but which contains different data. This situation is indicative of an attack. No retry would ever create this situation, as the resent message is never different from the first try. Either the message you just received is bogus, or the earlier one you responded to is bogus. The safe choice is to treat this as a protocol error, with all the consequences we discussed. (Ignoring the message you just received is safe, but it means that fewer forms of active attacks are detected as such. This has a detrimental effect on the detection and response parts of the security system.)

The third case is when you receive a message that is even older than the previous message you responded to. There is not much you can do with this. If you still know the original message you received at that phase in the protocol, you could check if it is identical. If it is, ignore it. If it is different, you have detected an attack and should treat it as a protocol error. Many implementations do not store all the messages that were received in a protocol execution, which makes it impossible to know whether the message you receive now is identical or not to the one originally processed. The safe option is to ignore these messages. You'd be surprised how often this actually happens. Sometimes messages get delayed for a long time. Suppose Alice sends a message that is delayed. After a few seconds, she sends a retry that does arrive, and both Alice and Bob continue with the protocol. Half a minute later, Bob receives the original message. This is a situation in which Bob receives a copy of—in protocol terms—a very old message.

Things get more complicated if you have a protocol in which there are more than two participants. These exist, but are beyond the scope of this book. If you ever work on a multiparty protocol, think carefully about replay and retries.

One final comment: it is impossible to know whether the last message of a protocol arrived or not. If Alice sends the last message to Bob, then she will never get a confirmation that it arrived. If the communication link is broken and Bob never receives the last message, then Bob will retry the previous message but that will not reach Alice either. This is indistinguishable to Alice from the normal end of the protocol. You could add an acknowledgment from Bob to Alice to the end of the protocol, but then this acknowledgment becomes the new last message and the same problem repeats. Cryptographic protocols have to be designed in a way that this ambiguity does not lead to insecure behavior.

Chapter 15

Key Negotiation Protocol

Finally we are ready to tackle the key negotiation protocol. The purpose of this protocol is to derive a shared key that can then be used for the secure channel we defined in chapter 8.

Complete protocols get quite complicated, and it can be confusing to present the final protocol all at once. Instead, we will present a sequence of protocols, each of which adds a bit more functionality. Keep in mind that the intermediate protocols are not fully functional, and will have various weaknesses.

15.1   The Setting

There are two parties in the protocol: Alice and Bob. Alice and Bob want to communicate securely. They will first conduct the key negotiation protocol to set up a secret session key k, and then use k for a secure channel to exchange the actual data.

For a secure key negotiation, Alice and Bob must be able to identify each other. This basic authentication capability is the subject of the third part of this book. For now, we will just assume that Alice and Bob can authenticate messages to each other. This basic authentication can be done using RSA signatures (if Alice and Bob know each other's keys or are using a PKI), or using a shared secret key and a MAC function.

But wait! Why do a key negotiation if you already have a shared secret key? There are many reasons why you might want to do this. First of all, the key negotiation can decouple the session key from the existing (long-term) shared key. If the session key is compromised (e.g., because of a flawed secure channel implementation), then the shared secret still remains safe. And if the shared secret key is compromised *after* the key negotiation protocol has been run, the attacker who learns the shared secret key still does not learn the session key negotiated by the protocol. So yesterday's data is still protected if you lose your key today. These are important properties: they make the entire system more robust.

There are also situations in which the shared secret key is a relatively weak one, like a password. Users don't like to memorize 30-letter passwords, and tend to choose much simpler ones. A standard attack is the *dictionary attack*, where a computer searches through a large number of simple passwords. A good key negotiation protocol can turn a weak password into a strong key. We will not go into these more advanced protocols in this chapter, however.

15.2   A First Try

We'll start with the simplest design we can think of, shown in figure 15.1. This is just the DH protocol in a subgroup with some added authentication. Alice and Bob perform the DH protocol using the first two messages. (We've left out some of the necessary checks, for simplicity's sake.) Alice then computes an authentication on the session key k and sends it to Bob, who checks the authentication. Similarly, Bob sends an authentication of k to Alice.

We don't know the exact form of the authentication at the moment. Remember, we said that we assume that Alice and Bob can authenticate messages to each other. So Bob is able to check $\text{AUTH}_A(k)$ and Alice is able to check $\text{AUTH}_B(k)$. Whether this is done using digital signatures or using a MAC function is not our concern here. This protocol just turns an authentication capability into a session key.

There are some problems with this protocol:

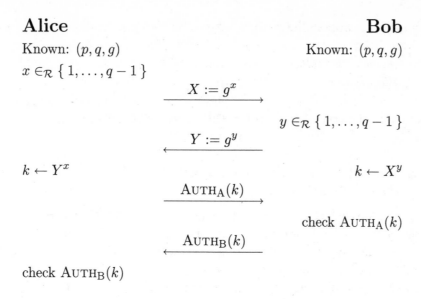

Figure 15.1: A first attempt at key negotiation.

- The protocol is based on the assumption that (p, q, g) are known to both Alice and Bob. Choosing constants for these values is a bad idea.

- It uses four messages, whereas it is possible to achieve the goal using only three.

- The session key is used as an input to the authentication function. This is not a problem if the authentication function is strong, but suppose the authentication function leaks a few bits about the session key. That would be bad. It certainly would require a new analysis of the entire protocol. A good rule of thumb is to use a secret only for a single thing. Here k will be used as a session key, so we don't want to use it in an argument to the authentication function.

- The two authentication messages are too similar. If, for example, the authentication function is a simple MAC using a secret key known to both Alice and Bob, then Bob could just send the authentication value that he received from Alice, and he would not need the secret key to complete the protocol. Thus Alice would not be convinced by the last authentication message.

- Implementations have to be careful not to use k until the authentication messages have been exchanged. This is not a major issue and is a rather simple requirement, but you wouldn't believe what some programmers think up when they try to optimize a program.

We will fix all of these problems in the course of this chapter.

15.3   Protocols Live Forever

We've emphasized the importance of designing systems to withstand the future. This is even more important for protocols. If you limit the size of database fields to 2000 bytes, it might be a problem for some users, but you can remove the limit in the next version. Not so for protocols. Protocols are run between different participants, and every new version needs to be interoperable with the old version. Modifying a protocol and still keeping it compatible with older versions is rather complicated. Before you know it, you have to implement several versions of the protocol, with a system to decide which version to use.

The protocol version switch becomes a point of attack, of course. If an older protocol is less secure, an attacker becomes interested in forcing you to use that older protocol. You'd be surprised at how many systems we've seen that suffer from what's known as a version-rollback attack.

It is of course impossible to know all the future requirements, so it might be necessary to define a second version of a protocol at some point in time. However, the cost of having several protocol versions is high, especially in overall complexity.

Successful protocols live almost forever (we don't care about unsuccessful ones). It is extremely difficult to completely remove a protocol from the world. So it is even more important to design protocols to be future-proof. This is why we can't specify a fixed set of DH parameters for our key negotiation protocol. Even if we chose them to be very large, there is always a danger that future cryptanalytical improvements might force us to change them.

15.4   An Authentication Convention

Before we go on, we will introduce an authentication convention. Protocols often have many different data elements, and it can be hard to figure out exactly which data elements need to be authenticated. Some protocols break because they neglect to authenticate certain data fields. We use a simple convention to solve these problems.

In our protocols, every time a party sends an authentication, the authentication data consists of all the data exchanged so far: all the previous messages, and all the data fields that precede the authentication in the authenticator's message. In the protocol shown in figure 15.1, Alice's authenticator would not be on k, but on X and Y. Bob's authenticator would cover X, Y, and AUTH_A.

This convention removes a lot of avenues of attack. It also costs very little. Cryptographic protocols don't exchange that much data, and authentication computations almost always start by hashing the input string. Hash functions are so fast that the extra cost is insignificant.

This convention also allows us to shorten the notation. Instead of writing something like $\text{AUTH}_A(X, Y)$ we simply write AUTH_A. As the data to be authenticated is specified by the convention, we no longer need to write it down explicitly. All further protocols in this book will use this convention.

Just as a reminder: authentication functions only authenticate a string of bytes. Each string of bytes to be authenticated must start with a unique identifier that identifies the exact point in the protocol where this authenticator is used. Also, the encoding of the previous messages and the data fields into this string of bytes must be such that the messages and fields can be recovered from the string without further context information. We've already talked about this in more detail, but it is an important point that is easily overlooked.

15.5   A Second Attempt

How do we fix the problems of the previous protocol? We don't want to use a constant DH parameter set, so we'll let Alice choose it and send it to Bob.

Alice   **Bob**

Choose suitable (p, q, g)

$x \in_{\mathcal{R}} \{1, \ldots, q-1\}$

$$\xrightarrow{\begin{array}{c} (p, q, g), \, X := g^x, \\ \text{Auth}_A \end{array}}$$

Check (p, q, g), X, Auth_A

$y \in_{\mathcal{R}} \{1, \ldots, q-1\}$

$$\xleftarrow{\quad Y := g^y, \, \text{Auth}_B \quad}$$

Check Y, Auth_B

$k \leftarrow Y^x$ $k \leftarrow X^y$

Figure 15.2: A second attempt at key negotiation.

We'll also collapse the four messages into two, as shown in figure 15.2. Alice starts by choosing DH parameters and her DH contribution, and sends it all to Bob with an authentication. Bob has to check that the DH parameters are properly chosen and that X is valid. (See chapter 12 for details of these checks.) The rest of the protocol is similar to the previous version. Alice receives Y and Auth_B, checks them, and computes the DH result.

We no longer have fixed DH parameters. We use only two messages, we don't use the authentication key directly in any way, and our authentication convention ensures that the strings that are being authenticated are not similar.

But now we have some new problems:

- What do we do if Bob wants a larger DH prime than Alice? Perhaps Bob has stricter security policies and thinks that the DH prime chosen by Alice isn't secure enough. Bob will have to abort the protocol. Maybe he could send an error message along the lines of "Require DH prime to be at least k bits long," but that gets messy and complicated. Alice would have to restart the protocol with new parameters.

- There is a problem with the authentication. Bob isn't sure he is talking to Alice at all. Anybody can record the first message that Alice sends, and then later send it to Bob. Bob thinks the message comes from Alice (after all, the authentication checked), and finishes the protocol, thinking he shares a key k with Alice. The attacker doesn't learn k, as he doesn't know x, and without k the attacker cannot break into the rest of the system that uses k. But Bob's logs will show a completed authenticated protocol with Alice, and that is a problem by itself, as it provides erroneous information to investigating administrators.

Bob's problem is called a lack of "liveness." He isn't sure that Alice is "alive," and that he's not talking to a replaying ghost. The traditional way to solve this is to make sure that Alice's authenticator covers a random element chosen by Bob.

15.6 A Third Attempt

We will fix these problems with a few more changes. Instead of Alice choosing the DH parameters, she will simply send her minimal requirements to Bob, and Bob will choose the parameters. This does increase the number of messages to three. (It turns out that most interesting cryptographic protocols require at least three messages. We don't know why, they just do.) Bob only sends a single message: the second one. This message will contain his authenticator, so Alice should send a randomly chosen element in the first message. We use a random nonce for this.

This leads to the protocol shown in figure 15.3. Alice starts by choosing s, the minimal size of the prime p she wants to use. She also chooses a random 256-bit string as nonce N_a and sends them both to Bob. Bob chooses a suitable DH parameter set and his random exponent, and sends the parameters, his DH contribution, and his authenticator to Alice. Alice completes the DH protocol as usual with the added authenticator.

There is one more problem to be solved. The final result k is a variable-sized number. Other parts of the system might find this difficult to work with. Furthermore, k is computed using algebraic relations, and leaving algebraic structure in a cryptographic system always scares us. There are a few places where you absolutely need such structure, but we avoid it wherever possible.

Alice   **Bob**

$s \leftarrow \min p$ size

$N_a \in_{\mathcal{R}} 0, \ldots, 2^{256} - 1$

$$\xrightarrow{\quad s,\ N_a \quad}$$

Choose (p, q, g)

$x \in_{\mathcal{R}} \{ 1, \ldots, q - 1 \}$

$$\xleftarrow{\quad (p,q,g),\ X := g^x, \atop \text{Auth}_\text{B} \quad}$$

Check (p, q, g), X, Auth_B

$y \in_{\mathcal{R}} \{ 1, \ldots, q - 1 \}$

$$\xrightarrow{\quad Y := g^y,\ \text{Auth}_\text{A} \quad}$$

Check Y, Auth_A

$k \leftarrow X^y$ $k \leftarrow Y^x$

Figure 15.3: A third attempt at key negotiation.

The danger of algebraic structure is that an attacker might find some way of exploiting it. Mathematics can be an extremely powerful tool. Over the past two decades we have seen many new proposals for public key systems, almost all of which have been broken, mostly due to the algebraic structure they contained. Always remove any algebraic structure that you can.

The obvious solution is to hash the final key. This reduces it to a fixed size, and also destroys any remaining algebraic structure.

15.7   Our Final Protocol

The final protocol is shown in short form in figure 15.4. This is the form that is easiest to read and understand. However, we've left a lot of verification steps out of the protocol to make it easy to read. We simply write "Check (p, q, g)," which stands for several verifications. To show you all the required cryptographic checks, the long form of the protocol is given in figure 15.5.

Alice **Bob**

$s \leftarrow \min p$ size

$N_a \in_{\mathcal{R}} 0, \ldots, 2^{256} - 1$

$$\xrightarrow{\quad s, N_a \quad}$$

Choose (p, q, g)

$x \in_{\mathcal{R}} \{ 1, \ldots, q-1 \}$

$$\xleftarrow{\quad (p, q, g),\ X := g^x, \quad \atop \text{AUTH}_B \quad}$$

Check (p, q, g), X, AUTH_B

$y \in_{\mathcal{R}} \{ 1, \ldots, q-1 \}$

$$\xrightarrow{\quad Y := g^y,\ \text{AUTH}_A \quad}$$

Check Y, AUTH_A

$k \leftarrow \text{SHA}_d\text{-256}(X^y)$ $k \leftarrow \text{SHA}_d\text{-256}(Y^x)$

Figure 15.4: The final protocol in short form.

Bob needs to choose a suitable size for p. This depends on the minimum size required by Alice and his own required minimum size. Of course, Bob should ensure that the value of s is reasonable. We don't want Bob to start generating 100,000-bit primes just because he received an unauthenticated message with a large value for s in it. Similarly, Alice should not start checking very large primes just because Bob sent them. Therefore, both Alice and Bob limit the size of p. Using a fixed maximum limits flexibility; if cryptanalytical progress suddenly forces you to use larger primes, then a fixed maximum is going to be a real problem. A configurable maximum brings with it all the problems of a configuration parameter that almost nobody understands. We've chosen to use a dynamic maximum. Both Alice and Bob refuse to use a prime that are more than twice as long as the prime they would prefer to use. A dynamic maximum provides a nice upgrade path and avoids excessively large primes. You can argue about whether the choice of the factor two is best. Maybe you should use three; it doesn't matter much.

Alice   **Bob**

$s_a \leftarrow \min p \text{ size}$

$N_a \in_{\mathcal{R}} 0, \ldots, 2^{256} - 1$

$$\xrightarrow{\quad s_a, N_a \quad}$$

$s_b \leftarrow \min p \text{ size}$

$s \leftarrow \max(s_a, s_b)$

$s \overset{?}{\leq} 2 \cdot s_b$

Choose (p, q, g) with $\log_2 p \geq s - 1$

$x \in_{\mathcal{R}} \{1, \ldots, q - 1\}$

$$\xleftarrow{\quad \substack{(p,q,g), \, X := g^x, \\ \text{AUTH}_\text{B}} \quad}$$

Check AUTH_B

$s_a - 1 \overset{?}{\leq} \log_2 p \overset{?}{\leq} 2 \cdot s_a$

$255 \overset{?}{\leq} \log_2 q \overset{?}{\leq} 256$

Check p, q both prime

$q \overset{?}{\mid} (p-1) \wedge g \overset{?}{\neq} 1 \wedge g^q \overset{?}{=} 1$

$X \overset{?}{\neq} 1 \wedge X^q \overset{?}{=} 1$

$y \in_{\mathcal{R}} \{1, \ldots, q - 1\}$

$$\xrightarrow{\quad Y := g^y, \, \text{AUTH}_\text{A} \quad}$$

Check AUTH_A

$Y \overset{?}{\neq} 1 \wedge Y^q \overset{?}{=} 1$

$k \leftarrow \text{SHA}_d\text{-}256(X^y)$ $k \leftarrow \text{SHA}_d\text{-}256(Y^x)$

Figure 15.5: The final protocol in long form.

The rest of the protocol is just an expansion of the earlier short form. If Bob and Alice are smart, they'll both use caches of suitable DH parameters. This saves Bob from having to generate new DH parameters every time, and it saves Alice having to check them every time. Applications can even use a fixed set of DH parameters, in which case you don't have to send them explicitly. A single DH parameter set identifier would be enough. All these changes are simple, direct optimizations of the protocol, so we will not discuss them in detail. Be careful, though. Optimizations can end up modifying the protocol enough to break it. There are no simple rules we can give you to check if an optimization breaks a protocol or not. Protocol design is still more an art than a science, and there are no hard rules to live by.

15.8   Different Views of the Protocol

There are a number of instructive ways to look at a protocol like this. There are a few properties that the protocol should have, and we can look at why the protocol provides them all.

15.8.1   Alice's View

Let's look at the protocol from Alice's point of view. She receives a single message from Bob. She's sure this message is from Bob because it is authenticated, and the authentication includes her random nonce N_a. There is no way anyone could forge this message or replay an old message.

Alice checks that the DH parameters are properly chosen, so the DH protocol has all its expected properties. So when she keeps y secret and sends out Y, she knows that only persons who know an x such that $g^x = X$ can compute the resulting key k. This is the basic DH protocol property. Bob authenticated X, and he only does that when he is following the protocol. Thus Bob knows the appropriate x, and is keeping it secret. Therefore, Alice is sure that only Bob knows the final key k that she derives.

So Alice is convinced that she is really talking to Bob, and that the key she derives can be known only to her and Bob.

15.8.2   Bob's View

Now let's look at Bob's side. The first message he receives gives him almost no useful information; it basically states that someone out there has chosen a value s_a and some random bits N_a.

The third message is different. This is a message that definitely came from Alice, because Alice authenticated it, and we assumed at the outset that Bob can verify an authentication by Alice. The authentication includes X, a random value chosen by Bob, so the third message is not a replay but has been authenticated by Alice specifically for this protocol run. Also, Alice's authentication covers the first message that Bob received, so now he knows that the first message was proper, too.

Bob knows the DH parameters are safe; after all, he chose them. So just like Alice, he knows that only someone who knows a y such that $g^y = Y$ can compute the final key k. But Alice authenticated the Y she sent, so she is the only person who knows the corresponding y. This convinces Bob that Alice is the only other person who can compute k.

15.8.3   Attacker's View

Finally we look at the protocol from the viewpoint of an attacker. If we just listen in on the communications we see all the messages that Alice and Bob exchange. But the key k is computed using the DH protocol, so as long as the DH parameters are safe, a passive attack like this is not going to reveal anything about k. In other words: we'll have to try an active attack.

One instructive exercise is to look at each data element and try to change it. Here we are quickly stopped by the two authentications. Alice's final authentication covers all the data that was exchanged between Alice and Bob. That means we can't change any data elements, other than to try a replay attack of a prerecorded protocol run. But the nonce and the random X value stop any replay attempts.

That doesn't mean we can't try to play around. We could, for example, change s_a to a larger value. As long as this larger value is acceptable to Bob, most of the protocol would complete normally. There are just three problems. First of all, increasing s_a isn't an attack because it only makes the DH prime larger, and therefore the DH parameters stronger. The second and third problems are the two authentications which will both fail.

In the real world, you will find many protocols where there are unauthenticated data elements. Most designers wouldn't bother authenticating s_a in our protocol, because changing it would not lead to an attack. (Both Alice and Bob independently verify that the size of p is large enough for them.) Allowing attackers to play around is always a bad idea. We don't want to give them any more tools than necessary. And we can certainly imagine a situation where not authenticating s_a can be dangerous. For example, assume that Bob prefers to use DH parameters from a list built into the program, and only generates new parameters when necessary. As long as Alice and Bob choose to use DH prime sizes that are still in the list, Bob never generates a new parameter set. But this also means that Bob's parameter generation code and Alice's parameter verification code are never used and therefore unlikely to be properly tested. A bug in the parameter generation and testing code could remain hidden until an attacker increases s_a. Yes, this is an unlikely scenario, but there are thousands of unlikely scenarios that are all bad for security. And thousands of low-probability risks add up to a high-probability risk. This is why we are so paranoid about stopping any type of attack anytime we can. It gives us defense in depth.

15.8.4   Key Compromise

So what happens if some other part of the system is compromised? Let's have a look.

If Alice merely loses her authentication key without it becoming known to an attacker, she simply loses the ability to run this protocol. She can still use session keys that were already established. This is very much how you'd expect the protocol to behave. The same holds for Bob if he loses his key.

If Alice loses the session key, without it becoming known to an attacker, she will have to run the key negotiation protocol again with Bob to establish a new session key.

Things get worse if an attacker manages to learn a key. If Alice's authentication key is compromised, the attacker can impersonate Alice from that moment on until the time that Bob is informed and stops accepting Alice's authentications. This is an unavoidable consequence. If you lose your car keys, anyone who finds them can use the car. That is one of the main functions of keys: they allow access to certain functions. This protocol does have the desirable property that past communications between Alice and Bob still remain secret. Even knowing Alice's authentication key doesn't let the attacker find the session key k for a protocol that has already finished, even if the attacker recorded all the messages. This is called *forward secrecy*.[1] The same properties hold with regard to Bob's authentication key.

Finally, we consider the situation where the session key is compromised. The key k is the hash of g^{xy}, where both x and y are randomly chosen. This provides no information about any other key. It certainly provides no information about Alice's or Bob's authentication keys. The value of k in one protocol run is completely independent of the k in another protocol run (at least it is if we assume that Alice and Bob use a good PRNG).

Our protocol offers the best possible protection against key compromises.

15.9   Computational Complexity of the Protocol

Let's have a look at the computational complexity of our solution. We'll assume that the DH parameter selection and verification are all cached, so we don't count them in the workload of a single protocol run. That leaves the following computations:

- Three exponentiations in the DH subgroup for both Alice and Bob.

- One authentication generation.

- One authentication verification.

- Various relatively efficient operations, such as random number generation, comparisons, and hash functions.

If symmetric-key authentication is used, then the run time of the protocol is dominated by the DH exponentiations. Let's look at how much work

---

[1] You sometimes see the term *perfect forward secrecy*, or PFS, but we don't use words like "perfect" because it never is.

that is. Bob and Alice each have to do three modular exponentiations with a 256-bit exponent. This requires about 1150 modular multiplications.[2] To get an idea of how much work this really is, we'll compare this to the computational cost of an RSA signature where the RSA modulus and the DH prime are the same size. For an s-bit modulus, the signature algorithm requires $3s/2$ multiplications if you do not use the CRT (Chinese Remainder Theorem). Using the CRT representation saves a factor of four, so the cost of an RSA signature on s-bit numbers is similar to the cost of doing $3s/8$ multiplications. This leads us to an interesting conclusion: RSA signatures are relatively slower than DH computations when the moduli are large, and relatively faster when the moduli are small. The break-even point is around 3000 bits. This is because DH always use 256-bit exponents, and for RSA the exponent grows with the modulus size.

We conclude that for the public-key sizes that we use, the DH computations cost roughly the same as an RSA signature computation. This is still the dominant factor in the computations for the protocol, but it is quite reasonable.

If RSA signatures are used for the authentication, the computational load more or less doubles. (We can ignore RSA verifications as they are very fast.) This still isn't excessive. CPU speeds are rapidly increasing, and in most practical implementations you'll see that communications delays and overhead take up more time than the computations.

15.9.1   Optimization Tricks

There are a few optimizations that can be applied to the DH operations. Using addition chain heuristics, each exponentiation can be done using fewer multiplications. Furthermore, Alice computes both X^q and X^y. You can use addition sequence heuristics to compute these two results simultaneously and save about 250 multiplications. See Bos [10, ch. 4] for a detailed discussion.

There are also various tricks that make it faster to generate a random y and compute g^y, but these tricks require so much extra system complexity that we'd rather not use them.

---

[2]This is for the simple binary exponentiation algorithm. A better-optimized algorithm reduces this to less than 1000 multiplications.

15.10   Protocol Complexity

This protocol is also an excellent example of why protocol design is so hideously difficult. Even a simple protocol like this quickly expands to a full page, and we didn't even include all the rules for DH parameter generation or the checks for the authentication scheme that are unknown at our abstraction level. Yet it is already difficult to keep track of everything that goes on. More complicated protocols get much larger. One particular smart card payment system that Niels worked on had a dozen or so protocols specified in 50 pages of symbols and protocol specifications, and that was using a proprietary, highly compact notation! There were 50 more densely written pages needed to cover the security-critical implementation issues.

Full documentation of a set of cryptographic protocols can run into hundreds of pages. Protocols quickly get too complicated to keep in your head, and that is dangerous. Once you don't understand it all, it is almost inevitable that a weakness slips in. The above-mentioned project was probably too complex to be fully understood, even by the designers.

A few years later Niels worked with another, commercially available smart card system. This was a well-known and established system that was widely used for many different smart card applications. One day Marius Schilder, a colleague, showed up with a question—or rather, with a large hole in the system. It turns out that two of the protocols had a destructive interference with each other. One protocol computed a session key from a long-term card key, a bit like the key negotiation protocol of this chapter. A second protocol computed an authentication value from the long-term card key. With a bit of tweaking, you could use the second protocol to let the smart card compute the session key, and then send half of the bits to you. With half of the key bits known, breaking the rest of the system was trivial. Oops! This bug was fixed in the next version, but it is a good illustration of the problems of large protocol specifications.

Real-world systems always have very large protocol specifications. Communicating is very complex, and adding cryptographic functions and distrust makes things even harder. Our advice: be very careful with protocol complexity.

One of the fundamental problems in this area is that there are no good modularization notations for protocols, so everything ends up being mixed together. We've already seen that here in this chapter: the DH parameter size negotiation, DH key exchange, and authentication are all merged together. This is not just a combination of loose parts; the specification and implementation mash them all together. It is rather like a really bad and complex computer program without any modularization. We all know what that leads to, but we've developed modularization techniques to deal with program complexity. Unfortunately, we lack modularization techniques for protocols. If you're looking for a long-term research project, this might be something for you. On the other hand, Niels once wrote a research proposal for exactly this issue, and had it accepted. There was funding for four years of research, but in the end he didn't take the project on because he realized he had no idea how to even approach the subject. The person who got the job never got anywhere with the subject either, but ended up doing four years of valuable research in a different area. The moral is that this is not an easy subject. It's going to be really hard to get that Ph.D. if the final conclusion after years of research is: "I haven't a clue."

15.11   A Gentle Warning

We've tried to make the design of the protocol look as easy as possible. Please don't be fooled by this. Protocol design is fiendishly difficult, and requires a lot of experience. Even with lots of experience, it is very easy to get wrong. Though we've tried very hard to get everything right in this book, there is always a possibility that the key negotiation protocol we designed here is wrong.

15.12   Key Negotiation from a Password

So far we've assumed that there is an authentication system to base the key negotiation on. In many situations, all you have is a password. You could just use a MAC keyed with the password to run this protocol, but there is a problem: given a transcript from this protocol (acquired by eavesdropping on the communications), you can test for any particular password. Just compute the authentication value and see whether it is correct.

The problem with passwords is that people don't choose them from a very large set. There are programs that search through all likely passwords. Ideally we'd like a key negotiation protocol where an eavesdropper cannot perform an offline dictionary attack.

Such protocols exist; probably the best-known example is SRP [97]. They provide a significant security improvement. Unfortunately, the entire area is a patent minefield. We haven't been able to find a suitable password-based key negotiation protocol that isn't tied up in patents. Stanford is giving away free patent licenses for a certain restricted set of uses of SRP, but there is at least one other patent that seems to cover SRP. This is such a confusing and complicated problem that we'd rather stay far away from it. And if we don't feel comfortable implementing these protocols, then we should not lead you, the reader, into temptation.

Chapter 16

Implementation Issues (II)

The key negotiation protocol we have designed leads to some new implementation issues.

16.1   Large Integer Arithmetic

The public-key computations all depend on large integer arithmetic. As we have already mentioned, it is not easy to implement large integer arithmetic properly.

Large integer routines are almost always platform-specific in one way or another. The efficiencies that can be gained by using platform-specific features are just too great to pass up. For example, most CPUs have an add-with-carry to implement addition of multiword values. But in C or almost any other higher-level language, you cannot access this instruction. Doing large integer arithmetic in a higher-level language is typically several times slower than an optimized implementation for the platform. And these computations also form the bottleneck in public-key performance, so there is a significant gain to be had by using platform-specific code for the large integer routines.

We won't go into the details of how to implement large integer arithmetic. There are other books for that. Knuth [55] is a good start. To us, the real question is how to *test* large integer arithmetic.

In cryptography we have different goals from those of most implementers. We consider a failure rate of 2^{-64} (about one in 18 million trillion) unacceptable, whereas most engineers would be very happy to achieve this. Many programmers seem to think that a failure rate of 2^{-20} (about one in a million) is acceptable, or even good. We have to do much better because we're working in an adversarial setting.

Most block ciphers and hash functions are rather easy to test.[1] Very few implementation bugs lead to errors that are hard to find. If you make a mistake in the S-box table of AES, it will be detected by a test of a few AES encryptions. Simple random testing exercises all the data paths in a block cipher or hash function and quickly finds all systematic problems. The code path taken does not depend on the data provided, or only in a very limited way. Any decent test set for a symmetric primitive will exercise all the possible flows of control in the implementation.

Large integer arithmetic is different. The major difference is that in most implementations, the code path depends on the data. Code that propagates the last carry is used only rarely. Division routines often contain a piece of code that is used only once every 2^{32} divisions or even once every 2^{64} divisions. A bug in this part of the code will not be found by random testing. This problem gets worse as we use larger CPUs. On a 32-bit CPU you could still run 2^{40} random test cases and expect that each 32-bit word value had occurred in each part of the data path. But this type of testing simply does not work for 64-bit CPUs.

The consequence is that you have to do extremely careful testing of your large integer arithmetic routines. You have to verify that every code path is in fact taken during the tests. To achieve this, you have to carefully craft test vectors: something that takes some care and precision. Not only do you have to use every code path, but you also need to run through all the boundary conditions. If there is a test with $a < b$, then you should test this for $a = b - 1$, $a = b$, and $a = b + 1$, but of course only as far as these conditions are possible to achieve.

Optimization makes this already bad situation even worse. As these routines are part of a performance bottleneck, the code tends to be highly optimized.

---

[1]Some notable exceptions are IDEA and MARS which often use separate code for special cases.

This in turn leads to more special cases, more code path, etc., all of which make the testing even harder.

A simple arithmetic error can have catastrophic security effects. Here is an example. While Alice is computing an RSA signature, there is a small error in the exponentiation modulo p but not modulo q. (She is using the CRT to speed up her signature.) Instead of the proper signature σ, she sends out $\sigma + kq$ for some value of k. (The result Alice gets is correct modulo q but wrong modulo p, so it must be of the form $\sigma + kq$.) The attacker knows $\sigma^3 \bmod n$, which is the number Alice is computing a root of, and which only depends on the message. But $(\sigma + kq)^3 - \sigma^3$ is a multiple of q, and taking the greatest common divisor of this number and n will reveal q and thus the factorization of n. Disaster!

So what are we to do? First of all, don't implement your own large integer routines. Get an existing library. If you want to spend any time on it, spend your time understanding and testing the existing library. Second, run really good tests on your library. Make sure you test every possible code path. Third, insert additional tests in the application. There are several techniques that you can use.

16.1.1 Wooping

The technique we describe in this section has the rather unusual name of *wooping*. During an intense discussion between David Chaum and Jurjen Bos, there was a sudden need to give a special verification value a name. In the heat of the moment one of them suggested the name "woop," and later the name stuck to the entire technique. Bos later described the details of this technique in his Ph.D. thesis [10, ch. 6], but dropped the name as being insufficiently academic.

The basic idea behind wooping is to verify a computation modulo a randomly chosen small prime. Think of it as a cryptographic problem. We have a large integer library that tries to cheat and give us the wrong results. Our task is to check whether we get the right results. Just checking the results with the same library is not a good idea, as the library might make consistent errors. Using the wooping technique, we can verify the library computations as long as we assume that the library is not actually malicious in the sense that it tries very hard to corrupt our verification computations.

First we generate a relatively small random prime t, in the order of 64–128 bits long. The value of t should not be fixed or predictable, but that is what we have a PRNG for. The value of t is kept secret from all other parties. Then for every large integer x that occurs in the computations, we also keep $\tilde{x} := (x \bmod t)$. The $\tilde{x}$ value is called the *woop* of x. The woop values have a fixed size, and are generally much smaller than the large integers. Computing the woop values is therefore not a great extra cost.

So now we have to keep woop values with every integer. For any input x to our algorithm we compute $\tilde{x}$ directly as $x \bmod t$. For all our internal computations we shadow the large integer computations in the woop values to compute the woop of the result without computing it from the large integer result.

A normal addition computes $c := a + b$. We can compute $\tilde{c}$ using $\tilde{c} = \tilde{a} + \tilde{b}$ $(\bmod\ t)$. Multiplication can be handled in the same way. We could verify the correctness of $\tilde{c}$ after every addition or multiplication by checking that $c \bmod t = \tilde{c}$, but it is more efficient to do all of the checks at the very end.

Modular addition is only slightly more difficult. Instead of just writing $c = (a + b) \bmod n$, we write $c = a + b + k \cdot n$ where k is chosen such that the result c is in the range $0, \ldots, n - 1$. This is just another way to write the modulo reduction. In this case k is either 0 or -1, assuming both a and b are in the range $0, \ldots, n - 1$. The woop version is $\tilde{c} = (\tilde{a} + \tilde{b} + \tilde{k} \cdot \tilde{n}) \bmod t$. Somewhere inside the modulo addition routine, the value of k is known. All we have to do is convince the library to provide us with k, so that we can compute $\tilde{k}$.

Modular multiplication is somewhat more difficult to do. Again we have to write $c = a \cdot b + k \cdot n$, and to compute $\tilde{c} = \tilde{a} \cdot \tilde{b} + \tilde{k} \cdot \tilde{n} \pmod{t}$ we need $\tilde{a}$, $\tilde{b}$, $\tilde{n}$, and $\tilde{k}$. The first three are readily available, but $\tilde{k}$ will have to be teased out of the modular multiplication routine in some way. That can be done when you create the library, but it is very hard to retrofit to the library. A generic method is to first compute $a \cdot b$, and then divide that by n using a long division. The quotient of the division is the k we need for the woop computation. The remainder is the result c. The disadvantage of this generic method is that it is significantly slower.

Once you can keep the woop value with modular multiplications, it is easy to do so with the modular exponentiation as well. Modular exponentiation routines simply construct the modular exponentiation from modular multiplications. (Some use a separate modular squaring routine, but that can be extended with a woop value just like the modular multiplication routine.) Just keep a woop value with every large integer, and have every multiplication compute the woop of the result from the woops of the inputs.

The woop-extended algorithms compute the woop value of the results based on the woop values of the inputs: if one or more of the woop inputs is wrong, the woop output is almost certainly wrong, too. So once a woop value is wrong, the error propagates to the final result.

We check the woop values at the end of our computation. If the result is x, all you have to do is check that $(x \bmod t) = \tilde{x}$. If the library made any mistakes, the woop value will not match. We assume that the library doesn't carefully craft its mistakes in a way that depends on the value t that we chose. After all, the library code was fixed long before we chose t, and the library code is not under control of the attacker. It is easy to show that any error that the library might make will be caught by the overwhelming majority of t values. So adding a woop verification to an existing library gives us an extremely good verification of the computations.

What we really want is a large integer library that has a built-in woop verification system. But we don't know of one.

How large should your woop values be? That depends on many factors. For random errors, the probability of the woop value not detecting the error is about $1/t$. But nothing is ever random in our world. Suppose there is a software error in our library. We've got to assume that the attacker knows this. He can choose the inputs to our computation, and not only trigger the error but also choose the difference that the error induces. This is why t must be a random, secret number; without knowing t, the attacker cannot target the error in the final result to a difference that won't be caught by our wooping.

So what would you do if you were an attacker? You would try to trigger the error, of course, but you would also try to force the difference to be zero modulo as many t's as you can. The simplest countermeasure is to require that t be a prime. If the attacker wants to cheat modulo 16 different 64-bit primes, then he will need to carefully select at least $16 \cdot 64 = 1024$ bits of the input. As most computations have a limited number of input bits that can be chosen by an attacker, this limits the probability of success of the attack.

Larger values for t are better. There are so many more primes of larger sizes that the probability of success rapidly disappears for the attacker. If we were to keep to our original goal of 128-bit security, we would need a 128-bit t, or something in that region.

Woop values are not the primary security of the system; they are only a backup. If a woop verification ever fails, we know that we have a bug in our software that needs to be fixed. The program should abort whatever it is doing and report a fatal error. This also makes it much harder for an attacker to perform repeated attacks on the system. Therefore, we suggest using a 64-bit random prime for t. This will reduce the overhead significantly compared to using a 128-bit prime, and it is good enough in practice. If you cannot afford the 64-bit woop, a 32-bit woop is always better than nothing. Especially on most 32-bit CPUs, a 32-bit woop can be computed very efficiently as there are direct multiplication and division instructions available.

If you ever have a computation where the attacker could provide a large amount of data, then you should check the intermediate woop values as well. Each check is simple: $(x \bmod t) \stackrel{?}{=} \tilde{x}$. By checking intermediate values that depend on only a limited number of bits from the attacker, you make it harder for him to cheat the woop system.

Using a large integer library with woop verifications has our strong preference. It is a relatively simple method of avoiding a large number of potential security problems. And we believe that it is less work to add woop verification to the library once than to add application-specific verifications to each of the applications that uses the library.

16.1.2   Checking DH Computations

If you don't have a woop-enabled library you will have to work without one. The DH protocol we described already contains a number of checks, namely that the result should not be 1 and that the order of the result should be q. Unfortunately, the checks are not performed by the party doing the computation, but by the party receiving the result of the computation. In general, you don't want to send out any erroneous results, because they could leak information, but in this particular case it doesn't seem to do much harm. If the result is erroneous, the protocol will fail in one way or another, so the error will be noticed. The protocol safety only breaks down when your arithmetic library returns x when asked to compute g^x, but that is a type of error that normal testing is very likely to find.

Where needed, we would probably run DH on a library without woop-verification. The type of very rare arithmetical errors that we worry about here are unlikely to reveal x from a g^x computation. Any other mistake seems harmless, especially since DH computations have no long-term secrets. Still, we will use a wooping library wherever possible, just to feel safe.

16.1.3   Checking RSA Encryption

RSA encryption is more vulnerable and needs extra checks. If something goes wrong you might leak the secret that you are encrypting, or even your secret key.

If woop-verification is not available, there are two other methods to check the RSA encryption. Suppose the actual RSA encryption consists of computing $c = m^5 \bmod n$, where m is the message and c the ciphertext. To verify this, we could compute $c^{1/5} \bmod n$ and compare it to m. The disadvantages are that this is a very slow verification of a relatively fast computation, and that it requires knowledge of the private key which is typically not available when we do RSA encryption.

Probably a better method is to choose a random value z and check that $c \cdot z^5 = (m \cdot z)^5 \bmod n$. Here we have three computations of fifth powers: the $c = m^5$; the computation of z^5; and then finally the check that $(mz)^5$ matches $c \cdot z^5$. Random arithmetical errors are highly likely to be caught by this verification. By choosing a random value z we make it impossible for any attacker to target the error-producing values. In our designs, we only use RSA encryption to encrypt random values, so the attacker cannot do any targeting at all.

16.1.4   Checking RSA Signatures

RSA signatures are really easy to check. The signer only has to run the signature verification algorithm. This is a relatively fast verification, and arithmetical errors are highly likely to be caught. Every RSA signature computation should verify the results by checking the signature just produced. There is no excuse not to do this.

16.1.5   Conclusion

Let us make something quite clear. The checks we have been talking about are *in addition* to the normal testing of the large integer libraries. They do not replace the normal testing that any piece of software, and especially security software, should undergo.

If any of these checks ever fail, you know that your software just failed. There is not much you can do in that situation. Continuing with the work you are doing is unsafe; you have no idea what type of software error you have. The only thing you can really do is log the error and abort the program.

16.2   Faster Multiplication

There are a lot of ways in which you can do a modulo multiplication faster than a full multiply followed by a long division. If you have to do a lot of multiplications, then Montgomery's method [68] is the most widely used one. Unfortunately, Montgomery's article is hard to read, so see [26] for a more readable description of his method.

The basic idea behind Montgomery's method is a technique to compute $(x \bmod n)$ for some x much larger than n. The traditional "long division" method is to subtract suitable multiples of n from x. Montgomery's idea is simpler: divide x repeatedly by 2. If x is even, we divide x by two by shifting the binary representation one bit to the right. If x is odd, we first add n

(which does not change the value modulo n, of course) and then divide the even result by 2. (This technique only works if n is odd, which is always the case in our systems. There is a simple generalization for even values of n.) If n is k bits long, and x is not more than $(n-1)^2$, we perform a total of k divisions by 2. The result will always be in the interval $0, \ldots, 2n-1$, which is an almost fully reduced result modulo n.

But wait! We've been dividing by 2, so this gives us the wrong answer. Montgomery's reduction does not actually give you $(x \bmod n)$, but rather $x/2^k \bmod n$ for some suitable k. The reduction is faster, but you get an extra factor of 2^{-k}. There are various tricks to deal with this extra factor.

One bad idea is to simply redefine your protocol to include an extra factor 2^{-k} in the computations. This is bad because it mixes different levels. It modifies the cryptographic protocol specification to favor a particular implementation technique. Maybe you'll want to implement the protocol on another platform later, but you find that you don't want to use Montgomery multiplication at all. (Maybe that platform is slow but has a large integer coprocessor that performs modular multiplication directly.) In that case, the 2^{-k} factors in the protocol become a real hindrance.

The standard technique is to change your number representation. A number x is represented internally by $x \cdot 2^k$. If you want to multiply x and y, you do a Montgomery multiplication on their respective representations. You get $x \cdot 2^k \cdot y \cdot 2^k$, but you also get the extra 2^{-k} factor from the Montgomery reduction, so the final result is $x \cdot y \cdot 2^k \bmod n$, which is exactly the representation of xy. The overhead cost of using Montgomery reduction therefore consists of the cost of converting the input numbers into the internal representation (multiplication by 2^k) and the cost of converting the output back to the real result (division by 2^k). The first conversion can be done by performing a Montgomery multiplication of x and $(2^{2k} \bmod n)$. The second conversion can be done by simply running the Montgomery reduction for another k bits, as that divides by 2^k. The final result of a Montgomery reduction is not guaranteed to be less than n, but in most cases it can be shown to be less than $2n-1$. In those situations a simple test and an optional subtraction of n will give the final correct result.

In real implementations, the Montgomery reduction is never done on a bit-by-bit basis, but per word. Suppose the CPU uses w-bit words. Given a value x, find a small integer z such that the least significant word of $x + zn$ are all zero. You can show that z will be one word, and can be computed by multiplying the least significant word of x with a single word constant factor that only depends on n. Once the least significant word of $x + zn$ is zero, you divide by 2^w by shifting the value a whole word to the right. This is much faster than a bit-by-bit implementation.

16.3   Side-Channel Attacks

We discussed timing attacks and other side-channel attacks briefly back in section 9.5. The main reason we were brief there is not because these attacks are benign. It is, rather, that timing attacks are most useful against public-key computations.

As we have already mentioned, symmetric-key computations tend to have a simple code path for each computation. The time it takes to compute a block cipher will therefore be constant. Well, relatively constant. There are all kinds of cache-related variable timings that are almost impossible to predict. We have not yet seen anyone attack a symmetric-key system on PC-like equipment using cache-induced timing differences, although this is a theoretical possibility.

Some ciphers invite implementations that use different code paths to handle special situations. IDEA [61, 62] and MARS [13] are two examples. Other ciphers use CPU operations whose timing varies depending on the data they process. On some CPUs, multiplication (used by RC6 [78] and MARS) or data-dependent rotation (used by RC6 and RC5 [80]) has an execution time that depends on the input data. This can enable timing attacks. The primitives we have been using in this book do not use these types of operations.

Public-key cryptography is more vulnerable to timing attacks. Public-key operations often have a code path that depends on the data. This almost always leads to different processing times for different data. Timing information, in turn, can lead to attacks. Imagine a secure Web server for e-commerce. As part of the SSL negotiations, the server has to decrypt an RSA message chosen by the client. The attacker can therefore connect to the server, ask it to decrypt a chosen RSA value, and wait for the response.

The exact time it takes the server to respond can give the attacker important information. Often it turns out that if some bit of the key is one, inputs from set A are slightly faster than inputs from set B, and if the key bit is zero, there is no difference. The attacker can use this difference to attack the system. He generates millions of queries from both sets A and B, and tries to find a statistical difference in the response times to the two groups. There might be many other factors that influence the exact response time, but you can average those out by using enough queries. Eventually you will gather enough data to measure whether the response times for A and B are different. This gives the attacker one bit of information about the key, after which the attack can proceed with the next bit.

This all sounds far-fetched, but it has been done in the laboratory, and could very well be done in practice [56].

16.3.1   Countermeasures

There are several ways to protect yourself against timing attacks. The most obvious one is to ensure that every computation takes a fixed amount of time. But this requires the entire library be designed with this goal in mind. Furthermore, there are sources of timing differences that are almost impossible to control. Some CPUs have a multiplication instruction that is faster for some values than for others. Many CPUs have complicated cache systems, so as soon as your memory access pattern depends on nonpublic data, the cache delays might introduce a timing difference. It is almost impossible to rid public-key operations of all timing differences. We therefore need other solutions.

An obvious idea is to add a random delay at the end of each computation. But this does not eliminate the timing difference. It just hides it in the noise of the delay. An attacker who can take more samples (i.e., get your machine to do more computations) can average the results and hope to average out the random delay that was added. The exact number of tries that the attacker needs depends on the magnitude of the timing difference the attacker is looking for, and the magnitude of the random delay that is added. In real timing attacks there is almost always a lot of noise, so any attacker who tries a timing attack is already doing the averaging. The only question is the ratio of the signal to the noise.

A third method is to make an operation constant-time by forcing it to last a standardized amount of time. During development you choose a duration d that is longer than the computation will ever take. You then mark the time t at which the computation started, and after the computation you wait until time $t+d$. This is slightly wasteful, but it is not too bad. We like this solution, but it only provides protection against pure timing attacks. If the attacker can listen in on the RF radiation that your machine emits or measure the power consumption, the difference between the computation and the delay is probably detectable, which in turn allows timing attacks as well as other attacks. Still, an RF-based attack requires the attacker to be physically close to the machine. That enormously reduces the threat, compared to timing attacks that can be done over the Internet.

You can also use techniques that are derived from blind signatures [56]. For some types of computations they can hide (almost) all of the timing variations.

There is no perfect solution to the problem of timing attacks. It is simply not possible to secure the computers you can buy against a really sophisticated attack such as an RF-based one. But although you can't create a perfect solution, you can get a reasonably good one. Just be really careful with the timing of your public-key operations. An even better solution than just making your public-key operations fixed-time is to make the entire transaction fixed-time using the technique mentioned above. That is, you not only make the public-key operation fixed-time, but you also fix the time between when the request comes in and the response goes out. If the request comes in at a time t, you send the response at time $t+C$ for some constant C. But to make sure you never leak any timing information, you had better be sure that the response will be ready at time $t+C$. To guarantee this, you will probably have to limit the frequency at which you accept incoming requests to some fixed upper limit.

16.4   Protocols

Implementing cryptographic protocols is not that different from implementing communication protocols. The simplest method is to maintain the state in the program counter, and simply perform each of the steps of the protocol in turn. Unless you use multithreading, this stops everything else in the program while you wait for an answer. As the answer might not be forthcoming, this is often a bad idea.

A better solution is to keep an explicit protocol state, and update the state each time a message arrives. This message-driven approach is slightly more work to implement, but it provides much more flexibility.

16.4.1   Protocols Over a Secure Channel

Most cryptographic protocols are executed over insecure channels, but sometimes you run a cryptographic protocol over a secure channel. This makes sense in some situations. For example, each user has a secure channel to a key distribution center; the key distribution center uses a simple protocol to distribute keys to the users to allow them to communicate to each other. (The Kerberos protocol does something like this.) If you are running a cryptographic protocol with a party you have already exchanged a key with, then you should use the full secure channel functionality. In particular, you should implement the replay protection. This is very easy to do, and it prevents a large number of attacks on the cryptographic protocol.

Sometimes the secure channel allows the protocol to use shortcuts. For example, if the secure channel provides replay protection, the protocol itself does not have to. Still, the old modularization rule states that the protocol should minimize its dependency on the secure channel.

For the rest of our protocol implementation discussion, we are going to assume that the protocol runs over an insecure channel. Some of the discussion does not quite apply to the secure channel case, but the solutions can never hurt.

16.4.2   Receiving a Message

When a protocol state receives a message, there are several checks that have to be made. The first is to see if the message belongs to the protocol at all. Each message should start with the following fields:

Protocol identifier. Identifies exactly which protocol and protocol version this is. Version identifiers are important.

Protocol instance identifier. Identifies which instance of the protocol this message belongs to. Perhaps Alice and Bob are running two key negotiation protocols simultaneously, and we don't want to confuse the two runs.

Message identifier. Identifies the message within the protocol. The easiest method is to simply number them.

Depending on the situation, some of these identifiers can be implicit. For example, for protocols which run over their own TCP connection, the port number and its associated socket uniquely identify the protocol instance. The protocol identifier and version information only need to be exchanged once. Note that it is important to exchange them at least once to make sure they get included in any authentication or signature used in the protocol.

After checking the protocol identifier and instance identifier, we know which protocol state to send the message to. Let us assume that the protocol state has just sent message $n - 1$ and is expecting to receive message n.

If the received message is indeed message n, things are easy. Just process it as the protocol rules specify. But what if it has a different number?

If the number is larger than n or less than $n - 1$, something very weird is going on. Such a message should not have been generated and therefore must be a forgery of some kind. You must ignore the contents of the forged message.

If the received message is message $n - 1$, message n that you sent might not have arrived. At least, this could happen if you are running the protocol over an unreliable transport system. As we want to minimize dependencies on other parts of the system, this is exactly what we will assume.

First of all, check that the newly received message $n-1$ is absolutely identical to the previous message with number $n - 1$ that you received. If they are different, you must ignore the new message. Sending a second answer will break the security of many protocols. If the messages are identical, you just resend message n. Of course, the version that you resend must be identical to the previous version of message n that you sent.

If you ignored the received message due to any of these rules, you have a second decision to make. Should you abort the protocol? The answer depends to some extent on the application and situation. If you have been running a protocol over a secure channel, something is very wrong. Either the secure channel is compromised, or the party you are talking to is misbehaving. In either case, you should abort the protocol and the channel. Simply delete the protocol state and the channel state, including the channel key.

If you're running the protocol over an insecure channel, then any of the ignored messages could be from an attacker trying to interfere with the protocol. Ideally, you would ignore the attacker's messages and just complete the protocol. This is, of course, not always possible. For example, if the attacker's forged message $n - 1$ reaches you first, you will send a reply. If you later receive the "real" message $n - 1$, you are forced to ignore it. There is no recovery from this situation, as you cannot safely send a second reply. But you have no idea which of the two messages $n - 1$ you received was the real one, so in order to have the best chance of completing the protocol successfully you should just log the second message $n - 1$ as an error and continue as usual. If the message you replied to came from the attacker, the protocol will fail eventually because cryptographic protocols are specifically designed to prevent attackers from successfully completing the protocol with one of the participants.

16.4.3 Timeouts

Any protocol run includes timeouts. If you don't get a response to a message within a reasonable time, you can resend your last message. After a few resends, you have to give up. There is no point continuing with a protocol when you cannot communicate with the other party.

The easiest way to implement timeouts is to send timing messages to the protocol state. You can use timers explicitly set by the protocol, or use timing messages that are sent every few seconds or so.

One well-known attack is to send lots of "start-of-protocol" messages to a particular machine. Each time you receive a start-of-protocol message, you initialize a new protocol execution state. After receiving a few million of these you run out of memory, and everything stops. A good example is the

SYN flood attack. There is no easy method to protect yourself against these
flooding attacks, but they do show that it is important to delete old protocol
states. If a protocol is stalled for too long, you should delete it.

The proper timing for resends is debatable. In our experience, a packet on
the Internet either arrives within a second or so, or is lost forever. Resending
a message if you haven't received a reply within five seconds seems reasonable. Three retries should be enough; if the message loss rate is so high that
you lose four consecutive messages spread out over 15 seconds, then you're
not going to get a whole lot done over that connection. We prefer to inform
the user of a problem after 20 seconds, rather than require the user to sit
there and wait for a minute or two.

Part III

Key Management

Chapter 17

The Clock

Before we begin a detailed discussion of key management, we need to discuss one more primitive function: the clock. At first glance, this is a decidedly *un*-cryptographic primitive, but because the current time is often used in cryptographic systems, we need a reliable clock.

17.1 Uses for a Clock

There are several cryptographic uses for a clock. Key management functions are often linked to deadlines. The current time can provide both a unique value and a complete ordering of events. We will discuss each of these uses in more detail.

17.1.1 Expiration

In many situations, we want to limit the validity period of a document. We see limited validity periods a lot in the real world, too. Checks, open airline tickets, vouchers, coupons, and even copyrights all have limited validity periods. The standard way to limit the validity period of a digital document is to include the expiration time in the document itself. But to check whether a document has expired, we need to know the current time. Hence the need for a clock.

17.1.2   Unique Value

Another useful function of a clock is that it provides a unique value for a single machine. We've been using nonces in several places. The important property of a nonce is that any single value is never used twice, at least within some defined scope. Sometimes the scope is limited, such as the nonce we use in the secure channel, and the nonce can be generated using a counter. In other situations the nonce has to be unique across reboots of the computer. There are two generic ways of generating nonce values. The first one is to use the current time of the clock with some mechanism to ensure that you never use the same time code twice. The second one is to use a PRNG, which we discussed in some detail in chapter 10. The disadvantage of using a random nonce is that it needs to be rather large. To achieve a security level of 128 bits, we would need to use a 256-bit random nonce. Not all primitives support such a large nonce. Furthermore, a PRNG can be very hard to implement on certain platforms. A reliable clock is an attractive alternative way to generate nonces.

17.1.3   Monotonicity

One of the useful properties of time is that it always keeps going forward. It never stops or reverses. There are cryptographic protocols that use this property. Including the time in a cryptographic protocol prevents an attacker from trying to pass off old messages as ones which belong to the current protocol. After all, the time encoded in those messages is not within the time-span of the current protocol.

Another really important application of the clock is auditing and logging. In any kind of transaction system, it is very important to keep a log of what happened. If there is ever a dispute, the audit logs provide the necessary data to trace the exact sequence of events. Including the time in each logging event is important; without a time stamp it is very hard to know which events belong to the same transaction, and in which order the events occurred. As well-synchronized clocks do not deviate (very much) from each other, the time stamps allow events from different logs on different machines to be correlated.

17.1.4   Real-Time Transactions

Our next example comes from Niels's work on electronic payment systems. To support real-time payments the bank needs to run a real-time financial transaction system. To allow an audit to be performed, several requirements have to be met. First of all, there should be a clear sequence of transactions. Given two transactions A and B, it is important to know which of the two was performed first, because the result of one of them could depend on whether the other one has been performed yet or not. The simplest way to record this sequence is to give a time stamp to each transaction. This only works if you have a reliable clock.

An unreliable clock might give the wrong time. There is no harm done if the clock accidentally moves backward: it is easy to check that the current time is greater than the time stamp of the last transaction performed. There is a problem, however, if the clock moves forward. Suppose half an hour's worth of transactions were done with the clock set in 2020. You can't just change the time stamps of those transactions; it is not acceptable to modify financial records by hand. You can't perform any new transactions with a time stamp before 2020 because that would upset the order of the transactions, which is determined by the time stamp. There are solutions to this problem, but a reliable clock is certainly preferable.

17.2   Using the Real-Time Clock Chip

Most desktop computers contain a real-time clock chip and a small battery. This is really a small digital watch built into your machine. This is how your computer knows what time it is when you start it up in the morning. Why not simply use this clock time?

The real-time clock chip is adequate for normal use, but in a security system we have to impose higher standards. As part of the security system, the clock should give the correct time even if an enemy tries to manipulate the clock. A second reason is the consequences of a failed clock. For normal uses, a clock that shows the wrong time is irritating but not dangerous. If the clock is part of the security system, then clock failures can result in much greater damage.

The real-time clocks in typical hardware are not as reliable and secure as we need. We have personally experienced several real-time clock chip failures in the last decade. Moreover, those failures were spontaneous, without a malicious attacker trying to corrupt the clock. Most failures are simple. On an old machine the battery runs low and the clock stops or resets to 1980. Or one day you start the machine and the clock has been set to some date in 2028.

Apart from the accidental errors in real-time clocks, we have to consider active attacks. Someone might try to manipulate the clock in some way. Depending on the details of the computer, changing the clock time can be easy or hard. On some systems you need special administrator access to change the clock; others have clocks that can be changed by anyone.

17.3   Security Dangers

There are several types of attack that could be mounted against a system with a clock.

17.3.1   Setting the Clock Back

Suppose the attacker can set the clock to some arbitrary time in the past. This might allow all kinds of mischief. The machine mistakenly believes it lives in the past. Maybe an attacker once had access to some data because he was a temporary employee, but that access has now expired. With the wrong time on the clock, a computer might now allow this ex-employee access to the sensitive data. This problem occurs every time some access is revoked from a user. Setting the clock back might restore his access, depending on how the rest of the system was designed.

Another interesting avenue of attack is automated tasks. An HR computer makes the salary payments automatically at the end of the month using direct deposit. Automated tasks like this are initiated by a program that checks the time and has a list of tasks to perform. Repeatedly setting the clock back can trigger the tasks repeatedly. If the task is set to start at midnight, the attacker sets the clock to 23:55 (11:55 pm), and waits for the task to be started. After the task finishes, the attacker sets the clock back again. He can repeat this until the bank balance of the company is exhausted.

Another problem occurs in financial systems. It is important to get the time of a transaction right because interest computations give different results depending on when a transaction was performed. If you carry a large balance on your credit card, it would be very advantageous to convince your bank's computer that the online payment you just made actually happened six months ago, and avoid paying six months of interest.

17.3.2   Stopping the Clock

Every designer lives with the instinctive understanding that time does not stand still. It is an unspoken assumption, too obvious to even document. The systems they design rely on the time behaving normally. But if the clock is stopped, time appears to stand still. Things might not get done. And many systems behave in unpredictable ways.

The simple problems are things like getting the wrong time on audit logs and reports. The exact time of a transaction can have large financial consequences, and sending out formal paperwork with the wrong date and time on it can lead to serious complications.

Other problems might happen with real-time displays. Maybe the GUI programmer uses a simple system to display the current situation at the real-time broker. Every ten seconds he refreshes the display with the latest data. But not all reports of financial transactions arrive with the same speed, due to various delays. Just reporting the latest data that was received is going to give an inconsistent view of the financial situation. Maybe one part of a transaction has already been reported, but the other half has not. The money could show up on the bank balance before the shares move from the stock holdings. Accountants do not like to get reports where the numbers do not add up.

So the programmer does something clever. Each report of a financial transaction is time-stamped and stored in a local database. To display a consistent report, he takes a particular point in time and reports the financial situation at that point in time. For example, if the slowest system has a five-second delay in reporting, then he displays the financial situation of seven seconds ago. It increases the display delay a bit, but it guarantees a consistent report. That is, until the clock is stopped. Suddenly, the display reports the same situation over and over again: the situation of seven seconds ago relative to the (failed) clock. Oops!

17.3.3   Setting the Clock Forward

Setting the clock forward makes the computer think it lives in the future. This leads to simple denial-of-service attacks. With the clock set four years in the future, all credit card transactions are suddenly refused because all the cards have expired. You cannot book online airline tickets either, because there is no airline schedule out yet for those dates.

Substantial bidding at eBay auctions happens in the last seconds. If you can move eBay's clock forward just a little bit, you cut out many of the other bidders and can obtain the item at a cheaper price.

A friend of ours had a problem of this nature with his billing system. Due to a software error, the clock jumped ahead by about 30 years. The billing system started to bill all his customers for 30 years of unpaid bills. In this case it didn't result in a direct financial loss, but it could have been different if he had been using automatic debits from bank accounts or credit cards. It certainly wasn't good customer relations.

There are also direct security risks involved with clocks set to a future time. There are many situations in which certain data is to be kept secret until a specific time, and to be made public after that time. In an automated system, setting the clock forward provides access to the data. If this is a profit warning for a publicly traded company, quite a bit of profit can be made from accessing this data prematurely.

17.4   Creating a Reliable Clock

We don't have a simple solution to the clock problem. We can suggest some ideas and techniques, but the details depend too much on the exact working environment and the risk analysis for us to be able to give universal answers.

Most computers have, or can implement, a counter of some sort that starts when the computer is booted. This might be a count of the number of CPU clock cycles, a refresh counter, or something similar. This counter can be used to keep track of the time since the last reboot. It is not a clock, as it provides no information about what the time is, but it can be used to measure elapsed time between events as long as both events happened since the last reboot.

The main use for the counter, at least in relation to our clock problem, is to check for accidental errors in the real-time clock. If the real-time clock doesn't run properly it will show discrepancies with the clock counter. This is simple to test for, and provides some warning for certain error modes of the clock chip. Note that the correspondence between clock time and counter value has to be modified if the clock time is changed by an authorized user.

A second simple check is to keep track of the time of the last shutdown, or the last time data was written to disk. The clock should not jump backwards. If your machine suddenly boots in the year 1980, it is obvious that something is wrong. It is also possible to stop the clock jumping forward too much. Most computers are booted at least once a week. Perhaps you should get the user to confirm the correct date if the machine hasn't been booted for a week.[1] That would catch the case of the clock jumping more than a week forward.

There are other methods of checking the time. You could ask a time server on the Internet or intranet. There are widely used time synchronization protocols such as NTP [66] or SNTP [67]. Some of these protocols even provide for authentication of the time data so that an attacker cannot spoof the machine. Of course, the authentication requires some kind of keying infrastructure. The shared key with the time server could be a manually configured symmetric key, but manually configuring keys is a hassle. It can also be done using a PKI, but as we will see in chapter 19, most PKI systems need a clock, which results in a chicken-and-egg problem. Be careful if you rely on the cryptographic protection offered by a clock synchronization protocol. The security of your entire system could hinge on the security

---

[1]As users will hit the OK button without looking at the message, it is probably better to ask the user to enter the current date without showing him what the clock-date is.

of the protocol, and we have not seen any cryptographic reviews of these protocols yet.

17.5   The Same-State Problem

This brings us to a serious problem that you find on some hardware platforms. We're talking here about small embedded computers—something like a door lock or a remote smart card reader. These typically consist of a small CPU, a small amount of RAM, nonvolatile memory (e.g., flash) to store the program, some communication channels, and further task-specific hardware.

You will notice that a real-time clock is often not included. Adding a real-time clock requires an extra chip, an oscillator crystal, and most importantly, a battery. Apart from the extra cost, adding a battery complicates the device. You now have to worry about the battery running out. Batteries can be sensitive to temperature fluctuations, and the toxic chemicals in some batteries can even lead to problems with shipping the hardware. For all of these reasons, many small computers do not have a real-time clock.

Every time such a small computer is booted, it starts in exactly the same state. It reads the same program from the same nonvolatile memory, initializes the hardware, and starts operations. As this is a book about cryptography, we will assume that some kind of cryptographic protocol is used in the communication with other pieces of the system. But here is the problem: without a clock or hardware random number generator, the embedded system will always repeat the exact same behavior. Suppose the attacker waits until the gate computer needs to open the gate because a truck needs to pass through. She reboots the gate computer just before the gate needs to open (e.g., by interrupting the power supply momentarily). After some initialization procedures, the central system will command the gate computer to open the gate via the communication channel. The next day the attacker reboots the gate computer again, and sends exactly the same messages as were sent the first time. As the gate computer starts in the same state and sees the same inputs, it behaves the same and opens the gate. This is bad. Note that it doesn't matter if the gate computer uses a time synchronization protocol. The protocol messages can be replayed from yesterday, and the gate computer has no way of detecting this. The same-state problem is not solved by any protocol.

A real-time clock chip solves this problem. The small embedded computer can encrypt the current time with a fixed secret key to generate highly random data. This data can in turn be used as a nonce in a cryptographic protocol. As the real-time clock never repeats its state, the embedded computer can avoid falling into the same-state trap.

A hardware random number generator has the same effect. It allows the embedded computer to behave differently each time it is rebooted.

But if you don't have a real-time clock or a random number generator, you have a big problem. Sometimes you can fudge a bit and try to extract randomness from the clock skew between the local clock oscillator and the network timing, but it is very hard to extract enough entropy from this within a short time. Taking 10 minutes to reboot an embedded computer is simply unacceptable.

We've seen the same-state problem come up again and again. The upshot is that the hardware has to change before you can do useful cryptography on such small computers. This is hard to sell to managers, especially since the hardware is often already in the field and they don't want to hear that something cannot be done. But there is no magic security sauce that you can pour over an existing insecure system to make it secure. If you don't design the security into the system from the very start, you almost never get good security.

There is one more possible solution, though it rarely works in practice. Sometimes you can keep a reboot counter in the nonvolatile memory. Each time the CPU reboots, it increments a counter in nonvolatile memory. This solution is fraught with problems. Some nonvolatile memories can only be updated a few thousand times, which makes the machine wear out if you keep updating the counter. Some nonvolatile technologies require an additional power voltage to be programmable, which is often not available in the field. In some designs you can only set bits in nonvolatile memory, or wipe all of the nonvolatile memory. The latter option is not viable, as you'd lose the main program of the machine. Even if all these problems are overcome, it is very difficult to modify nonvolatile memory in such a way that the counter always reliably increases even if the power supply to the machine can be interrupted at arbitrary points in time. This nonvolatile counter option is only viable in a minority of the cases we've seen.

17.6   Time

While we're discussing clocks, we have a few short comments on which time base to choose. Stay away from local time. Local time is the time we use on our watches and other clocks. The problem is, local time changes with daylight savings time. These changes pose problems: some time values are repeated each year when clocks are set back an hour in the fall, which means that the time is no longer unique or monotonic. Some time values are impossible when clocks are set forward an hour in the spring. Furthermore, the exact date on which daylight savings time starts and stops is different in different countries. In some countries the rules change every few years, and you don't want to have to update your software for that. And people who travel with laptops might change the time on their laptops to the local time, which just makes these problems worse.

The obvious choice is to use UTC time. This is an international time standard based on atomic clocks, and is widely used throughout the world. Any single computer can keep track of the offset of local time with regard to UTC and use this knowledge in the interactions with the user.

There is one problem with UTC: the leap seconds. To keep UTC synchronized with the Earth's rotation, there is a leap second once every few years or so. So far all leap seconds have been extra seconds; there is a particular minute that gets 61 seconds. It is also theoretically possible to have a missing second. It all depends on the rotation of the Earth. The problem for computers is that the leap seconds are unpredictable. Ignoring leap seconds leads to inaccuracies in measuring time intervals across a leap second. This is not really a cryptographic problem, but if you want to make a good clock you might as well do it right. All computer software always assumes that each minute has 60 seconds. If you synchronize directly to a real UTC clock, the insertion of a leap second can lead to problems. Most likely this results in your internal clock repeating itself for one second. It is a minor problem, but again, it destroys the uniqueness and monotonicity of time values.

For most applications, the exact synchronization of the clock is less important than the monotonicity and uniqueness of the time stamps. As long as you make sure the clock never jumps backwards at a leap second, it doesn't matter how you solve this problem.

More information about different time scales, such as UTC, GMT, TAI, and UT1, can be found on the Internet.

17.7   Conclusion

Unfortunately, we have no ideal solution for you. Creating a reliable clock is very tricky, especially in a cryptographic setting where you assume that there are malicious attackers. The best solution depends on your local situation. Good luck!

Chapter 18

Key Servers

At last we turn to key management. This is, without a doubt, the most difficult issue in cryptographic systems, which is why we left it until the end. We've discussed how to encrypt and authenticate data, and how to negotiate a shared secret key between two participants. Now we need to find a way for Alice and Bob to recognize each other over the Internet. As you will see, this gets very complex very quickly. Key management is especially difficult because it involves people instead of mathematics, and people are much harder to understand and predict.

Before we start, let us make one thing clear. We talk only about the cryptographic aspects of the key management, not the organizational aspects. The organizational aspects include things like a policy of whom to issue keys to, which keys get access to which resources, how to verify the identity of the people that get keys, policies on the security of the stored keys, verification mechanisms that these policies are being adhered to, etc. Every organization will implement these differently, depending on their requirements and their existing organizational infrastructure. We will only concern ourselves with the parts that directly affect the cryptographic system.

One way to handle the key management is to have a trusted entity to hand out all the keys. We'll call this entity the *key server*.

18.1   Basics

The basic idea is simple. We assume that everybody sets up a shared secret key with the key server. For example, Alice sets up a key K_A that is known only to her and to the key server. Bob sets up a key K_B that is known only to him and to the key server. Other parties set up keys in exactly the same fashion.

Now suppose Alice wants to communicate with Bob. She has no key she can use to communicate with Bob, but she can communicate securely with the key server. The key server in turn can communicate securely with Bob. We could simply send all the traffic to the key server and let the key server act as a giant post office. But that is a bit hard on the key server, as it would have to handle enormous amounts of traffic. A better solution is to let the key server set up a key K_{AB} that is shared by Alice and Bob.

18.2   Kerberos

This is the basic idea behind Kerberos, a widely used key management system [58]. Kerberos is based on the Needham-Schroeder protocol [76].

At a very basic level, here is how it works. When Alice wants to talk to Bob, she first contacts the key server. The key server sends Alice a new secret key K_{AB} plus the key K_{AB} encrypted with Bob's key K_B. Both these messages are encrypted with K_A so that only Alice can read them. Alice sends the message that is encrypted with Bob's key to Bob. Bob decrypts it and gets K_{AB}, which is now a session key known only to Alice and Bob—and to the key server, of course.

One of the features of Kerberos is that the key server, called the KDC in Kerberos terminology, does not have to update its state very often. Of course, the key server has to remember the key that it shares with each user. But when Alice asks the KDC to set up a key between her and Bob, the KDC performs the function and then forgets all about it. It does not keep track of which keys between users have been set up. This is a nice property because it allows a heavily loaded key server to be distributed over several machines in a simple manner. As there is no state to be updated, Alice can talk to one copy of the key server one moment and to another copy the next moment.

It turns out that the cryptographic protocols needed for a Kerberos-style system are very complicated. Initially designing such protocols looks quite easy to do, but even experienced cryptographers have published proposals only to have them broken later on. The flaws that creep in are very subtle. We're not going to explain these protocols here, as we consider them to be too dangerous. Even we shy away from designing this type of protocol anew. If you want to use a protocol of this sort, use the latest version of Kerberos. It has been around for quite a while and many competent people have looked at it.

18.3   Simpler Solutions

Sometimes it is not possible to use Kerberos. The protocol is far from simple, and it imposes some restrictions. Servers have to memorize all tickets that they have accepted, and every participant needs a reliable clock. There are several situations in which these requirements cannot be met.

We can create a simpler and more robust solution if we don't put so much emphasis on efficiency. It turns out to be especially useful to allow the key server to maintain state. Modern computers are far more powerful than they were in the days when Kerberos was first designed, and they should not have any trouble maintaining state for tens of thousands of participants. Even a very large system with 100,000 participants is not a problem: if each participant requires a 1 kilobyte state in the key server, storing all states requires only 100 megabytes of memory. The key server still needs to be fast enough to set up all the requested keys, but that too is much less of a problem with modern, fast computers.

We will only discuss the situation in which there is a single key server. There are techniques that you can use to distribute the key server state over several computers. We won't go into the details because you really don't want to have a key server for tens of thousands of participants; it's too risky. The danger of large key servers is that *all* the keys are in a single place. That makes the key server a very attractive target for attack. The key server must also be online at all times, which means an attacker can always communicate with the key server at will. The current state of the art does not protect computers from network attacks very well, and putting all your keys in a single place is an invitation to disaster. For smaller systems, the total "value" of the keys kept by the key server is smaller, so this threat is reduced.[1] In the next few chapters we will talk about a solution to the key management system that is better suited to very large systems. We will restrict our discussion of key servers to fairly small systems—up to a few thousand participants or so.

18.3.1 Secure Connection

Here is a brief description of our simpler solution. First of all, we assume that Alice and the key server share a key K_A. Instead of using this key directly, they use it to run a key negotiation protocol, like the ones we discussed in chapter 15. (If K_A is a password, you'd really prefer to use one of the protocols suitable for low-entropy passwords that we discussed in section 15.12, but that involves all the patent problems.) The key negotiation protocol sets up a fresh key K_A' between the key server and Alice. All other participants also perform the same protocol with the key server, and they all set up fresh keys.

Alice and the key server use K_A' to create a secure communication channel (see chapter 8 for details). Using the secure channel, Alice and the key server can communicate securely. Confidentiality, authentication, and replay protection are all provided by the secure channel. All further communications happen over this secure channel. All other participants create a similar secure channel with the key server.

18.3.2 Setting Up a Key

It is now much easier to design a protocol that sets up a key between Alice and Bob. We only need to consider the case where messages get lost, or are deleted by the attacker, because the secure channel protects us from

---

[1]We don't like to leave any threat in the system, but in key management you always end up with a compromise solution.

all other types of manipulation. The protocol can now be something fairly simple. Alice asks the key server to set up a key between her and Bob. The key server responds by sending a new key K_{AB} to both Alice and Bob. The key server can even send the message to Bob through Alice, so that it does not need to communicate with Bob directly.

This does pose one limitation on the system: Bob must run the key negotiation protocol with the key server before Alice asks the key server to set up a shared key with Bob. Whether this turns out to be a problem depends on the exact circumstances, as do the possible solutions to this limitation.

18.3.3   Rekeying

Like all keys, the K'_A key must have a limited lifetime. This is easy to arrange as Alice can always rerun the key negotiation protocol (using the original key K_A for authentication) to set up a fresh K'_A key. A key lifetime of a few hours seems reasonable for most situations.

Because we can always rekey, the key server does not have to store the secure channel state in a reliable manner. Suppose the key server crashes and loses all state information. As long as it remembers K_A (and the corresponding keys for the other participants), there is no problem. All we have to do to recover is to run the key negotiation protocol between the key server and every participant again. So, although the key server is not stateless, it does not have to modify its long-term state—the part that is stored on nonvolatile media—when running the protocols.

18.3.4   Other Properties

Perhaps our solution is not simpler than Kerberos from an implementation point of view, but it is simpler from a conceptual point of view. The secure channel makes it much easier to oversee the possible lines of attack against the protocol. Using the key negotiation protocol and the secure channel we already designed is a good example of how modularization can help in the design of cryptographic protocols.

Using the key negotiation protocol to set up the secure channel has another advantage: we get forward secrecy. If Alice's key K_A is compromised today, then her old secure channel keys K'_A are not revealed, and therefore all her old communications are still secure.

In the earlier parts of the book we gave a detailed example design of the cryptographic function we discussed. We won't do that here, nor will we for the rest of the book. The cryptography is fairly straightforward, and we could certainly have described a key server system, but it would not be very useful. Designing key management systems is more a problem of collecting a suitable set of requirements for the particular application and getting the user interface right than a problem of cryptography. To be able to explain the design choices for a concrete example here, we would have to invent and document the entire surrounding social and organizational structure, the threat environment, and the application that needs the key management. That would be more suitable for a book on fictional cryptography than one on practical cryptography.

18.4   What to Choose

If you want to implement a central key server, you should use Kerberos if possible. It is widely available and widely used.

In those situations where Kerberos is not suitable, you will have to design and build something like the solution we described, but that will be a major operation. For the most common type of cryptographic applications that we have seen, you should count on spending as much time on the key server system as you did on the entire application.

Chapter 19

The Dream of PKI

In this chapter we will give the standard presentation of what a PKI is, and how it solves the key management problem. It is important to understand this first. In the next chapter we'll talk about why a PKI doesn't really work that well in practice, but for this chapter we'll visit the perfect world where a PKI solves all your problems.

19.1   A Very Short PKI Overview

A PKI is a *Public-Key Infrastructure*. It is an infrastructure that allows you to recognize which public key belongs to whom. The classical description is as follows.

There is a central authority that is called the *Certificate Authority*, or CA for short. The CA has a public/private key pair (e.g., an RSA key pair) and publishes the public key. We will assume that everybody knows the CA's public key. As this key remains the same over long periods of time, this is easy to accomplish.

To join the PKI, Alice generates her own public/private key pair. She keeps the private key secret, and takes the public key PK_A to the CA and says: "Hi, I'm Alice and PK_A is my public key." The CA verifies that Alice is who she says she is, and then signs a digital statement that states something like

"Key PK_A belongs to Alice." This signed statement is called the *certificate*. It certifies that the key belongs to Alice.

If Alice now wants to communicate with Bob, she can send him her public key and the certificate. Bob has the CA's public key, so he can verify the signature on the certificate. As long as Bob trusts the CA, he also trusts that PK_A actually belongs to Alice.

Using the same procedures, Bob gets his public key certified by the CA, and sends his public key and certificate to Alice. They now know each other's public key. These keys in turn can be used to run the key negotiation protocol to establish a session key for secure communications.

What is required is a central CA that everybody trusts. Each participant needs to get his public key certified, and each participant needs to know the CA's public key. After that, everybody can securely communicate with everybody else.

That sounds simple enough.

19.2   PKI Examples

To make the rest of this chapter easier to understand, we'll first give some examples of how PKIs can be implemented and used.

19.2.1   The Universal PKI

The ultimate dream is a universal PKI. A large organization, like the post office, certifies everybody's public key. The beauty of this is that every person only needs to get a single key certified, as the same key can be used for every application. Because everybody trusts the post office, or whatever other organization becomes the universal CA, everybody can communicate securely with everybody else, and they all live happily ever after.

If our description sounds a bit like a fairy tale, that is because it is. There is no universal PKI, and there never will be.

19.2.2 VPN Access

A more realistic example would be a company that has a VPN to allow its employees to access the corporate network from home or from their hotel room when they are traveling. The VPN access points must be able to recognize the people who have access and exactly what level of access they have. The IT department of the company acts as the CA and gives every employee a certificate that allows the VPN access points to recognize the employee.

19.2.3 Electronic Banking

A bank wants to allow its customers to perform financial transactions on the bank's Web site. Properly identifying the customer is vital in this application, as is the ability to produce proof acceptable in court. The bank itself can act as the CA and certify the public keys of its customers.

19.2.4 Refinery Sensors

A refinery complex is very large. Spread out between miles of pipes and access roads are hundreds of sensors that measure things like temperature, flow rate, and pressure. Spoofing sensor data is a very serious attack on the refinery. It might not be too difficult to send false sensor data to the control room, tricking the operators into taking actions that lead to a large explosion. Therefore, it is imperative that the control room get the proper sensor readings. We can use standard authentication techniques to ensure that the sensor data has not been tampered with, but to be sure that the data actually comes from the sensor, some kind of key infrastructure is needed. The company can act as a CA and build a PKI for all the sensors so that each sensor can be recognized by the control room.

19.2.5 Credit Card Organization

A credit card organization is a cooperative venture between a few thousand banks spread out all over the world. All of these banks must be able to exchange payments. After all, a user who has a credit card from bank A must be able to pay the merchant that banks with bank B. Bank A will need to settle with bank B in some way, and that requires secure communications. A PKI allows all banks to identify each other and perform secure transactions. In this situation, the credit card organization can act as the CA that certifies the keys of each bank.

19.3   Additional Details

In real life, things become somewhat more complicated, so various extensions to the simple PKI scheme are often used.

19.3.1   Multilevel Certificates

In many situations, the CA is split into multiple pieces. For example, the central credit card organization is not going to certify each bank directly. Instead, they will have regional offices to deal with the individual banks. You then get a two-level certificate structure. The central CA signs a certificate on the regional CA's public key that says something like: "Key PK_X belongs to regional office X and is allowed to certify other keys." Each regional office can then certify the individual bank keys. The certificate on the bank's key consists of two signed messages: the central CA's delegation message that authorizes the regional office's key, and the regional office's certification of the bank's key. This is called the *certificate chain*, and such a chain can be extended to any number of levels.

Such multilevel certificate structures can be very useful. It basically allows the CA functionality to be split into a hierarchy, which is easy to handle for most organizations. Almost all PKI systems have a multilevel structure. One disadvantage of this structure is that the certificates grow larger and require more computations to verify, but this is a relatively small cost in most situations. Another disadvantage is that each extra CA that you add to the system provides another point of attack, and thereby reduces overall system security.

One way to reduce the disadvantage of the large multilevel certificates that we have not seen in practice is to collapse the certificate hierarchy. To continue with our example above, once the bank has its two-level certificate, it could send it to the central CA. The central CA verifies the two-level certificate and replies with a single certificate on the bank's key using the master CA key. Once the key hierarchy is collapsed like this, the cost of adding extra levels to the hierarchy becomes very small. But then again, adding extra layers might not be such a good idea; many-layered hierarchical structures are rarely effective.

You have to be careful in chaining certificates together like this. They add more complexity, and complexity is always bad. Here is a recent example. Secure sites on the Internet use a PKI system to allow browsers to identify the correct Web site. In practice this system isn't very secure, if only because most users don't verify the name of the Web site they are using. But last year a fatal bug showed up in a library that validates certificates on all Microsoft operating systems. Each element of the certificate chain contains a flag that specifies whether the key it certifies is a CA key or not. CA keys are allowed to certify other keys. Non-CA keys are not allowed to certify other keys. This is an important difference. Unfortunately, the library in question didn't check this flag. So an attacker could buy a certificate for the domain `nastyattacker.com` and use it to sign a certificate for `amazon.com`. Microsoft Internet Explorer used the faulty library. It would accept `nastyattacker.com`'s certification of a fake Amazon key, and show the fake Web site as the real Amazon Web site. Thus a worldwide security system that cost a fortune to build was completely outflanked by a simple little bug in a single library. Once the bug was published, a patch was released (it took several tries to fix all the problems), but this remains a good example of a minor bug destroying the security of an entire system. No doubt, there are still people using the unpatched version of the library.

19.3.2   Expiration

No cryptographic key should be used indefinitely; there is always a risk that the key will be compromised. Regular key changes let you recover from the compromise, albeit slowly. A certificate should not be valid forever either, because both the CA's key and the public key that is being certified expire. Apart from these cryptographic reasons, expiration is important in keeping information up-to-date. When a certificate expires, a new one will have to be reissued, and this creates an opportunity to update the information in the certificate. A typical expiration interval is somewhere between a few months and a few years.

Almost all certificate systems include an expiration date and time. Nobody should accept the certificate after this date and time. This is why participants in a PKI need a clock.

Many designs include other data in the certificate. Often certificates have a not-valid-before time in addition to the expiration time. There can be different classes of certificates, certificate serial numbers, date and time of issue, etc. Some of this data is useful, some useless.

The most commonly used format for certificates is X.509 v3, which includes an inordinate amount of junk. Should you ever wish to go insane, take a look at Peter Gutmann's X.509 style guide [40]. If you work on a system that doesn't have to be interoperable with other systems, you are much better off forgetting X.509. If you must use X.509, you have our condolences.

19.3.3   Separate Registration Authority

Sometimes you will see a system with a separate registration authority. The problem is a political one. It is the HR department of a company that decides who is an employee. But the IT department has to run the CA; that is a technical job that they are not going to allow the HR department to do.

There are two good solutions to this. The first one is to use a multilevel certificate structure and let the HR department be its own sub-CA. This automatically provides the necessary flexibility to support multiple sites. The second solution is much like the first one, except that once a user has a two-level certificate he exchanges it for a one-level certificate at the central CA. This eliminates the overhead of checking a two-level certificate each time it is used, at the cost of adding a simple two-message protocol to the system.

The really bad solution is to add a third party to the cryptographic protocol. The project specifications will talk about the CA and another party that might be called something like the RA (Registration Authority). The CA and RA are treated as completely separate entities, which adds more than

100 pages of documentation to the system. That is bad in itself. Then there is the need to specify the RA–CA interaction. We've even seen three-party protocols in which the RA authorizes the CA to issue a certificate. This is madness, but it is a good example of the problem of imposing user requirements on a technical solution. User requirements only specify the outside behavior of a system. The company needs to have separate functionality for the HR and IT departments. But that does not mean that the software has to have different code for the HR and IT departments. In many situations, and certainly in this one, the two departments can use much of the same functionality, and thus much of the same code. Using a single set of certificate functions leads to a design that is simpler, cheaper, more powerful, and more flexible than one based directly on the original requirements which included both a CA and an RA entity. A two-level CA scheme allows HR and IT to share most of the code and protocols. The differences in this case are mostly in the user interface and should be easy to implement. That translates to maybe a few hundred lines of extra code, not a few hundred extra pages of specifications that turn into tens of thousands of lines of code.

19.4   Conclusion

What we have described is a dream, but a very important dream. PKI is the first and last word on key management for most of our industry. People have been brought up on this dream, and see it as something so obvious that it doesn't need stating. To be able to understand them you must understand the PKI dream, because a lot of what they say is within the context of the dream. And it feels *so* good to think that you have a solution to the key management problem. . . .

Chapter 20

PKI Reality

Time to destroy a dream. There are some fundamental problems with the basic idea of a PKI. Not in theory, but then, theory is something very different from practice. PKIs simply don't work in the real world like they do in the dream. This is why the PKI hype of a few years ago never matched the reality.

20.1 Names

We'll start with a relatively simple problem: the concept of a name. The PKI ties Alice's public key to her name. What is a name?

Let's begin in a simple setting. In a small village, everybody knows everybody else by sight. Everybody has a name, and the name is either unique or will be made unique. If there are two Johns, they will quickly come to be called something like Big John and Little John. For each name there is one person, but one person might have several names; Big John might also be called Sheriff.

The name we are talking about here is not the name that appears on legal documents. It is the name that people use to refer to you. A name is really any kind of data that is used to refer to a person, or more generally, to an entity. Your "official" name is just one of many names, and for many people it is one that is rarely used.

As the village grows into a town, the number of people increases until you no longer know them all. Names start losing their immediate association with a person. There might only be a single J. Smith in town, but you might not know him. Names now start to lead a life of their own, divorced from the actual person. You start talking about people you have never actually met. Maybe you end up talking in the bar about the rich Mr. Smith who just moved here and who is going to sponsor the high-school football team next year. Two weeks later you find out that this is the same person that joined your baseball team two months ago, and whom you know by now as John. People still have multiple names, after all. It just isn't obvious which names belong together, and which person they refer to.

As the town grows into a city, this changes even more. Soon you will only know a very small subset of the people. What is more, names are no longer unique. It doesn't really help to know that you are looking for a John Smith if there are a hundred of them in the city. The meaning of a name starts to depend on the context. Alice might know three Johns, but when at work she talks about "John," it is clear from the context that she means the John upstairs in sales. Later at home it might mean John the neighbor's kid. The relationship between a name and a person becomes even fuzzier.

Now consider the Internet. Soon a billion people will be online. What does the name "John Smith" mean there? Almost nothing: there are too many of them. So instead of more traditional names we use e-mail addresses. You now communicate with jsmith533@yahoo.com. That is certainly a unique name, but in practice it does not link to a person in the sense of someone you will ever meet. Even if you could find out information such as his address and phone number, he is just as likely to live on the other side of the world. You are never going to meet him in person unless you really set out to do so. Not surprisingly, it is not uncommon for people to take on different online personalities. And as always, each person has multiple names. Most users acquire multiple e-mail addresses after a while. (We have a dozen between us.) But it is extremely difficult to find out whether two e-mail addresses refer to the same person. And to make things more complicated, there are people who share an e-mail address, so that "name" refers to them both.

There are large organizations that try to assign names to everybody. The best-known ones are governments. Most countries require each person to have a single official name, which is then used on passports and other official documents. The name itself is not unique—there are many people with the same name—so in practice it is often extended with things like address, driver's license number, and date of birth. This still does not guarantee a unique identifier for a person, however.[1] Also, several of these identifiers can change over the course of a person's life. People change their addresses, driver's license numbers, names, and even gender. Just about the only thing that doesn't change is the date of birth, but this is compensated for by the fact that plenty of people lie about their date of birth, in effect changing it.

Just in case you thought that each person has a single government-sanctioned official name, this isn't true either. Some people are stateless and have no papers at all. Others have dual nationalities, with two governments each trying to establish an official name—and for various reasons, they may not agree on what the official name should be. The two governments might use different alphabets, in which case the names cannot be the same. Some countries require a name that fits the national language, and will modify foreign names to a similar "proper" name in their own language.

To avoid confusion, many countries assign unique numbers to individuals, like the Social Security number (SSN) in the United States or the SoFi number in the Netherlands. The whole point of this number is to provide a unique and fixed name for an individual so that his actions can be tracked and linked together. To a large degree these numbering schemes are successful, but they also have their weaknesses. The link between the actual human and the assigned number is not very tight, and false numbers are used on a large scale in certain sectors of the economy. And as these numbering schemes work on a per-country basis, they do not provide global coverage or global uniqueness.

One more aspect of names deserves mention. In Europe there are privacy laws that restrict what kind of information an organization can store about people. For example, a supermarket is not allowed to ask for, store, or otherwise process an SSN or SoFi number for its loyalty program. This restricts the reuse of government-imposed naming schemes.

So what name should you use in a PKI? Because many people have many different names, this becomes a problem. Maybe Alice wants to have two keys, one for her business and one for her private correspondence. But she

---

[1]Driver's license numbers are unique, but not everybody has one.

might use her maiden name for her business and her married name for her private correspondence. Things like this quickly lead to serious problems if you try to build a universal PKI. This is one of the reasons why smaller application-specific PKIs work much better than a single large one.

20.2   Authority

Who is this CA that claims authority to assign keys to names? What makes that CA authoritative with respect to these names? Who decides whether Alice is an employee who gets VPN access or a customer of the bank with restricted access?

For most of our examples this is a question that is simple to answer. The employer knows who is an employee and who isn't; the bank knows who is a customer. This gives us our first indication of which organization should be the CA. Unfortunately, there doesn't seem to be an authoritative source for the universal PKI. This is one of the reasons why a universal PKI cannot work.

Whenever you are planning a PKI you have to think about who is authorized to issue the certificates. For example, it is easy for a company to be authoritative with regard to its employees. The company doesn't decide what the employee's name is, but it does know what name the employee is known by *within the company*. If "Fred Smith" is officially called Alfred, this does not matter. The name "Fred Smith" is a perfectly good name within the context of the employees of the company.

20.3   Trust

Key management is the most difficult problem in cryptography, and a PKI system is one of the best tools that we have to solve it with. But everything depends on the security of the PKI, and therefore on the trustworthiness of the CA. Think about the damage that can be done if the CA starts to forge certificates. The CA can impersonate anyone in the system, and security completely breaks down.

A universal PKI is very tempting, but trust is really the area where it fails. If you are a bank and you need to communicate with your customers, would you trust some dot-com on the other side of the world? Or even your local government bureaucracy? What is the total amount of money you could lose if the CA does something horribly wrong? How much liability is the CA willing to take on? Will your local banking regulations allow you to use a foreign CA? These are all enormous problems. Just imagine the damage that can occur if the CA's private key is published on a Web site....

Think of it in traditional terms. The CA is the organization that hands out the keys to the buildings. Most large office buildings have guards, and most guards are hired from an outside security service. The guards verify that the rules are being obeyed: a rather straightforward job. But deciding who gets which keys is not something that you typically outsource to another company because it is a fundamental part of the security policy. For the same reason, the CA functionality should not be outsourced.

No organization in the world is trusted by everybody. There isn't even one that is trusted by *most* people. Therefore there will never be a universal PKI. The logical conclusion is that we will have to use lots of small PKIs. And this is exactly the solution we suggest for our examples. The bank can be its own CA; after all, the bank trusts itself, and all the customers already trust the bank with their money. A company can be its own CA for the VPN, and the credit card organization can also run its own CA.

An interesting observation here is that the trust relationships that are used by the CA are ones that already exist and are based on contractual relationships. This is always the case when you design cryptographic systems: the basic trust relationships that you build on are all based on contractual relationships.

20.4 Indirect Authorization

Now we come to a big problem with the classical PKI dream. The PKI ties keys to names, but most systems are not interested in the name of the person. The banking system wants to know which transactions to authorize. The VPN wants to know which directories to allow access to. None of these

systems cares *who* the key belongs to, only *what* the keyholder is authorized
to do.

To this end, most systems use some kind of *access control list*, or ACL.
This is just a database of who is authorized to do what. Sometimes it is
sorted by user (e.g., Bob is allowed the following things: access files in the
directory /usr/bob, use the office printer, access the file server), but most
systems keep the database indexed by action (e.g., charges to this account
must be authorized by Bob or Betty). Often there are ways to create groups
of people to make the ACLs simpler, but the basic functionality remains the
same.

So now we have three different objects: a key, a name, and permission to
do something. What the system wants to know is which key authorizes
which action, or in other words, whether a particular key has a particular
permission. The classical PKI solves this by tying keys to names and using
an ACL to tie names to permissions. This is a roundabout method that
introduces additional points of attack [28].

The first point of attack is the name–key certificate provided by the PKI. The
second point of attack is the ACL database that ties names to permissions.
The third point of attack is name confusion: with names being such fuzzy
things, how do you compare whether the name in the ACL is the same as
the name in the PKI certificate? And how do you avoid giving two people
the same name?

If you analyze this situation, you will clearly see that the technical design
has followed the naive formulation of the requirements. People think of
the problem in terms of identifying the key holder and who should have
access—that is how a security guard would approach the problem. Automated systems can use a much more direct approach. A door lock doesn't
care who is holding the key, but allows access to anyone with the key.

20.5   Direct Authorization

A much better solution is to directly tie the permissions to the key, using
the PKI. The certificate no longer links the key to a name; it links the key
to a set of permissions [28].

All systems that use the PKI certificates can now decide directly whether to allow access or not. They just look at the certificate provided and see if the key has the appropriate permissions. It is direct and simple.

Direct authorization removes the ACL and the names from the authorization process, thereby eliminating these points of attack. Some of the problems will, of course, reappear at the point where certificates are issued. Someone must decide who is allowed to do what, and ensure that this decision is encoded in the certificates properly. The database of all these decisions becomes the equivalent of the ACL database, but this database is less easy to attack. First of all, it is easy to distribute to the people making the decisions, removing the central ACL database and its associated vulnerabilities. Decision makers can just issue the appropriate certificate to the user without further security-critical infrastructure. This also removes much of the reliance on names, because the decision makers are much further down in the hierarchy and have a much smaller set of people to deal with. They often know the users personally, or at least by sight, which helps a great deal in avoiding name confusion problems.

So can we just get rid of the names in the certificates then?

Well, no. Though the names will not be used during normal operations, we do need to provide logging data for audits and such. Suppose the bank just processed a salary payment authorized by one of the four keys that has payment authority for that account. Three days later, the CFO calls the bank and asks why the payment was made. The bank knows the payment was authorized, but it has to provide more information to the CFO than just a few thousand random-looking bits of public-key data. This is why we still include a name in every certificate. The bank can now tell the CFO that the key used to authorize the payment belonged to "J. Smith," which is enough for the CFO to figure out what happened. But the important thing here is that the names only need to be meaningful to humans. The computer never tries to figure out whether two names are the same, or which person the name belongs to. Humans are much better at dealing with the fuzzy names, whereas computers like simple and well-specified things such as sets of permissions.

20.6 Credential Systems

If you push this principle further, you get a full-fledged credential system. This is the cryptographer's super-PKI. Basically, it requires that you need a credential in the form of a signed certificate for every action you perform. If Alice has a credential that lets her read and write a particular file, then she can delegate some or all of her authority to Bob. For example, she could sign a certificate on Bob's public key that reads something like "Key PK_{Bob} is authorized to read file X by delegated authority of key PK_{Alice}." If Bob wants to read file X, he has to present this certificate and a certificate proof that Alice has read access to file X.

A credential system can add additional features. Alice could limit the time validity of the delegation by including the validity period in the certificate. Alice might also limit Bob's ability to delegate the authority to read file X.[2]

In theory, a credential system is extremely powerful and flexible. In practice, they are rarely used. There are several reasons for this.

First of all, credential systems are quite complex and can impose a noticeable overhead. Your authority to access a resource might depend on a chain of half-a-dozen certificates, each of which has to be transmitted and checked.

The second problem is that credential systems invite a micromanagement of access. It is so easy to split authorities into smaller and smaller pieces that users end up spending entirely too much time deciding exactly how much authority to delegate to a colleague. This time is often wasted, but a bigger problem is the loss of the colleague's time when it turns out he doesn't have enough access to do his job. Maybe this micromanagement problem can be solved with better user education and better user interfaces, but that seems to be an open problem. Some users avoid the micromanagement problem by delegating (almost) all their authority to anyone who needs any kind of access, effectively undermining the entire security system.

---

[2]This is an often-requested feature, but we believe it may not be a good one. Limiting Bob's ability to delegate his authority just invites him to run a proxy program so that other people can use his credential to access a resource. Such proxy programs undermine the security infrastructure and should be banned, but this is only tenable if there are no operational reasons to run a proxy. And there are always operational reasons why someone needs to delegate authority.

The third problem is that you need to develop a credential and delegation language. The delegation messages need to be written in some sort of logical language that computers can understand. This language needs to be powerful enough to express all the desired functionality, yet simple enough to allow fast chaining of conclusions. It also has to be future-proof. Once a credential system is deployed, every program will need to include code to interpret the delegation language. Upgrading to a new version of the delegation language can be very difficult, especially since security functionality spreads into every piece of a system. Yet it is effectively impossible to design a delegation language that is general enough to satisfy all future requirements, since we never know what the future will bring. This remains an area of further research.

The fourth problem with credential systems is probably insurmountable. Detailed delegation of authority is simply too complex a concept for the average user. There doesn't seem to be a way of presenting access rules to users in a manner they can understand. Asking users to make decisions about which authorities to delegate is bound to fail. We see that in the real world already. In some student houses it is customary for one person to go to the ATM and get cash for several people. The other students lend him their ATM card and PIN code. This is an eminently stupid thing to do, yet it is done by some of the supposedly smarter people in our society. As consultants, we've visited many companies and sometimes had work-related reasons to have access to the local network. It is amazing how much access we got. We've had system administrators give us unrestricted access to the research data, when all we needed to do was look at a file or two. If system administrators can't get this right, ordinary users certainly won't.

As cryptographers, we'd love the idea of a credential system if only the users were able to manage the complexity. There is undoubtedly a lot of interesting research to do on human interactions with security systems.

There is, however, one area where credentials are very useful and should be mandatory. If you use a hierarchical CA structure, the central CA signs certificates on the keys of the sub-CAs. If these certificates do not include any kind of restriction, then each sub-CA has unlimited power. This is bad security design; we've just multiplied the number of places where system-critical keys are stored.

In a hierarchical CA structure, the power of a sub-CA should be limited by including restrictions in the certificate on its key. This requires a credential-like delegation language for CA operations. Exactly what type of restrictions you'd want to impose depends on the application. Just think about what type of sub-CAs you want to create and how their power should be limited.

20.7   The Modified Dream

Let's summarize all the criticism of PKIs we've presented so far and present a modified dream. This is a more realistic representation of what a PKI should be.

First of all, each application has its own PKI with its own CA. The world consists of a large number of small PKIs. Each user is a member of many different PKIs at the same time.

The user must use different keys for each PKI, as he cannot use the same key in different systems without careful coordination in the design of the two systems. The user's key store will therefore contain dozens of keys, requiring tens of kilobytes of storage space.

The PKI's main purpose is to tie a credential to the key. The bank's PKI ties Alice's key to the credential that allows access to Alice's account. Or the company's PKI ties Alice's key to a credential that allows access to the VPN. Significant changes to a user's credentials require a new certificate to be issued. Certificates still contain the user's name, but this is mainly for management and auditing purposes.

This modified dream is far more realistic. It is also more powerful, more flexible, and more secure than the original dream. It is very tempting to believe that this modified dream will solve your key management problems. But in the next section we will encounter the hardest problem of all—one that will never be solved fully and will always require compromises.

20.8 Revocation

The hardest problem to solve in a PKI is revocation. Sometimes a certificate has to be withdrawn. Maybe Bob's computer was hacked and his private key was compromised. Maybe Alice was transferred to a different department or even fired from the company. You can think of all kinds of situations where you want to revoke a certificate.

The problem is that a certificate is just a bunch of bits. These bits have been used in many places and are stored in many places. You can't make the world forget the certificate, however hard you try. Bruce lost a PGP key almost a decade ago; he still gets e-mail encrypted with the corresponding certificate.[3] Even trying to make the world forget the certificate is unrealistic. If a thief breaks into Bob's computer and steals his private key, you can be certain that he also made a copy of the certificate on the corresponding public key.

Each system has its own requirements, but in general, revocation requirements differ in three variables:

- *Speed of revocation.* What is the maximum amount of time allowed between the revocation command and the last use of the certificate?

- *Reliability of revocation.* Is it acceptable that under some circumstances revocation isn't fully effective? What residual risk is acceptable?

- *Number of revocations.* How many revocations should the revocation system handle at a time?

There are two workable solutions to the revocation problem: revocation lists and fast expiration.

20.8.1 Revocation List

A *certificate revocation list*, or CRL, is a database that contains a list of revoked certificates. Everybody who wants to verify a certificate must check the CRL database to see if the certificate has been revoked.

---

[3]PGP has its own strange PKI-like structure called the *web of trust*. In practice, it is too complicated to explain to users, and it is used only on a limited scale.

A central CRL database has nice properties. Revocation is almost instantaneous. Once a certificate has been added to the CRL, no further transactions will be authorized. Revocation is also very reliable, and there is no direct upper limit on how many certificates can be revoked.

The central CRL database also has significant disadvantages. Everybody must be online all the time to be able to check the CRL database. The CRL database also introduces a single point of failure: if it is not available, no actions can be performed. If you try to solve this by authorizing parties to proceed whenever the CRL is unavailable, then attackers will use denial-of-service attacks to disable the CRL database and destroy the revocation capability of the system.

An alternative is to have a distributed CRL database. You could make a redundant mirrored database using a dozen servers spread out over the world, and hope it is reliable enough. But such redundant databases are so expensive to build and maintain that they are normally not an option. Don't forget, nobody wants to spend money on security.

Some systems simply send copies of the entire CRL database to every device in the system. The U.S. military STU-III encrypted telephone works in this manner. This is similar to the little booklets of stolen credit card numbers that used to be sent to each merchant. It is relatively easy to do. You can just let every device download the updated CRL from a Web server every half hour or so, at the cost of increasing the revocation time. However, this solution restricts the size of the CRL database. Most of the time you can't afford to copy hundreds of thousands of CRL entries to every device in the system. We've seen systems where the requirements state that every device must be capable of storing a list of 50 CRL entries. No prize for figuring out how to attack such a system.

In our experience, CRL systems are expensive to implement and maintain. They require their own infrastructure, management, communication paths, and so on. A considerable amount of extra functionality is required just to handle the comparatively rarely used functionality of revocation.

20.8.2   Fast Expiration

Instead of revocation lists, you can use fast expiration. This makes use of the already existing expiration mechanism. The CA simply issues certificates with a very short expiration time, ranging anywhere from 10 minutes to 24 hours. Each time Alice wants to use her certificate, she gets a new one from the CA. She can then use it for as long as it remains valid. The exact expiration speed can be tuned to the requirements of the application, but a certificate validity period of less than 10 minutes does not seem to be very practical.

The major advantage of this scheme is that it uses the already available certificate issuing mechanism. No separate CRL is required, which significantly reduces the overall system complexity. All you need to do to revoke a permission is to inform the CA of the new access rules. Of course, everybody still needs to be online all the time to get the certificates reissued.

Simplicity is one of our main design criteria, so we prefer fast expiration to a CRL database. Whether fast expiration is possible depends mostly on whether the application demands instantaneous revocation, or whether a delay is acceptable.

20.8.3   Revocation Is Required

Because revocation can be hard to implement, it becomes very tempting not to implement it at all. Some PKI proposals make no mention of revocation. Others list the CRL as a future extension possibility. In reality, a PKI without some form of revocation is pretty useless. Real-life circumstances mean that keys *do* get compromised, and access has to be revoked. Operating a PKI without a working revocation system is somewhat like operating a ship without a bilge pump. In theory, the ship should be watertight and it shouldn't need a bilge pump. In practice, there is always water collecting in the bottom of the ship, and if you don't get rid of it, the ship eventually sinks.

20.9   So What Is a PKI Good For?

At the very beginning of our PKI discussion we stated that the purpose of having a PKI is to allow Alice and Bob to generate a shared secret key, which they use to create a secure channel, which they in turn use to communicate securely with each other. Alice wants to authenticate Bob (and vice versa) without talking to a third party. The PKI is supposed to make this possible.

But it doesn't.

There is *no* revocation system that works offline. It is easy to see why. If neither Alice nor Bob contacts any outside party, neither of them can ever be informed that one of their keys has been revoked. So the revocation checks force them to go online. Both our revocation solutions require online connections.

But if we are online, then we don't need a big complex PKI. We can achieve our security by simply setting up a central key server, such as the ones we described in chapter 18.

Let's compare the advantages of a PKI over a key server system:

- A key server requires everybody to be online in real time. If you can't reach the key server, you can't do anything at all. There is no way Alice and Bob can recognize each other. A PKI gives you some advantages. If you use expiration for revocation, then you only need to contact the central server once in a while; for applications that use certificates with validity periods of hours, the requirement for real-time online access is significantly relaxed. Even if you use a CRL database, you might have rules on how to proceed if the CRL database cannot be reached. Credit card systems have rules like this. If you can't get automatic authorization, any transaction up to a certain amount is okay. These rules would have to be based on a risk analysis, including the risk of a denial-of-service attack on the CRL system, but at least you get the option of proceeding; the key server solution provides no alternatives.

- The key server is a single point of failure. Distributing the key server is difficult, since it contains all the keys in the system. You really don't want to start spreading your secret keys throughout the world. The CRL database, in contrast, is much less security-critical and is easier to distribute. The fast-expiration solution makes the CA a point of failure. But large systems almost always have a hierarchical CA, which means that the CA is already distributed and failures affect only a small part of the system.

- In theory, a PKI should provide you with nonrepudiation. Once Alice has signed a message with her key, she should not be able to later deny that she signed the message. A key server system can never provide this; the central server has access to the same key that Alice uses and can therefore forge an arbitrary message to make it look as if Alice sent it. In real life, nonrepudiation doesn't work because people cannot store their secret keys sufficiently well. If Alice wants to deny that she signed a message, she is simply going to claim that a virus infected her machine and stole her private key.

- The most important key of a PKI is the CA root key. This key does not have to be stored in a computer that is online. Rather, it can be stored securely, and only loaded into an offline computer when needed. The root key is only used to sign the certificates of the sub-CAs, and this is done only rarely. In contrast, the key server system has the master key material in an online computer. Computers that are offline are much harder to attack than those that are online, so this makes a PKI potentially more secure.

So there are a few advantages to PKIs. They are nice to have, but none of them gives you a really critical advantage. These advantages only come at a stiff price. A PKI is much more complex than a key server system, and the public-key computations require a lot more computational power.

20.10 What to Choose

So how should you set up your key management system? Should you use a key server–type scheme or a PKI-type scheme? As always, this depends on your exact requirements.

For small systems, the extra complexity of a PKI is not warranted. We think it is easier to use the key server approach. This is mainly because the advantages of a PKI over the key server approach are more relevant for large installations than for small ones.

For large systems, the additional flexibility of a PKI is still attractive. A PKI can be a more distributed system. Credential-style extensions allow the central CA to limit the authority of the sub-CAs. This in turn makes it easy to set up small sub-CAs that cover a particular area of operations. As the sub-CA is limited in the certificates it can issue by the certificate on its own key, the sub-CA cannot pose a risk to the system as a whole. For large systems, such flexibility and risk limitation are important.

If you are building a large system, we would advise you to look very seriously at a PKI solution, but do compare it to a key server solution. You'll have to see if the PKI advantages outweigh its extra cost and complexity. One problem might be that you really want to use credential-style limitations for your sub-CAs. To do this, you must be able to express the limitations in a logical framework. There is no generic framework in which this can be done, so this ends up being a customer-specific part of the design. It probably also means that you cannot use an off-the-shelf product for your PKI, as they are unlikely to have an appropriate certificate restriction language.

Chapter 21

PKI Practicalities

If you need a PKI, you will have to decide whether to buy it or build it. You can buy PKI products, although if you did that you wouldn't need this book. This is an engineering book, not a buyer's guide. Therefore, we'll assume you're rolling your own. We'll discuss some of the practical considerations that occur when designing a PKI system.

21.1 Certificate Format

Whatever you do, stay away from X.509 certificates. If you need a reason, read [40] and weep. Doing it yourself is probably easier. A certificate is just a data type with multiple and optional fields. This is a straightforward software engineering problem that we won't discuss in detail. Note that it is important that the encoding of a particular data structure be unique, because in cryptography we often hash a data structure to sign it or compare it. A format like XML, which allows several representations of the same data structure, requires extra care to ensure that signatures and hashes always work as they should.

21.1.1   Permission Language

For all but the simplest of PKI systems, you really want to be able to restrict the certificates that a sub-CA can issue. To do that you need to encode a restriction into the sub-CA's certificate, which in turn requires a language in which to express the key's permissions. This is probably the hardest point of the PKI design, and we can't help you with it. The restrictions that you are going to need depend on your application. If you can't find sensible restrictions, you should rethink your decision to use a PKI. Without restrictions in the certificates, every sub-CA effectively has a master key— and that is a bad security design. You could restrict yourself to a single CA, but then you would lose many of the advantages of a PKI over a key server system.

21.1.2   The Root Key

To do anything, the CA must have a public/private key pair. Generating this pair is straightforward. The public key needs to be distributed to every participant, together with some extra data, such as the validity period of this key. To simplify the system, this is normally done using a self-certifying certificate, which is a rather odd construction. The CA signs a certificate on its own public key. Although it is called self-certifying, it is nothing of the sort. The name self-certification is a historical misnomer that we are stuck with. The certificate doesn't certify the key at all, and it proves nothing about the security properties of the key, because anyone can create a public key and self-certify it. What the self-certification does is tie additional data to the public key. The permission list, validity period, human contact data, etc., are all included in the self-certificate. The self-certificate uses the same data format as all other certificates in the system, and all participants can reuse the existing code to check this additional data. The self-certificate is called the root certificate of the PKI.

The next step is to distribute the root certificate to all the system's participants in a secure manner. Everybody must know the root certificate, and everybody must have the right root certificate.

The first time a computer joins the PKI, it will have to be given the root certificate in a secure manner. This can be as simple as pointing the computer at a local file or a file on a trusted Web server, and telling the machine that this is the root certificate for the PKI in question. Cryptography cannot help with this initial distribution of the root certificate, because there are no keys that can be used to provide the authentication. The same situation occurs if the private key of the CA is ever compromised. Once the root key is no longer secure, an entirely new PKI structure will have to be initialized, and this involves giving every participant the root certificate in a secure manner. This should provide a good motivation for keeping the root key secure.

The root key expires after a while, and the central CA will have to issue a new key. Distributing the new root certificate is easier. The new root certificate can be signed with the old root key. Participants can download the new root certificate from an insecure source. As it is signed with the old root key, it cannot be modified. The only possible problem is if a participant does not get the new root certificate. Most systems overlap the validity of the root keys by a few months to allow sufficient time for switching to the new root key.

There is a small implementation issue here. The new CA root certificate should probably have two signatures—one with the old root key so that users can recognize the new root certificate, and one (self-certifying) signature with the new root key to be used by new devices that are introduced after the old key expires. You can do this either by including support for multiple signatures in your certificate format, or by simply issuing two separate certificates for the same new root key.

21.2 The Life of a Key

Let's consider the lifetime of a single key. This can be the CA's root key, or any other public key. A key goes through several phases in its life. Not all keys require all phases, depending on the application. As an example we'll use Alice's public key.

Creation The first step in the life of a key is creation. Alice creates a public/private key pair and stores the private part in a secure manner.

Certification The next step is certification. Alice takes her public key to the CA or the sub-CA, and has it certify her key. This is the point where the CA decides which permissions to give to Alice's public key.

Distribution Depending on the application, Alice might have to distribute her certified public key before she can use it. If, for example, Alice uses her key for signatures, each party that could potentially receive Alice's signature should have her public key first. The best way to do this is to distribute the key for a while before Alice uses it the first time. This is especially important for a new root certificate. When the CA switches to a new root key, for example, everybody should be given the chance to learn the new root certificate before being presented with a certificate signed with the new key.

Whether you need a separate distribution phase depends on your application. If you can avoid it, do so. A separate distribution phase has to be explained to the users, and becomes visible in the user interface. That, in turn, creates lots of extra work, because many users won't understand what it means and will not use the system properly.

Active use The next phase is when Alice uses her key actively for transactions. This is the normal situation for a key.

Passive use After the active use phase, there must be a period of time where Alice no longer uses her key for new transactions, but everybody still accepts the key. Transactions are not instantaneous; sometimes they get delayed. A signed e-mail could very well take a day or two to reach its destination. Alice should stop using her key actively and allow a reasonable period for all pending transactions to be completed before the key expires.

Expired Finally, the key expires and it is not considered to be valid anymore.

How are the key phases defined? The most common solution is to include explicit times for each phase transition in the certificate. The certificate contains the start of the distribution phase, the start of the active use phase, the start of the inactive use phase, and the expiration time. Unfortunately, all of these times have to be presented to the user, because they affect the way the certificate works, and this is probably too complicated for ordinary users to handle.

A more flexible scheme is to have a central database that contains the phase of each key, but this introduces a whole new raft of security issues, which we'd rather not do. And if you have a CRL, it can override the chosen phase periods and expire a key immediately.

Things become even more complicated if Alice wants to use the same key in several different PKIs. In general, we think this is a bad idea, but sometimes it cannot be avoided. Suppose Alice uses a small tamper-resistant module that she carries with her. This module contains her private keys and performs the necessary computations for a digital signature. Such modules have a limited storage capacity. Alice's certificates on her public key can be stored on the corporate intranet without size limitations, but the small module cannot store an unlimited number of private keys. In situations like this, Alice ends up using the same key for multiple PKIs. It also implies that the key lifetime schedule should be similar for all the PKIs Alice uses. This might be difficult to coordinate.

If you ever work on a system like this, make sure that a signature used in one PKI cannot be used in another PKI. You should always use a single digital signature scheme, such as the one explained in section 13.7. The signed string of bytes should not be the same in two different PKI systems or in two different applications. The simplest solution is to include data in the string to be signed that uniquely identifies the application and the PKI.

21.3   Why Keys Wear Out

We've mentioned several times that keys have to be replaced regularly, but why is this?

In a perfect world, a key could be used for a very long time. An attacker who has no system weaknesses to work with is reduced to doing exhaustive searches. In theory, that reduces our problem to one of choosing large enough keys.

The real world isn't perfect. There are always threats to the secrecy of a key. The key must be stored somewhere, and an attacker might try to get at it. The key must also be used, and any use poses another threat. The key has to be transported from the storage location to the point where the relevant computations are done. This will often be within a single piece of equipment, but it opens up a new avenue of attack. If the attacker can eavesdrop on the communication channel used for this transport, then he gets a copy of the key. Then there is the cryptographic operation that is done with the key. There are no useful cryptographic functions that have a proof of security. They are all based on ad hoc arguments, along the lines of: "Well, none of us has found a way to attack this function, so it looks pretty safe."[1]

The longer you keep a key, and the more you use it, the higher the chance that an attacker might manage to get your key. If you want to limit the chance of the attacker knowing your key, you have to limit the lifetime of the key. In effect, a key wears out.

There is another reason to limit the lifetime of a key. Suppose something untoward happens and the attacker gets the key. This breaks the security of the system, and causes damage of some form. (Revocation is only effective if you find out that the attacker has the key; a clever attacker would try to avoid detection.) This damage lasts until the key is replaced with a new key. By limiting the lifetime of a single key, we limit the window of exposure to an attacker who has been successful.

There are thus two advantages to short key lives. They reduce the chance that an attacker gets a key, and they limit the damage that is done if he nevertheless succeeds.

So what is a reasonable lifetime? That depends on the situation. There is a cost to changing keys, so you don't want to change them too often. On the other hand, if you only change them once a decade, you can be sure that the change-to-a-new-key function will not work at the end of the decade. As a general rule, a function or procedure that is rarely used or tested doesn't

---

[1]What is often called a "proof of security" for cryptographic functions is no such thing. These proofs are merely reductions: if you can break function A, you can also break function B. They are valuable in allowing you to reduce the number of primitive operations you have to assume are secure, but they do not provide a real-world proof of security.

work.[2] Probably the biggest danger in having long-term keys is that the change-key function is never used, and therefore will not work well when it is needed. A key lifetime of one year is probably a reasonable maximum.

Key changes in which the user has to be involved are relatively expensive, so they should be done infrequently. Reasonable key lifetimes are from one month and upwards. Keys with shorter lifetimes will have to be managed automatically.

21.4 So What Should You Do?

We cannot give you a detailed answer without knowing considerably more about the application you are working on, and the environment in which it is supposed to operate. We can give detailed advice on encryption functions, and even key negotiation protocols, but key management is not so much a cryptographic problem as it is a problem of interfacing with the real world. We've given you a number of general guidelines, and we realize these are not enough to design your key management system. But we feel it is impossible to give accurate advice without knowing the particular situation you are facing, and a book is not a good vehicle for giving personalized advice.

---

[2]This is a generally applicable truism, and is the main reason why you should always test emergency procedures, such as fire drills.

Chapter 22

Storing Secrets

We discussed the problem of storing transient secrets, such as session keys, back in section 9.3. But how do we store long-term secrets, such as passwords and private keys? We have two opposing requirements. First of all, the secret should be kept secret. Second, the risk of losing the secret altogether (i.e., not being able to find the secret again) should be minimal.

22.1 Disk

One of the obvious ideas is to store the secret on the hard drive in the computer or on some other permanent storage medium. This works, but only if the computer is kept secure. If Alice stores her keys (without encryption) on her PC, then anyone who uses her PC can use her keys. Most PCs are used by other people, at least occasionally. Alice won't mind letting someone else use her PC, but she certainly doesn't want to grant access to her bank account at the same time! Another problem is that Alice probably uses several computers. If her keys are stored on her PC at home, she cannot use them while at work or while traveling. And should she store her keys on her desktop machine at home or on her laptop? We really don't want her to copy the keys to multiple places; that only weakens the system further.

A better solution would be for Alice to store her keys on her PDA. A PDA is less likely to be lent out, and it is something that she takes with her everywhere she goes. (An alternative for the PDA would be her cell phone or wristwatch, but to use them requires updates to the infrastructure that are outside our scope.)

You'd think that security would improve if we encrypt the secrets. Sure, but with what? We need a master key to encrypt the secrets with, and that master key needs to be stored somewhere. Storing it next to the encrypted secrets doesn't give you any advantage. This *is* a good technique to reduce the number and size of secrets though, and it is widely used in combination with other techniques. For example, a private RSA key is several thousand bits long, but by encrypting it with a symmetric key we can reduce the size of the required secure storage by a significant factor.

22.2 Human Memory

The next idea is to store the key in Alice's brain. We get her to memorize a password, and encrypt all the other key material with this password. The encrypted key material can be stored anywhere—maybe on a disk, but it could also be stored on a Web server where Alice can download it to whatever computer she is using at the moment.

Humans are notoriously bad at memorizing passwords. If you choose very simple passwords, you don't get any security. There are simply not enough simple passwords for them to be really secret: the attacker can just try them all. Using your mother's maiden name doesn't work very well; her name is quite often public knowledge—and even if it isn't, there are probably only a few hundred thousand surnames that the attacker has to try to find the right one.

A good password must be unpredictable. In other words, it must contain a lot of entropy. Normal words, such as passwords, do not contain much entropy. There are about half a million English words—and that is counting all the very long and obscure words in an unabridged dictionary—so a single word as password provides at most 19 bits of entropy. Estimates of the amount of entropy per character in English text vary a bit, but are in the neighborhood of 1.5–2 bits per letter.

We've been using 256-bit secret keys throughout our systems to achieve 128 bits of security. In most places, using a 256-bit key has very little additional cost. However, in this situation the user has to memorize the password (or key), and the additional cost of larger keys is high. Trying to use passwords with 256 bits of entropy is too cumbersome; therefore, we will restrict ourselves to passwords with only 128 bits of entropy.[1]

Using the optimistic estimate of 2 bits per character, we'd need a password of 64 characters to get 128 bits of entropy. That is unacceptable. Users will simply refuse to use such long passwords.

What if we compromise and accept 64 bits of security? That is already very marginal. At 2 bits of entropy per character, we need the password to be at least 32 characters long. Even that is too long for users to deal with. Don't forget, most real-world passwords are only 6–8 letters long.

You could try to use assigned passwords, but have you ever tried to use a system where you are told that your password is "7193275827429946905186"? Or how about "aoekjk3ncmakwe"? Humans simply can't remember such passwords, so this solution doesn't work. (In practice users will write the password down, but we'll discuss that in the next section.)

A much better solution is to use a passphrase. This is similar to a password. In fact, they are so similar that we consider them equivalent. The difference is merely one of emphasis: a passphrase is much longer than a password.

Perhaps Alice could use the passphrase, "Pink curtains meander across the ocean." That is nonsensical, but fairly easy to remember. It is also 38 characters long, so it probably contains about 57–76 bits of entropy. If Alice expands it to "Pink dotty curtains meander over seas of Xmas wishes," she gets 52 characters for a very reasonable key of 78–104 bits of entropy. Given a keyboard, Alice can type this passphrase in a few seconds, which is certainly much faster than she can type a string of random digits. We rely on the fact that a passphrase is much easier to memorize than random data. Many mnemonic techniques are based on the idea of converting random data to things much closer to our passphrases.

---

[1]For the mathematicians: passwords chosen from a probability distribution with 128 bits of entropy.

Some users don't like to do a lot of typing, so they choose their passphrases slightly differently. How about "Wtnitmtstsaaoof,ottaaasot,aboet."? This looks like total nonsense; that is, until you think of it as the first letters of the words of a sentence. In this case we used a sentence from Shakespeare: "Whether 'tis nobler in the mind to suffer the slings and arrows of outrageous fortune, or to take arms against a sea of troubles, and by opposing end them." Of course, Alice should not use a sentence from literature; literary texts are too accessible for an attacker, and how many suitable sentences would there be in the books on Alice's bookshelf? Instead, she should invent her own sentence, one that nobody else could possibly think of.

Compared to using a full passphrase, the initial-letters-from-each-word technique requires a longer sentence, but it requires less typing for good security because the keystrokes are more random than consecutive letters in a sentence. We don't know of any estimate for the number of bits of entropy per character for this technique. Maybe somebody can do the research and write a paper on various ways of choosing passphrases.

Passphrases are certainly the best way of storing a secret in a human brain. Unfortunately, many users still find it difficult to use them correctly. And even with passphrases, it is extremely difficult to get 128 bits of entropy in the human brain.

22.2.1   Salting and Stretching

To squeeze the most security out of a limited-entropy password or passphrase, we can use two techniques that sound as if they come from a medieval torture chamber. These are so simple and obvious that they should be used in every password system. There is really no excuse not to use them.

The first is to add a *salt*. This is simply a random number that is stored alongside the data that was encrypted with the password. If you can, use a 256-bit salt.

The next step is to *stretch* the password. Stretching is essentially a very long computation. Let p be the password and s be the salt. Using any cryptographically strong hash function h, we compute

$$x_0 := 0$$
$$x_i := h(x_{i-1} \,\|\, p \,\|\, s) \qquad \text{for } i = 1, \ldots, r$$
$$K := x_r$$

and use K as the key to actually encrypt the data. The parameter r is the number of iterations in the computation, and should be as large as practical. (It goes without saying that x_i and K should be 256 bits long.)

Let's look at this from an attacker's point of view. Given the salt s and some data that is encrypted with K, you try to find K by trying different passwords. Choose a particular password p, compute the corresponding K, decrypt the data and check whether it makes sense. If it doesn't, then p must have been false. To check a single value for p you have to do r different hash computations. The larger r is, the more work the attacker has to do.

In normal use, the stretching computation has to be done every time a password is used. But remember, this is at a point in time where the user has just entered a password. It has probably taken several seconds to enter the password, so using 200 ms for password processing is quite acceptable. Here is our rule to choose r: choose r such that computing K from (s, p) takes 200–1000 ms on the user's equipment. Computers get faster over time, so r should be increasing over time as well. Ideally, you determine r experimentally when the user first sets the password, and store r alongside s. (Do make sure that r is a reasonable value, not too small or too large.)

How much have we gained? If $r = 2^{20}$ (just over a million) then the attacker has to do 2^{20} hash computations for each password she tries. Trying 2^{60} passwords would take 2^{80} hash computations, so effectively using $r = 2^{20}$ makes the effective key size of the password 20 bits longer. The larger r you choose, the larger the gain.

Look at it another way. What r does is stop the attacker from benefiting from faster and faster computers, because the faster computers get, the larger r gets, too. It is a kind of Moore's law compensator, but only in the long run. Ten years from now, the attacker can use the next decade's technology to attack the password you are using today. So you still need a decent security margin and as much entropy in the password as you can get.

This is another reason to use a key negotiation protocol with forward secrecy. Whatever the application, it is quite likely that Alice's private keys end up being protected by a password. Ten years from now, the attacker will be able to search for Alice's password and find it. But if the key that is encrypted with the password was only used to run a key negotiation protocol with forward secrecy, then the attacker will find nothing of value. Alice's key is no longer valid (it has expired), and knowing her old private key does not reveal the session keys used ten years ago.

The salt stops the attacker from taking advantage of an economy of scale when she is attacking a large number of passwords simultaneously. Suppose there are a million users in the system, and each user stores an encrypted file that contains her keys. Each file is encrypted with the user's stretched password. If we did not use a salt, then the attacker can attack as follows: guess a password p, compute the stretched key K, and try to decrypt each of the key files using K. The stretch function only needs to be computed once for every password, and the resulting stretched key can be used in an attempt to decrypt each of the files.

This is no longer possible when we add the salt to the stretching function. All the salts are random values, so each user will use a different salt value. The attacker now has to compute the stretching function once for each password/file combination, rather than once for each password. This is a lot more work for the attacker, and it comes at a very small price for the users of the system.

So how large a salt value do you need? We can't be bothered to do a detailed analysis. Maybe you can get away with 128 bits (if there are no possible birthday attacks), but why bother? Bits are cheap, and using a 256-bit salt is simpler for everybody.

By the way, do take care when you do this. We once saw a system that implemented all this perfectly, but then some programmer wanted to improve the user interface by giving the user a faster response as to whether the password he had typed was correct or not. So he stored a checksum on the password, which defeated the entire salting and stretching procedure. If the response time is too slow, you can reduce r a bit, but make sure that there is no way to recognize whether a password is correct or not without doing at least r hash computations.

22.3   Portable Storage

The next idea is to store key material outside the computer. The simplest form of storage is a piece of paper with passwords written on it. Most people have that in one form or another, even for noncryptographic systems like Web sites. Many users have at least half a dozen passwords to remember— we certainly have—and that is simply too much, especially for systems where you use your password only rarely. So to remember passwords, users write them down. The limitation to this solution is that the password still has to be processed by the user's eyes, brain, and fingers every time it is used. To keep user irritation and mistakes within reasonable bounds, this technique can only be used with relatively low-entropy passwords and passphrases.

As a designer, you don't have to design or implement anything to use this storage method. Users will use it for their passwords, no matter which rules you make and however you create your password system.

A more advanced form of storage would be a portable memory of some form. This could be a memory-chip card, a floppy disk, a magnetic stripe card, or any other kind of digital storage. Digital storage systems are always large enough to store at least a 256-bit secret key, so we can eliminate the low-entropy password. The portable memory becomes very much like a key. Whoever holds the key has access, so this memory needs to be held securely.

22.4   Secure Token

A better—and more expensive—solution is to use something we call a secure token. This is a small computer that Alice can carry around. The external shape of tokens can differ widely, ranging from a smart card (which looks just like a credit card), to an iButton, USB dongle, or PCMCIA card. The main properties are a nonvolatile memory (i.e., a memory that retains its data when power is removed) and a CPU.

The secure token works primarily as a portable storage device, but with a few security enhancements. First of all, access to the stored key material can be limited by a password or something similar. Before the secure token will let you use the key, you have to send it the proper password. The token can protect itself against attackers that try a brute-force search for the password by disabling access after three or five failed attempts. Of course, some users mistype their password too often, and then their token has to be resuscitated, but you can use longer, higher-entropy passphrases or keys that are far more secure for the resuscitation.

This provides a multilevel defense. First of all, Alice protects the physical token; for example, by keeping it in her wallet or on her key chain. An attacker has to steal the token to get anywhere, or at least get access to it in some way. Then the attacker needs to either physically break open the token and extract the data, or find the password to unlock the token. Tokens are often tamper-resistant to make a physical attack more difficult.[2]

Secure tokens are currently one of the best and most practical methods of storing secret keys. They can be relatively inexpensive and small enough to be carried around conveniently.

One problem in practical use is the behavior of the users. They'll leave their secure token plugged into their computer when going to lunch or to a meeting. As users don't want to be prompted for their password every time, the system will be set to allow hours of access from the last time the password was entered. So all an attacker has to do is walk in and start using the secret keys stored in the token.

You can try to solve this through training. There's the "corporate security in the office" video presentations, the embarrassingly bad "take your token to lunch" poster that isn't funny at all, and the "if I ever again find your token plugged in unattended, you are going to get another speech like this" speeches. But you can also use other means. Make sure the token is not only the key to access digital data, but also the lock to the office doors, so that users have to take their token to get back into their office. Fix the coffee machine to only give coffee after being presented with a token. This motivates employees to bring their token to the coffee machine and not leave it plugged into their computer while they are away. Sometimes security consists of silly measures like these, but they work far better than trying to enforce take-your-token-with-you rules by other means.

---

[2]They are tamper-resistant, not tamper-proof. Tampering is always possible; tamper-resistance merely makes tampering more expensive.

22.5   Secure UI

The secure token still has a significant weakness. The password that Alice uses has to be entered on the PC or some other device. As long as we trust the PC this is not a problem, but we all know PCs are not terribly secure, to say the least. In fact, the whole reason for not storing Alice's keys on the PC is because we don't trust it enough. We can achieve a much better security if the token itself has a secure built-in UI. Think of a secure token with a built-in keyboard and display. Now the password, or more likely a PIN, can be entered directly into the token without the need to trust an outside device.

Having a keyboard on the token protects the PIN from compromise. Of course, once the PIN has been typed, the PC still gets the key, and then it can do anything at all with that key. So we are still limited by the security of the whole PC.

To stop this, we have to put the cryptographic processes that involve the key into the token. This requires application-specific code in the token. The token is quickly growing to a full-fledged computer, but now a trusted computer that the user carries around. The trusted computer can implement the security-critical part of each application on the token itself. The display now becomes crucial, since it is used to show the user what action he is authorizing by typing his PIN. In a typical design, the user uses the PC's keyboard and mouse to operate the application. When, for example, a bank payment has to be authorized, the PC sends the data to the token. The token displays the amount and a few other transaction details, and the user authorizes the transaction by typing her PIN. The token then signs the transaction details and the PC completes the rest of the transaction.

In reality, tokens with a secure UI are too expensive for most applications. Maybe the closest thing we have is a PDA, such as a Palm. However, people download programs onto their PDAs, and a PDA is not designed from the start as a secure unit, so perhaps the PDA is not significantly more secure than a PC.

This is an excellent example of the conflict between security and functionality. People like to be able to download programs and run them any time they want. They also like to be able to trust their computer with valuable information. Given the current state of the art in operating system security, it is not possible to combine in a single machine the flexibility of downloadable programs with the security that we need. And given the choice between security and downloading a program that will show dancing pigs on the screen, users will choose dancing pigs just about every time.

22.6   Biometrics

If we want to get really fancy, we can add biometrics to the mix. You could build something like a fingerprint or iris scanner into the secure token. At the moment, biometric devices are not very useful. Fingerprint scanners can be made for a reasonable price, but the security they provide is abysmal. In 2002, cryptographer Tsutomu Matsumoto, together with three of his students, showed how he was able to consistently fool all the commercially available fingerprint scanners he could buy, using only household and hobby materials [64]. Even making a fake finger from a latent fingerprint (i.e., the ones you leave on every shiny surface) is nothing more than a hobby project for a clever high-school student.

The real shock to us wasn't that the fingerprint readers could be fooled. It was that fooling them was so incredibly simple and cheap. What's worse, the biometrics industry has been telling us how secure biometric identification is. They never told us that forging fingerprints was this easy. Now suddenly a mathematician (not even a biometrics expert) comes along and blows the whole process out of the water. There are two possibilities: either the industry knew about this and has been lying to us, or they didn't know about it, and they are therefore obviously incompetent. You really have to wonder how secure other biometric systems are.

Still, even though they are easy to fool, fingerprint scanners can be very useful. Suppose you have a secure token with a small display, a small keyboard, and a fingerprint scanner. To get at the key, you need to get physical control of the token, get the PIN, and forge the fingerprint. That is more work for the attacker than any of our previous solutions. It is probably the best practical key storage scheme that we can currently make. On the other hand, this secure token is going to be rather expensive, so it won't be used by many people.

Fingerprint scanners could also be used on the low-security side rather than the high-security side. Touching a finger to a scanner can be done very quickly, and it is quite feasible to ask the user to do that relatively often. A fingerprint scanner could thus be used to increase the confidence that the proper person is in fact authorizing the actions that the computer is taking. This makes it more difficult for employees to lend their password to a colleague. Rather than trying to stop sophisticated attackers, the fingerprint scanner could be used to stop casual breaches of the security rules. This might make a more important contribution to security than trying to use the scanner as a high-security device.

As a side note, Matsumoto's work might have serious repercussions for the use of fingerprint evidence in criminal cases. It turns out to be relatively easy to make a fake finger from a latent fingerprint. So how about putting a bit of sweat on the fake finger and using it to place someone else's fingerprint somewhere? Up to now this has been the stuff of spy movies, but it might be rather easy to do. Suddenly, the fingerprints on the murder weapon don't mean nearly as much as they used to. It could easily take a decade or more for the legal system to adapt to the idea that fingerprints can be forged with relative ease; meanwhile it remains a perfect tool for framing someone.

22.7 Single Sign-On

Because the average user has so many passwords, it becomes very appealing to create a single sign-on system. The idea is to give Alice a single master password, which in turn is used to encrypt all the different passwords from her different applications.

To do this well, all the applications must talk to the single sign-on system. Any time an application requires a password, it should not ask the user but rather the single sign-on program for it. In practice, this just plain doesn't work. There is no widely-used standard for this process, and until there is, it won't happen automatically. Just think of all the different applications that would have to be changed to automatically get their passwords from the single sign-on system.

A simpler idea is to have a small program that stores the passwords in a text file. Alice types her master password and then uses the copy and paste functionality to copy the passwords from the single sign-on program to the application. Bruce designed a public domain program called Password Safe to do exactly this. But it's just the digital version of the piece of paper that Alice writes her passwords on. It is useful, and an improvement on the piece of paper if you always use the same computer, but not the ultimate solution that the single sign-on idea would really like to be.

22.8   Risk of Loss

But what if the secure token breaks? Or the piece of paper with the passwords is left in a pocket and run through the washing machine? Losing secret keys is always a bad thing. The cost can vary from having to reregister for each application to get a new key, to permanently losing access to important data. If you encrypt your Ph.D. thesis that you have been working on for five years with a secret key and then lose the key, you no longer have a Ph.D. thesis. You just have a file of random-looking bits. Ouch!

It is hard to make a key storage system both easy to use and highly reliable. A good rule of thumb, therefore, is to split these functions. Keep two copies of the key—one that is easy to use, and another one that is very reliable. If the easy-to-use system ever forgets the key, you can recover it from the reliable storage system. The reliable system could be very simple. How about a piece of paper in a bank vault?

Of course, you want to be careful with your reliable storage system. By design, it will quickly be used to store all of your keys, and that would make it a very tempting target for an attacker. You'll have to do a risk analysis to determine whether it is better to have a number of smaller reliable key storage places or a single large one.

22.9   Secret Sharing

There are some keys that you need to store super-securely—for example, the private root key of your CA. As we have seen, storing a secret in a secure manner can be difficult. Storing it securely and reliably is even more difficult.

There is one cryptographic solution that can help in storing secret keys. It is called *secret sharing*, which is a bit of a misnomer because it implies that you share the secret with several people. You don't. The idea is to take the secret and split it into several different shares. It is possible to do this in such a way that, for example, three out of the five shares are needed to recover the secret. You then give one share to each of the senior people in the IT department. Any three of them can recover the secret. The real trick is to do it in a manner such that any two people together know absolutely nothing about the key.

Secret sharing systems are very tempting from an academic point of view. Each of the shares is stored using one of the techniques we talked about before. A k-out-of-n rule combines a high security (at least k people are necessary to retrieve the key) with a high reliability ($n - k$ of the shares may be lost without detrimental effect). There are even fancier secret sharing schemes that allow more complex access rules, along the lines of (Alice and Bob) or (Alice and Carol and David).

In real life, secret sharing schemes are rarely used because they are too complex. They are complex to implement, but more importantly, complex to administrate and operate. Most companies do not have a group of highly responsible people who distrust each other. Try telling the board members that they will each be given a secure token with a key share, and that they will have to show up at 3 a.m. on a Sunday in an emergency. Oh yes, and they are not to trust each other, but to keep their own shares secure even from other board members. They will also need to come down to the secure key-management room to get a new key share every time someone joins or leaves the board. In practice, this means that using the board members is out. The CEO isn't very useful for holding a share either, because the CEO tends to travel quite a bit. Before you know it, you are down to the two or three senior IT management people. They could use a secret sharing scheme, but the expense and complexity make this unattractive. Why not use something much simpler, such as a safe? Physical solutions such as safes or bank vaults have several advantages. Everybody understands how they work, so you don't need extensive training. They have already been tested extensively, whereas the secret-reconstruction process is hard to test because it requires such a large number of user interactions—and you really don't want to have a bug in the secret-reconstruction process that results in you losing the root key of your CA.

We will not explain how secret sharing schemes operate in detail. That explanation requires quite a bit of mathematical background, and since secret sharing schemes are so rarely used, there is no point in including them here.

22.10   Wiping Secrets

Any long-term secret that we store eventually has to be wiped. As soon as a secret is no longer needed, its storage location should be wiped to avoid any future compromise. We discussed the problems of wiping memory in section 9.3. Wiping long-term secrets from permanent storage is much harder.

The schemes for storing long-term secrets that we discussed in this chapter use a variety of data storage technologies: hard disk, paper, floppy disk, magnetic stripe card, EPROM, EEPROM, flash memory, or battery-maintained RAM. None of these storage technologies comes with a documented wiping functionality that guarantees that the data it stored is no longer recoverable.

22.10.1   Paper

Destroying a password written down on paper is typically done by destroying the paper itself. One possible method is to burn the paper, and then grind the ashes into a fine powder, or mix the ashes into a pulp with just a little bit of water. Shredding is also an option, although many shredders leave the paper in large enough pieces that reconstructing a page is relatively easy.

22.10.2   Magnetic Storage

Magnetic media are very hard to wipe. There is surprisingly little literature about how to do this; the best paper we know of is by Peter Gutmann [39], although the technical details of that paper are probably outdated now.

Magnetic media store data in tiny magnetic domains; the direction of magnetization of a domain determines the data it encodes. When the data is overwritten, the magnetization directions are changed to reflect the new data. But there are several mechanisms that prevent the old data from being completely lost. The read/write head that tries to overwrite old data is never exactly aligned, and will tend to leave some parts of the old data untouched. Overwriting does not completely destroy old data. You can think of it as repainting a wall with a single coat of paint. You can still vaguely see the old coat of paint under it. The magnetic domains can also migrate away from the read/write head either to the side of the track or deeper down into the magnetic material, where they can linger for a long time. Overwritten data is typically not recoverable with the normal read/write head, but an attacker who takes apart a disk drive and uses specialized equipment might be able to retrieve some or all of the old data.

In practice, repeatedly overwriting a secret with random data is probably the best option. There are a few points to keep in mind:

- Each overwrite should use fresh random data. Some researchers have developed particular data patterns that are supposed to be better at wiping old data, but the choice of patterns depends on the exact details of the disk drive. Random data might require more overwriting passes for the same effect, but it works in all situations and is therefore safer.

- Overwrite the actual location that stored the secret. If you just change a file by writing new data to it, the file system might decide to store the new data in a different location, which would leave the original data intact.

- Make sure that each overwrite pass is actually written to disk and not just to one of the disk caches. Disk drives that have their own write-cache are a particular danger, as they might cache the new data and optimize the multiple overwrite operations into a single write.

- It is probably a good idea to wipe an area that begins well before the secret data and that ends well after it. Because the rotational speed of a disk drive is never perfectly constant, the new data will not align perfectly with the old data.

As far as we know, there is no reliable information on how many overwrite passes are required, but there is no reason to choose a small number. You only have to wipe a single key. (If you have a large amount of secret data, store that data encrypted under a key, and only wipe the key.) We consider 50 or 100 overwrites with random data perfectly reasonable.

It is theoretically possible to erase a tape or disk using a degaussing machine. However, modern high-density magnetic storage media resist degaussing to such an extent that this is not a reliable wiping method. In practice, users do not have access to degaussing machines, so this is a nonissue.

Even with extensive overwriting, you should expect that a highly specialized and well-funded attacker could still recover the secret from the magnetic medium. To completely destroy the data, you will probably have to destroy the medium itself. If the magnetic layer is bonded to plastic (floppy disk, tape), you can consider shredding and then burning the media. For a hard disk, you can use a belt sander to remove the magnetic layer from the platters, or use a blowtorch to melt the disk platters down to liquid metal. In practice, you are unlikely to convince users to take such extreme measures, so repeated overwriting is the best practical solution.

22.10.3   Solid-State Storage

Wiping nonvolatile memory, such as EPROM, EEPROM, and flash, poses similar problems. Overwriting old data does not remove all traces, and the data retention mechanisms we discussed in section 9.3.4 are also at work. Again, repeatedly overwriting the secret with random data is the only practical solution, but it is by no means perfect. As soon as the solid-state device is no longer needed, it should be destroyed.

Part IV

Miscellaneous

Chapter 23

Standards

We've conspicuously avoided standards in this book. There is a good reason for that. Security standards rarely work. But if you do any cryptographic engineering, you are going to encounter standards, so you need to know a bit about them.

23.1 The Standards Process

For those who have not been involved in the standards development process, we'll first describe how standards are made. It starts out with some standardization body, such as the Internet Engineering Task Force (IETF), the Institute of Electrical and Electronics Engineers (IEEE), the International Organization for Standardization (ISO), or the European Committee for Standardization (CEN). This standardization body sets up a committee in response to some perceived need for a new or improved standard. The committee goes by different names: working group, task group, or whatever. Sometimes there are hierarchical structures of committees, but the basic idea remains the same. Committee membership is typically voluntary. People apply to join, and pretty much anyone is accepted. Often there are some procedural hoops to jump through, but there is no significant selection of members. These committees vary in size up to several hundred members, but big committees split themselves into smaller subcommittees (called task group, study group, or whatever). Most work is done in a committee of up to a few dozen people.

Standardization committees have regular meetings, once every few months. All members travel to a city and meet in a hotel for a few days. In the months between meetings, members of the committee will do some work, create proposals and presentations, etc. At the meetings, the committee decides which way to proceed. Usually there is a single editor who gets the job of putting all the proposals together into a single standards document. Creating a standard is a slow process and often takes many years.

So who turns up to join these committees? Well, being a member is expensive. Apart from the time it takes, the travel and hotels are not cheap. So everybody there is sent by their company. Companies have several motivations to be represented. Sometimes they want to sell products that must interoperate with products from other companies. This requires standards, and the best way to keep track of the standardization process is to be there. Companies also want to keep an eye on their competitors. You don't want to let your competitor write the standards, because they will do something to put you at a competitive disadvantage—perhaps skew it toward their own technology or requirements, or include techniques for which they themselves hold a patent. Sometimes companies don't want a standard, so they show up at the committee meetings to try to slow the process down to allow their proprietary solution time to capture the market. In real life, all these motivations, plus several more, are all mixed together in varying proportions to create a very complex political environment.

Not surprisingly, quite a number of standardization committees fail. They either never produce anything, or produce something atrociously bad, or they end up being deadlocked and overtaken by the market, and then they standardize whatever system captured the market. Successful committees manage to produce a standards document after a few years.

Once the standard has been written, everybody goes and implements it. This, of course, leads to systems that do not interoperate, so there is a secondary process where interoperability is tested and the different manufacturers adapt their implementations to work together.

There are many problems with this process. The political structure of the committee puts very little emphasis on creating a good technical standard.

The most important thing is to reach consensus. The standard is finished when everybody is equally *un*happy with the result. To pacify the different factions, standards have many options, extended functionalities, useless alternatives, etc. And as each faction has its own ideas, opinions, and focus points, the best compromise is often contradictory. Many standards are internally inconsistent, or even contradict themselves.

This whole process is made even more complex by the fact that companies are creating implementations while they are still standardizing, based on drafts of the standard. This makes it even harder to change something, because somebody has already implemented it and doesn't want to do it again. Of course, different companies will implement things in different ways and then fight in the committee to get the standard adjusted to fit their implementation. Sometimes the only compromise is to choose something that neither company has implemented, just to ensure that they are equally unhappy. Technical merit does not really feature in this type of discussion.

23.1.1 The Standard

One of the results is that most standards are extremely hard to read. The standards document is a design by committee, and there is no pressure within the process to make the document clear, concise, accurate, or readable. In fact, a highly unreadable document is easier to work with, because only a few of the committee members will understand it, and they can work on it without being bothered by the other members. Digging through hundreds of pages of badly written documentation is no fun, so most committee members end up not reading the full draft and only checking the limited portions of the standard they are interested in.

23.1.2 Functionality

As we already mentioned, interoperability testing is always required. And of course, different companies implement different things. Quite often, what ends up being implemented is subtly different from what the standard defines, and as each company is already marketing its products, it is sometimes too late to change things. We've seen products of brand *A* that recognize the implementations of brand B by their deviations from the standard, and then adjust their own behavior to make things work.

Standards often include a very large number of options, but the actual implementations will only use a particular set of options, with a few restrictions and extensions, of course, because the standards document itself describes something that doesn't work. And the difference between the actual implementations and the standard are, of course, not documented.

Overall, the entire process works—kind of—but only for central functionality. A wireless network will allow you to connect, but management functionality is unlikely to work across products from different vendors. Simple HTML pages will display correctly on all browsers, but more advanced layout features give different results on different browsers. We've all become so used to this that we hardly notice it.

It really is a sad state of affairs. As an industry, we seem unable to create standards that are even readable or correct, let alone provide interoperability of different products for all but the most basic functionality.

23.1.3   Security

These failings mean that the typical method of producing standards simply doesn't work for security purposes. In security, we have an active attacker who will seek out the most remote corner of the standard. Security also depends on the weakest link: any single mistake can be fatal.

We've already hammered on the importance of simplicity. Standards are anything but simple. The committee process precludes simplicity and invariably produces something that is more complex than anyone in the committee can fully understand. For that reason alone, the result can never be secure.

When we've spoken to some standardization people about this problem, we often get responses along the lines of: "Well, the techies always want to make a perfect standard." ... "Political realities are that we have to make a compromise." ... "That is just how the system works." ... "Look at what we have achieved." ... "Things are working pretty well." We're sorry, but in security that is not good enough. The very fact that interoperability testing is required after the standard has been set demonstrates that committee standards don't work in security. If the functional part of the standard (i.e., the easy part) isn't good enough to result in interoperable systems without testing, then the security part cannot possibly achieve security without testing. And as we know, it isn't possible to test for security. Sure, it might be possible to create an implementation that includes a subset of the functionality of the standard that is also secure, but that is not sufficient for a security standard. A security standard claims that if you adhere to it, you will achieve a certain level of security. Security is simply too difficult to leave to a committee.

We don't know of a single committee-written security standard that is worthwhile, so whenever someone suggests using a cryptography standard, we are always extremely reluctant—and sometimes even hostile.

There are a few useful standards in this field, none of which was written by a committee. Sometimes you get just a small group of people who create a single coherent design. And sometimes the result is adopted as a standard without a lot of political compromises. These standards can be quite good. We'll discuss the most important two below.

23.2 SSL

SSL is the security protocol used by Web browsers to connect securely to Web servers. The first widely used version was SSL 2, which contained several security flaws. The improved version is known as SSL 3 [37]. It was designed by three people without any further committee process. SSL 3 has been widely used, and is generally acknowledged as a good protocol.

A warning: SSL is a good protocol, but that does not mean that any system that uses SSL is secure. SSL relies on a PKI to authenticate the server, and the PKI client embedded in most browsers is so permissive that the overall security level is rather low. One of our browsers has 108 different root certificates from 35 different CAs. So even before we start looking at active attacks, there are 35 different organizations spread throughout the world that we have to trust with all of our Web information.

SSL was never really standardized. It was simply implemented by Netscape, and became a de facto standard. Standardization and further development of SSL is being done under the name TLS by an IETF working group. We have not studied TLS in detail. So far the changes seem fairly minor, and we have no reason to believe that TLS is not as good as SSL 3. But given the IETF's recent record with designing security protocols such as IPsec [33], there is certainly a danger of the committee effect once again asserting itself and destroying a good standard.

23.3   AES: Standardization by Competition

To us, AES is the shining example of how to standardize security systems. AES is not a design by committee, but rather a design by competition. The process is rather simple. First you specify what the system is supposed to achieve. Developing the specifications can be done in a reasonably small group with inputs from many different sources.

The next step is a call for proposals. You ask experts to develop complete solutions that satisfy the given requirements. Once the proposals are in, all that remains is to choose among the proposals. This is a straightforward competition in which you judge them by a variety of criteria. As long as you make security the primary criterium, the submitters have a vested interest in finding security weaknesses in their competitors' proposals. With a bit of luck, this will lead to useful feedback. In other situations, you might have to pay to get security evaluations done by outside experts.

In the end, with a bit of luck, you will be able to select a single proposal, either unchanged or with minor changes. This is not the time to make an amalgamation of the different proposals; that will just lead to another committee design. If none of the proposals satisfy the requirements, and it seems possible to create something better, you should probably ask for new proposals.

This is exactly how NIST ran the AES competition, and it worked incredibly well. The 15 original proposals were evaluated in a first round and reduced to five finalists. A second round of evaluations on the finalists led to the selection of the winner. Amazingly enough, any one of the five finalists would have been a good standard, and certainly a better standard than any committee design.

The competition model of standardization doesn't work if you don't have enough experts to create at least a few competing designs. But in our opinion, if you don't have enough experts to generate several proposals, you should not be standardizing any security systems. For reasons of simplicity and consistency, which are crucial to the overall security, a security system must be designed by a small group of experts. Then you need other experts to analyze the proposal and attack it, looking for flaws. To have any hope of getting a good result—whatever process you use—you need enough experts to form at least three proposal groups. If you have that many experts, you should use the competition model, as it is the only model so far that has demonstrated that it can produce good security standards.

Chapter 24

Patents

Patents have a far greater effect on cryptography than we are comfortable with. We understand the business rationale of patents, and both of us have our names on quite a few patents. (Often they're results of consulting work we've done, and are owned by the companies that hired us.) But patents often mean that we can't use the mathematical tools we need and force us to compromise in ways we don't like. More importantly, we don't believe that patents serve the security community. There are several aspects of the current patent system that make it unworkable in practice.

24.1 Prior Art

You are not supposed to be able to get a patent on something that is already known. Anything that is already publicly known before the patent is applied for is called *prior art*. But, as anyone who works with the current patent system knows, that doesn't stop you from claiming things that are already known. In 2001 a guy in Australia patented the wheel, or rather a "circular transportation facilitation device" [52]. You'd think that there would be some prior art for that. This was an attempt to show how bad the patent system is. Most patents are not that blatant in their abuse of the system, but time and time again we've seen patent claims extend to cover prior art. We've even seen a patent filed by one person six months after attending a conference where the very technique he patented was presented by someone else.

The reason that prior art gets usurped by a patent is that the patent office simply cannot check whether a patent claim covers prior art. There is just too much prior art around; you can't find it all. The problem is that once a patent has been issued, it is *presumed* to be valid. That is, if you have been using a cipher for years in your products, and someone else files a patent claim that covers your prior art, *you* have to assume the burden of proof that your use is prior art. The patent holder can just sit back and let you do all the hard work. This is, of course, expensive. It involves patent lawyers, and makes such patents an excellent vehicle for legal blackmail: buy a cheap license, or spend ten times as much on your lawyers.

24.2   Continuations

The patent system has an even weirder property. We don't quite understand how it works, but it is a patent lawyer's trick. For any technology that you've patented, you always keep one or two patents "open"; i.e., you keep it in the patent process. When you file a patent, you have to file a disclosure document that describes the technology. The disclosure document cannot be changed later, but the patent claims can. And it is quite easy to delay the patent issuing process by procedural means. So you delay a few continuation patents (extensions of your basic patent). Now suppose a competitor starts using a technique that is significantly different from the one you patented, but related. You then try to rewrite the claims of the continuation patent to cover your competitor's techniques. Getting the claims approved is a negotiation process between you and the patent office, and the patent office doesn't know what your competitor is using, so you have a good chance of getting them approved. You then let the continuation patent issue, with the claims that directly cover your competitor's techniques, and sue your competitor for patent infringement. It sounds like fraud to us, but this is standard practice, and apparently legal.

24.3   Vagueness

A patent is supposed to describe the technique clearly so that others can implement the patented technology. That is part of the patent bargain. In return for disclosing the technology, the patent holder is granted a 20-year monopoly on it. In practice, patents are deliberately written to be vague, unclear, and difficult to read. Very often the patent holder will *not* describe the best way to use his techniques, even though that is a requirement of the patent process.

Suppose you are working on a system and you think that a particular patent might be a problem. You can just get the patent, read it, and decide whether it covers your work, right? Wrong! It is extremely complex to figure out whether a patent covers a particular system. In the end, it is decided by a judge who has no technical background. Predicting the outcome is almost as accurately done by tossing a coin.

24.4   Reading Patents

One word of advice: never read a patent. That's right. You'd think that reading patents to see what they cover is a good idea. It is not. If you infringe on a patent without having known that you did so, you may end up paying damages to the patent holder. But if they can prove that you willfully infringed (because you knew about their patent), you may end up paying triple damages. So if you read a patent, you automatically increase your liability for infringing that patent by a factor of three.

And now for the real stinger: even if you read a patent and decide, as an expert in your field, that your work is not covered by the patent, the judge might still find that you willfully infringed. You see, you as an expert are not qualified to judge what a patent covers. Only a patent lawyer can do that. So if you want to avoid the possibility of having to pay triple damages, you have to pay a patent lawyer to figure out whether you are infringing the patent or not. There are millions of patents out there, and you cannot possibly afford to pay a patent lawyer to read every one of them.

Therefore, the safest solution is to never read a patent. At least you can then claim that you didn't willfully infringe on the patent.

24.5   Licensing

If Alice has a patent and Bob wants to use that technology, Alice can sell a license to Bob. This is a very common thing to do. Many large companies cross-license all their patents with each other. They basically trade the patent licenses on all the patents they have, without paying each other in money. Smaller companies have to buy a license. In many areas of engineering, this is not a significant problem. If you need to use a patent, you can get a license on reasonable terms.

Somehow, things are different in cryptography. In the 1980s, the field was distorted by some very basic initial patents on RSA and DH—in those days the only two useful public-key systems. For years and years these very fundamental patents were extremely difficult and expensive to license. There are stories of companies trying to buy a license and simply being refused.

The patent holders decided to use these patents to control the development of the technology by limiting the licensing. That effectively made these technologies unavailable to the rest of the market. In theory, that is what patents are supposed to support, but the overall effect can be unfortunate if a needed security technology cannot be used because of a patent, and the patent holder refuses to license it.

We recently had a difficult situation with some of the new block cipher modes XCBC, IACBC, and OCB. There are three inventors, at least two of whom built on the work of the previous ones. All three filed for patents, but due to the delay in the patent issuing process, no patents have been issued yet. Because they have not yet issued, the patent claims are not known, so it is impossible to know which patent covers what. As all applicants can still craft their claims knowing what the other inventors did (the patent claims have not yet been fixed) it is quite possible that anyone who uses any of these inventions has to get a license for all three patents. Maybe it is possible to use XCBC with only a single patent license, but that involves putting a great deal of faith in the sanity of the patent system—something we do not advise.

So if you want to use, say, OCB, you may need three patent licenses—for patents that have yet to issue. That means three contracts to negotiate, with three different lawyers, assuming they all are willing to license their patents. Don't be too surprised if negotiations take half a year or more. We've seen situations where, after a protracted negotiation, the patent holder at the very last moment decided not to license his patent. This spells disaster for a company developing a product. Trying to license a patent delays product development, imposes huge upfront cost (if only for the legal fees), and putting the entire product line at risk from arbitrary actions by the patent holders and their lawyers. Also, the longer you negotiate with them, the worse your negotiating position becomes, because you already invested in the process and the product, and you really need to get it to market right now.

It would seem logical for these three inventors to get together and pool their patents to make it easy for everybody to get a single license for all of their patents. There were attempts at organizing this, but the last we heard was that the inventors could not agree.

The licensing problems surrounding XCBC, IACBC, and OCB are exactly what motivated the development of CCM (see section 8.5). CCM is half the speed, but patent-free. That's an advantage that greatly outweighs the extra computations it requires.

Even in cases where the patent has issued and it is quite clear what it covers, the transaction cost of licensing a patent can be very high. Most patent holders make it difficult to get a license. Standard licensing terms are often nonexistent or too onerous to use. As soon as lawyers are needed to start negotiating appropriate licensing terms, the up-front costs explode. Patent holders often do not seem to understand that there are alternatives to the use of their patent, and that getting a license has to be made easy and relatively cheap.

24.6   Defensive Patents

Many companies file patents not so much to enforce them, but to defend themselves. If you have a whole pile of patents, and your competitor sues you over one of his patents, you can always find one of your patents that he infringed, or at least one that you can allege that he infringed. It is a bit like MAD: mutually assured destruction. If you sue me, I'll sue you, and we both lose enormous amounts of money (on legal fees and lost opportunities). Sometimes we see two companies involved in this game of chicken. Quite often they settle after a year or so, once cooler heads realize that a mutual suicide pact doesn't provide much shareholder value.

24.7   Fixing the Patent System

Our current patent system is completely out of control. At best, patents are a necessary evil. At worst, they are an entirely legal form of fraud and blackmail. Patents are supposed to help inventors by rewarding them for the results of their research. In our opinion, the cost of the current patent system for the IT industry far outweighs the advantages. Patents are valid for 20 years—effectively eternity in the IT world. Just getting a patent takes several years, which translates to several product cycles in the industry. The time scale of the IT industry is so much faster that the patent system cannot keep up.

There is, of course, one group of people that consistently benefits from the patent system: the lawyers. No prizes for guessing which professional group claims that the current system is workable, or even good.

An often-heard claim is that patents protect the little inventor against the big company. Humbug. You might find isolated examples of that, but most of the time it works the other way around. A single inventor or a small company develops a really new product. They invest their time and money to develop it and bring it to market. But once they start to threaten the market of a large firm, they are threatened with a patent lawsuit. Small companies cannot afford to fight a patent in court, which leaves them wide-open to blackmail. We personally know of at least one small company with an innovative product that experienced this, and in the end they had to sell out to the large firm at a very modest price. The current patent system gives huge powers to large firms that have patent lawyers on salary and enough money to create a believable threat of patent litigation.

We think that the IT industry would be better off without patents than with patents. Some of our friends have different views, and this is certainly a point open for debate. But the current system is simply not working.

At a minimum, we'd like to speed up the patent system. Issue the patents within three months of filing, and limit the patent to three to five years. Allow patents to be challenged based on prior art by anyone, even after they have been issued. And create a system for determining whether a particular product infringes on a patent, a system that works on a time scale of months rather than years. There is no benefit to the IT industry in having a judge rule that someone infringed a patent five years ago. You need an answer within the time scale of the industry, which is at most a few months.

This is, of course, just our opinion. The patent system won't be fixed, because there is simply no political gain to be made in this area. So we'll have to live with the system, and that probably means that people will keep filing patents for anything they invent, just to protect themselves against their competitors. And designers in cryptography will spend their time and effort to avoid patented areas.

24.8 Disclaimer

We are not lawyers. We don't even look like lawyers. Don't take our advice in legal matters. In other words: you're on your own, unless you pay a patent lawyer a few hundred dollars per hour. Welcome to the wonderful world of patents.

Chapter 25

Involving Experts

There is something strange about cryptography: everybody thinks they know enough about it to design and build their own system. We never ask a second-year physics student to design a nuclear power plant. We wouldn't let a trainee nurse who claims to have found a revolutionary method for heart surgery operate on us. Yet people who have read a book or two think they can design their own cryptographic system. Worse still, they are sometimes able to convince management, venture capitalists, and even some customers that their design is the neatest thing since sliced bread.

Among cryptographers, Bruce's first book, *Applied Cryptography* [87, 88], is both famous and notorious. It is famous for bringing cryptography to the attention of tens of thousands of people. It is notorious for the systems that these people then designed and implemented on their own.

A recent example is 802.11, the wireless network standard. The initial design included a secure channel called *wired equivalent privacy* (WEP) to encrypt and authenticate wireless communications. The standard was designed by a committee which didn't include any cryptographers. The results were horrible. The decision to use the RC4 encryption algorithm was not the best one, but not a fatal flaw in and of itself. However, RC4 is a stream cipher and needs a unique nonce. WEP didn't allocate enough bits for the nonce, with the result that the same nonce value had to be reused, which in turn resulted in many packets being encrypted with the same key stream. That defeated the encryption properties of the RC4 stream cipher, and allowed a smart attacker to break the encryption. A more subtle flaw was not hashing the secret key and nonce together before using it as the RC4 key, which eventually led to key-recovery attacks [36]. A CRC checksum was used for authentication, but since CRC computations are linear, it was trivial (using some linear algebra) to modify any packet without any chance of detection. A single shared key was used for all users in a network, making key updates much more difficult to do. The network password was used directly as the encryption key for all communications, without using any kind of key negotiation protocol. And finally, encryption was turned off by default, which meant that most implementations never bothered turning encryption on in the first place. WEP wasn't just broken; it was robustly broken.

Designing a replacement for WEP was not easy, because it had to be retrofitted to existing hardware. But there was no choice; the security of the original standard was abysmal. The replacement is called WPA and should now be available.

The WEP story is not exceptional. It got more press than most bad cryptographic designs because 802.11 is such a successful product, but we have seen many similar situations in other systems. As a colleague once told Bruce: "The world is full of bad security systems designed by people who have read *Applied Cryptography*."

Practical Cryptography is likely to have the same effect.

That makes this a very dangerous book. Many people will read this book, and then turn around and design a cryptographic algorithm or protocol. When they're finished they'll have something that looks good to them, and maybe even works, but they will get the security disastrously wrong. Maybe they'll get 70% right. If they're very lucky, they may get 90% right. But there is no prize for being almost right in cryptography. A security system is only as strong as its weakest link; to be secure, *everything* must be right. And that is something you simply can't learn from reading books.

So why did we write this book if it will lead to bad systems? We wrote it because people who want to learn how to design cryptographic systems must learn it somewhere, and we didn't know of any other suitable books. Consider this book as an introduction to the field, even though it is not a manual or textbook. We also wrote it for the other engineers involved in

a project. Every part of a security system is of critical importance, and
everybody who works on a project has to have a basic understanding of
the security issues and techniques involved. This includes the programmers,
testers, technical writers, management, and even sales people. Each person
needs to understand enough about security issues to do his or her work properly. We hope this book provides an adequate background to the practical
side of cryptography.

If we can leave you with one piece of advice, it is to use cryptographic experts
if at all possible. If your project involves cryptography, then you need input
from an experienced cryptographic designer. Involve one in your project at
the beginning. The earlier you consult a cryptographic expert, the cheaper
and easier it will be in the long run. Many a time we've been called to
projects well underway, only to poke holes in parts that had long since been
designed or implemented. The end result is always expensive, either in terms
of effort, project schedule, and cost, or in terms of the security for the user
of the end product.

Cryptography is fiendishly difficult to do right. Even the systems designed
by experts fail regularly. It doesn't matter how clever you are, or how much
experience you have in other fields. Designing and implementing cryptographic systems requires specialized knowledge and experience, and the only
way to get experience is to do it over and over again. And that, of course,
also involves making mistakes. So why get an expert if he makes mistakes
as well? For the same reason you get a qualified surgeon to operate on you.
It is not that they don't make mistakes; it is that they make a lot fewer
and less serious mistakes. And they work in a conservative manner so that
the small mistakes do not lead to catastrophic results; they know enough to
fail well.

Implementing cryptographic systems is almost as much a specialty as designing them is. Cryptographic designers are available for hire. Cryptographic
implementers are much harder to come by, in part because you need more
of them. A single designer can create work for ten to twenty implementers.
Most people don't think of cryptographic implementation as a specialty.
Programmers will move from database programming to GUI work to cryptographic implementations. It's true that database programming and GUI
work are also specialties, but an experienced programmer can, with a bit of

study, get reasonable results. This does not hold for implementing cryptography, where everything must be right.

The best way we know to implement cryptographic systems is to take competent programmers and train them for this task. This book might be part of their training, but mostly it requires experience and the right mindset. And just like any other special IT skill, it takes years before someone is truly good at it. Given the long time it takes to gather this experience, you must be able to retain these people once they achieved it. That's another problem, and one we will gladly leave to others to solve.

Maybe even more important than this, or any other, book is the project culture. "Security first" should not just be a slogan; it has to be woven into the very fabric of the project and the project team. Everybody has to live, breathe, talk, and think security all the time. This is incredibly hard to achieve, but it can be done. DigiCash had a team like that in the 1990s. The aviation industry has a similarly pervasive safety culture. This is something that cannot be achieved in the short term, but it is certainly something which you can strive toward. This book is merely a primer on the most important security issues intended for the more technical people on the team.

As Bruce wrote in *Secrets and Lies*: "Security is a process, not a product." In addition to the security culture, you also need a security process. The aviation industry has an extensive safety process. Most of the IT industry doesn't even have a process for producing software, let alone a process for high-quality software, much less a process for security software. Writing good security software is probably beyond the current state of the art in our industry. That does not mean we should give up, though. As information technology becomes more and more critical to our infrastructure, our freedom, and our safety, we *must* improve the security of our systems. We have to do the best we can.

We hope this book can contribute somewhat to the improvement of our security systems by teaching those who are working on security systems the basics of practical cryptography.

Acknowledgments

This book is based on our collective experience over the many years we have worked in cryptography. We are heavily indebted to all the people we worked with. They made our work fun and helped us reach the insights that fill this book. We would also like to thank our customers, both for providing the funding that enabled us to continue our cryptography research and for providing the real-world experiences necessary to write this book.

Certain individuals deserve special mention. Beth Friedman conducted an invaluable copyediting job, and Denise Dick greatly improved our manuscript by proofreading it. John Kelsey provided valuable feedback on the cryptographic contents. And the Internet made our collaboration possible. We would also like to thank Carol Long and the rest of the team at Wiley for bringing our ideas to reality.

And finally, we would like to thank all of the programmers in the world who continue to write cryptographic code and make it available, free of charge, to the world.

Bibliography

[1] Ross J. Anderson. *Security Engineering: A Guide to Building Dependable Distributed Systems.* John Wiley & Sons, Inc., 2001. ISBN 0-471-38922-6. [Page 20]

[2] Ross Anderson, Eli Biham, and Lars Knudsen. Serpent: A proposal for the Advanced Encryption Standard. In National Institute of Standards and Technology [72]. See http://www.cl.cam.ac.uk/~rja14/serpent.html or http://www.nist.gov/aes. [Page 58]

[3] Mihir Bellare, Ran Canetti, and Hugo Krawczyk. Keying Hash Functions for Message Authentication. In Neal Koblitz, editor, *Advances in Cryptology—CRYPTO '96*, volume 1109 of *Lecture Notes in Computer Science*, pages 1–15. Springer-Verlag, 1996. [Page 101, 102]

[4] Mihir Bellare, Joe Kilian, and Phillip Rogaway. The Security of Cipher Block Chaining. In Yvo G. Desmedt, editor, *Advances in Cryptology—CRYPTO '94*, volume 839 of *Lecture Notes in Computer Science*, pages 341–358. Springer-Verlag, 1994. [Page 101]

[5] Charles H. Bennett and Gilles Brassard. An update on quantum cryptography. In G.R. Blakley and David Chaum, editors, *Advances in Cryptology, Proceedings of CRYPTO 84*, volume 196 of *Lecture Notes in Computer Science*, pages 475–480. Springer-Verlag, 1984. [Page 157]

[6] Eli Biham, Orr Dunkelman, and Nathan Keller. The Rectangle Attack—Rectangling the Serpent. In Birgit Pfitzmann, editor, *Advances in Cryptology—EUROCRYPT 2001*, volume 2045 of *Lecture Notes in Computer Science*, pages 340–357. Springer-Verlag, 2001. [Page 58]

[7] Eli Biham. New Types of Cryptanalytic Attacks Using Related Keys. In Tor Helleseth, editor, *Advances in Cryptology—EUROCRYPT '93*, volume 765 of *Lecture Notes in Computer Science*, pages 398–409. Springer-Verlag, 1993. [Page 45]

[8] J. Black, S. Halevi, H. Krawczyk, T. Krovetz, and P. Rogaway. UMAC: Fast and Secure Message Authentication. In Michael Wiener, editor, *Advances in Cryptology—CRYPTO '99*, volume 1666 of *Lecture Notes in Computer Science*, pages 216–233. Springer-Verlag, 1999. [Page 104, 105]

[9] Jurjen Bos. Booting problems with the JEC computer. Personal communications, 1983. [Page 141]

[10] Jurjen Bos. *Practical Privacy*. PhD thesis, Eindhoven University of Technology, 1992. Avalable from `http://www.macfergus.com/niels/lib/bosphd.html`. [Page 205, 275, 281]

[11] Gilles Brassard and Claude Crépeau. Quantum Bit Commitment and Coin Tossing Protocols. In A.J. Menezes and S.A. Vanstone, editors, *Advances in Cryptology—CRYPTO '90*, volume 537 of *Lecture Notes in Computer Science*, pages 49–61. Springer-Verlag, 1990. [Page 157]

[12] Karl Brincat and Chris J. Mitchell. New CBC-MAC forgery attacks. In V. Varadharajan and Y. Mu, editors, *Information Security and Privacy, ACISP 2001*, volume 2119 of *Lecture Notes in Computer Science*, pages 3–14. Springer-Verlag, 2001. [Page 100]

[13] Carolynn Burwick, Don Coppersmith, Edward D'Avignon, Rosario Gennaro, Shai Halevi, Charanjit Jutla, Stephen M. Matyas Jr., Luke O'Connor, Mohammad Peyravian, David Safford, and Nevenko Zunic. MARS—a candidate cipher for AES. In National Institute of Standards and Technology [72]. See `http://www.research.ibm.com/security/mars.html` or `http://www.nist.gov/aes`. [Page 61, 288]

[14] Christian Cachin. *Entropy Measures and Unconditional Security in Cryptography*. PhD thesis, ETH, Swiss Federal Institute of Technology, Zürich, 1997. See `ftp://ftp.inf.ethz.ch/pub/publications/dissertations/th12187.ps.gz`. [Page 161]

[15] Lewis Carroll. *The Hunting of the Snark: an Agony, in Eight Fits*. Macmillan and Co., London, 1876. [Page 142]

[16] Florent Chabaud and Antoine Joux. Differential Collisions in SHA-0. In Hugo Krawczyk, editor, *Advances in Cryptology—CRYPTO '98*, volume 1462 of *Lecture Notes in Computer Science*, pages 56–71. Springer-Verlag, 1998. [Page 88]

[17] Nicolas Courtois and Josef Pieprzyk. Cryptanalysis of Block Ciphers with Overdefined Systems of Equations. Cryptology ePrint Archive, Report 2002/044, 2002. `http://eprint.iacr.org/`. [Page 62]

[18] Joan Daemen and Vincent Rijmen. AES Proposal: Rijndael. In National Institute of Standards and Technology [72]. See http://www.esat.kuleuven.ac.be/~rijmen/rijndael/ or http://www.nist.gov/aes. [Page 56]

[19] Don Davis, Ross Ihaka, and Philip Fenstermacher. Cryptographic Randomness from Air Turbulence in Disk Drives. In Yvo G. Desmedt, editor, *Advances in Cryptology—CRYPTO '94*, volume 839 of *Lecture Notes in Computer Science*, pages 114–120. Springer-Verlag, 1994. [Page 156]

[20] Bert den Boer and Antoon Bosselaers. Collisions for the compression function of MD5. In Tor Helleseth, editor, *Advances in Cryptology—EUROCRYPT '93*, volume 765 of *Lecture Notes in Computer Science*, pages 293–304. Springer-Verlag, 1993. [Page 87]

[21] Whitfield Diffie and Martin E. Hellman. New Directions in Cryptography. *IEEE Transactions on Information Theory*, IT-22(6):644–654, November 1976. [Page 83]

[22] Whitfield Diffie and Martin E. Hellman. New Directions in Cryptography. *IEEE Transactions on Information Theory*, IT-22(6):644–654, November 1976. [Page 207, 208]

[23] Edsger W. Dijkstra. The Humble Programmer. *Communications of the ACM*, 15(10):859–866, 1972. Also published as EWD340, http://www.cs.utexas.edu/users/EWD/ewd03xx/EWD340.PDF. [Page 132]

[24] Giovanni Di Crescenzo, Niels Ferguson, Russel Impagliazzo, and Markus Jakobsson. How To Forget a Secret. In Christoph Meinel and Sophie Tison, editors, *STACS 99*, volume 1563 of *Lecture Notes in Computer Science*, pages 500–509. Springer-Verlag, 1999. [Page 143]

[25] Hans Dobbertin. Cryptanalysis of MD4. *J. Cryptology*, 11(4):253–271, 1998. [Page 87]

[26] Stephen R. Dussé and Burton S. Kaliski Jr. A Cryptographic Library for the Motorola DSP56000. In I.B. Damgård, editor, *Advances in Cryptology—EUROCRYPT '90*, volume 473 of *Lecture Notes in Computer Science*, pages 230–244. Springer-Verlag, 1990. [Page 286]

[27] Morris Dworkin. *Recommendation for Block Cipher Modes of Operation—Methods and Techniques*. National Institute of Standards and Technology, December 2001. Available from http://csrc.nist.gov/publications/nistpubs/800-38a/sp800-38a.pdf. [Page 75]

[28] Carl Ellison. Improvements on Conventional PKI Wisdom. In Sean Smith, editor, *1st Annual PKI Research Workshop—Proceedings*, pages 165–175, 2002. Available from http://www.cs.dartmouth.edu/~pki02/Ellison/. [Page 328]

[29] Jan-Hendrik Evertse and Eugène van Heyst. Which New RSA-Signatures Can Be Computed from Certain Given RSA-Signatures? *J. Cryptology*, 5(1):41–52, 1992. [Page 231]

[30] H. Feistel, W.A. Notz, and J.L. Smith. Some Cryptographic Techniques for Machine-to-Machine Data Communications. *Proceedings of the IEEE*, 63(11):1545–1554, 1975. [Page 52]

[31] Niels Ferguson, John Kelsey, Stefan Lucks, Bruce Schneier, Mike Stay, David Wagner, and Doug Whiting. Improved Cryptanalysis of Rijndael. In Bruce Schneier, editor, *Fast Software Encryption, 7th International Workshop, FSE 2000*, volume 1978 of *Lecture Notes in Computer Science*, pages 213–230. Springer-Verlag, 2000. [Page 56]

[32] Niels Ferguson, John Kelsey, Bruce Schneier, and Doug Whiting. A Twofish Retreat: Related-Key Attacks Against Reduced-Round Twofish. Twofish Technical Report 6, Counterpane Systems, February 2000. See http://www.counterpane.com/twofish.html. [Page 45]

[33] Niels Ferguson and Bruce Schneier. A Cryptographic Evaluation of IPsec, 1999. See http://www.counterpane.com/ipsec.html. [Page 117, 370]

[34] Niels Ferguson, Richard Schroeppel, and Doug Whiting. A simple algebraic representation of Rijndael. In Serge Vaudenay and Amr M. Youssef, editors, *Selected Areas in Cryptography, 8th Annual International Workshop, SAC 2001*, volume 2259 of *Lecture Notes in Computer Science*. Springer-Verlag, 2001. [Page 57]

[35] Niels Ferguson. Collision attacks on OCB. Unpublished manuscript, 2002. [Page 127]

[36] Scott Fluhrer, Itsik Mantin, and Adi Shamir. Weaknesses in the Key Schedule Algorithm of RC4. In Serge Vaudenay and Amr M. Youssef, editors, *Selected Areas in Cryptography, 8th Annual International Workshop, SAC 2001*, volume 2259 of *Lecture Notes in Computer Science*. Springer-Verlag, 2001. [Page 382]

[37] Alan O. Freier, Philip Karlton, and Paul C. Kocher. The SSL Protocol, Version 3.0. Internet draft, Transport Layer Security Working Group, November 18, 1996. Available from http://home.netscape.com/eng/ssl3/. [Page 369]

[38] Ian Goldberg and David Wagner. Randomness and the Netscape Browser. *Dr. Dobb's Journal*, pages 66–70, January 1996. Available from www.cs.berkeley.edu/~daw/papers/ddj-netscape.html. [Page 155]

[39] Peter Gutmann. Secure Deletion of Data from Magnetic and Solid-State Memory. In *USENIX Security Symposium Proceedings*, 1996. Available from http://www.auckland.ac.nz/~pgut001. [Page 141, 142, 360]

[40] Peter Gutmann. X.509 Style Guide, October 2000. Available from `http://www.cs.auckland.ac.nz/~pgut001/pubs/x509guide.txt`. [Page 320, 339]

[41] D. Harkins and D. Carrel. The Internet Key Exchange (IKE). RFC 2409, November 1998. [Page 104, 220]

[42] Intel. *Intel 82802 Firmware Hub: Random Number Generator, Programmers Reference Manual*, December 1999. Available from the Intel web site. [Page 157]

[43] International Telecommunication Union. *X.680-X.683: Abstract Syntax Notation One (ASN.1), X.690-X.693: ASN.1 encoding rules*, 2002. Available from `www.itu.int/ITU-T/studygroups/com17/languages/x680-x693_0702.pdf`. [Page 254]

[44] Jakob Jonsson. On the Security of CTR+CBC-MAC. In *Selected Areas in Cryptography, 9th Annual International Workshop, SAC 2002*, 2002. See `http://csrc.nist.gov/encryption/modes/proposedmodes/ccm/ccm-ad.pdf`. [Page 126]

[45] Robert R. Jueneman. Analysis of Certain Aspects of Output Feedback Mode. In David Chaum, Ronald L. Rivest, and Alan T. Sherman, editors, *Advances in Cryptology, Proceedings of Crypto 82*, pages 99–128. Plenum Press, 1982. [Page 74]

[46] David Kahn. *The Codebreakers, The Story of Secret Writing*. Macmillan Publishing Co., New York, 1967. [Page 20]

[47] John Kelsey, Bruce Schneier, and Niels Ferguson. Yarrow-160: Notes on the Design and Analysis of the Yarrow Cryptographic Pseudorandom Number Generator. In Howard Heys and Carlisle Adams, editors, *Selected Areas in Cryptography, 6th Annual International Workshop, SAC '99*, volume 1758 of *Lecture Notes in Computer Science*. Springer-Verlag, 1999. [Page 160]

[48] John Kelsey, Bruce Schneier, David Wagner, and Chris Hall. Cryptanalytic Attacks on Pseudorandom Number Generators. In Serge Vaudenay, editor, *Fast Software Encryption, 5th International Workshop, FSE'98*, volume 1372 of *Lecture Notes in Computer Science*, pages 168–188. Springer-Verlag, 1998. [Page 160]

[49] John Kelsey, Bruce Schneier, David Wagner, and Chris Hall. Side Channel Cryptanalysis of Product Ciphers. *Journal of Computer Security*, 8(2–3):141–158, 2000. See also `http://www.counterpane.com/side_channel.html`. [Page 150]

[50] John Kelsey, Bruce Schneier, and David Wagner. Key-Schedule Cryptanalysis of IDEA, G-DES, GOST, SAFER, and Triple-DES. In Neal Koblitz, editor, *Advances in Cryptology—CRYPTO '96*, volume 1109 of *Lecture Notes in Computer Science*, pages 237–251. Springer-Verlag, 1996. [Page 45]

[51] S. Kent and R. Atkinson. Security Architecture for the Internet Protocol. RFC 2401, November 1998. [Page 125]

[52] John Keogh. *Circular transportation facilitation device.* Australian Patent Office, August 2001. Granted Innovation Patent No. AU2001100012 A4, available from `http://www.ipmenu.com/archive/AUI_2001100012.pdf`. [Page 373]

[53] Joe Killian and Phillip Rogaway. How to Protect DES Against Exhaustive Key Search. In Neal Koblitz, editor, *Advances in Cryptology—CRYPTO '96*, volume 1109 of *Lecture Notes in Computer Science*, pages 252–267. Springer-Verlag, 1996. [Page 46]

[54] Lars R. Knudsen and Vincent Rijmen. Two Rights Sometimes Make a Wrong. In *Workshop on Selected Areas in Cryptography (SAC '97)*, pages 213–223, 1997. See `http://adonis.ee.queensu.ca:8000/sac/sac97/papers.html`. [Page 44]

[55] Donald E. Knuth. *Seminumerical Algorithms*, volume 2 of *The Art of Computer Programming*. Addison-Wesley, 1981. [Page 158, 194, 197, 279]

[56] Paul C. Kocher. Timing Attacks on Implementations of Diffie-Hellman, RSA, DSS, and Other Systems. In Neal Koblitz, editor, *Advances in Cryptology—CRYPTO '96*, volume 1109 of *Lecture Notes in Computer Science*, pages 104–113. Springer-Verlag, 1996. [Page 289, 290]

[57] Paul Kocher, Joshua Jaffe, and Benjamin Jun. Differential Power Analysis. In Michael Wiener, editor, *Advances in Cryptology—CRYPTO '99*, volume 1666 of *Lecture Notes in Computer Science*, pages 388–397. Springer-Verlag, 1999. [Page 151]

[58] J. Kohl and C. Neuman. The Kerberos Network Authentication Service (V5). RFC 1510, September 1993. [Page 310]

[59] H. Krawczyk, M. Bellare, and R. Canetti. HMAC: Keyed-Hashing for Message Authentication. RFC 2104, February 1997. [Page 101, 102]

[60] T. Krovetz, J. Black, S. Halevi, A. Hevia, H. Krawczyk, and P. Rogaway. UMAC: Message Authentication Code using Universal Hashing. RFC draft draft-krovetz-umac-01.txt, 2000. [Page 104, 105]

[61] Xuejia Lai and James L. Massey. A Proposal for a New Block Encryption Standard. In I.B. Damgård, editor, *Advances in Cryptology—EUROCRYPT '90*, volume 473 of *Lecture Notes in Computer Science*, pages 389–404. Springer-Verlag, 1990. [Page 288]

[62] Xuejia Lai, James L. Massey, and Sean Murphy. Markov Ciphers and Differential Cryptanalysis. In D.W. Davies, editor, *Advances in Cryptology—EUROCRYPT '91*, volume 547 of *Lecture Notes in Computer Science*, pages 17–38. Springer-Verlag, 1991. [Page 288]

[63] Arjen K. Lenstra and Eric R. Verheul. Selecting Cryptographic Key Sizes. *J. Cryptology*, 14(4):255–293, August 2001. [Page 37, 217]

[64] T. Matsumoto, H. Matsumoto, K. Yamada, and S. Hoshino. Impact of Artificial "Gummy" Fingers on Fingerprint Systems. In *Proceedings of SPIE, Vol #4677, Optical Security and Counterfeit Deterrence Techniques IV*, to appear. See also `www.itu.int/itudoc/itu-t/workshop/security/present/s5p4.pdf`. [Page 356]

[65] Alfred J. Menezes, Paul C. van Oorschot, and Scott A. Vanstone. *Handbook of Applied Cryptography*. CRC Press, 1996. ISBN 0-8493-8523-7. [Page 20]

[66] David L. Mills. Network Time Protocol (Version 3). RFC 1305, March 1992. [Page 303]

[67] D. Mills. Simple Network Time Protocol (SNTP) Version 4. RFC 2030, October 1996. [Page 303]

[68] P. Montgomery. Modular Multiplication without Trial Division. *Mathematics of Computation*, 44(170):519–521, 1985. [Page 286]

[69] National Institute of Standards and Technology. *DES Modes of Operation*, December 2, 1980. FIPS PUB 81, available from `http://www.itl.nist.gov/fipspubs/`. [Page 75]

[70] National Institute of Standards and Technology. *Data Encryption Standard (DES)*, December 30, 1993. FIPS PUB 46-2, available from `http://www.itl.nist.gov/fipspubs/`. [Page 51, 53]

[71] National Institute of Standards and Technology. *Secure Hash Standard*, April 17, 1995. FIPS PUB 180-1, available from `http://www.itl.nist.gov/fipspubs/`. [Page 88]

[72] National Institute of Standards and Technology. *AES Round 1 Technical Evaluation, CD-1: Documentation*, August 1998. See `http://www.nist.gov/aes`. [Page 55, 387, 388, 389, 394]

[73] National Institute of Standards and Technology. *Data Encryption Standard (DES)*, 1999. DRAFT FIPS PUB 46-3, available from `http://csrc.ncsl.nist.gov/fips/`. [Page 51]

[74] National Institute of Standards and Technology. *Proc. 3rd AES candidate conference*, April 2000. [Page 55]

[75] National Institute of Standards and Technology. *Secure Hash Standard (draft)*, 2001. Draft FIPS PUB 180-2, available from `http://csrc.nist.gov/encryption/shs/dfips-180-2.pdf`. [Page 89]

[76] Roger M. Needham and Michael D. Schroeder. Using Encryption for Authentication in Large Networks of Computers. *Communications of the ACM*, 21(12):993–999, December 1978. [Page 310]

[77] Bart Preneel and Paul C. van Oorschot. On the Security of Two MAC Algorithms. In Ueli Maurer, editor, *Advances in Cryptology—EUROCRYPT '96*, volume 1070 of *Lecture Notes in Computer Science*, pages 19–32. Springer-Verlag, 1996. [Page 102]

[78] Ronald L. Rivest, M.J.B. Robshaw, R. Sidney, and Y.L. Yin. The RC6 Block Cipher. In National Institute of Standards and Technology [72]. See `http://www.rsasecurity.com/rsalabs/rc6/` or `http://www.nist.gov/aes`. [Page 61, 288]

[79] Ronald L. Rivest. The MD4 Message Digest Algorithm. In A.J. Menezes and S.A. Vanstone, editors, *Advances in Cryptology—CRYPTO '90*, volume 537 of *Lecture Notes in Computer Science*, pages 303–311. Springer-Verlag, 1990. [Page 87]

[80] Ronald L. Rivest. The RC5 Encryption Algorithm. In B. Preneel, editor, *Fast Software Encryption, Second International Workshop, FSE'94*, volume 1008 of *Lecture Notes in Computer Science*, pages 86–96. Springer-Verlag, 1995. [Page 288]

[81] Ronald Rivest, Adi Shamir, and Leonard Adleman. A Method for Obtaining Digital Signatures and Public-Key Cryptosystems. *Communications of the ACM*, 21:120–126, February 1978. [Page 223]

[82] R. Rivest. The MD5 Message-Digest Algorithm. RFC 1321, April 1992. [Page 87]

[83] Phillip Rogaway, Mihir Bellare, John Black, and Ted Krovetz. OCB: A Block-Cipher Mode of Operation for Efficient Authenticated Encryption. In *Eighth ACM Conference on Computer and Communications Security (CCS-8)*, pages 196–205. ACM, ACM Press, 2001. [Page 76, 126]

[84] Phillip Rogaway, Mihir Bellare, John Black, and Ted Krovetz. OCB: A Block-Cipher Mode of Operation for Efficient Authenticated Encryption, September 2001. Available from `http://www.cs.ucdavis.edu/~rogaway`. [Page 76, 126]

[85] RSA Laboratories. *PKCS #1 v2.1: RSA Cryptography Standard*, January 2001. Available from `http://www.rsasecurity.com/rsalabs/pkcs`. [Page 236]

[86] Bruce Schneier, John Kelsey, Doug Whiting, David Wagner, Chris Hall, and Niels Ferguson. *The Twofish Encryption Algorithm, A 128-Bit Block Cipher.* Wiley, 1999. [Page 45, 59]

[87] Bruce Schneier. *Applied Cryptography, Protocols, Algorithms, and Source Code in C.* John Wiley & Sons, Inc., 1994. ISBN 0-471-59756-2. [Page 381]

[88] Bruce Schneier. *Applied Cryptography, Second Edition, Protocols, Algorithms, and Source Code in C.* John Wiley & Sons, Inc., 1996. ISBN 0-471-12845-7. [Page 20, 381]

[89] Bruce Schneier. *Secrets and Lies, Digital Security in a Networked World.* John Wiley & Sons, Inc., 2000. ISBN 0-471-25311-1. [Page 3, 20]

[90] Dr. Seuss. *Horton Hears a Who!* Random House, 1954. [Page 109]

[91] C.E. Shannon. A Mathematical Theory of Communication. *The Bell Systems Technical Journal*, 27:370–423 and 623–656, July and October 1948. See `http://cm.bell-labs.com/cm/ms/what/shannonday/paper.html`. [Page 155]

[92] David Wagner, Niels Ferguson, and Bruce Schneier. Cryptanalysis of FROG. In *Proc. 2nd AES candidate conference*, pages 175–181. National Institute of Standards and Technology, March 1999. [Page 44]

[93] David Wagner and Bruce Schneier. Analysis of the SSL 3.0 protocol. In *Proceedings of the Second USENIX Workshop on Electronic Commerce*, pages 29–40. USENIX Press, November 1996. Revised version available from `http://www.counterpane.com`. [Page 109]

[94] Doug Whiting, Russ Housley, and Niels Ferguson. Counter with CBC-MAC (CCM), June 2002. See `http://csrc.nist.gov/encryption/modes/proposedmodes/ccm/ccm.pdf`. [Page 126]

[95] Michael J. Wiener. Cryptanalysis of short RSA secret exponents. *IEEE Transactions on Information Theory*, 36(3):553–558, May 1990. [Page 232]

[96] Robert S. Winternitz. Producing a One-way Hash Function from DES. In David Chaum, editor, *Advances in Cryptology, Proceedings of Crypto 83*, pages 203–207. Plenum Press, 1983. [Page 45]

[97] Thomas Wu. The Secure Remote Password Protocol. In *Proceedings of the 1998 Network and Distributed System Security (NDSS'98) Symposium*, March 1998. [Page 278]

Index

Crypto-Gram

Stay abreast of the latest developments in cryptography and computer security—subscribe to the free newsletter Crypto-Gram. Delivered monthly to your e-mail address, Crypto-Gram is written by Bruce Schneier, and is packed with news summaries, analyses, insights, and commentaries.

To subscribe to Crypto-Gram, visit:
http://www.counterpane.com/crypto-gram.html
Or send a blank message to **crypto-gram-subscribe@chaparraltree.com**
Back issues of Crypto-Gram are available at:
http://www.counterpane.com/crypto-gram.html

Here are some of the subjects that appeared in previous issues of Crypto-Gram:

January 2003	• *Militaries and Cyber-War* • *The RMAC Authentication Mode*
December 2002	• *Counterattack* • *Crime: The Internet's Next Big Thing*
November 2002	• *Security Notes from All Over: Japanese Honeybees*
October 2002	• *National Strategy to Secure Cyberspace* • *One-Time Pads*
September 2002	• *AES News* • *Microsoft Word 97 Vulnerability*
August 2002	• *Palladium and the TCPA* • *License to Hack* • *Arming Airline Pilots*
July 2002	• *Embedded Control Systems and Security* • *Perrun Virus*
June 2002	• *Fixing Intelligence Failures* • *More on Security and Secrecy*
May 2002	• *Secrecy, Security, and Obscurity* • *Fun with Fingerprint Readers*
April 2002	• *How to Think About Security* • *Is 1024 Bits Enough?*
March 2002	• *SNMP Vulnerabilities* • *Richard Clarke on 9/11's Lessons*
February 2002	• *Microsoft and "Trustworthy Computing"* • *Judging Microsoft*
January 2002	• *Windows UPnP Vulnerability*
December 2001	• *National ID Cards* • *Judges Punish Bad Security* • *Computer Security and Liabilities*
November 2001	• *Full Disclosure* • *GOVNET*
October 2001	• *Cyberterrorism and Cyberhooliganism* • *SSSCA* • *SANS Top 20*
30 Sept 2001	• *Special issue on the September 11 terrorist attacks and their aftermath*
September 2001	• *11 September 2001* • *NSA's Dual Counter Mode*
August 2001	• *Code Red Worm* • *Adobe, Elcomsoft, and the DMCA*
July 2001	• *Phone Hacking: Next Generation* • *Monitoring First*